Understanding and Shaping Curriculum

To SDH, our family, and Miss Trivitt, who was in my lap until the end

Understanding and Shaping Curriculum

What We Teach and Why

Thomas W. Hewitt
University of South Alabama (Retired)

SAGE Publications
Thousand Oaks ▪ London ▪ New Delhi

For information:

Sage Publications, Inc.
2455 Teller Road
Thousand Oaks, California 91320
E-mail: order@sagepub.com

Sage Publications Ltd.
1 Oliver's Yard
55 City Road
London EC1Y 1SP
United Kingdom

Sage Publications India Pvt. Ltd.
B-42, Panchsheel Enclave
Post Box 4109
New Delhi 110 017 India

Printed in the United States of America

Library of Congress Cataloging-in-Publication Data

Hewitt, Thomas W.
Understanding and shaping curriculum: What we teach and why / Thomas W. Hewitt.
    p. cm.
Includes bibliographical references and index.
ISBN 0-7619-2868-5 (cloth)
   1. Education—Curricula—Philosophy. 2. Curriculum planning.
3. Curriculum evaluation. I. Title.
LB1570.H5 2006
375′.001—dc22

                                 2005024322

This book is printed on acid-free paper.

06 07 08 09 10 9 8 7 6 5 4 3 2 1

Acquisitions Editor:	Diane McDaniel
Editorial Assistant:	Erica Carroll
Associate Editor:	Margo Crouppen
Production Editor:	Denise Santoyo
Copy Editor:	Brenda Weight
Permissions Editor:	Karen Wiley
Typesetter:	C&M Digitals (P) Ltd.
Indexer:	Mary Mortensen
Cover Designer:	Michelle Lee Kenny

Contents

LIST OF FIGURES

Chapter 9   **225**

Chapter 10   **259**

Chapter 11   **287**

Chapter 12   **315**

PREFACE

The purpose of this textbook is to explore and illuminate curriculum. It has been my experience that students preparing to teach often comment that curriculum seems amorphous. They are remarking on the confusing ways curriculum is used. Often it seems to be a word for what is taught, the subjects or content. At other times, it is presented as forms of practice; a subset of general teacher activities about "what" to teach, such as content development or lesson planning; a set of theories; or as a special school knowledge like elementary, middle, or high school curriculum. Sometimes it is used to refer to particular kinds of curriculum, a college curriculum or a church school curriculum, examples that simply clarify the place and purpose in a general way. However, the central association is curriculum in schools and that, along with the schooling process, creates the context for learning about curriculum.

What does curriculum mean in each of those instances and what brings coherence in understanding curriculum? What does it mean to do curriculum work and be a curriculum worker? To consider such questions, you would need to develop a response that conveys your own professional, critical perspective in thinking about and working in curriculum. In the spirit of seeking a critical perspective, you will come to consider what preconceptions you hold about teaching and, more specifically, your predispositions toward curriculum, instruction, and the learning process. Personal introspection about preconceptions and predispositions is an important characteristic of self-regulation as a professional. In that sense of the critical, it is also important for me as the author to set out my perspective because it affects the content and organization of this text.

ONE AUTHOR'S VIEW

There are two aspects that demarcate the conceptualization behind this textbook; one is about the nature of understanding, the other about teacher education. I hold that understanding a thing—what we come to know about it—is to determine its characteristics and render it complete, to give it a wholeness of form or structure, whether it is a physical object, a poem, or a concept. That is, of course, personalized meaning. There are coalescing characteristics about curriculum that give it meaning. First is the familiar association of curriculum with schooling and society, what you were taught and, it's hoped, learned, the personal and social meaning curriculum derives from the school experience over some 12 years. It is in the common history of that experience, everyone's shared and personal familiarity with it, that curriculum exists and has existed. Second, because it is found in schools or the equivalent in all societies and social groups, curriculum can be studied in terms of place and location. Third, curriculum is an activity in people's work, teachers and students especially, and we can study those and other activities that help us understand curriculum. Fourth, curriculum at any given time is a documentary of the tensions that exist in society about what schools should do and what they should teach; for instance, should intelligent design be given equal time with evolution? Curriculum is also a summation of conserved change, a record that if revisited can inform the present; curriculum documents will tell us if a decision to give equal time to evolution and intelligent design became policy. The confluence of those characteristics leads to a centering conception of curriculum as what schools are about—without curriculum they have no reason to exist.

The second aspect in my conceptualizing of why curriculum is important involves the preparation of teachers. The vital center of schooling is the interaction of the teacher and students, and that interaction is over the curriculum. Because of that important connection, curriculum plays an indispensable part in preparing teachers to teach. With instruction, the learning process, and assessment-evaluation, curriculum forms the core of what students preparing to teach need to study. If curriculum is central to schooling, it is also central to teacher preparation. That distinguishing confluence is essential to this textbook and to thinking about curriculum.

THE STRATEGY BEHIND THE BOOK

Authoring begins simply enough in deciding to write. The next step, devising a plan and strategy for doing it, is harder. Paraphrasing an important curriculum requirement, you have to decide what purposes your work will serve, and then what writings or other tools will create the path a reader will follow. The strategy is in two interdependent parts. The first, organizational considerations, is based on my perspective as discussed in the preceding section, and necessitates organizing the content in a different way than is traditionally done in curriculum textbooks. The second is about writings and tools, the text and pedagogies that will inform and help the reader.

The organizational plan corresponds to four purposes that frame the book. The first is to overview what is known and introduce the reader to the big picture, where you are going, an entry-level view of the world of curriculum and particularly its relationship to schools and schooling. A second is to focus on what you, the student, need to know about curriculum, the knowledge bases that are essential to develop the world of curriculum. The third purpose is to emphasize the practice aspect of curriculum, curriculum work, not only as curriculum practice but also as a coequal knowledge base in curriculum. Finally, part of being a practitioner is to understand the inevitability of change and the necessity to keep current about issues and trends that are important and will affect both knowledge and the work of curriculum.

The second aspect of the strategy, the writing and pedagogies, is the more problematic and depends on the capacity of the author to convey and translate into helpful forms what curriculum is all about. The text must blend organization and content to build meaning as it goes and continuously cross-reference ideas that may seem concrete but move toward abstraction. The text as written message should move in a simple to complex way that would enhance the readers' engagement and understanding. Simple does not refer to being simplistic but to the meaning intended or conveyed, as in an initial encounter, a mention in passing, or an introduction, as in a brief definition or description to get you started. You will note that concepts, terms, and ideas are introduced and then recur as you progress in your study of curriculum and move from surface to deeper meaning. Comprehending the lean or rich meaning intended often depends on contextual elaboration. Whenever possible, examples are provided appropriate to the level of discussion about the particular idea or concept. This recurring character of discussion is meant to refresh, review, extend, or expand on something previously encountered. Thus, something discussed in one chapter is viewed as a building block for something in a future chapter.

THE ORGANIZATION OF THE BOOK

Based on the strategy outlined, the text is divided into four parts, and in each chapter, pedagogical tools and resources are embedded to support discussion. **Part I**, The World of Curriculum, is an overview of curriculum that initiates you into the problems of defining, conceptualizing, and describing curriculum. It introduces you to the genesis of the field of curriculum, the nature of curriculum work in professional practice, the roles and functions of curriculum workers, the process of creating curriculum, and curriculum as a dialogue among its professional practitioners. The idea melding the four chapters in Part I is that curriculum exists as a discipline that both creates knowledge and uses that knowledge to create more of a working dialectic among practitioners in diverse settings. **Part II** is about the knowledge base for curriculum. It explores the basics of curriculum and sources of the knowledge that serve curriculum. In Chapters 5 through 8, there are discussions about tools (models, theories, and critiques) to learn about and use in curriculum; special knowledge unique to curriculum; and the historical, sociocultural, and intellectual knowledge of the discipline. These chapters also refer to the diversity of relevant knowledge from other fields and the interdisciplinary nature of knowledge and practice. **Part III** is a guide to curriculum work and what curriculum practitioners do, especially in the contexts of schools and schooling. Chapters 9 through 12 examine processes of planning, policy making, curriculum development and adaptation, implementation, integrated management, research, and evaluation. **Part IV** addresses challenges of curriculum change, with the final two chapters, 13 and 14, focusing on curriculum issues, trends, and the future.

The strategy, as noted, emphasizes pedagogical features and resources embedded in the chapters and the end of the book to aid or extend your study of curriculum. A **Perspective Into Practice** box in each chapter offers concrete examples illustrating the relevance of an idea or ideas in the chapter to both elementary and secondary school settings and contexts. There are graphic organizers in each chapter to illustrate, provide examples, or further expand understanding of key ideas, events, or actions in curriculum. At the end of each chapter you will find **Critical Perspective** questions with suggested activities and a **Resources for Curriculum Study** section offering selected books, journals, other media, and online resources to explore for more information. In addition to the resources section, each chapter closes with a **References** section listing works cited in the chapter. Additional resources for student use include a **Glossary** of terms a **Recommended Readings** of additional resources that were not included in the end-of-chapter references, a **List of Figures**, and the **Index.**

Acknowledgments

I want to acknowledge the reviewers who were gracious with their time and provided thoughtful comments and very useful suggestions:

Cynthia Chapel, Lincoln University

Linda T. Coats, Mississippi State University

Christopher R Gareis, The College of William & Mary

Barbara Gonzalez-Pino, The University of Texas at San Antonio

Michael Grady, St. Louis University

Angela Rhone, Florida Atlantic University

Robert A. Schultz, The University of Toledo

Allen Seed, University of Memphis

Ted Singletary, Boise State University

Editors, as I have learned, make the enterprise happen, and I don't believe there could be a better crew than the Sage team. I'm extremely grateful to Diane McDaniel, my acquisitions editor, and Marta Peimer, her able assistant, who were with me from the beginning in shaping the book and providing sound advice, support, and encouragement. To my editorial gurus, Margo Crouppen and Brenda Weight, who came on in the later phases of finalizing and production, thanks for always being assuring, guiding my struggles with text and format, always asking the right question and, most important, always being there for the question. I have learned much from all of you and appreciate your patience, support, and the always-collaborative sense of "our" project you conveyed. To Art Pomponio, my gratitude for thinking I could do this venture, and to

Mary Ellen Lepionka, thanks for helping me figure out how to get where I wanted to go.

There are always those who have been mentors and friends along the professional path and whose ideas and counsel have been instrumental in my career and in shaping my understanding of curriculum and education. To Dell Felder and Carl Schomburg, for the friendship, intellectual mentoring, and encouragement, a very special thanks. Collegial friendships play an important part in academic life. Along the way, the maturing of ideas and shared experiences with Jay Mulkey, Bob Newhouse, Mary Harris, and Mike Grady were instrumental in helping me form ideas about curriculum. I would be remiss if I didn't acknowledge Norb Maertens, who has left us but whose ideas, ways of doing things, and love of life carry on. In the end, it is the author who must take responsibility, and I do so hoping the effort will be useful to others.

Chapter 1

INTRODUCTION

Congratulations! You have chosen to study in the field of education and join one of the most historic and honored callings, a life of professional work in schooling, schools, and curriculum. Depending on where you are in your program of study, you have taken various courses to prepare you. In this textbook you will explore the world of schooling and curriculum. Before proceeding, there are several preliminaries to address. One is to understand the significance of schooling in society and the place of curriculum within that. A second is to establish the importance of thinking about ways to look at curriculum: what is critical in the sense of essentials in thinking and forming your thoughts into a perspective that guides your work as a professional. Finally, there are some key ideas that should guide your study, what you will read and discuss related to this text, and the course in which it is being used. These might be thought of as certain caveats, or cautions, you need to keep in reflection as you proceed. Those are the starting points as you begin your journey into the education field and the particulars of teaching, learning, and curriculum knowledge essential in professional practice.

SOCIETY AND SCHOOLING

The English professor turns on the tape recorder in the freshman composition class. Students prepare to take notes for an essay to be turned in at the end of the session. The tape is a short dialogue between a Hopi mother and child about the latter's actions and inappropriate behavior emanating from a situation in which the child had failed to share a toy with another. The mother was coaching the child to understand sharing behavior and the cooperative nature of Hopi life. The tape ended with the mother's admonition, "but that is not the Hopi Way!" a closing comment reflecting several observations about being a Hopi. In the Hopi community, the people in manner and conduct have distinct characteristics that mark acceptable behavior. Further, there exists some "code" that informs the young Hopi about how to behave. And perhaps most important, the Hopi Way is knowledge to be learned.

This illustration of Hopi life suggests several strands or themes that weave in and out as you explore curriculum. One strand is the importance of "schooling," what in this informal sense the Hopi parent is doing by instructing the child in the ways of Hopi life. A second is the nature of and need for schools in any society. Although the mother's instruction is not formal schooling in a building as you have experienced it, it is school in the Hopi sense; the Hopi family and all the community is a school in the social and cultural sense. Third, there are important relationships between and among schooling as a process, schools as institutions, and curriculum. In Hopi life, the "code" is the curriculum to be learned in the "school" of the family-community. The teaching of that code is the schooling the Hopi child encounters.

Each of you is, in a sense, a Hopi. You acquire the social and cultural codes whether you are a member of some indigenous group in a rain forest, a nomadic Bedouin tribesman, or a supposedly sophisticated urban dweller. Anthropologists refer to this acquiring process as *enculturation,* the learning of one's *culture,* the ways of behaving and thinking as a member. Culture, enculturation, and behavior are fundamental socio-cultural processes that, depending on the type of human organizational unit—group, tribe, society, or nation—are acquired in some way, from the very simple one-on-one contact of parent and child to the organized classroom of the school. Think of culture in a broader context as knowledge, what a group or a society determines is important to pass on to its members. What constitutes that knowledge and how it is conveyed will vary. What is familiar to you in America is the special knowledge that is passed on through schools and other approved institutional units such as the family and home. That special body of knowledge is what is to be learned, and you are "schooled" in it.

Schooling and Learning

The school provides you with the opportunity to learn the knowledge you need to make a life for yourself and be an effective participant in your society. Schooling, the process that engages that knowledge, is usually institutionalized in schools but can occur in different ways, as the Hopi life example suggests. In its formal sense, knowledge is identified in different ways, often being referred to as content or subject matter taught in schools. In the early years of the American colonies and the young republic, it consisted of reading, writing, and arithmetic. The various references and ways of describing curriculum as the substance of schooling over the past hundred years have gradually been embodied in the word *curriculum.*

The curriculum is the knowledge you are to learn. Returning to the way of the Hopi, what the child is expected to learn, the knowledge of Hopi society and culture, has its counterpart in the modern school curriculum. Hopi knowledge is about the ways of life and the Hopi worldview. Think of this knowledge as two things, content and ways of thinking with that content, which is what defines being a Hopi. These content and perspective matters are central to conceptualizing curriculum. Not only is there more to curriculum today, but also it is far more complex and requires greater sophistication in thought. Being new does not make the modern curriculum more important; that is a relative determination of time and place. What it does suggest is that human learning from past to present is a cumulative encounter with some form of curriculum.

Curriculum is complex and possesses a richness of expression. According to one classic source, there are four forms that curriculum may take, the (a) explicit curriculum, (b) implicit curriculum, (c) hidden curriculum, and (d) null curriculum (Eisner, 1985). Each serves a purpose that may or may not be explicitly stated but which is nonetheless inclusive in curriculum thinking and work. The intent is to understand curriculum as multidimensional. The *explicit curriculum* is that of mathematics, science, and so forth, the subject matter specified in documents that guide teachers. The *implicit curriculum* is what is being taught or engaged by the teacher and students, the actual curriculum-in-use. The *hidden curriculum* is what is not explicit but often subliminal and unintended, perhaps the behaviors that are circumscribed in the rules of the classroom. The *null curriculum* refers to what is not being taught, perhaps issues about sex or alternate lifestyles. Other curriculum scholars have proposed different terms, and some of these are presented in Figure 1.1. Obviously, which terms are used give shaded meanings to curriculum. You will find this a recurring issue, so you need to be sure which terms you want to use, understand the nuances, and be prepared to explain what you mean by their use. As you will encounter shortly in this chapter, the use of terms and the precision of their use is a critical element in any practice and profession, but in none more so than the practice of building and using knowledge about schooling and curriculum. This is a process of perspective building that will recur in different contexts as you explore curriculum in the chapters that follow.

Curriculum-Practitioner Connections

Curriculum is the substance of schooling and the reason for schools. Through schooling, curriculum links the person and society, the person and culture, and the society and culture. American society has deemed schools as appropriate, sanctioned

Figure 1.1   Curriculum Labels

Curriculum, depicted in different terms by scholars and others, often implies a similar meaning. The choice of words is often a reflection of the writer's perspective.

- **Perspective 1:** Curriculum that is required to be taught is specified in official documents and often described as the *implicit* or *intended* or *planned* or *formal* curriculum.
- **Perspective 2:** Curriculum that is not stated or made explicit but might be implemented by a teacher is often referred to as the *unintended* or *hidden* or *informal* or *implied* curriculum.
- **Perspective 3:** Curriculum from the position of the implementer, most likely the teacher, but it might be the learner, is often categorized as the *taught* or *delivered* or *implemented* curriculum.
- **Perspective 4:** Curriculum from the recipient's position, usually the student, has been referred to as the *learned* or *received* or *experienced* or *studied* curriculum.
- **Perspective 5:** Curriculum as viewed from the position of the general public or parents of children in school is not often discussed, but if it were, it might be referred to using the labels in Perspective 1, or as the *public* or *private* or *parochial* curriculum or the *remembered* curriculum of personal experience or the *political* curriculum of special interest, advocacy, or community organizations.

Source: Sources consulted in developing these perspectives are Eisner (1985), Eisner and Vallance (1974), Jackson (1992a), and Kelly (2004).

institutions for developing a common approach to acculturating people in all things American. The largest schooling experience is, of course, public schooling. Regardless of whether it is institutionalized in a public, private, parochial, or some alternative school form, curriculum is intimately associated with the purposes schools serve, as well as embodying the various kinds of knowledge (vocational, humanities, sciences, etc.) transmitted through schooling.

The curriculum serves as a connector in another important way: it connects the academic and practical creation of knowledge about curriculum itself. This is a dualistic characteristic of curriculum; it exists both as a body of knowledge about itself *and* about the curriculum of the school. As a body of formal knowledge about curriculum itself, it includes special terms and language, theories, modes of thinking, specialized tools for curriculum work, and scholarly discourse traditions, all deriving from the work of scholarly academics, schoolteachers, and other educational practitioners. Through their common focus on curriculum, academics, classroom teachers, curriculum and instructional designers, and other practitioners are connected. That connection is not always clear or strong. Reasons for this include a tendency to treat curriculum as an academic subject rather than as a matter of practice, viewing curriculum as the province of scholars and researchers rather than that of the teacher, student, and classroom and a historic divide in how curriculum work evolved. Nevertheless, curriculum has advanced as a distinct body of knowledge and professional work linking a variety of practitioners in various contexts. To understand curriculum is to come to know it as a body of knowledge and professional work. Thus curriculum, as depicted in Figure 1.2, can be

Figure 1.2   The World of Curriculum

CURRICULUM WORK

Academic Practitioners

Create knowledge about curriculum through study, inquiry, and working with educational institutions and school constituents.

School Practitioners

Create knowledge about curriculum as teachers, policymakers, creators of curriculum and materials, and appliers of academic knowledge, theorizing from practice.

Other Practitioners

Other people in different roles and locations also contribute to curriculum knowledge as curriculum practitioners; these include state and district school personnel, foundations, organizations, interest groups, publishers, and other organizations with an educational interest.

CURRICULUM KNOWLEDGE

Academic Sources

Scholars and researchers study curriculum and create knowledge; they share it through teaching and training professional practitioners, publications, and interchanges as consultants with educational agents and institutions.

Practice Sources

School practitioners, teachers, curriculum specialists, and other school-related personnel create knowledge by applying academic knowledge and practice knowledge that emerges from using curriculum.

Related Sources

Knowledge related to curriculum also comes from other disciplines such as history, political science, and business.

---

defined as both acculturated knowledge and a body of work that flows from both curriculum as practice and as a field of study.

This formulation constitutes what you might commonly refer to as a frame of reference, a mental structuring, a particular way of considering things, or, in a word, a perspective. The mental activity of forming any frame of reference is to personally make sense of things. Collectively, multiple frames of reference that are generally understood and used in a society can lead to a common ordering of knowledge and a worldview. The concepts of nationhood and nationalism and their presentation in the study of American history, civics, and literature are examples of social purposes served by curriculum.

Curriculum as Frames of Reference

The opening story about the Hopi Way signifies the universal quest to make sense of the world, to construct a reality that works and can be passed on. This framing for understanding is often shared with immediate family and affiliate groups, especially peers. Throughout life, you generate new frames of reference and modify old ones. This human capacity for framing things to give them a common meaning and power in their use is both a cognitive process and a result of that process. Frames of reference can also include worldviews, ideologies, and personal outlooks. How people individually and collectively see the world is a matter of self-perspective and an acquired public frame of reference. It is important to consider these framing devices in understanding both curriculum and your views on curriculum. Contemporary issues about what should be included in curriculum—matters of cultural inclusiveness bound up in the culture wars of the 1990s or about the place of evolution and intelligent design, for example—evolve around differing frames of reference. Whatever consensus is achieved reflects an arrival at some common frame of reference, one that is shared. That shared consensus might, for example, be about what it means to be an American, in which you and others would describe or characterize what defines the national character. Similarly, members of professional learning communities also share specialized ways of characterizing their work. And, both the societal and professional framing processes are factored by the conceptual looseness or tightness of meaning, the range of situations in which they can be used, the knowledge required to develop them, and a commitment to continuously explore and validate them. Figure 1.3 summarizes the framing process, both in its societal and professional contexts. While frame of reference is probably acceptable for a broader, more general, societal conceptualizing of what it means, for example, to be American, a different approach is appropriate in the narrower academic, professional sense of developing knowledge and investigating problems, where randomness must give way to canons of practice and structural forms that create a commonplace of knowledge and work. Two ideas, (a) the critical and (b) perspective, need to be discussed as you start your exploration.

THE IMPORTANCE OF THE CRITICAL PERSPECTIVE

As you study to become a professional, you will acquire a specialized kind of perspective. What is a perspective and where does it come from? What is a perspective made of and what makes one perspective more useful or powerful than another? And, what makes a perspective critical? The first question is asking about the sources for forming a perspective: What are the supposed truths and knowledge on which it is based? The second question asks you to consider different kinds of and uses for perspectives and what is the basis for using one and not another. The last question highlights the

Figure 1.3   Curriculum Frames of Reference

Factor	Societal Frames	Professional Frames
Conceptual	Focus is on universal ideas about what it means to be an American, the institutional structures of society, and appropriate civic conduct transmitted through schools	Conceptual focus is dedicated to studying schools as specific institutions and creating knowledge about them as institutions serving society
Range of View	General in that the focus is not on schools per se but their institutional mandate to serve educational needs and whether they are effective in that charge	Focus is on curriculum-school-schooling relationships
Knowledge	Reliance is on general knowledge for social uses such as the historical development of a society and its beliefs, like those acquired in schooling	Reliance is on using and generating specialized knowledge about schooling-curriculum relationships in fulfilling the general institutional expectations of society
Validation	Society is law centered and governance is based on a constitution	Continuous reflection about practice and dependence on verification in knowledge produced and used

importance of a particular professional process, that of the critical perspective and developing a critical perspective. This mode of thought, the *critical,* is associated with such terms as *critical analysis, critical pedagogy, critical perspective,* and *critical theory,* which are summarized in Figure 1.4. If you were to read about any of those terms, critical thinking, for example, you would note that the terms *critical* and *thinking* are linked together but that the term critical is seldom introduced and discussed separately to suggest how it fixes a meaning for a term like critical thinking.

The Critical and Perspective

Let's consider the idea of the critical first. The critical in literature and the arts is qualitative; it means the application of stated or implied criteria in careful judgment or judicious evaluation of, perhaps, a book, performance, or art object. Its use in the medical field refers to that stage of a disease at which an abrupt change for better or

Figure 1.4   Meanings and Uses of the Critical

Critical is a widely used word referring loosely to seeing something clearly and truly in order to make a fair judgment. Implied in that is the identification or creation of some criterion or criteria to be used in making a judgment.

Critical analysis refers to forming a set of criteria (the critical) to use in studying or exploring something to delineate its parts, structure, or other constituent elements. It is used widely in various areas of scholarly works, retaining its central meaning but changed by the area of knowledge in which it is used.

Critical pedagogy has been used as a term subsuming those teaching and learning practices designed to raise learner consciousness and transform oppressive social conditions to create a more egalitarian society.

Critical perspective refers to a specialized way of viewing or studying something, the critical referring to the preparatory act of identifying the criteria or elements that configure the view, as in creating a lens through which to observe. A critical perspective is particular to scholarship and professional practice.

Critical theory is a broad term associated with the humanities and social sciences characterized by very loose boundaries as to its precise meaning and application. It has two main foci: (a) to study human identity and its nature in private and public spheres of life and (b) to specify ways social and cultural institutions (media, religion, government, etc.) shape identity.

worse may be expected. In the education field, critical is usually coupled with thinking to create the idea of critical thinking (Weill & Anderson, 2000). The *critical* in critical thinking means an effort to see a thing clearly and truly in order to judge it fairly. *Thinking* simply refers to your cognitive capacity. Together, as *critical thinking,* they convey a capability to think that promotes clarity and judgment, desired characteristics in those who will study and practice in the education field. Turning to the matter of *perspective,* in Western thought, especially since the Enlightenment, the matter of perspective has been an issue of scholarly interest. Descartes' famous statement, "I think, therefore I am" is a declaration of perspective. He was decoupling from the religious to the secular world and claiming the human ability to create knowledge and truth. Similarly, as David Blacker (1998) reminds us, anthropologist and noted French postmodernist Michel Foucault claimed that perspectives come from the subjective side of human interpretative skills rather than from truths, forming a kind of "politics of truth." What he is suggesting is that all perception, what can be individually known, is subjective. Whatever is claimed as "truth" in the secular sense is not neutral; it has a subjective reality, and it is political. Accepting something as true, real, useful, that which is proved, and then using it, is a political act in that you seek to have it accepted and must be prepared in the forensic way to "prove" it for acceptance by others. The emphasis on truth and proof is essential in building a scholarly perspective. Similar insights about this process of creating perspectives come from religion scholar Elaine Pagels and the hermeneutical tradition. Discussing the nature of interpretation, she notes that "what each of us perceives and acts upon as true has much to do with our situation, social, political, cultural, religious, or philosophical" (1988, p. xxvii). In addition to self-knowing you as a unique person, she is pointing to at least five potential knowledge sources for "grounding" a perspective: society, politics, culture, religion, and philosophy.

Qualities of a Critical Perspective

Grounding is an interesting word and, in the sense of your firmament, "standing your ground," or having your feet planted firmly, it is an important quality in building a critical perspective. This sense of *grounding* is to render a perspective real and verifiable rather than contrived or speculative, a necessary condition in scholarly work and establishing reliable knowledge. Verifiability is fundamental to establishing the legitimacy of a perspective. And legitimacy is important in the professional world of teachers, academicians, or any practitioner concerned with knowledge creation where scholarship is essential to discussion. Grounding is also characterized by high-quality discourse in the work of a practice community, particularly the professions.

In the marketplace of knowledge creation, an idea gains credibility if the perspective that shapes it is also plausible. Plate tectonics, for example, was an idea put forth in the 19th century but only validated in the mid-20th century. As an explanation for the movement of the earth's crust and its subsequent insight into earthquakes and volcanic action, it seems obvious to us today. It evolved from the development of one scientist's professional critical perspective and took a long time to gain acceptance and be validated. The process of establishing credibility is a critical process, what Thomas Popkewitz and Marie Brennan refer to as "a broad band of disciplined questioning of the ways . . . power works through the discursive practices and performance of schooling" (1998a, p. 4). If something is learned in school, it comes to you as legitimate and credible; you know you can use it. Children in elementary school tend to accept what they learn without question. As learners pass into middle and high school, they should begin to encounter that "broad band of disciplined questioning" to which Popkewitz and Brennan refer. That is, learners encounter the power of curriculum in two ways, the power of curriculum as accepted truth, and the transfer of that power in knowing something, its "empowerment." For the learner, learning to think critically is the empowerment! *Critical thinking* invokes reflection and introspection as elements of practice that suggest careful and principled evaluation or reasoned judgment. This suggests that grounding is more than knowing about and using knowledge and the ways to think from a perspective that grounds and legitimizes critical practice. It is, in Foucault's postmodern formulation, empowerment reflected in performance. An actor considering a role must think the character through, consider the contexts and conditions in which he or she will create the role and interpret the character in a particular way. In the broader context of a play or movie, an actor's grounded perspective creates an interpretation of how the character would behave. The actor is striving for a match between his or her perception of the role and those of the people attending the performance. Legitimacy is the match the actor makes between interpretation and audience expectation.

Legitimacy is also a factor in the work of school practitioners and curriculum workers. They must apply critical thought to a variety of knowledge forms, formal ones such as disciplines of knowledge and informal ones such as knowledge of the classroom, students, and school. In discussing critical practice, Joe Kincheloe comments, "Practitioner ways of knowing are unique, quite different from the technical, scientific ways of knowing, traditionally associated with professional expertise" (2000, p. 23). In teaching, a teacher employs a critical perspective in judging student performance, making instructional decisions, deliberating over educational policy issues, or conceptualizing a curriculum and how to develop it. Often these actions, like the actor's, are interpretive, a leap from the grounded knowledge and thought of what the teacher has learned formally to the tentativeness of knowledge as experience from practice. Think of this as a dialogue, your personal conversation about what you know formally and knowledge experienced in application. For teachers, there is often a discrepancy between knowledge learned in preparing to teach and the teaching experience. Reconciling such discrepancies is a matter of making judgments and actions legitimate, a matter of the critical perspective. Understanding and working from a critical perspective provides schooling professionals with a process for verifying decisions and legitimating performance. This is important because professional practitioners, particularly those working with curriculum, should be able to explain the perspective that guides the thinking and practice in their work. They do this by employing a critical perspective along with a metacognitive approach to understanding their critical perspectives. That is, one should be critical about being critical! This "self-regulation" is a quality of expertise (Facione, 1998) and should, as you will read about in Chapter 3, be exhibited often in professional behavior. Other qualities, in addition to grounding, credibility, legitimacy, and self-regulation, mark a perspective as critical. Summarizing from a number of writings about the critical (for example, see Bowers & Flinders, 1990; Kincheloe & Steinberg, 1993; Kincheloe, Steinberg, & Villaverde, 1999; Schon, 1983; Walkerdine, 1988), the following additional *personal* characteristics are relevant:

- *Thinking:* Being critical means accepting the ability to reason using active, sociocultural, cognitive constructions rather than inferred, stylized, static, psychological models of thinking.
- *Context:* To think critically is to contextualize, to perceive ecologically, in a sense, to think about the whole, the parts, and the relationships as an array of possible actions with imaginable consequences.
- *Self:* Awareness of who and what you are, your self, is central to understanding your critical perspective.

- *Reflection:* Cultivating introspection and reflection, thinking about consequences and how they might be connected to decisions, reinforces other qualities of critical perspective: self-awareness, contextualization, and critical thinking.

These characteristics are, to a degree, always considerations in the conscious effort to create a critical perspective. And developing that way of thinking is the responsibility of the person beginning his or her studies to become a teacher or other practitioner in schools and with curriculum. One way to understand this creative process of building a critical perspective is to consider what a critical perspective might look like in application.

Applying a Critical Perspective

A critical perspective is useful when applied to your personal interests or work in the field of education. Whether your intended work is called teaching, learning, schooling, education, or something else, there is a knowledge base with which you and any other professional in the field of education should be familiar. In education, this comprises at least the five areas, or domains of knowledge, referred to in Figure 1.5.

Indeed, teaching could be described in one way as the composite of decisions made by a teacher in each of these areas of knowledge. For any educational professional, there is a need to understand what curriculum is, how to use it, and how to provide effective instruction. Because learning is an individual, social, cultural, and biocognitive process, professional practitioners need appropriate knowledge from these areas. Professional preparation is not complete without familiarity with assessment and evaluation that assign meaning and value to learning outcomes and to personal and public expectations. In education, those domains of knowledge bound the broader world of educational practice and perspective. Teachers and others who work in and with curriculum acquire a special, or critical, perspective as differentiated from the broad

---

Figure 1.5   Domains of Knowledge in Education

1. **Curriculum:** whatever is designated to be taught and learned

2. **Instruction:** how you want to engage curriculum, the manner of delivery

3. **Learning:** the individualized process of how curriculum is acquired through instruction

4. **Assessment:** the monitoring of curriculum, learning, and instruction by using specific tools such as tests, observational schemes, or other techniques

5. **Evaluation:** the creation and application of a value or system of values in curriculum, instruction, or learning separately or in combination based on assessment

---

educational one. That specialization is important, it is the difference between just generally thinking about something from a frame of reference and acquiring and using a critical perspective bounded by the character and context of the work you are preparing for. Reiterating an important point made earlier, unlike a more general frame of reference, a critical perspective is a special acquisition through study and dialogue within a practitioner community. The critical perspective is the capacity for informed judgment, the heart of professional practice for those who will work in schools, enter into the process of schooling, and engage the curriculum.

PERSPECTIVE INTO PRACTICE:
Domains of Knowledge in a Social Studies Lesson

Critical Perspectives	Elementary Example	Secondary Example
Curriculum: Symbols of the American nation and their meaning.	Study the American flag: flag nomenclature, field, stars, stripes, and display. Flag etiquette.	Study national symbols and their use: the meaning of icons and symbols. Uses include patriotism, national identity, allegiance, and propaganda.
Instruction: Using concrete objects such as flags and pictures to convey abstract ideas associated with or embedded in them.	Introduce the key words: field, stars, stripes, design, display, and etiquette. Use a contemporary U.S. flag, a picture of the Betsy Ross flag, the "Don't Tread on Me" flag, or some other flag of American origin, to compare and contrast.	Gather several different examples of symbols and icons (different flag, cross, crescent, Coke bottle, etc.). Focus on the symbolism they represent. Consider how each evolved a symbolic meaning and how that relates to some aspect of American identity and character.
Learning: Using a variety of media to study symbols and their meaning. Emphasis on concrete, abstract, and comparative thinking.	Focus on parts of the flag (stars, stripes, etc.) from concrete examples to abstract meanings through symbols.	The emphasis is on doing a comparative analysis. Develop some initial criteria to work with and add or subtract criteria as they are discussed.
Assessment: Using written exam, discussion checklist, word-definition matching, essay options, and other forms of creating data.	Use grade-, age-, and competence-appropriate tools: blank paper flag fill-in, individual free draw and labeling of the parts, flag	The emphasis is on applying knowledge by using criteria in a story, drawing or painting a flag that would symbolize patriotism or

Emphasis is on providing equal-assessment tool options, especially for special need or second language students.	presentations, or choice of correct display from given examples.	national identity in a different way. Use music as another medium to convey and analyze symbols.
Evaluation: Linking the assessment responses or products (test, picture, etc.), standards of value, and summative reporting requirements to convey a performance level such as a grade in a prescribed reporting system.	Create value judgments based on assessment data, teacher perceptions of each student's individual performance, and students' own expectations for themselves. Specified standards-driven school-grade level performance requirements may also enter into the mix.	Develop and use informal school assessment data from nontraditional performance measures to extend students' experiences and provide an opportunity to match student characteristics with alternative modes of assessment.

KEY IDEAS TO GUIDE STUDY

Thinking about curriculum is an encounter with its multifaceted nature and the realization that there are sets of key ideas that play out in the study of schooling and curriculum. These in many ways reflect social and political ideals from and about the American experience. They play out in diverse contexts, a nuance of the particular time and the milieu in which they appear and reappear. Other ideas preface the nature of knowledge and how that affects your knowing about schooling and curriculum. One set of ideas is about curriculum and schooling, and the second is about approaching the study of curriculum.

Ideas About Curriculum and Schooling

Discussions about curriculum, either as practiced in schools or elsewhere, can't escape the social and cultural contexts in which it is embedded. Whether it is life in China, Mexico, or the United States, whatever the people collectively consider important for the ordered social good is expressed and passed throughout the society. The relationship between society and schooling is the curriculum, and there are a number of ideas about that relationship to consider.

1. *Schooling is a sociocultural process* in which a society or group seeks to transmit to the young (or to the newcomer) the knowledge, behaviors, and skills that it considers important to the welfare of the society. Depending on the particular human unit

(i.e., family group, state, nation), schooling may be informal, as in the family, or formal, as in the school as a social institution.

2. *The curriculum is central to schooling.* Simply put, the curriculum is the content that is being taught. It is the single important reason for the existence of schooling, either formally as in a public school district or informally as in, perhaps, a preschool for very young learners. In either case, there will be some stated curriculum and materials that represent that curriculum.

3. *Curriculum is values based.* Curriculum expresses what a society and culture regard as important to be passed on for the perpetuation of the society and its way of life. For example, consider the orientation of the curriculum to serve the college bound compared with the availability of vocational career options for those who do not want to go to college. What value does that convey? Or, consider the proportion of curriculum allocated to the study of science and mathematics compared with that for the arts. Considering knowledge alone, what is valued?

4. *Curriculum is a political tool.* In the world of nations, the curriculum is a means to order society and build loyalty to it, a pillar of nation building capable of creating unity, conformity, and performance of civic duty. The agenda of any special interest group or political party includes ideas about the purpose and use of education, and the schools are the conduit for implementing those ideas through policy making and curriculum development.

5. *Curriculum is a reflection of the society and cultures it serves.* If you were to study American textbooks both past and present, particularly those in history and literature, you would find that they promote being American. Civic participation, love of country, patriotism, democracy, constitutionalism, the rule of law—all come into play. Popular culture, a reflection of the society, a blur of lifestyle experiences, is recounted in textbooks and preserves the fading memory of one generation into another, statements of social and cultural change. This might give the impression that curriculum is obsolescent or irrelevant. That would be wrong! What this represents is the important conserving character of curriculum, a reflection of the society it serves. What is interesting about this characteristic of conservancy is the importance it places on teachers to know the content they are charged to teach.

6. *Schooling and curriculum are in a state of perpetual reform.* If there is anything the history of American schooling and curriculum suggests, it is that there is no state of rest or long period of quiet stability. As you are probably aware, the recent No Child Left Behind Act of 2001 seems to dominate discussions about schooling and is a hot topic in the news and the teachers' lounge. It is just one more manifestation of the perpetual reform that is a real characteristic of schooling and curriculum. These reform efforts are always proposed for the social good, and few would doubt the sincerity of the authors. The contesting that goes on is good in the sense that a democracy is often

a messy discussion about important issues and the direction a society is being challenged to take. The state of perpetual reform has to be accepted as part of the schooling experience and working in and with the curriculum.

Ideas About Curriculum Study

You may recall the feelings you had when going off to the first day of formal schooling, probably kindergarten. Or you may have had the experience of taking a child to school for the very first day. Think of how you were "prepped" for that experience or how you prepared that child. The idea was to be positive, to give you or that child some pointers on what the experience would be like and how to be ready. That is the intent here, to give you some thoughts to frame your approach as you encounter the world of curriculum and the knowledge and ideas about practice you will begin to consider as you begin your professional career. In starting out, these first thoughts might be useful:

1. *All knowledge should be considered tentative.* What existed as knowledge 50 or even 100 years ago has changed. Knowledge is constantly being created and revised, a condition that requires a constant state of reflection and review, a role for special scholars within a body of knowledge. The knowledge in the school curriculum you experienced has changed as new knowledge emerges. Imagine what a textbook and the curriculum in science were like pre-Sputnik and in view of current knowledge from the Hubble telescope and explorations and landings on Mars.

2. *Curriculum as a formal body of knowledge is a separate discipline within the field of education.* Education is a broad field comprising knowledge and knowledge-building activities divided into smaller units, or disciplines. Curriculum is one of those disciplines and exists as a special body of knowledge and work. There are relationships; no discipline or field made up of disciplines is isolated. Curriculum and instruction are not separate and unrelated. You need to study and learn about each discipline in itself and then begin to explore their interrelationships that emerge through study and are applied as practice in learning to teach.

3. *A discipline of knowledge has a particular structure* or organization and a particular set of issues or problems that are the focus of discourse in a scholarly community of practitioners. Curriculum, as a discipline, has such a structural character. Things to focus on in understanding that structure include the following:

- The extant *literature,* the writings, studies, and other scholarly endeavors that form a repository of knowledge
- The important *issues and questions* that drive participant discussions and are the focus of research and study
- The particular and special *language* that participants use in their discussion in the context of how it is used in the area of knowledge under study

- The *modes of inquiry,* how investigations proceed, the particular methods and tools used as scholars and others work, particularly as they pertain to special use in the area of knowledge.

7. *Within any discipline, you will find competing ideas and differing perspectives.* The good health of any body of knowledge and scholarly activity depends on generating new and often different ideas as well as periodically revisiting existing ideas and perspectives. This creates a vital tension, ensuring an intellectual vigor among participants and in the process of knowledge creation and use. You will encounter ambiguities about concepts and ideas in curriculum knowledge. For example, there is probably a conversational practitioner agreement on what curriculum means, but defining it, putting it into words and agreeing to a single definition, creates some interesting divergences.

8. *There are many curriculum workers and places of practice.* Curriculum activities occur across a variety of types of work, roles, institutions, and settings in which curriculum knowledge is both created and applied. For instance, corporations develop curriculum for training employees in special knowledge needed by the corporation. Publishing houses produce textbooks, professional books for scholars and teachers, and specialize in developing materials for a variety of instructional settings. Similarly, teachers have in-service sessions to gain knowledge about new curriculum content and teaching methods.

You began this chapter with a discussion of schooling and society and are closing it by reflecting on some key ideas about schools, schooling, curriculum, and the nature of curriculum study. These provide the starting points for continuing your journey exploring curriculum and schooling.

Summary and Conclusions

The subject of this textbook is curriculum, a body of knowledge and a field of study and work. Curriculum is the content of schooling, what is taught in schools and the reason schools exist in some form in a society. The study of schools and schooling is an integral part of the larger field of education. Formal curriculum study involves several communities of practitioners: One is the academic community that seeks to create knowledge about curriculum and schooling through specialized inquiry, and the other is the community of practitioners who deal with curriculum in schools and other locations and produce practice knowledge. This common curriculum enterprise, the curriculum, encompasses large numbers of people who require formal preparation for research, teaching, and other roles in curriculum work. That preparation entails learning the existing body of curriculum knowledge and the ways of inquiring about and doing curriculum work. Central to assuming a role as a professional practitioner is understanding and acquiring a critical perspective about schools, schooling, and curriculum. The concept of the *critical* necessitates focusing on the structure and content of a field of study as a distinct body of knowledge with particular ways of thinking about that knowledge. It is the application of perspective to practice that is continuous and has an acquired reflectivity. Sketching out your critical perspective begins by entering into and exploring the world of curriculum, keeping in mind the key ideas about curriculum that flow in and out of that exploration.

Critical Perspective

1. What aspects of "the American way" are encoded in curriculum?

2. How do schools and schooling in the United States reflect differences in critical perspectives about curriculum?

3. What is an example from your own schooling of each kind of curriculum that Eisner identifies?

4. What purposes and goals of schooling does curriculum serve in all societies?

5. Five ideas about schooling and society are discussed. Can you identify contemporary examples for each of them?

6. What is your connection to curriculum as a professional practitioner?

7. On what frames of reference is your present view of curriculum based? How would you explain that to another person?

8. Why is it important that you develop a critical perspective in your approach to curriculum?

Resources for Curriculum Study

1. Read an abstract of a study on the structure and content of doctoral programs in higher education in China (Wang, n.d.) at http://www3.baylor.edu/~Xin_Wang/pdf/abstract.pdf. What ideas presented in this chapter were supported in that study?

2. Survey a guidebook (http://www.alaskool.org/native_ed/curriculum/cupik_guidebook/Guidebook_Cupik.htm) for integrating culture and curriculum in an Alaska Native community (Reagle, 1998). How does this application suggest the

significance of social and cultural factors in shaping curriculum? What non-Native priorities appear to be part of the curriculum integration?

3. For an interesting online review by Aimee Howley (1998) of Ohio University of *Foucault's Challenge: Discourse, Knowledge, and Power in Education,* edited by Popkewitz and Brennan (1998b), go to http://edrev.asu.edu/reviews/rev18.htm

4. Find a bibliography of works by C. A. Bowers, which include his ideas about the relationship of social ecology to schooling, at http://www.education.miami.edu/ep/contemporaryed/C__A__Bowers/c__a__bowers.html

5. For your portfolio, for a lesson you have taught or observed or plan to teach, consider creating an example like those in Figure 1.3, applying interrelationships of the domains of education to a case.

6. In addition to the resources and references at the end of chapters, you should begin to build a personal file of useful resources on a computer disk, in a card file, or whatever suits your style. The following sources should be on your list. They are useful for a first look at curriculum terms, ideas, and so forth, and offer leads to advance your inquiry. The *Handbook of Research on Curriculum* (Jackson, 1992b) covers just about any topic in curriculum. *Understanding Curriculum* (Pinar, Reynolds, Slattery, & Taubman, 2002) offers insights from a postmodern perspective and is also comprehensive. *Curriculum Books: The First Hundred Years* (Schubert, Schubert, Thomas, & Carroll, 2002) approaches curriculum by focusing on historic trends in books about curriculum. You can cross-reference just about anything using these sources.

References

Blacker, D. (1998). Intellectuals at work and in power: Toward a Foucaultian research ethic. In T. Popkewitz & M. Brennan (Eds.), *Foucault's challenge: Discourse, knowledge, and power in education* (pp. 348–367). New York: Teachers College Press.

Bowers, C. A., & Flinders, D. (1990). *Responsive teaching: An ecological approach to classroom patterning of language, culture and thought.* New York: Teachers College Press.

Eisner, E. (Ed.). (1985). *Learning and teaching the ways of knowing: Eighty-fourth yearbook of the National Society for the Study of Education, part II.* Chicago: National Society for the Study of Education.

Eisner, E., & Vallance, E. (Eds.). (1974). *Conflicting onceptions of curriculum.* Berkeley, CA: McCutchan.

Facione, P. A. (1998). *Critical thinking: What it is and why it counts* [Electronic version]. Millbrae, CA: California Academic Press. Retrieved December 2003 from http://www.insightassessment.com/pdf_files/what&why98.pdf

Howley, A. (1998). [Review of the book *Foucault's challenge: Discourse, knowledge, and power in education*]. Retrieved January 2004 from http://edrev.asu.edu/reviews/rev18.htm

Jackson, P. W. (1992a). Conceptions of curriculum and curriculum specialists. In P. W. Jackson (Ed.), *Handbook of research on curriculum* (pp. 3–40). New York: Macmillan.

Jackson, P. W. (Ed.). (1992b). *Handbook of research on curriculum.* New York: Macmillan.

Kelly, A.V. (2004). *The curriculum: Theory and practice* (5th ed.). London: Sage.

Kincheloe, J. L. (2000). Making critical thinking critical. In D. Weill & H. K. Anderson (Eds.), *Perspectives in critical thinking* (pp. 23–40). New York: Peter Lang.

Kincheloe, J. L., & Steinberg, S. (1993). A tentative description of post-formal thinking: The critical confrontation with cognitive theory. *Harvard Educational Review, 63*(3), 296–320.

Kincheloe, J. L., Steinberg, S., & Villaverde, L. (1999). *Rethinking intelligence: Confronting psychological assumptions about teaching and learning.* New York: Routledge.

Pagels, E. (1988). *Adam, Eve, and the Serpent.* New York: Vintage Books / Random House.

Pinar, W. F., Reynolds, W. M., Slattery, P., & Taubman, P. M. (2002). *Understanding curriculum.* New York: Peter Lang.

Popkewitz, T. S., & Brennan, M. (1998a). Restructuring of social and political theory in education: Foucault and a social epistemology of school practices. In T. S. Popkewitz & M. Brennan (Eds.), *Foucault's challenge: Discourse, knowledge, and power in education* (pp. 3–38). New York: Teachers College Press.

Popkewitz, T. S., & Brennan, M. (Eds.). (1998b). *Foucault's challenge. Discourse, knowledge, and power in education.* New York: Teachers College Press.

Reagle, C. (1998b). *Guidebook for integrating Cup'ik culture and curriculum.* Retrieved January 2004 from http://www.alaskool.org/native_ed/curriculum/cupik_guidebook/Guidebook_Cupik.htm

Schon, D. A. (1983). *The reflective practitioner.* New York: Basic Books.

Schubert, W. H., Schubert, A. L. L., Thomas, T. P., & Carroll, W. M. (2002). *Curriculum books: The first hundred years* (2nd ed.). New York: Peter Lang.

Walkerdine, V. (1988). *The mastery of reason: Cognitive development and the production of rationality.* New York: Routledge.

Wang, X. (n.d.). *A study of the curriculum structure and content of doctoral programs in higher education in the People's Republic of China.* Retrieved December 2003 from http://www3.baylor.edu/ ~Xin_Wang/pdf/abstract.pdf

Weill, D., & Anderson, H. K. (Eds.). (2000). *Perspectives in critical thinking.* New York: Peter Lang.

Part I

THE WORLD OF CURRICULUM

The past, present, and future are reflections of each other. The institutions in any given society mirror those reflections. To understand a society's sense of itself, the particular social character, what is valued, and what is expected of it members, look to its institutions. Among American institutions, schools and their process of schooling reflect America's sense of itself, signaling our character, values, and expectations. At the heart of the schooling enterprise lies the curriculum, and in Part I, you will take a first look at the world of curriculum, how it arose, and what the work comprises in curriculum, and be introduced to certain traditions of thought and practice.

Chapter 2

IN SEARCH OF CURRICULUM

Remember your years in school? Alphabets and numbers meant kindergarten. Reading, spelling, arithmetic, celebrating holidays, reading stories, planting seeds, observing birds and animals—these were primary and elementary school experiences. Then came middle and high school, a shift from the general learning in science, language arts, and social studies to more specific knowledge in biology, chemistry, literature, languages, history, algebra, and geography, among others. What you were learning was often referred to as the "knowledge" you needed to know or the "skills" you should learn, usually tucked into some rationale such as, "If you don't study all that, you won't be ready for life!" or "You need to know that to be successful and get ahead!" Mostly it was accepted without too much questioning, the "stuff" you didn't like, history or mathematics, perhaps, being the exception. So, why were you subjected to that knowledge during 12 years of schooling? Because the society, the community, the group of which you are a member, decided it was important for all its members to share in that common knowledge and learn about ideas, knowledge, skills, and experiences that the society decided were important. In the present, all those courses that students in American schools are supposed to experience and learn is summed up in a word, *curriculum*.

HISTORICAL CONSTRUCTIONS OF CURRICULUM

Curriculum as a word is not a recent invention. It does not simply refer to what is taught in schools or imply a listing of subjects taught. It is more complex, a word from antiquity that has evolved in meaning. Referring to a dictionary, you find that curriculum is from a Latin word, *currere* (probably of earlier Greek origin), referring to the running of a course as in a chariot race. Schooling could also be envisioned as a course to be run or gone over in the same way that a racecourse is a confined, known experience with a beginning and end. Beyond that initial definition, dictionaries variously define curriculum as an aggregate of courses of study given in a school, college, or university (sometimes cited collectively as educational institutions); a particular course of study; or both. Based on a consensus of dictionary sources, curriculum would simply mean "a course of study." However, if you search out what a "course of study" means, you come full circle—it is referred to as a curriculum! Left with that very limited dictionary definition, it will prove more fruitful to follow the trail about how this very complex word evolved through some very inventive times. Curriculum historians have traced the use of the word *curriculum* and its emergence into common use in books and published writings in the years from the 1890s to about 1918 (see Kliebard, 1986; Schubert, Schubert, Thomas, & Carroll, 2002). However, to understand its emergence as an idea and as a discipline in the field of education, the tale begins earlier in the rise of new knowledge in 19th-century America.

Science and Technology

In the mid-19th century, a series of important publishing events signaled a revolution in ideas and knowledge about human life and the physical world in which we live. In 1859, after a 20-year wait, Charles Darwin published *The Origin of Species* (Darwin, 1859/1995). In this book, and the two that followed, he presented and defended his theory of evolution. It is reasonable to say that those publications forever changed the direction of the study of biology and influenced thinking in all areas of knowledge. At about the same time that Darwin was voyaging on the Beagle and formulating his theory, Jacob Bigelow published *The Elements of Technology* (1829) and introduced that concept to American science. That term, in modern garb, conjures up such things as cell phones and nanotechnology. Thus evolution and technology were born, and physical science and life would never be the same from that time on. Their appearance marks two turns in scientific thinking, a new view of the physical world, and, with Darwin's second book in his trilogy, *The Descent of Man* (1871), the emergence of a new field, the scientific study of the human species. What does this have to do with curriculum? It has to do with the influence of evolution on the rising new discipline of sociology; the emergence of a new family of knowledge, the social sciences; and the public articulation and wedding of two key ideas, freedom and progress. Scientific ideas became the justification for freedom and progress, and together they became the purpose and content of what has become a distinctive American curriculum.

Freedom and Progress

In 19th-century America, one of the most influential sociologists was an Englishman, Herbert Spencer. Robert Nisbet sums up his influence this way, "It is impossible to think of any single name more deeply respected, more widely read among social philosophers and scientists, and more influential in a score of spheres, than was that of Herbert Spencer" (1980, p. 235). Spencer coined the term *Social Darwinism*, which essentially encompassed the following ideas: (a) A person has freedom to do what he or she wills as long as that does not transgress the same right for others, and (b) the individual and society are organic and evolving, and progress could be achieved through movement toward identified goals for the improvement of both. Spencer held that knowledge was the means to freedom and progress and, in one of his famous lectures, asked, "What knowledge was of most worth?" It is a short trip from that question to the matter of passing that "knowledge" to members of the society so that social and individual progress could be achieved. In short, what Spencer was staking out was an original curriculum question, "What ought to be taught?" His answer was to use science, mathematics, and the emerging social sciences (political science, economics, sociology, and anthropology) as knowledge to achieve whatever ends were determined in the name of progress and freedom.

Questions about purposes, content, and instruction in schooling were part of the larger knowledge revolution about the nature of American society playing out at the turning of the 19th into the 20th century. Spencer's question about what should be taught initiated thinking about subjects and instruction, basic elements in schooling. In much the same way that Darwin had unsettled complacent science with his ideas about evolution, Spencer and others applied it to social betterment through science, albeit with a large dose of racism—it was white society that they addressed. Bigelow's science-driven technology idea, manifest in new applications of electricity, industrial machinery, the railroad, and wireless and other inventions, seemed to substantiate the arguments of Darwin and Spencer. The confluence of those strands seemed to suggest a new unity of knowledge that could lead to improvement in all spheres of American life.

Figure 2.1   The Herbartian Method

- Preparation
  Review of new ideas related to old ones
- Presentation
  Presentation of the new material
- Association
  Association of old with new material
- Generalization
  Deriving of general principles (new knowledge) from the association of the old and new
- Application
  Applying the principles (new knowledge) to specific practical situations

Curriculum and Instruction

The problem was, what means of delivery could best serve to get the new message of the scientific gospel into society? The American solution, which took many years to achieve, was to provide this knowledge through some form of common schooling. What was taught prior to the new knowledge was variously referred to as "content" or "subject matter," based on disciplines of knowledge and the exercise of the mind consistent with the prevailing *faculty psychology*—a 19th-century concept of learning that saw the mind as consisting of separate powers, or faculties. The unwieldy task of enumerating or listing individual subject matter in addressing "what was to be taught" begged for a solution, some collective term. New pedagogical ideas entered the schooling dialogue and further complicated the matter of which subjects or what content. For example, in the 1880s and 1890s, the popular Herbartian movement in education (Kliebard, 1986) used the term *method* in ways that seem synonymous with content or subject matter. However, as depicted in Figure 2.1, method might also imply instruction or a template for devising a lesson plan addressing what was to be taught and how to do it.

This apparent mingling of subject matter and instruction as pedagogy seemed confusing: Were the matters of the subjects to be taught and instruction in those subjects the same or separate issues? Did it make any difference? These new pedagogical issues, the separate articulation of content issues from instructional ones, marked the emergence of new and important matters of practice. In pedagogical terms, instruction was understood to mean the delivery of what was to be taught. There remained the matter of the "what" that was to be delivered. The idea of using curriculum as a concept subsuming and replacing such words as content or subject matter had yet to gel. Notwithstanding its early appearance in the title of John Dewey's 1902 signal publication *The Child and the Curriculum,* the concept of curriculum had not gained educational prominence. It was not easy to replace the traditional use of subject matter and content designations with an economical word for what was taught in schools. The problems of meaning—using curriculum as synonymous with instruction, or implying both when using the term pedagogy—those matters of clarification also vexed curriculum's emergence as an area of study, a distinct, separate one of scholarly interest within the larger field of education.

The Applied and Academic Traditions

Exactly what was curriculum? What did it mean? From a Spencerian point of view, curriculum was "knowledge" to be transmitted, specifically that which was of "most worth." The issue was, then, just a matter of deciding which kind of knowledge. When Spencer asked his question, he did so from an academic point of view to advocate the application of scientific knowledge in the study of human evolution. Events and emerging ideas about the nature of society and the future would provide different and often competing meanings for curriculum and signify it in different ways. Mere definitions would not suffice; curriculum had to have attributes, defining qualities that would give it shape. That kind of thinking meant to conceptualize a new meaning for curriculum, a process that played out over the course of some 50 years, a period roughly from Dewey's 1902 publication *The Child and the Curriculum* to Ralph Tyler's *Basic Principles of Curriculum and Instruction,* published in 1949. Two developments affected the conceptual process, the rise of the social sciences and the question of the practical and academic nature of curriculum work. The rise of the social sciences, particularly sociology, shifted the focus to the study of human social institutions, of which schools were one. The second development, the matter of assigning responsibility over curriculum, centered on institutional decisions about whether curriculum was a practical or academic enterprise.

By the 1920s, activities such as curriculum development in mainly urban school districts—Denver, Chicago, and St. Louis, for example—gave curriculum a practical, applied, dimension (Cuban, 1984; Kliebard, 1986; McKelvey, 1963). Various state departments of education—Indiana and Alabama, for example—provided guides for doing curriculum development. Curriculum work meant curriculum development, at least at the school and teaching level. Publications from the National Education Association and the Progressive Education Association also spread the word about developmental processes and activities. However, it was at the academic level that the greatest influence was achieved.

Academicians, specifically those who would influence prospective teachers—those such as Boyd Bode at Ohio State; John Dewey at Chicago; and William Heard Kilpatrick, Harold Rugg, and George S. Counts at Teachers College, Columbia—were among many who published influential books about curriculum (see Schubert et al., 2002). These books were mainly of two orientations, those focusing on practical matters and those on the theoretical. Discussion about the practical focused on purposes for schooling and what content would best achieve those purposes, an early dialogue about aligning purposes and curriculum. Given contemporary discussions about purposes, you can understand that the debate was as lively then as now. The second approach was theoretical, not in the scientific sense but in a form that came to be called *curriculum theory.* These were proposals advocating a specific curriculum presented with extensive logical argument and representative examples of organization and content. With rare exception, what these texts represented were "ought to be" and "how to" perspectives rather than reports or suggestions based on research or scholarly studies of curriculum work. These developments meant, in effect, that curriculum was dividing into two distinct areas of work, one of academic text development and theorizing, the other of the school practitioner and curriculum development. The meaning of curriculum depended on what was expressed through text authority rather than what was known through practice, specifically through practical curriculum development activity. This was the great divide, the theory-based knowledge encountered in preparing to teach on the one hand and what was actually found about curriculum in the reality of school practice on the other hand. What influenced meaning and practice was what was published and disseminated about curriculum. Texts became the influential source, not the stories of practical work in schools and classrooms.

Classroom Teachers and Curriculum Scholars

The academic/school community divide also influenced the development of curriculum work in a broader sense. Conceptualizing and mapping out curriculum and curriculum work was moving along two paths. Going in one direction were those pursuing curriculum as an academic function. Steering a different course were those advocating the practical, understanding curriculum through its use by practitioners in schools and classrooms. The voices multiplied. Some addressed curriculum as the need to differentiate knowledge according to specific purposes. Others assumed the mantle of formal academic knowledge and asked which of the disciplines were of most worth in forming curriculum content. Still others forsook the knowledge issue in favor of beginning with aims or purposes to be served, or centering on the child, and then determining what knowledge or experience would meet those needs. Curriculum scholars have categorized those perspectives in various ways, calling them orientations, philosophical positions, ideologies, and so forth. Some of these frames of reference and their authors are summarized in Figure 2.2. Collectively, they are of historical and philosophical interest, a sampling of different scholarly perspectives on curriculum.

Taken collectively, these suggest two things. First, that curriculum was evolving as a larger focus beyond merely selecting "knowledge." There were other possibilities, other reasons for organizing curriculum, particularly those growing out of new knowledge from the social sciences about the relationships among people, society, its

Figure 2.2   Some Curriculum Frames of Reference

McNeill (1975)	Eisner & Vallance (1974)	Kliebard (1986)	Huebner (1966)	Tanner & Tanner (1980)
Prevailing Conceptions	*Concerns or Orientations*	*Interest Groups*	*Rationales*	*Curriculum Traditions*
Humanistic	Cognitive	Humanist	Technical	Traditional
Social	Processes	Developmentalist	Political	Essentialist
Reconstruction	Technology	Social Meliorist	Scientific	Experimental
Academic	Self-Actualization	Social Efficiency	Aesthetic	
Technological	Academic		Ethical	
	Rationalism			
	Social Reconstruction			

institutions, and what knowledge would serve their progress. Second, there was a growing differentiation between curriculum and instruction. New interest in the study of teaching, learning, and schooling—the Progressive Education Association's Eight-Year Study during the 1930s was one example—began to focus on the research complexities in working with curriculum and instruction, separately or in combination.

Whereas the general trend was toward research about learning and instruction and less about curriculum per se, the separate interests gave impetus to new interpretations and ideas about what constituted the world of curriculum. There was an interest in searching out and building a foundation of knowledge about curriculum, and there was increased interest in the nature of the classroom and particular aspects of teaching as curriculum (Cuban, 1984). The acts of teaching and learning highlight several interesting characteristics of curriculum. It is knowledge; it is practice. It is the relationship between knowledge and practice. It is content, as in science or literature, and it is a process, as in a particular way to think in and with each subject. Curriculum is also place-bound; it has the characteristics of being in a location, usually a classroom. Teachers and students in those places tend to be isolated, and creatively studying this "curriculum-in-context" is not easily done with traditional quantitative research methods. However, the availability of new qualitative methods from the social sciences— case study and ethnographic methods, for example—provided new tools of inquiry to study the classroom and teaching as microunits. Using those methods, researchers and other practitioners could explore and illuminate curriculum and, of course, other contextual elements such as instruction. A second advantage of the new inquiry methods was that the object of study was "happening"; it was in use. The reformulation of how and what to study, the recasting of how to look at curriculum as something alive rather than inert, propelled changes in thinking about curriculum and its constituent nature. Much of that impetus was owed to what came to be called the Tyler Rationale.

CURRICULUM INQUIRY AND THE TYLER RATIONALE

If a deeper understanding of curriculum was to be achieved, it had to begin with a rethinking of what was known and the articulation of new ways of thinking about and studying curriculum. The dilemma in advancing the notion of curriculum was twofold. There was a sense that traditional ways of studying curriculum—the speculative, logical, and theoretical—were unprogressive. Second, unlike other fields, such as the social and natural sciences with their growing traditions of foundational knowledge based on research, no similar inquiry tradition was developing, either generally in education or particularly about schooling and curriculum.

Competing Curriculum Ideas

Schooling discussions were not bereft of ideas. The reality was much discussion advocating one position or another but lacking any evidence validating a particular one. How does a *curricularist,* defined as anyone who works with curriculum, such as the teacher or the scholar, accept as valid certain new ideas about curriculum and purposes for schooling as well as linkages between purposes and curriculum? By the mid-1930s, the major focus was on the aims of schooling, and the force of curriculum thinking and work was on establishing the legitimacy of one of three main contending views. The traditionalist promoted knowledge and subject matter. A second group wanted curriculum to serve social purposes. A third thought curriculum should focus on the learner (more about these ideas in Chapters 4 and 7). The foundation for arguing any position was essentially logical scholarly argument, speculation, and theory. What was lacking was a way to establish the legitimacy of any one of the three views being advocated. There was no research-based knowledge to guide curriculum work or substantiate one set of proposals or theories as better than any other. What curriculum study needed was a fresh approach to inquiry that would lead to a new core of knowledge about curriculum and ways to study it in addition to the existing discourse of scholarly argument and theory building.

Curriculum Inquiry and Tyler's Work

Refocusing curriculum work meant asking new questions and devising new methods to study and guide curriculum work. The catalyst was Ralph Tyler's formulation of a way to think and do curriculum and instructional work that essentially derived

Figure 2.3   The Tyler Rationale

• STATE PURPOSES •
What educational purposes should the school seek to attain?

• IDENTIFY EXPERIENCES •
What educational experiences can be provided that are likely to attain these purposes?

• ORGANIZE EXPERIENCES •
How can these educational experiences be effectively attained?

• EVALUATE EXPERIENCES •
How can we determine whether these purposes are being attained?

Source: Tyler, 1949, pp. 1–2.

from his experience as evaluator for the seminal 1930s Eight-Year Study of the Progressive Education Association. Although more is written about this study and Tyler in Chapter 7, it is important to mention it in this discussion about the development of curriculum as a discipline within the education field. Tyler, through a series of steps (Figure 2.3), established a process for working with curriculum that was elegant in its focus, was easily used, and centered inquiry and thinking.

Tyler's Rationale, as it has come to be known, bridged the curriculum dualities—curriculum as what was to be taught in schools and curriculum as a scholarly body of knowledge, and curriculum as knowledge building about content to be taught and as knowledge about the processes to construct that knowledge. Using Tyler's Rationale gave curriculum a new meaning and prompted the search for additional ways to study curriculum and create new knowledge. Curriculum was moving beyond definitional discussions, theory formulation, and speculative curriculum development practices. Looking at curriculum from the perspective of the university scholar or the teacher practitioner meant encounters with complexity and greater levels of abstraction, a perception that there were more layers of curriculum knowledge to be uncovered. The new knowledge required validation through research, practice, or both.

In effect, curriculum work could evolve from Tyler's Rationale; it suggested a cycle of knowledge production about curriculum functioning in a disciplined way, joining together practitioners in all phases of curriculum activity in a bounded discourse community. This does not mean a community of kindred souls all enveloped in the same ideas. It does mean a community with a disciplined sense of itself, one that is framed by a common focus in a discussion with different views: A belief that progress is made through the creation of knowledge, acceptance that in the creative process there will be a struggle to maintain an equilibrium of engagement, and awareness that curiosity—the casual observation or unexpected question—could change or challenge that balance. Tyler's contribution to curriculum is much like Darwin's contribution to biology; it changed and recentered discussion and energized the search for knowledge through different methods of inquiry.

Tyler's Rationale added a new dimension to understanding curriculum. It was no longer a matter of understanding by definition; rather, curriculum would be understood in different ways. The process Tyler envisioned moved curriculum from a passive to an active mode. Curriculum in the old, passive sense had functioned as a speculative venture about knowledge to be taught, arguments over subject matter inclusions, or theories about how to frame a curriculum. Tyler introduced a way to "think about" and "do" curriculum that could be used by anyone anywhere. It opened up a range of different ways to understand curriculum—through a definition, as a concept, and by experiencing it—and to give meaning to it in all its forms—from the simple and concrete use of a textbook to the complex and abstract formulation of a single K–12 curriculum.

CURRICULUM RECONCEPTUALIZED AND REDEFINED

As noted previously, a brief definition for curriculum would be "a course of study." You or I might define curriculum as "all the subjects taken in school"—history, languages, and physics, for example. Neither definition would be in error, and either would convey a simple meaning that would be understood, at least by any American. Curriculum scholars have also weighed in with definitions. A sample of those efforts is found in Figure 2.4.

Figure 2.4   Some Definitions and Descriptions of Curriculum

A *series of things*, which children and youth must do and experience, by way of developing abilities to do the things well that make up the affairs of adult life. (Bobbitt, 1918, p. 42)

Curriculum is all the experiences children have under the guidance of teachers. (Caswell & Campbell, 1935, p. 5)

The total effort of the school to bring about desired outcomes in school and out-of-school situations (Saylor & Alexander, 1974, p. 3)

Curriculum encompasses all learning opportunities provided by the school. (Saylor & Alexander, 1974, p. 7)

The curriculum is what is learned. (Macdonald, 1986)

The "curriculum," as we use the term, refers not only to the official list of courses offered by the school—we call that the "official curriculum"—but also to the purposes, content, activities, and organization of the educational program actually created in schools by teachers, students, and administrators. (Walker & Soltis, 1997, p. 1)

A set of decision-making processes and products that focuses on the preparation, implementation, and assessment of general plans to influence students' behaviors and insights. (Armstrong, 2003, p. 4)

Glancing through those selections, you can discern both differences and similarities. There appears to be some consensus that curriculum is some kind of a planned experience, that it relates to learners, and that it has a location, the school. Beyond those elements, the characterizations vary. There is a sense that those definitions can only provide surface meanings. Students of curriculum, especially scholars, have for years attempted to establish a standardized meaning for curriculum, and they will continue to do so. Understanding curriculum beyond definitions requires other ways of thinking about it—as a concept, as an activity, as experience.

Curriculum as Concept

Concepts are complex meanings wrapped into one or several words. They are meanings created by conceptualization, a process of elaboration using ways to think about something, as in picturing, perceiving, imagining, or experiencing it. As a way of creating meaning, concepts go beyond accepted definitions, descriptions, or simple sensory experience. To think conceptually is to use your mind to create knowledge about something—intrinsic knowledge already possessed and the external knowledge that must be acquired. Moving through the process of defining, describing, and conceptualizing, you encounter tiers of knowing, a migration from surface to deeper meaning involving degrees of simplicity and complexity. Moving from the simple and concrete to the complex and abstract in thinking is a passage through knowledge creation. In a sense, this is moving from general to more specialized meaning. For example, the words *car, vehicle,* and *automobile* are a set of concepts. Each is different, yet each relates in limited ways to the others. A car is an automobile and a vehicle; it can also be a vehicle but not an automobile, as in a train "car" that is a piece of railroad rolling stock. Vehicles include more than cars, but an automobile has a specific set of attributes and anything else either has them or it doesn't. The applicability of meanings to such concepts involves levels of simplicity, complexity, concreteness, and abstractness. Curriculum can be made immediate and concrete, as in textbooks or guides you can see, touch, and read. A student and teacher can experience curriculum in a classroom. The classroom serves as a context, a set of circumstances that can shape meanings you acquire about curriculum as you experience it.

Curriculum as Activity

Studying how curriculum is created and used, what curriculum workers such as teachers actually do with it, gives specialized meaning to curriculum as an activity. Observing a teacher using the curriculum in a classroom adds an applied dimension. The knowledge about curriculum the teacher needs in order to use curriculum differs from the knowledge required in other worker roles. The particular roles of different curriculum workers also refine its meaning. Other professionals—professors, curriculum researchers, and curriculum specialists—may have work- or role-related needs that require a different conceptualizing of curriculum. The individual or role-related personal need to know, the level of understanding, and the knowledge requirements of a particular role or work context depend on the way people use curriculum and make decisions about it in their work.

Different activities define curriculum in different ways by how they represent curriculum and the kind of curriculum knowledge they use and in turn create about curriculum. What, for example, do a textbook company and a teacher have in common? Each is involved in curriculum work—the teacher in the fluid events of using the curriculum in the classroom and having to adjust it in relation to the students, time, plans, and other factors. The textbook worker is producing a static textbook, something inert until it is used. There are two dimensions at work that unite them. The teacher uses the text as the platform for classroom work and is guided by it as it represents the curriculum. The textbook producer is creating the platform the teacher will use. There has to be congruence through the text as representing what the teacher needs and what the textbook company provides based on a common foundation of knowledge about curriculum and the purposes it is to serve. More will be said about this curriculum as activity in Chapter 3, which introduces you to curriculum work, and in Chapters 8 through 12, where you will study the various roles and the interactive nature of curriculum work.

Curriculum as Experience

Some things acquire meaning through our experiencing them. This is a special characteristic of curriculum. In your schooling, you passed through the curriculum mediated by the time and place of that journey. Your individual and shared encounters with the curriculum shaped individual and collective meaning of curriculum. If you asked a diverse sample of people—from various states, of different ages, who attended different types of schools—and asked them what they were taught in any grade, they would with minor variations describe a similar curriculum. They shared experiences in common even though these occurred in different settings.

Teachers and other school personnel who work with curriculum also experience curriculum but in a different way. They directly experience the curriculum as *curriculum-in-use*. This has multiple meanings. From the teacher's perspective, it is what is being taught—reading, literature, science, and so forth. From the students' point of view, it is what they individually attend to and receive or experience, an idiosyncratic process. Ask a group of students what they studied in school today and they will give you different answers that, taken as a whole, depict the curriculum. Parents and the general public also have perceptions of the curriculum-in-use. They observe and discuss from a distance. The distance from the event coupled with demands in the daily circumstances of living seem to scatter perceptions of the curriculum. For them, curriculum-in-use tends to become a selective remembering of what it was when they were in school. Parents who criticize "that new math" or suggest that teachers ought to get back to the "solid" subjects they had in school are reacting to the "then" and "now" aspect of curriculum-in-use.

A Curriculum, The Curriculum, Your Curriculum

The idea of curriculum-in-use evokes other meanings attained in the curriculum experience: The curriculum is illuminated in teaching and learning; teachers teach the curriculum, students learn it. That shared set of experiences involves a general sense of engagement in *a* curriculum, one that is generic in nature; *the* curriculum, that which is intended and specific to the moment; and *your* curriculum, what is experienced personally. Considered as questions, what does experiencing *a* curriculum, *the* curriculum, and *your* curriculum mean?

The first encounter (what is *a* curriculum?) strives to characterize a generic, universal meaning for curriculum. There are essentially two views about that. The first is that curriculum embraces schools and schooling; it is what is taught there. The second view is that curriculum is not specific to a place or setting but can exist in many forms as a set of experiences. Schubert et al. (2002, p. 499) put it thus: "[Homes], peer groups, formal youth organizations, jobs, and the media profoundly influence children and youth. I submit these are curricula in their own right." In this latter view, curriculum could be anything and mean anything.

The second question (what is *the* curriculum?) refers to curriculum as de jure and as de facto. *De jure* refers to curriculum as a legal entity. It is established through constitutions and other laws prescribing what should be in the school curriculum, that is to say, what should be taught. By *de facto* is meant the actual, daily, moment-to-moment existence of curriculum in schools, the reality of what is taught in the classroom by the teacher and experienced by the students. The existence of curriculum is a fact; it is the curriculum-in-use. Curriculum, as you recall from Chapter 1, has been described in various ways; two ways you have not yet encountered refer to its formal and informal nature. *Formal* curriculum (de jure in this sense) refers to what is made explicit in such documents as a state curriculum guide or course of study or teacher's lesson plan. It is *informal* in the ways it is adjusted by the teacher's decisions as it is taught, the modification or exclusion of what is formalized. Two other aspects of the informal curriculum (see Chapter 1) have been labeled the *hidden curriculum* and the *null curriculum*. The hidden curriculum refers to unwritten, and often unintended, things students learn in school. An elementary student learns to walk in a line when moving, to wait turns for the drinking fountain, and to raise a hand to speak. These and other rules are not stipulated in the formal, or de jure, curriculum; they are part of the hidden curriculum. There is also what Elliot Eisner (1994) refers to as the null curriculum: that which is not taught. This concept highlights the power of particular mindsets in education, which also affect decisions over what purposes the curriculum should serve. Eisner identified a "small chunk" mindset in curriculum practice, for example, in which factual details are emphasized over "big picture" understandings. These unifying observations, because they are not taught, are part of the null curriculum. As another example, until recently, the achievements of women and minorities also tended to be part of the null curriculum.

Your curriculum refers to the individual, personal understanding of curriculum—what teachers, students, and others perceive as the curriculum. As a teacher, your curriculum is what you plan and engage through instruction. It is the taught curriculum. As a student, your curriculum is the received curriculum that you encounter under the direction of the teacher. Note that it is possible that what a teacher prepares, the intended curriculum, may not be what the students receive. Your curriculum is also historical. It includes the personal memories and remembrances often at odds with the reality of the contemporary curriculum in general or the particular curriculum-in-use.

Curriculum as History and Expectations

Mid–20th-century thinking among scholars in all areas of knowledge anticipated the advances to be made in human progress through science. The Salk polio vaccine, advances in jet propulsion and rocketry, the Great Society programs, and the civil rights movement seemed to reflect what General Electric claimed and Ronald Reagan spoke, "At General Electric, progress is our most important product." That comment about progress from the 1950s suggests the tone or theme of a particular phase in the historical development of schooling and curriculum in America. These periods are sketched in Figure 2.5. Referring to that figure for a moment, you will note that central to the social progress of the 1950s was the role of educational institutions and the potent empowerment they received from the famous post–World War II GI Bill. In 1944, the United States Congress created a vast "right" to a schooling opportunity, first for

Figure 2.5   The Changing American Curriculum

- **Formative Period (c. 1860s–1900s):** The discourse evolves about schooling and conceptualizing the substance of what is taught as curriculum.
- **Curriculum Creation (c. 1900s–1970s):** Curriculum is emphasized as practice through curriculum development work in schools. Theory work tends toward linking theory and practice. The Great Depression and two world wars distract attention from schooling.
- **Theory and Discourse (c. 1970s–1980s):** Speculative academic discussions about theory and reconceptualizing tend to dominate discourse and separate school and academic communities in curriculum work.
- **The Contemporary Scene (c. 1980s–2005):** Starting in 1983, a flow of school reform movements brings debate about purposes for public schooling, outcomes, accountability, and equity in and access to the curriculum.

returning veterans and later extended to all who served. The other direct recipients of that largesse were postsecondary training institutions, colleges, and universities—expansion of educational opportunities meant more schools and programs to meet the demands of returning veterans. The message was progress through education, and education for all meant from kindergarten through college. There was, however, no systematic linking of schooling from kindergarten through college, and only a minimal articulation of what learning or other requirements were necessary for entry at any particular point from kindergarten to college. The fundamental question was what did they need to know (knowledge) or to do (skills) preparatory to exercising their educational rights? This was the quintessential issue: the curriculum.

The upshot was that for the next 50-some years and into the 21st century, curriculum and its scope and sequence, from preschool to graduate school, became a primary concern. That learning flow became the focus of numerous reform efforts. Still, the questions remained. To the perennial one, what exactly is curriculum, were added several others. One—how do you go about doing curriculum?—prompted the study of curriculum as work, a collection of behaviors and decisions. A second focused on the dual character of curriculum, the content of what was taught and the process itself as something to be studied. A third followed from earlier wrestling with various meanings curriculum had begun to accrue, one anchored in fact, the other in future thinking. These are the questions of "how" the curriculum got the way it is and "what" it is likely to be in the future, twin reflections that frame thinking about the meanings of curriculum like bookends. Both depend on understanding that curriculum is a social product, a reflection of the society it serves. Referring again to Figure 2.5, the curriculum and what it has come to mean have evolved through four epochs. During each epoch, some ideology or practice was added, forming a distinctly American system of schooling. Those constructions represent consensual responses American society made about the need for schools and the purposes for schooling. The organization and content of the curriculum suggest national values, what it means to be an American—the knowledge, skills, and experiences that an American ought to possess, and our place in the world. The curriculum reflects a collective sense of self, an American character, the institutional structures that are important, and the ideologies that power how we view the future.

Since before nationhood, American schooling traditions have been shaped by obvious and subtle issues and conflicts among various parties: public, parochial, private, political, lay, and professional. Among the enduring issues have been two: "What purposes should schools serve?" and "What should schools teach?" Both questions are curriculum questions because they arrive at the issue of curriculum substance, what is to be taught, the content, the "course to be run." The response given to one requires consideration of the other regardless of which is asked first. It is not a matter of the starting point; what curriculum has been, its past meaning, and what it will mean tomorrow are bookends framing what it means in the present.

PERSPECTIVE INTO PRACTICE: Curriculum Reconceptualized and Redefined		
Definitions	*Elementary Classroom*	*Secondary Classroom*
Curriculum as **Activity:** Lessons from life sciences	Develop the life cycle concept: planting a flower or vegetable seed in dirt or a potato in water, a simple activity mirroring curriculum discussions about planning, organizing, and implementing curriculum material.	Study the life cycle concept: Viewing a video on the life cycle of the salmon and developing a comparable cycle for other life forms. How a teacher plans, organizes, and implements a lesson employing comparative analyses to promote higher thinking and development.
Curriculum as **Experience:** Lessons from life sciences	The *teacher* highlights the development of the plant and creates a master chart of progress. The *student* observes the growth and creates a daily chart with comments and follows his or her own personal plant's development.	The *teacher* presents other life cycle examples (i.e., mice, elephants, etc.) for species variation. The *student* prepares a chronology of their life cycles reflecting the various developments and presented in a chart summary and personal narrative.
Curriculum as **History** and **Expectations:** Lessons from life sciences	The life cycle concept is applicable to every species. It can be charted as historical approach. It is a basic concept schools are expected to teach in increments of depth.	The concept of a life cycle moves personal thinking to consider the simple and concrete, as in watching a seed develop, and the complex and abstract, as in the development of humans. Learning to think in this way is a threshold to professions such as teaching, medicine, and theology.

PERCEPTIONS ABOUT CURRICULUM

Curriculum has a history and multiple meanings. Out of that history and the collective meanings that give it shape, what perceptions should guide further exploration? From the discussion to this point, some perceptions seem warranted and have been alluded to previously, whereas others are new extrapolations. These perceptions do not promote a particular perspective. Rather, they frame a threshold of knowledge from which to begin exploring curriculum. They provide the landscape of possible perceptions out of which a picture of curriculum knowledge and practice arise. This picture is based on seeing curriculum as dynamic, powerful, ubiquitous, and multipurpose.

Curriculum Is Dynamic

Curriculum is always in a state of becoming even though it is captured in the passive confines of a book or picture or some other medium used to present and engage it. A classroom textbook presents "canned" information to be learned. If a teacher opts not to read certain pages or sections, the curriculum represented in the book's content has been changed. These on-the-spot changes are the professional decisions a teacher makes. They change the curriculum into a different one that may or may not be what was intended. In making those kinds of decisions, the teacher is guided by knowledge about curriculum gained from course work and from classroom practice. Other factors also influence curriculum activity. There is always the possibility that the curriculum planned for a specified time will have to be altered. If the time allocation changes, something will be omitted. Teacher plans for Thursday may not be met because of schedule changes such as an unannounced assembly or a scheduled emergency drill. This can mean some learners get what was planned whereas others get nothing or an abbreviated version. Students also get sick, they leave early for sporting events, and they are taken out of school for parental reasons. All these factors influence how the curriculum is or isn't received in the intended way. The upshot is that circumstances, not students, often interdict curricular intent. Curriculum becomes differentiated by circumstances as well as by variations in students. And that is another problem. No student is the same as another, and some, such as immigrants and students with special needs, must be considered specifically. These variations in the population of students force curriculum to be dynamic, to be considered in multiple contexts. This is a perspective of curriculum as vibrant and not static. The initial encounter with curriculum is a face-off with anticipated but unknown outcomes.

Curriculum Is Powerful

Control of the school curriculum is an exercise in power. The forces determining the shape of the curriculum can subtly influence the social, cultural, political, and economic directions in a society. The curriculum is indoctrination for good or evil. It can be liberating and conserving, promote individual development or group allegiances. In America, school curriculum promotes individual development through a core of common studies: reading, language arts, mathematics, and others of what are considered the liberal arts. Those studies are presumed to "liberate" the person to develop critical ways to think. The curriculum also allows a choice of electives that promote individual student interests. On the other hand, what the curriculum offers is traditional; that is, it is much the same curriculum that has existed over the last two or three generations. The history of American curriculum is not one of dramatic or quick change. The nature of a democracy, the inherent need for discussion and to search for consensus, mitigates. As a society becomes more democratic, including more persons in the decision process,

agreeing on school purposes becomes more complex. Various stakeholders, (i.e., political parties, special interest groups, businesses, advocacy groups, etc.) expect to participate. They bring with them diverse, often conflicting views about the purposes schools
and curriculum should serve. Decisions also are often subject to shifting views of the
momentary majority. Usually the result is a "negotiated curriculum."

In America, the curriculum also mirrors the transitional impact social and political
movements, leaders, and events have had on the question of purposes schools should
serve. For example, a perusal of textbooks used during World Wars I and II shows how
governments used propaganda about the enemy to stir nationalistic feelings and support
for the war. Unfortunately, the curriculum has also been used to foster racism and dis-
parage other cultures. How and why these exploits have occurred suggest two things. In
democratic societies such as the United States, curriculum negotiation is characterized
by its contentious, fragile nature. Censorship discussions about what should or should
not be included in textbooks or what books students should read exemplify this fragility.
Second, democracies by their very nature have untidy decision-making processes. In
many ways, the curriculum is an artifact, documenting how ideas and politics have
played out. Various episodes—the progressive movement of the early 20th century, censorship during the McCarthy era of the 1950s, and the effect of the Russian Sputnik in
1957—influenced the writing of curricula and textbooks by shifting the emphasis and
content. More recently, the arrival of the standards-based curriculum movement in the
1980s and 1990s and the No Child Left Behind Act of 2001 have given curriculum a
more prescriptive appearance. There has been a standardization of curricular expectations and a gradual transfer of curriculum responsibility from local schools and districts
to state, regional, and national organizations including the federal government. This
movement has tended to lessen local curriculum initiatives and control. Curriculum thus
both reflects and engenders power.

Curriculum Is Everywhere

Curriculum involves many people at different levels and in different locations.
Consider your state, for example. Locally, the curriculum exists in the classroom, the
school, and the central district office. Statewide, it is in all classrooms, schools, and
school districts. Curriculum is also a function of the state department of instruction or
department of education, as the case may be, which exercises authority over the curriculum for all schools and districts in the state. There are regional organizations such
as the Southern Association of Colleges and Schools, national entities such as the
Association for Supervision and Curriculum Development, and quasi-public ones like
the Council of Chief State School Officers that are all involved in some way with curriculum work. There are others—commercial textbook publishers, school supply specialists, manufacturers, and special interest groups—that produce curriculum materials
for classroom use.

Across the nation, a variety of sanctioned and unsanctioned materials is available. The distinction is important. A state or district board approves "sanctioned materials," mostly those in the form of textbooks. "Unsanctioned materials" are offered on a discretionary basis in the hope they will find their way into the classroom, serving the interests of those creating the materials. Curriculum materials can often be flash points for controversy, especially if they seem to contravene public perceptions of local standards. Materials of a religious nature or those pertaining to sex or sexual practices are some examples.

Curriculum is ubiquitous. Other than public and quasi-public contexts for curriculum, there are parochial institutions, such as the Roman Catholic Church, which provide special religious-oriented curriculum for their schools. Private schools also have curricula that can vary. There is also the Waldorf Curriculum and others available for home schooling or other schooling alternatives. Despite the many and varied curricula, however, ultimate authority over what they will contain and what will be regarded as minimums is under the authority of the individual state in which the school or schooling activity is located. How that authority is exercised will vary from state to state.

Curriculum Serves Many Purposes

Curriculum is what schools and schooling are all about. It is also important because, in the school setting, it can be a defining, shared American experience. Through curriculum, we have the opportunity to develop and share in common citizenship, language, history, and specialized knowledge in the sciences and the arts. It is interesting that a school-age child in any grade can change schools from one state to another and find that the curriculum from school to school, state to state, is virtually the same. This will hold true in public schooling and is usually true for private and parochial schools as well. This suggests that in a general sense, a common, unofficial curriculum exists. The existence of this supposed common curriculum is curious because no national curriculum exists in the United States. Other nations, the United Kingdom and Germany, for example, have national curricula. Why don't we? Under the United States Constitution, the federal government does not have a specific, direct grant of power to establish or control schools. In America, schools are traditionally creatures of the individual states in accordance with each state's constitutional provisions. By custom, the exercise of a state's constitutional authority has been one of "local control" by the authorized subunit usually designated as the school "district." What unites this decentralized and dispersed quality of schooling and schools? The curriculum! The state may establish by law what shall be taught in all schools—parochial, private, and public—and for those taught at home. The authority to determine what the curriculum will be is a powerful social, cultural, economic, and political tool. This involves two important kinds of work, policy making and planning, which are the subjects for discussion in Chapter 9.

Schools and curriculum serve important social and cultural purposes for the societies and cultures in which they are embedded. Perceptions of curriculum and schools are part of our individual and collective social and cultural experiences. In the United States, schooling and curriculum serve both to represent and facilitate an evolving American society and nation. For example, elementary schooling in reading and writing, the basic literacy skills, seeks to ensure communication in a common language. Young children also learn about American traditions, holidays, and other symbols of our civic heritage. Curriculum represents a common connecting of people through experience and ideas. This implies a certain commonality in what schools collectively do, what they are to achieve, their reasons for existing in and serving society.

Individualism and personal development are honored American ideals served by curriculum. Considering curriculum's social-cultural nature, what purposes or expectations of the individual derive from that milieu, and how are they determined? As social-cultural beings and recipients of social-cultural knowledge embedded in curriculum, the emphasis is to develop personal reflection about our own values and beliefs, and those inherent in the larger society and culture to which we belong. Central to that is considering how the individual is valued. Totalitarian regimes, dictatorships, and theocracies resolve those questions easily; a person or a select few determine what schools will teach. In other types of societies and their governmental dispositions, the importance of the individual varies in accordance with the state apparatus and the interests that control it. In some third-world countries, controlling elites can determine how and for whom individualism is defined and who is eligible for schooling. Scholarly studies (Apple, 1983; Argyris & Shon, 1993; Cowen, 2002) suggest that to whom knowledge and information is given determines the health of a society and its institutions; the degree of egalitarianism and democracy permitted enhances stability and progress.

The statement is often made that "all politics is local." We can also say that "all curriculum is local," in that it is particular to and serves the purposes people in a community regard as important to be reflected in what is taught in their schools. There is an interesting dynamic among how curriculum is viewed in the local community, on a statewide basis, and nationally. Popular perceptions of purposes schools serve and what should be the curriculum content are often differentiated according to one's location and distance from them. The parent with a school-age child has more curriculum awareness than parents with children who have graduated. Parents with young adults in college are more cognizant of the curriculum connection between K–12 schooling and preparation for effective college work. In communities where life opportunities are keyed to local employment patterns, curriculum and school concerns are tied more to preparation for an effective work life. Annually, various polls ask people about schools and schooling to determine public perceptions about schooling, expectations, and how successful schools are. That is, pollsters ask if schools do what the asked person wants them to or thinks they ought to do. With few exceptions, poll results suggest that the more local and proximate the school is to the respondent, the more favorable the rating. By implication, so is their view of curriculum.

Although polling may give an impression of diverse local differences and fluidity concerning the basic purposes for schooling and curriculum, there is a long-term thread of continuity with state, regional, and national purposes. One, the development of "citizenship," takes in several subpurposes. Through citizenship, we are taught about civic duties, participation in politics, voting, being informed, and honoring the concept of law. Studying history, we achieve a sense of common heritage or nationhood. Flag and pledge engender patriotism. English is studied as a primary language of common discourse. These examples provide insights into how the curriculum is used to socialize and assimilate Americans.

Schools also provide access to "knowledge." People who are informed and have access to knowledge are thought to develop productive lives. This school-based knowledge promotes intellectual growth by introducing learners to various formal ways of thinking such as historically, scientifically, and philosophically. Study in this formal knowledge base promotes intelligent thought, a critical capability in individual development, and motivation to pursue further knowledge. In addition to this formal knowledge, schooling introduces us to informal knowldege, an often subtle, hidden knowledge that is cultural and social. We learn how to act in a variety of settings, the home, classroom, and other social and public places. Social-cultural learning is not usually stated as a purpose; it is carried in the unwritten standards of the local community, in classroom rules, and in the subtleties of student-to-teacher and student-to-student interactions.

Citizenship and knowledge provide convenient categories under which to cluster purposes. However, it is important to remember that in any given historical period, citizenship and knowledge may be considered differently. This is an important distinction because purposes need to be understood in context. We will be returning to this matter of alternative purposes and differing contexts in future chapters.

ENVISIONING CURRICULUM AS A FIELD OF STUDY

If curriculum is found in diverse settings among many different workers, what ties it together as a discipline, an object of study? What knowledge is held in common regardless of role or setting? As suggested in this chapter, answering such questions requires an understanding of how curriculum has evolved in meaning and as a body of knowledge and practice, each aspect informing the other and together constituting curriculum as a formal discipline of study. Envisioning curriculum as a discipline in education as a field of study warrants attention because it is fundamental to schools and schooling. It is personally necessary because you are preparing for a role as, perhaps, teacher or curriculum specialist. As this conversation about curriculum continues in the chapters to follow, it is appropriate to consider the shape of the curriculum as a field of study and its constituent elements, and as a realm of knowledge and practice within a larger field called education.

Studying Curriculum as Knowledge

To study something is to contemplate it, to apply your mental capacities, to think about it. There are several considerations in developing your ways of studying things. As noted in Chapter 1, formulating a critical perspective is important in the contemplative process. Another facet is to look for the way a body of knowledge is put together, how it is structured, much like understanding the human body by learning about its structure of systems. Uncovering how a body of knowledge is formed provides insight into how it works, how to think in and work with the content of a particular body of knowledge. This is not to say that all knowledge pursuits are structured in exactly the same way. Mathematics and philosophy, for instance, differ in form and content, but either can be illuminated by studying how it is organized, its structure. Knowledge organized into disciplines and fields becomes working units of formal inquiry and scholarly work. Another matter is to look across all bodies of knowledge to examine what supporting, enhancing information might come from other disciplines such as history and the humanities like philosophy, the arts, and the social sciences. Because all knowledge is related in some way, specific knowledge produced in one discipline or field may prove relevant in another, particularly in curriculum. Processes such as research methods used in one discipline might be useful to investigations in others. For example, some curriculum work might rely on historical methods to study curriculum history or on case study methods to focus on how a teacher works with curriculum in a classroom. These important matters of "inquiry" are foundational aspects of curriculum work, particularly evaluation, discussed in Chapter 12.

Studying Curriculum as Practice

A second aspect of studying curriculum is to focus on the different types of curriculum practice and the settings in which they occur. This requires an exploration of the types of curriculum work and the multiple layers of institutions and agencies in which the various types of work are done, from schools and academic research settings to commercial publishing houses and federal and state governmental agencies. For example, what does the Council of Chief State School Officers have to do with curriculum and what curriculum work do they carry out? What do you know about policy making or the role of the federal government in Washington in educational matters and particularly curriculum? Questions such as those frame the study of curriculum and help you to perceive the magnitude of existing knowledge to be understood, not only for teachers but for anyone working in and with curriculum. Often the assumption appears to be that the created knowledge you are studying to become a practitioner derives solely from knowledge made by scholars and those who inquire about education generally or curriculum in particular. Teachers and other school professionals can also contribute to that knowledge base, and often it is in the actual practice of teaching that that knowledge develops, not in textbooks or college classrooms. Practice knowledge from experience contributes an experimental, tentative knowledge that in the immediacy of the classroom life with the curriculum-in-use sustains practice and, as it proves out, enters into the knowledge base.

Earlier in this chapter, it was suggested that, like all human endeavors, creating knowledge and organizing it into various fields and disciplines is a work in progress. Curriculum as a young discipline evolving to its current state has etched a historical path from its formation to the present. What constitutes curriculum as a specific body of knowledge is the subject of Part II. It suffices at this point to note that "knowing" the knowledge base is essential to curriculum work. You would not be expected to walk into a dentist's office and function as a dental hygienist without the appropriate knowledge and practice; likewise, you should not be expected to do curriculum work as a teacher or specialist without the same kind of grounding in curriculum knowledge and practice.

Summary and Conclusions

Today's school curriculum differs from that of 50 or 100 years ago. If you were to take a textbook used in the 1920s or 1930s, one from the 1960s, and a current one, you would have a comparative snapshot of what was important then and now and how curriculum, as the content or subject matter of what was to be taught, has changed over time. Historical events, forces, and invented ideas such as evolution and technology influence how a people, a society, think about what is important and what the American people think its institutions should promote. Freedom and progress are distinctive, very American, ideals. School curriculum is also a reflection of the clash of ideas over social, political, cultural, and economic purposes schools should serve, what should be taught, the subjects that would best reflects those purposes, how schools should be organized, and who should attend them. Interestingly, it is not a story of rapid, rampant change in response to whimsical issues and fads. Because curriculum at any given time reflects the push and pull over issues in a society, it has a conserving presence, not quickly changed yet subject to gradual alteration as those issues are resolved. Curriculum has evolved as a composite term for content or subject matter. It has also become a particular field of study with an identifiable structure, defining characteristics of practice, and a body of grounded knowledge.

Critical Perspective

1. From your personal experiences, what examples can you cite that reflect the ideas of freedom and progress through the school curriculum?

2. Ideas have power. Can you identify ideas that are now in your education that were not in your curriculum when you were in school?

3. How do you differentiate curriculum from instruction? Do you think it is important for a teacher or other educational professional to do so?

4. In what ways has the development of social science influenced thinking about curriculum?

5. The Herbartian method and the Tyler Rationale both offer a process for thinking about curriculum and instruction in teaching. What comparisons can be drawn about the two approaches?

6. What does the term *curriculum-in-use* mean? Do any of the definitions in Figure 2.4 reflect that meaning?

7. The text refers to various "types" of curriculum (e.g., formal, de jure) that amplify or extend the meaning of curriculum. Make a list of terms and (a) identify examples for them from your knowledge about curriculum and (b) given the sample definitions in Figure 2.4, determine if any of the terms fit within those definitions.

8. What examples can you identify from your personal schooling experience or from your understanding of curriculum that fit into the perceptions of curriculum discussed in the text?

Resources for Curriculum Study

1. Two excellent sources for understanding the gradual changes in the content of the American school curriculum during the 20th century to the present are the following books by Herbert Kliebard: *The Struggle for the American Curriculum* (1986) and *Forging the American Curriculum* (1992). Daniel and Laurel Tanner's *History of the School Curriculum* (1990) is also useful. Larry Cuban's *How Teachers Taught* (1984) offers glimpses of curriculum in the classroom.

2. Throughout the development of American schooling, colleges and universities have had a strong influence on the content and organization of the school

curriculum. Frederick Rudolph's book *Curriculum* (1978) is an excellent source for understanding the usually top-down relationship between what was in the college curriculum and how that influenced the school curriculum.

3. Biographical sketches are available online for any of the people mentioned in the chapter. Type in a name, Herbert Spencer, for example, and use several sites to compare the information. For a more contextual discussion of people mentioned in the chapter, see the end-of-chapter references or consult the Recommended Readings section for further study.

4. For an interesting discussion of the original moral intent of the Herbartian method (Schimmels, n.d.), go online to http://faculty.leeu.edu/~bestes/resources/white paper.htm

5. It is important to look at curriculum and how it is understood through other than American eyes. From a British perspective, Mark K. Smith offers an excellent discussion of curriculum's rise and development in his article "Curriculum Theory and Practice." You can retrieve this online at http://www.infed.org/biblio/b-curric.htm

References

Apple, M. W. (1983). *Education and power.* New York: Routledge.

Argyris, C., & Shon, D. (1993). *Knowledge for action.* San Francisco: Jossey-Bass.

Armstrong, D. G. (2003). *Curriculum today.* Upper Saddle River, NJ: Merrill Prentice Hall.

Bigelow, J. (1829). *The elements of technology.* Boston: Boston Press.

Caswell, H., & Campbell, D. (1935). *Curriculum development.* New York: American Book.

Cowen, T. (2002). The fate of culture. *Wilson Quarterly, 29*(4), 62–77.

Cuban, L. (1984). *How teachers taught: Constancy and change in American classrooms, 1890–1980.* White Plains, NY: Longman.

Darwin, C. (1871). *The descent of man.* London: John Murray.

Darwin, C. (1995). *On the origin of species.* New York: Gramercy Books/Random House. (Original work published 1859)

Dewey, J. (1902). *The child and the curriculum.* Chicago: University of Chicago Press.

Eisner, E. (1994). *The educational imagination: On the design and evaluation of school programs* (3rd ed.). New York: Macmillan.

Kliebard, H. M. (1986). *The struggle for the American curriculum, 1893–1958.* Boston: Routledge & Kegan Paul.

Kliebard, H. M. (1992). *Forging the American curriculum.* London: Routledge.

Macdonald, J. B. (1986). The domain of curriculum. *Journal of Curriculum and Supervision, 1*(3), 205–214.

McKelvey, B. (1963). *The urbanization of America, 1860–1915.* New Brunswick, NJ: Rutgers University Press.

Nisbet, R. (1980). *The history of the idea of progress.* New York: Basic Books.

Rudolph, F. (1967). *Curriculum* (Carnegie Council on Policy Studies in Higher Education). San Francisco: Jossey-Bass.

Saylor, G., & Alexander, W. (1974). *Curriculum planning for schools.* New York: Holt, Rinehart, & Winston.

Schimmels, C. (n.d.). *A white paper on lesson planning.* Retrieved February 2004 from http://faculty.leeu.edu/~bestes/resources/whitepaper.htm

Schubert, W. H., Schubert, A. L. L., Thomas, T. P., & Carroll, W. M. (2002). *Curriculum books: The first hundred years* (2nd ed.). New York: Peter Lang.

Smith, M. K. (1996, 2000). *Curriculum theory and practice.* Retrieved February 2004 from http://www.infed.org/biblio/b-curric.htm

Tanner, D., & Tanner, L. (1990). *History of the school curriculum.* New York: Macmillan.

Tyler, R. W. (1949). *Basic principles of curriculum and instruction.* Chicago: University of Chicago Press.

Walker, D. F., & Soltis, J. F. (1997). *Curriculum and aims.* New York: Teachers College Press.

Chapter 3

CURRICULUM WORK AND PROFESSIONAL PRACTICE

Remember being asked what you wanted to be when you grew up? Your first recollection is probably of a casual question or comment by your dad, your mom, a relative, or perhaps a friend. The question probably popped up numerous times later in school and in conversations with your friends. Then there was a new awareness, the pressure that began as early as middle or junior high school to decide about a college or noncollege, perhaps a vocational or general curriculum track. For most young Americans, growing up there were jobs like baby-sitting, working at the corner store, kitchen work, busing or waiting tables, lawn service work, construction work, and numerous other introductory experiences to the world of work. In most instances, all you needed was to be age appropriate according to state law and to secure whatever certificate was necessary, a food handler's permit, for example. Regardless of how you started, you had to learn the work. Now you are taking a course leading to a degree and probably a certificate to teach. You are entering the world of professional work, and that requires learning a designated body of knowledge and demonstrating proficiency in applying that knowledge. You can eventually be a teacher working with curriculum as you teach, or you could be doing other curriculum work, perhaps as a curriculum and instructional specialist in a school or at the district office. There are others—a publisher, a school board member, a parent, an educational researcher, or president of a foundation—whose work with curriculum may not be so obvious.

CURRICULUM WORKERS

What do people who specialize in curriculum work actually do? Although the nature of the work varies, there are certain parameters that characterize it. Location, for example, where the work is performed, can mean the classroom or the state department of education offices in the capital. Jurisdiction for curriculum work, the assigned responsibility and authority, can vary from that of the teacher in the classroom to that of the state board of education and imply different commitments of time. Of those who work with curriculum, you are more familiar with teachers and other school personnel such as the academic counselor, the principal, and perhaps an assigned curriculum specialist. Looking beyond schools and workers in administrative levels relating to them, though, you will find many other persons who perform curriculum work in education.

Teachers and Curricularists

You are aware that a teacher's role is complex, a series of actions constituting a set of interrelated practices about curriculum, instruction, assessment, evaluation, and learning. The teaching role requires knowledge in all those areas. What flows through all that activity, whether as part of instruction, a conversation with another teacher, preparing the lessons for tomorrow, or attending an in-service, is some consideration of curriculum. A classroom teacher is involved with curriculum all day, perhaps not every minute, but continuously. Curriculum flows in and out of everything a teacher does. Teaching is in part the act of applying curriculum knowledge of several kinds, the kind about the subjects taught (school curriculum) and curriculum practice knowledge. It is also how to interrelate and blend curriculum, instruction, assessment, and evaluation individually for learners. Teachers, who probably make up the largest segment of people who work *with* curriculum, differ from those whose work roles are specifically for working *in* the curriculum. The nuance between *with* and *in* is important. Whereas the curriculum weaves in and out of teaching as a teacher works *with* curriculum, the *in* differentiates the important generalist like the teacher from a more contained or specialized curriculum work. Curricularist, a term first discussed in Chapter 1, is often used to designate a specialization in curriculum. As such, it does not indicate a specific role with exclusive attributes. It does refer to more specialized roles such as the curriculum specialist, a position often found in a school district central office. The key point is the degree to which the role or work is exclusively *in* curriculum. Obviously, the teacher's role is broader and inclusive of other functions whereas that of the curriculum specialist is narrowly defined. Unfortunately, confusion often attends such distinctions when specialists are variously titled as curriculum specialists, instructional specialists, or curriculum and instructional specialists. The use of such titles in school districts is quite arbitrary, and the reality is that a person-designated specialist may or may not have expertise in either curriculum or instruction. Obviously, you would have to observe what kind of specialization the person is required to perform.

Other Curriculum Roles

There are many other roles in curriculum work in addition to teachers and curricularists. Workers in publishing houses producing textbooks and other materials for the classroom are doing curriculum work. College and university faculty engage in curriculum work, both as specialists in the content that forms the school curriculum and in scholarly activities that study curriculum as part of their interest in teaching and learning. There are also those who, like teachers, work directly with curriculum but may not have the same entry-level degree and certification. Classroom aides, teacher assistants, and library or media assistants are several examples. Others working with curriculum are found in places far removed from the classroom. Employees in state and federal government agencies deal with curriculum within the larger scope of educational programs. School board members and parents are also part of the curriculum community. The student in the classroom can also be considered to be involved with curriculum work. A new and growing area of curriculum work involves assessment and evaluation, what can be classified as monitoring the curriculum. Item writers, creators of tests and other assessment instruments, all key their work to the existing curriculum. Evaluation experts study assessment data and interpret meaning in curriculum terms. All those workers are keeping the curriculum under surveillance at a distance. The instrumentation goes to the classroom or school or both, and is strapped, in a metaphorical sense, to the curriculum like the electronic monitoring devices attached to a heart patient that monitor pulse, blood pressure, and other functions. Those monitoring the devices are removed from the direct association a teacher has, but they are similarly connected to the daily work by virtue of the instruments they use. Evaluation and monitoring could be considered curriculum work through technological extension.

CURRICULUM WORK

Work in curriculum is complex and differs in several ways. For instance, expectations and requirements for performance outcomes may vary. Elementary teachers are especially prepared to teach reading, a crucial skill, and expectations will be measured in the resulting number of children who can read at a given level of proficiency for a specific grade. A secondary teacher's performance is similarly related to the knowledge proficiency demonstrated by students in the subjects they teach. Others working with curriculum will have different preparation and performance expectations matched to the particulars of their work. Another factor that differentiates among curriculum workers is the proximity of particular work roles to the heart of curriculum work—school, classroom, students, and teacher. Moving out from that center, you encounter other roles and supporting curriculum work. The district curriculum specialist is closest to the classroom, removed from it but in a direct line of contact and support. In comparison, a publisher of curriculum materials is very far removed, not in a direct line of support, and has a seemingly incidental role in curriculum work, yet the publisher's products, a textbook or other materials, are essential to both the teacher and specialist in their curriculum work. Given such diversity, how can curriculum work be organized in order to understand it? Curriculum work seems always to be in progress, a variety of activities playing out in various places. Curriculum work would seem to defy any orderly classification. In fact, curriculum work is not easily classified except in a general way. If you were to survey the curriculum literature, particularly textbooks, you would find these commonly used work classifications: knowledge making, policy making, planning, development, management, assessment, evaluation, and research. These shape an initial structure in which to consider and order curriculum work, a world of knowledge and practice. As a preliminary set of terms about curriculum work, they are described in Figure 3.1. Depending on the context in which they are used, keep in mind that in different settings, there may be multiple functions performed by one practitioner or several people in combinations. For example, a curriculum planner might also work in development, or someone involved in development might be dealing with assessment-evaluation. The purpose here is to briefly familiarize you with these kinds of curriculum work so you will recognize them as the discussion proceeds.

Knowledge Making

Knowledge is being created at the very moment you read this. There is the knowledge of information, data, news, gossip, and conversation, the informal kinds of unvalidated, everyday public knowledge. There is also a formal knowledge, the validated kinds of academic conversation, research, and scholarly inquiry associated with the academy. The *academy* refers to the colleges and universities and some research institutions that contribute to curriculum work and knowledge production. Obviously, they are located in different places in the United States and throughout the world. Academics study schooling and curriculum for a variety of reasons, including research, theory building, and other scholarly pursuits related to their academic roles. They contribute to curriculum work by the knowledge they produce, which may or may not emerge

Figure 3.1   A First Look at Curriculum Work

Knowledge making: As it suggests, the creating of knowledge about curriculum as a process, how it is done, and the subject matter or content it contains.

Policy making: Creating the authority that sets the direction for creating curriculum, much like a law does.

Planning: This refers to the preliminary thinking about the actions and scope needed to implement something and determine the preliminary activities or elements needed.

Development: The activities to create something, in this case a curriculum, the actual production of a math curriculum, for example.

Management: The continuous activities that are repetitive, umbrella-like, to carry on what has been decreed by policy, planned for, and implemented. These activities also occur in each of those kinds of work (e.g., managing, policymaking, or planning).

Assessment: It is important to find out how a policy, plan, or management process is doing, so data about it must be gathered, usually on a continuous basis, for making further judgments. Sending out a questionnaire and giving a test are examples of assessment activities.

Evaluation/Research: Activities that can range from simply gathering information about car insurance to undertaking a long-term study of a particular medicine's effects or how a particular curriculum compares with another one in terms of ease of learning.

directly from involvement with schools and schooling. Traditionally, they have produced curriculum theory, been involved with curriculum development, and trained people such as teachers for curriculum work. What academics and other curriculum workers share is a reliance on the same curriculum knowledge foundation. Their critical role is to know that foundation and convey it to those entering curriculum work. They also contribute from a distance by thinking about the curriculum knowledge being created and how it can be structured so it can be passed on and understood. For example, data from assessments related to school and learner performance have no particular use as curriculum knowledge until they are given that value though analysis and interpretation, usually the work of an academically situated person. There is another dimension to knowledge making that is often overlooked. That is the knowledge about the particular ways of doing things in any type of curriculum work, what is referred to as the practice of curriculum and the knowledge culture, the cocoon in which the thinking, doing, and relating about the work occurs. It is not like knowing subject matter in the school curriculum or the foundational knowledge of curriculum, it is the knowledge that each worker comes to hold about the way to do his or her work and participate with others in that work (Clancey, 1997; Danielson, 2004; Uneo, 2000). You have probably experienced that sense of knowing about the work, not only how to do it but also the nuances and subtleties of what to do and not do as a participant in that work, including the moral and ethical allowances of work behavior. All those elements, the mores, traditions, customs, and ways of doing things, are part of that work culture of practice.

People who stay in a type of work for a long period of time acquire that particular cultural knowledge (tacit knowledge) and, as they become senior workers, contribute to the culture and pass it on to others.

Policy Making

Presidents, governors, mayors, and legislators always seem to have something they want to change, start, or improve. What they propose usually starts out as an expression like "we need a policy . . ." and then they add whatever is on their mind. Listen to a newscast or pick up a newspaper and you find references to some policy about this or that. Is it just another word thrown around indiscriminately in public conversation or does it have important and significant meaning? What is policy making? *Policy* refers to a defined course or method of action, a coherent plan selected to guide and determine present and future decisions. *Policy making,* then, simply refers to the creation of policy.

The formal study of policy and policy making has essentially been the province of historians and political scientists. Policy studies in the education field began to emerge in the 1950s, focusing on policy formulation and its effects on efforts to reform schools, such as the comprehensive high school movement and the federally supported curriculum initiatives later in that decade and into the early 1960s. The education literature is sparse but growing (see Stein, 2004; Warren, 1978) with some useful discussions of policy making and curriculum (Elmore & Sykes, 1992). Two examples of political initiatives that established important public policy involved international affairs. One familiar example you should recall from your history courses is the Monroe Doctrine, which in effect told 19th-century adventuring European nations to stay out of the Americas. Another, more contemporary one is the famous containment thesis of George Kennen, which after World War II became the guide for American foreign policy to control the spread of communism and the Soviet Union. Concerning schools and schooling, there are two familiar contemporary examples. The report of the National Commission on Excellence in Education of 1983, *A Nation at Risk,* initiated a national school reform movement that took different forms depending on how political parties and interest groups coalesced on particular aspects of the report. The legacy of that report, the impetus to and emphasis on reform, continues today. The importance of the report was not its effect on direct policy making but on promoting different approaches to reform rather than using the governing apparatus of the state and the law. That changed with the most recent reform initiative, the No Child Left Behind (NCLB) Act of 2001, signed into law in 2002. This act is the latest reincarnation of the Elementary and Secondary Education Act dating from the 1960s. The NCLB Act is a comprehensive accountability program based on extensive testing and increased financial support for schools keyed to meeting particular mandates such as developing curriculum standards, establishing comparative student performance levels across states, and assuring teacher quality in their areas of curriculum expertise. Reform, standards, associated costs, and the NCLB Act are major educational policy issues with important curriculum implications. The importance is the shift from policy initiatives resulting from reports and reformers to direct policy making by law.

Planning

Policy gives direction to planning. Policy says, here is what is to be done, and planning takes policy from idea or statement and shapes it into a vision to guide later development actions. *Curriculum planning* identifies the elements and forms that will be necessary, the assemblage of ways to think about and work through the elements to be used in creating the curriculum. A similar process might be the preparation of a blueprint for a building or a computer-assisted design—both are representations of what is anticipated. In planning a building, consideration is given to the purposes or functions to be served and particulars such as the number and type of rooms and the heating, cooling, plumbing, electrical, and other systems that are needed. Curriculum planning also takes in the purposes to be served; what content elements, subject matter such as science, mathematics, and so forth, will be included; and how the curriculum will be organized—the broad scope of what is to be embraced and sequenced, and the overall organizational designs to fit the schooling pattern. In a general sense, planning bridges policy and what is to result, the development that is intended to carry out the policy and implement the plan. Think of the policy-planning relationship this way: Policy is the authority for implementing the purpose or idea to be carried out, whereas planning is the activity to shape the parameters for development work. The degree of planning and who does it will vary depending on the given planning unit, its location, capability, and grant of authority for planning work. Policy making and planning are developed in more detail in Chapter 9.

Development

Curriculum development is probably the most well-known activity in curriculum work. Unfortunately, *curriculum development* is often used interchangeably with the word *curriculum,* creating the impression that they are one and the same. They are not! Curriculum development is a type of curriculum work; it is not curriculum, either as encompassing all curriculum activity or as curriculum, the body of knowledge. Think of curriculum development as those activities that create curriculum and its representative materials for use in some school or comparable setting. There are two primary ways to think about development as an idea. Some authors mate planning and development as a single process. Others separate them as connected but different activities. If it helps, substitute the word *construction* as synonymous with *development,* as W. W. Charters did in *Curriculum Construction* (1923), or substitute *making* for *development,* as in *curriculum making,* the term used by another pioneer in curriculum development, Franklin Bobbitt (1924). As a key type of work, curriculum development contributes to and relies on the curriculum knowledge bases that you will begin to explore in Part II, Chapters 5–8. The knowledge about developing curriculum, a product of scholarly study of practitioner activity, enters into the curriculum knowledge base. That knowledge is then passed on to new workers who study curriculum and then become practitioners. Their work in turn produces knowledge that again cycles into the knowledge base. As one kind of work, curriculum development both relies on and contributes to the curriculum knowledge base. The commentary here is meant only to introduce you to development very generally. A broader discussion of development in creating curriculum waits in Chapter 4, and a discussion of the developmental process as a key kind of curriculum work is in Chapter 10.

Management

The school curriculum, like anything else, has to be looked after and kept in repair; in a word, it has to be *managed. Curriculum management* entails a number of activities you will recognize: official curriculum materials such as district or state curriculum guides have to be distributed, and textbooks must be issued and later requests for replacements or additional ones handled. These activities depend on dedicated storage space, often a central repository, and a distribution system. Management and maintenance are needed to keep the curriculum viable, a process of managing and maintaining the basic materials, the supporting resources, and the procedures that connect all curriculum workers in the management process, be it at the school, district, or some other level or place in curriculum work. Management work might mean responding to a request for the reproduction of materials within the school or at the district office. Outside workplaces might include a publishing house that produces texts or other needed material. Management work might mean contact with curriculum vendors who supply such common curriculum materials as software, hardware, paper and other consumables, and maps and other materials. These are images of traditional curriculum management functions, acquisition, storage, and distribution, which on the surface seem to require little curriculum knowledge. Management and maintenance as a kind of curriculum work are discussed extensively in Chapter 11.

Monitoring

It is important to know how a curriculum is working with reference to itself or students and if it is meeting goals or reaching stated outcomes. Securing such knowledge should not be a reaction to problems that arise suddenly, demands of the moment, or forces outside curriculum. It should be knowledge available from data derived through a systematic process inclusive of assessment, evaluation, and research. The term *monitoring* is used here to refer to those particular activities that are continuous and embedded in curriculum work rather than random or ad hoc. Referring again to Figure 3.1, assessments are the tools used in evaluation—tests, observation ratings, checklists, and so forth—to establish some measurement, some form of data. Evaluation is the matter of establishing or placing a unit or units of value on the data. Put a little differently, evaluation gives the assessment meaning. Considered in the context of monitoring, assessment-evaluation should be continuous, like the monitoring that occurs in a water filtration process where instrumentation is strategically placed to provide a flow of data. In planning and constructing curriculum, one of the important considerations should be to establish a monitoring process. Research in monitoring has a more specialized purpose as a tool for formal study of more complex questions and issues about curriculum, usually indicating a need for large-scale investigation, perhaps across multiple activities such as curriculum and instruction. Summarizing, monitoring as a concept refers to assessment-evaluation and related research functions that generally fall into the category of inquiry methods. Chapter 12 is devoted to further elaboration of those ideas in curriculum work.

SETTINGS FOR CURRICULUM WORK

Curriculum work and practice are layered. Probably the most important layer and the focus of all curriculum work is the classroom or similar setting as the point of interaction between the curriculum and the student or other designated recipient. The purpose for almost all kinds of curriculum work is to ultimately affect that place and what goes on there. The matter of place as the location where there is curriculum activity is important (Hutchison, 2004). There are several ways to consider the matter of place and location in curriculum work. One is as layers of locations: the states taken individually or as a group; national as in considering the nation as a single unit, the United States of America; or regional/sectional as in the South, Midwest, or Southwest. Another approach is to consider units of control, places empowered to do curriculum work: the state of Idaho, the federal government, or the local school district. The problem with either approach is that certain variants of curriculum work cannot be easily accommodated. A publisher does not fit easily within classifications of location by state or other political units in describing where and what they do that is important in curriculum work. There are also the peculiarities of how curriculum work is assigned across such units. The federal role in curriculum work is unlike that of the various states, which themselves empower curriculum work in different ways. A third approach, using both the place-location and political units of control, will be used in this overview and introduction to where curriculum work is done.

Academic Departments

The academy is the keeper of knowledge. While both academic and school practitioner work creates or seeks to create knowledge, one important role of the academic is to collect, interpret, and organize knowledge in disciplined ways. William Wraga's (1997) discussion of what he calls the "professional knowledge" of curriculum suggests that the primary resource of curriculum knowledge is the literature about curriculum. Determining the specific literature constituting that knowledge is based on various studies of what literature the professors of curriculum consider important. The literature so specified subsumes studies of synoptic texts, orientation or philosophies of curriculum, curriculum activities, and shared expert judgments. Certainly teachers, curriculum specialists and others directly involved with schools, and independent researchers and others who study schooling also create knowledge in addition to what professors and other academics say is important. That knowledge from practice (e.g., from teachers, curriculum specialists, professors, researchers) is itself important curriculum knowledge. Regardless of which workers participated in creating that knowledge, it belongs to all. Knowledge of work, of role, and of the culture of both is part of the professional conversation about knowledge from practice. The academic community acts as the arbiter of what knowledge is important for inclusion in the discipline: the appropriate rubrics of discourse, canons of practice, and other formal matters that set the parameters for work in curriculum.

Classrooms and Schools

With the possible exception of students who are home schooled, the central focus of curriculum work is the classroom and school. Any aspect of curriculum thought, activity, and work has some expression in the local classroom and school. Your classrooms and schools are also what you personally remember about curriculum. The often-used political expression referred to previously, all politics is local, suggests that it is local politics and community matters that prevail in how you see the world. It can also be said in the same spirit that all schooling is local. What both mean is that what is experienced, lived, as local, as community, as what is relational to your sense of place and location, is immediate and personal. Think of the neighborhood elementary school, what is first experienced, the stepping outside the home into a new world of peers. It is the first place of curricular engagement. It is a world of teachers, principals, support personnel, and students, all working with curriculum in various ways in a particular place. There are a host of other roles, from custodial workers to members of the school board. The local school, the first school experience, sets the tone and, for better or worse, personalizes the meaning of schooling through the people students encounter and how they are guided into learning. The importance of the initial local school experience suggests several observations about curriculum at the level of school and classroom.

- Implementing the curriculum requires shared engagement of common material—in its simplest form, the curriculum is the textbook.
- Curriculum is the heart of schooling—whether it is as a textbook or in some other form, it is the reason for schools and the most common shared experience of citizenship.
- The availability of a common curriculum in the form of the traditional commercially published textbook is economically cost efficient. No single school, district, or state can generate the numbers of texts and materials needed for schooling in the United States.
- The obvious and most important roles in working with curriculum are the students and the teachers. Less visible are the workers who produce the curriculum or those whose work supports classroom engagement of the curriculum.

The classroom, school, and textbook signify the basic sources from which the need for all curriculum work springs. Most important, there would not be a need for policy making, development, or other curriculum functions if schools did not exist.

Districts, Regions, and States

Beyond the local school, other units are involved with curriculum work, the most important being the local school district. The administrative officials, school board, and teachers and students are the core constituents. There are also a number of important community and interest groups and affiliations. Among those with a direct connection are the student-parent-teachers association (SPTA) or equivalent. Others not as directly associated, as is the SPTA, include interest groups such as the Chamber of Commerce, local unions, and other service organizations, all of which have been traditional supporters of schools in local communities. While those organizations and agencies do not do curriculum work by creating it, they do become involved with policy and planning activities when citizens and groups in a community are called on to serve on school committees, either for their own children in a particular school or on advisory boards the district superintendent or school board may create for consultative purposes or to tap expertise in the community. There are also local philanthropic organizations that become involved with gifts, such as a new pool for the high school or new American flags for all the schools. Sometimes these "gifts" can lead to controversies; consider, for example, placing the Ten Commandments in a school lobby and you will probably incite an immediate public storm.

There are 50 autonomous state governments, each operating under a constitution that sets the basic law or laws regarding schools. As pointed out before, schools are creatures of the state. However, no particular state is isolated, and states with contiguous boundaries work out reciprocal relationships where schools are concerned. This has occurred where schooling sits astride the state boundary lines and when different state jurisdictions apply. This can mean problems arising from different state authorities over funding, health requirements, busing, and other school matters. Often this leads to special laws or agreements by two different states to address these unusual local problems. An example might be a city school district bounding two states where the city schools take in students from an adjacent state. Which state's laws are controlling? What if the per-pupil expenditures and the lines of support differ? These kinds of questions get into issues of reciprocity, funding, and control—all matters of policy requiring coordination, planning, and legislative and executive involvement. Curriculum requirements and textbook selection procedures may differ. What if one state forbids the use of the term *evolution* in science texts and the other doesn't? Those kinds of questions point both to curriculum's importance and to the importance of curriculum and schooling events at the state level. Sometimes matters like those affect a number of states. This can lead to a regional solution involving negotiation of protocols, special legislation, and sometimes funding. Recently, these interstate compacts have become important for pooling common resources, credentialing, and eliminating duplicate educational services, especially in higher education. The ventures of particular interest for curriculum are those coordinating access to Internet electronic libraries and similar resources.

National and International Domains

You are aware that there is a United States Department of Education. You may not know that it was created as recently as 1977. Prior to that, the federal involvement with education and schooling was through the United States Office of Education, established in the latter part of the 19th century and headed by a Commissioner of Education. Among the more illustrious commissioners have been Henry Barnard, William Torrey Harris, and Francis Keppel. Federal involvement has been slow to develop for several reasons. Foremost is the lack of any direct grant of power in the United States Constitution to the federal government. Over time, court cases have expanded the federal role from one of limited advocacy, as it was under the old Office of Education, to more extensive involvement via the general welfare clause and, in the 1950s, by extension, through national defense. An associated reason for the federal reticence is the traditional issue of local control discussed previously. There is and always has been a tension between local/state and state/federal interests where schools and schooling are concerned. Schooling has been considered the province of the state. Economic upheavals such as the Great Depression, international conflicts, and the rise of America as an international power have increased pressure for excellence in schooling to keep pace with other nations. Those pressures have at various times overridden traditional concern about state-federal separation. As examples like Head Start, federal programs for special education, and the recent NCLB Act attest, the role and influence of the government in Washington are still being defined.

Although the conversation about curriculum work and practice has been limited to the United States and the American experience, it would be naive to assume the school curriculum is strictly an American phenomenon. Much of the curriculum knowledge base is informed by work in other national settings (Gamoran, 1998; Kelly, 2004). In the early development of American institutions, critical knowledge, key ideas, and influential practices about schooling emanated from Europe. Now, American colleges and universities are a mecca for foreign students wanting cutting-edge knowledge and to understand American institutions such as our schools. As a world leader, the United States is also economically and ideologically competitive, and the success of the American curriculum in keeping pace with other nations educationally is important internationally. Indeed, the International Assessment of Educational Progress and international educational activities under the auspices of the United Nations suggest the size and importance of the world enterprise. Unfortunately, a discussion of international education and curriculum has to be limited for two reasons. First, that telling is a whole other book. Second, there is the matter of the translation of educational traditions and policies in other societies and nations and the differing cultural implications from one location, society, or culture to another. This refers to the assumption that a finding about schools and schooling deemed beneficial in one culture or society is transferable to another, or that international test results in themselves allow for comparisons about schooling across nations. Those are contentious issues with potential political implications outside the purview of this book and the narrower considerations of American curriculum.

BECOMING A PROFESSIONAL CURRICULUM PRACTITIONER

Professional practitioners of whatever stripe form a collective of people working in the area where the matter of proficiency, of applied expertise and judgment, is crucial. They are a community of conversation, a disciplined discourse, to establish the standards for attaining proficiency, expertise, or competence and an agent or agency to certify that achievement. Those who wish to participate in such a learning community must acquire the knowledge, the ways of knowing, and the qualities of practice that define the conditions of participation. These prepractice and practice requirements are presented in Figure 3.2. They suggest the elements of professional performance that a potential curriculum practitioner should acquire.

Figure 3.2   Elements of Professional Practice

Preparation for Practice	Practice
Acquiring Knowledge	Activating Knowledge
Organizing Knowledge	Communicating Curriculum
Building Perspective	Envisioning Curriculum
Building Expertise	Reflecting on Curriculum

Building Knowledge

The usual introduction to curriculum begins in course work and a textbook. Each textbook represents one author's view of curriculum and is intended to do several things. First, it is to articulate the knowledge that exists about curriculum. The second function is role related; it focuses primarily on understanding the curriculum-teacher relationship, with secondary attention to others, like the curriculum supervisor or specialist in the school district. With varying degrees of emphasis, all contemporary texts address curriculum development, curriculum theorizing, and curriculum evaluation and curriculum history. In addition, there are varying treatments of contributing knowledge from philosophy, cognition, learning theory, and sociology. Knowing curriculum work is not just acquiring the academic knowledge about the functions of each type of work, it is also about the manner of practical application; the roles and functions particular to curriculum work; the various institutional places and locations where the various types or categories of curriculum work take place; and the breadth of that work, the levels of institutional concern inclusive of the type of work, roles, and places of work.

Introductions to curriculum knowledge are also about the various ways to describe knowledge and how it can be organized. You are probably familiar with knowledge categorized as the humanities, sciences, and the arts. There are other ways to understand knowledge and organize it. There is knowledge as content to be learned: mathematics and biology are familiar to you as examples of knowledge in the school curriculum. All knowledge is personal and "encompasses all that a person knows or believes is true, whether or not it is verified as true in some sort of objective or external way" (Alexander, Schallert, & Hare, 1991, p. 317). Knowledge, as you recall from discussions in the preceding chapters, can be generally classified as formal or informal, but the modes or ways of knowing in and across any knowledge are more complex. A sample of ways to organize knowledge and ways or the manner of knowing is provided in Figure 3.3. Although caution is advised in generalizing as to whether ways of knowing are particular to either domain in the figure, there is a tendency to understand them as more applicable in the formal domain. For example, knowledge can be characterized by how

Figure 3.3   Modes of Knowing and Forms of Knowledge

Basic Organizations or Domains of Knowledge

Formal knowledge refers to knowledge and modes of knowing from a discipline such as biology or a field of study such as medicine where it is stipulated and intended by its very organization. Logical knowing is associated with formal knowledge.

Informal knowledge derives from experience and is usually characterized as vicarious and unintended rather than as expected and intended, as in formal knowledge. The knowledge gleaned from everyday living, interrelationships, and the location-place in life.

Knowledge as Modes of Knowing

Conceptual knowing is understanding relationships among discrete bits of things and uses, thought, and reflection, as in knowing the concept of tree and being able to place objects that seem to be trees in that category by virtue of their common characteristics, the links among them.

Contextual knowing is conditional knowledge about where and when to apply what you know as in a setting, a fit of knowledge within the current place one is experiencing.

Declarative knowing is what you know and can verbalize or declare about something.

Focus knowing is different from tacit knowing in that you know about something in your focus by describing or otherwise characterizing it without depending on what you might already know about it.

Logical knowing is understanding correct and incorrect reasoning, as in problem solving, and is distinguished from irrational thinking.

Practice knowing is knowledge generated by specialized actions in very defined settings or contexts such as those of a teacher, a doctor or other medical personnel, or an electrician.

Procedural knowing deals with rules, ordered procedures, sequences, and the like, as in counting or word use or ordering of symbols.

Tacit knowing is knowledge you already have and bring to thinking about something that is in your focus. Usually not verbalized, as in the automatic way you know how to open a door even while conversing with another person.

---

you acquire it and use it, what Elizabeth Vallance (1999) referred to as the "modes of knowing." *Content knowledge* (think of book learning) is often associated with formal knowledge (Alexander et al., 1991). Such content, once learned, remains as something to be recalled or remembered on some occasion and is often referred to as *declarative knowledge*. Knowledge is also a demonstration of having learned something and the manner of being able to use that knowledge. This is sometimes called *conceptual* and *procedural knowledge*. In applying what you study, you read the contextual environment in which you practice, acquiring what Sternberg (1990) calls contextual intelligence. Applying that contextual intelligence yields *contextual knowledge*. For example, doing curriculum work as a teacher is not just the application of knowledge about curriculum; often it is the received knowledge about a need to adjust the curriculum being taught in the immediacy of the classroom environment as it changes from moment to moment.

That is a daunting task. Metaphorically, it is a game of engagement in which the outcome is the assessment of curricular moment-to-moment intake by the learner. The teacher functions as a manager, a game master, aware of the governing rules but prepared to officiate others as they would seem appropriate to the moment and the probable future. It is practice in which worker actions are guided by unspoken rules so familiar they are taken for granted, an example of what Michael Polanyi (1958) labeled *tacit knowledge.* Kinds of knowledge and modes of knowing aren't fixed or necessarily rooted in the curriculum knowledge base; they are also social and situational, embedded in the coordinated activities of professional practice as *practice knowledge.* Collectively, these modes and forms of knowledge are part of what Pierre Teilhard de Chardin (1975) refers to as the "noosphere" of human social and cultural consciousness. Similarly, psychologist Jerome Bruner points out in *Acts of Meaning* (1990) that individual human knowing of the world and self is a self, social, and culturally created process.

Knowledge, as noted earlier, can also be categorized as simply formal or informal. Expanding on the idea of informal knowledge, there are two aspects to consider. One is that the informal can be personal or shared knowledge. As personal knowledge, it is held without being verifiable or made credible in other ways—it is our own creation. Second, when shared, it may not be necessarily held to be the same by others even though in using it they may seem to convey or exhibit a common understanding (Clancey, 1997; Davenport & Prusak, 1998). Those aspects taken together differentiate formal and informal knowledge. *Personal informal knowledge* is distinctive walk-about knowledge: ways to behave, rules, the ordinary social and culturally acquired things that guide our daily ways of living and participation in public life. In school, this is learning how to play with others, walk in the halls, be orderly in the classroom, and obey rules. In contrast to personal informal knowledge, *personal formal knowledge* is consensual knowing: something validated or standardized and made useful as being true or applicable under specifiable conditions. Examples include the empirical knowledge of science and scholarly inquiry, and the formal knowledge of the farmer, electrician, plumber, engineer, draftsman, or medical practitioner that represents technical and commercial knowledge validated in applied ways. It is also the knowledge of academic and professional work, the logical knowledge of created facts, concepts, ideas, procedures, and multiform data held together by a system or systems of thought. There is also formal knowledge that is philosophical and literary, for want of a better term: a literate, humanistic knowledge, what is knowable and true in the arts and literature (see Wood, 2003). It is knowledge that is valid and reliable in the sense of scholarly rationality rather than empirical-scientific. In the real world of teaching and learning, no work role is purely one way of thinking or relies on one specific base of knowledge. The student learning about curriculum needs to be familiar with the forms of knowledge and modes of knowing that will be encountered in doing curriculum. This mix of various ways of knowing and the formal and practice knowledge configures the practical, the essence of the role-work-knowledge relationship in practice, what is realized in the actual doing of curriculum work.

Building Perspectives

In general, roles in curriculum work share certain attributes associated with being a professional practitioner. None is more important than that of perspective building. In Chapter 1, the concept of a *critical perspective* was introduced, which included reference to your own personal perspective and the one you build as a professional and practitioner. As a composite, they represent how you see yourself, the way others see you, and how you perceive and do curriculum or any kind of work. In education and curriculum, perspectives have various qualities such as being scholarly; an inquirer; an expertise builder; and an on-your-feet classroom learner, a professional practitioner who can work with whatever is at hand. Perspective building begins with the perceptions and other sensory sources; they are the raw materials used in developing frames of reference, your ways of making sense of the world. The word *perspective* serves in an economizing way to represent other words or phrases (e.g., frame of reference, point of view, etc.) generally conveying the same meaning. Perspective building includes what beliefs you hold about life, politics, religion, and social relations that you act on. Perspectives are the "up-front" expressions, the rationales you give for what you say or how you behave. Perspectives represent getting to "know" the world, what Weick (1995) and Coburn (2001) refer to as "sensemaking," the personal making sense of perceptions, creating meaning that is personal, cultural, and social in significance. In the plural, involving many persons, shared perceptions and perspectives result in collective sense making. Perspectives represent a synthesis of perceptions, a cognitive hub that filters the possibilities for knowledge and action. The idea of the critical perspective is that it acts as the governor of other perspectives, the personal and professional ones you and I create as practitioners.

Personal Perspective

The personal perspective refers to things in our everyday life: the family and religion, the beliefs and values a person holds about life. These develop from social and cultural experiences, family and peer relationships, how you are brought up, and a mix of things that with biological inheritances generate a sense of self, an identity. Personal perspective can also be affected by encounters with ideology, identity, and social-cultural contexts.

Ideology

Ideology refers to the idiosyncratic and culture-bound ways of thinking and the prevailing ideas that characterize a person or a group. Terms like *democracy, freedom,* and *civil rights* reflect ideological considerations that are Judaic-Christian and European, hallmarks of Western civilization. Curriculum taught in schools is an ideological product, a way to think American. In the mainstream curriculum that most students take, history choices include American and perhaps a world history course. Literature offerings are, again, mainly American and European, with possibly some prose and poetry to suit local students from special cultural backgrounds. The American curriculum is constructed to Americanize, to create an American ideal.

Ideology also enters into the preparation of professionals. Earning a degree places you in classrooms where faculties introduce different ideas about education and schooling. There are the "isms," progressivism and constructivism, for example, and the "ists," such as the cognitivists, modernists, and postmodernists. These are ideologies of the academic culture that you encounter and about which you must make rational decisions as you prepare to be a professional. The critical perspective becomes important in thinking about these ideas.

Identity

Who are you? What do you believe? How would you describe yourself?

Those are questions of identity. Sociologist George Herbert Meade conceptualized the self as what we know about ourselves and what we receive back from others about ourselves, something he called the "generalized other." There is personal identity, social identity, cultural identity, and identity with work roles. The personal folding of those into one designates the self. The clarification of yourself to others is often referred to as your character. Identity refers to the individual's sense of who and what he or she is. Identity enters into curriculum work in our presentation of self as a worker, thinker, and personality. Am I a good listener, a cooperative coworker?

Sociocultural Context

Society and culture provide us with the social and cultural experiences that are among the strongest influences in our development as humans. Neighborhood, community, peer group, and school experiences create perceptions about place-location from which we build personal and collective perspectives about what it is like to live in a city, in the suburbs, or on a farm. Our interactions with others often make us aware of perceptual differences, the recognition that we don't see things the same way, especially when religious and political matters are at issue. Ethnic associations, for example, create subtle perceptions based on skin color, movement, dress, and language. Consideration of factors such as place, location, and ethnicity is also recognition that things in our focus have multiple characteristics; we may focus on the same thing but have different perceptions because we fix on different qualities. Our self-understanding, our sociocultural personhood, who and what we think we are, the self-perceptions we hold, is a composite of knowledge acquired in the experience of living, from family views of life in general and personal sociocultural background. These qualities shape how and on what we focus in developing our idiosyncratic construction of meaning.

Figure 3.4   Attributes of a Professional Perspective

- Critical Perspective
  To promote reflective thought and guide thinking in all its aspects, thinking about thinking itself and the objects of thought.

- Personal Perspective
  The self-knowledge necessary in continually understanding yourself, both separately as a person and as a person in a professional role.

- Knowledge Perspective
  Discerning what perspectives are embedded in knowledge as ways of thinking in a body of knowledge or across several bodies of knowledge.

- Other Attributes
  Cultivating a scholarly outlook, being an inquirer or researcher, building expertise.

Professional Perspective

A professional perspective is formally acquired as one learns a vocation or profession. Some aspects of a professional perspective are practice based, others are academic related, and some are both. One way to think of a professional perspective is as a superperspective that takes in other perspectives, as suggested in Figure 3.4. These, like the critical perspective discussed in Chapter 1, have been mentioned in previous discussions and are now brought together as elements in a professional perspective. In each case, it is a body of requisite knowledge, whether it is self-knowledge or the knowledge of thought that should become part of the professional person's development. The professional perspective continues to evolve and mature through work in the practice setting, continuing academic study, and the interrelating of the two. Your professional perspective guides how you view curriculum and perform curriculum work. Professional perspectives should not be dogmatic; they should include learned correctives, the suspending of judgment, the capacity to meditate, the ability to detach and stand outside oneself, and the idea of the critical perspective. An applied professional perspective should suggest behaviors with certain transcending qualities: an appreciation of scholarship and research, the development of a grounded expertise, and the capacity for on-the-feet learning. In addition to those perspectives, certain other elements of the professional should be cultivated, things such as a scholarly outlook, a dedication to research and inquiry in all its forms, and a commitment to expertise.

Scholarly Outlook

Scholars, suggests A. D. Nuttall, are not just intelligent or bright, they have a "dedication to detail and a passion for accuracy" (2003, p. 60). Scholarship has a "quality of completeness" about it he describes as "complete, though not redundant, documentation; complete accuracy, *even with reference to matters not crucial to the main argument;*

and, together with all this, a sense that the writer's knowledge at the fringe of the thesis is as sound as his or her knowledge of the core material" (p. 61). The scholarly way is a struggle to get everything right and complete, what Nuttall calls the "abstract altruism of the intellect." Scholarship is accuracy and completeness, as in having copious foot- or endnotes, appropriate and useful citations, and applicable references and indexes. Finding such things suggests good form and a respect for others in the enterprise. The quest for accuracy stands equally beside the scholar's obligation to truth, not just in the factual sense but the interpretive and analytical as well. Whereas the scholarly path is concerned with truth and accuracy, those quests are bound by moral and ethical dispositions to be encountered, experienced, and acquired in becoming a professional. Matters of plagiarism, failure to attribute to others their due, and failure in collegial relationships can become pitfalls in scholarly work.

Being an Inquirer

A curriculum practitioner should also cultivate a sense of curiosity, a need to find out, to know, to be an inquirer. Inquiry in its informal meaning refers to an attitude, a perspective. In its formal sense, there are two aspects of inquiry: one is being a researcher, and the other is being a consumer or user of research. All professional preparation programs address those dimensions of inquiry. Somewhere in the program there will be an encounter with a component (usually a series of courses) that introduces inquiry as practice, the matter of being a researcher. Prevailing models of research in the discipline of interest are studied. The emphasis is on familiarizing oneself with the models, then developing a research proposal using either a qualitative or quantitative method, all in preparation for being involved directly as a participant in some research enterprise. There being no lock on the research door, anyone can participate as long as they adhere to the practices and judgments about what is appropriate research according to currently accepted standards by researchers and practitioners in the particular knowledge community of interest. Not every curriculum worker needs to be a researcher, but everyone needs to be ready to be a participant and a consumer of research.

Appreciator of Research

Although associated with inquiry, it is important to be an appreciator and consumer of research. As part of preparation, professional practitioners explore research to understand criteria for appraising the investigative process and the findings that result. The practitioner as a consumer of research is in an important position to judge the utility of the research findings as applied in classrooms with learners. In the work of creating curriculum, one of the most important tasks is piloting materials with a variety of teachers and students across different classroom settings. This is an important level of inquiry, to determine if the curriculum fits the intended purposes and the ways it works out with teachers and students alike.

Building Expertise

The professional practitioner starting out is a novice. Attaining the cloak of the expert awaits continued study and the experience of practice. Expertise has a number of interpretations. There is expertise by professional standing, an acknowledgement of expertise in a field of work. For example, in physics, few would doubt the expertise of a Stephen Hawking or an Albert Einstein. Standing can also refer to affiliation or association: being employed by a particular college or university or place of practice such as a clinic, medical complex, or hospital; being selected to membership on a team led by a renowned professional; being elected to office in a premier professional organization; or, vicariously, being a student or associate of a particular scholar or practitioner. Expertise by authority refers to the interesting manner in which the legal system identifies a person as an expert to give testimony. The United States court system relies on *Rules of Evidence for United States Courts and Magistrates* (2003), specifically Rule 702, in considering what is an expert. Individual state judicial systems also have rules on expertise that differ in the particular gradations made by each state's judiciary or legislature.

What all those examples convey is the common reliance on personal knowledge, skills, experience, training, or education to classify individuals as experts—they are experts by virtue of what they know and have done. More recently, the focus has been on what are called expert studies (Brint, 1994). The idea is that, by analyzing the learning process of persons considered experts, it will be possible to understand what cognitive functions are needed in going from novice to expert in selective arenas of work such as education, medicine, mathematics, and sports (Bereiter & Scardamalia, 1993). The idea is that a composite of such studies would suggest a set of common cognitive functions to assist the transition of workers from the novice state to that of the expert. Patricia Alexander (2003) has provided a useful introduction to this work. Robert Sternberg (2003) also provides insights into the thinking dimension of domain work, the expertise-wisdom relationship in critical cognitive functioning experts use in working within their particular domain of knowledge such as physics, history, or fine arts. In curriculum, it would be equivalent to studying the way an expert understands and uses the knowledge base in curriculum to do curriculum work. There are several caveats to this research. One is that the studies are domain specific (physics, languages, etc.), and the nature of a domain of knowledge itself might mean that the expert pattern in one knowledge domain may vary from that in another. For example, two secondary school teachers, one in math and the other in history, would find the ways they have to operate in and with their domain of knowledge different. Second, what one knows, a person's expert knowledge, is in part learned in idiosyncratic ways and it may not be possible to generalize expert learning across all domains or persons. Third, it is important to keep in mind the transitional, dynamic quality of all knowledge and thinking. What delineates a novice or expert at any given time shifts and changes; today's expert may not be the same as the expert of tomorrow because what constitutes expertise will change. Regardless, traversing the road to expertise in curriculum work begins in the basic knowledge of curriculum and curriculum practice.

On-the-Feet Learner

In addition to being scholarly, being concerned about carefully constructing a professional perspective, developing expertise, and becoming an inquiring professional, a curriculum practitioner must be ready to invent and take actions based on what is *at* hand, not what he or she would like to have *in* hand. It is a matter of immediacy, the making do with the available tools, ideas, strategies, and so forth. Anthropologist Claude Lévi-Strauss (1966) associated this with the French word *bricolage,* meaning a construction of something from what is at hand. A professional practitioner often has to work as a *bricoleur,* a person who makes things or takes action with what is available. Applied to you as a learner, it means to think and act on your feet. For the teacher practitioner, it means being an on-the-feet learner as you teach. Teachers in their classroom curriculum work would immediately recognize the importance of this professional characteristic. Often in a classroom, there is an immediate need to substitute or swap curriculum materials to enhance learning opportunities. A curriculum specialist may get a priority request from a school for different texts. The bricoleur's strategy might mean a quick trip to a book repository, the copying of some material, or procuring whatever else is "at hand" to complete the work. Curriculum work can involve the unexpected, such as a curriculum question or inquiry asked on the fly while walking with a parent or staff member, or an on-the-spot discussion about curriculum materials. All those situations require immediate responses that may be dependent on the professional's formal knowledge of curriculum or the experience knowledge gained from working with curriculum. Circumstances like those are part of curriculum work.

<table>
<tr><td colspan="3" align="center">PERSPECTIVE INTO PRACTICE:
Application of Personal and Professional Perspectives
in an Elementary and Secondary Classroom</td></tr>
<tr><td>Perspective</td><td>Elementary Classroom</td><td>Secondary Classroom</td></tr>
<tr><td>Professional Aspects

Inquiring</td><td>The teacher observes how different children respond to word recognition, spelling, and sounding out words and wonders what curriculum options there are.</td><td>A civics teacher notes that in teaching about the U.S. Constitution, different perspectives enhance the curriculum organization.</td></tr>
<tr><td>Appreciating Research</td><td>In talks with other teachers and a district curriculum specialist, the teacher identifies available knowledge from research.</td><td>Recalling from a curriculum course, the teacher considers alternate curriculum patterns, such as a spiral or other format, and seeks out appropriate research with other teachers and the district specialist.</td></tr>
</table>

Applying Research	With the assistance of the specialist, several research-proven curriculum alternatives are applied to special-case learning problems in spelling and word recognition.	The teacher decides to teach the Constitution by proceeding from the idea of structure (the branches of government) related to the local experiences of students and work toward state and federal examples using patterns from a research study.
On-the-Feet Learning	Application of new knowledge in realistic teaching situations and how an approach to spelling works by itself or in combination with other applications gives experience in adjusting the curriculum as you go.	Even with research-based curriculum options, implementation with learners requires movement between one pattern and another as student responses indicate.
Expertise Building	The teacher now has increased knowledge and experience from implementation that is available to others in the school and district.	By identifying alternative ways to organize the civics curriculum's study of constitutions, the teacher becomes an experience base of knowledge for others and can model the curriculum option.
Personal Aspects		
Ideology	Professional behavior is tied to flexibility in thinking about a problem or circumstance and teacher role to enhance possible learning opportunities.	The realization that there is no one best way to organize curriculum and teach it. Flexibility, like rigidity, is its own ideology. Experience and knowledge of practice promote personal learning.
Identity	Positive sense making, a trait of a confident person, evolves into a positive professional identity.	Personal confidence in the knowledge and use of curriculum is both a matter of knowing the subject (civics) and knowing curriculum knowledge; both are essential to a teacher's identity.
Sociocultural Contact	Recognition that the learners' capability to learn to spell and sound out words may be a function of home and group language learning pattern and that, as a teacher, you exhibit similar personal use of speech.	Interest in civics and history is related to what knowledge is considered important and relevant by a learner. Personal sociocultural contexts influence what a person wants to learn.

DOING CURRICULUM WORK

The practical in curriculum is thoughtful action. In its most applied sense, a teacher working with students finds it in the employment of knowledge about curriculum. It is a curriculum worker's personal dialogue between knowledge used, knowledge received in that use, and new knowledge about curriculum created in the context and circumstances of being applied. The dynamics of curriculum practice are little studied. Summarizing from Walter Doyle's (1992) review of curriculum and pedagogy, with the exception of a few studies about teachers' work with curriculum, research specifically looking at the characteristics of other curriculum work and roles is very limited. Based on the literature available, curriculum roles and work would seem to have these qualities in common: activation of knowledge and its communication, a speculative turn of mind, envisioning the result or effect of some action or idea, and reflection—the reviewing, the rethinking, the ruminating about what has happened from start to finish. Using the teacher role as an example, each quality can be illuminated.

Activating Curriculum

Activation involves two curriculum dimensions. One is the content or subject matter knowledge—what is to be taught—which is the school dimension of curriculum. The other knowledge of curriculum is the teaching dimension of curriculum, working the subject matter through knowledge of curriculum concepts such a scope or sequence. If one has studied the knowledge base in curriculum and rehearsed its deployment, for example in student teaching, then the impression of a command of curriculum has been established. Activating that curriculum knowledge implies two aspects. One is to make that command of knowledge, what is to be taught, explicit and accessible to the intended, the students. Second, the application should demonstrate competence in operationalizing the intended formal content of the school curriculum carried as the message through instruction. Activation in curriculum work, a teacher's enacting of the content to be taught, mirrors the grasp, or mastery, of knowledge about curriculum in both the school and teaching dimension of curriculum.

Given opportunity and experience, the activation character of curriculum practice becomes tacit knowledge. One studies curriculum by learning to organize content, plan lessons or units, and present them through instruction. Along the way, the novice teacher picks up cues about different ways to organize knowledge, alternate knowledge options, and other insights that are unwritten in a text or materials about curriculum but that are important in practice. You learn to think "curriculum" on your feet and discern the shadow of new understandings between your thoughts and your actions. In practice, a teacher differentiates among thoughts and actions that simultaneously contain curricular, instructional, and other applied elements in the set of actions that circumscribe teaching.

Communicating Curriculum

Teaching is a process of engagement, a communication, the sending and receiving of curriculum. Imagine a kindergarten teacher working with numbers, that being the "content," or message being delivered. There is a confluence of two important bases of knowledge. One is the teacher's curriculum knowledge, how to organize the curriculum, plan an order of presentation, and arrange the context of engagement for the learners. Those curriculum concerns inform the teacher about the second, content dimension of curriculum work, determining what needs to be modified in the organization of knowledge about numbers. The curriculum becomes a participatory, shared creation as a communicated experience. It is a collective understanding about specified content deriving from interaction between teacher and students. In that sense, what is learned is held in common, an assumption of mutual belief and knowledge. The teacher learns, the students learn.

Curriculum is also communication of the expected. The curriculum the parent experienced is what is expected for the child. The larger social and cultural purposes for schools are carried in those experiences and expectations. The teacher, indeed any curriculum worker, should be able to explain the curriculum goals and understand the popular expectations, to answer a student's basic question, "Why do I have to learn this?" Being able to respond to such questions or situations is why there is a need to study the knowledge base in curriculum, particularly curriculum history and politics. The curriculum has been used throughout the American experience to communicate the message of citizen loyalty, to direct the knowledge resources toward economic ends, and to create a sense of nationhood and influence the direction of the society. The curriculum practitioner often walks a fine line among personal views about what the curriculum should teach, the purposes for which it exists, and what it actually contains. The school curriculum and the curriculum worker can become embroiled unwillingly in the contesting of curriculum messages by external forces, from the initiation of curriculum work when choices are made in planning a curriculum, through the creation of materials that represent it, to the classroom enactment of the curriculum.

Envisioning Curriculum

Curriculum practice is open ended, there is no finality, and it is always in a state of becoming. Even when a teacher has taught a lesson or a curriculum specialist has prepared a curriculum guide, there is an acceptance that the knowledge imparted as subject matter, the curriculum-in-use, has been modified, is outdated, or has become obsolete. There is also awareness of possible limitations in the capacity of existing curriculum discipline knowledge to guide practice. For example, knowledge production in curriculum or any discipline is always subject to the time lag in validating and disseminating new knowledge. However, another characteristic of practice is that it is a proactive endeavor necessitating some practical vision of future practice. For the practitioner, *envisioning* is a process of imagining, anticipating, or "hunching" the practical knowledge necessitated by curriculum practice. Often, curriculum workers engage in the possibilities of what might be: a consideration of what exists, whether it can or should be influenced by considering new relationships, and how it would appear if placed in different contexts, modified as a tool, or recast in some other way. It is a form of practice knowledge that Schon (1983) refers to as the *nonpropositional* knowledge derived from meditation-in-action, what can be called *efferent knowing*. In the disciplinary sense of knowledge production, this is the raw knowledge of individual practice that begins the journey to becoming part of a discipline's knowledge base, either as a result of formal research into practice or as authenticated in the collective discourse among practitioners about what works in actual practice. Teachers *envision* in planning the curriculum from one day to the next, when they anticipate content organization and order of presentation. A district curriculum supervisor, in planning for new curriculum materials such as new textbooks, has to envision how the materials fit the existing curriculum.

Reflecting on Curriculum

Another aspect of practice is reflection, the conceptualizing of what is transpiring or is ongoing. It is a different process: an overarching thinking about practice from beginning to end that subsumes envisioning, communication, and activation aspects of practice. *Reflection-in-practice* has several meanings. There is a form of reflection that occurs as one thinks about what one is doing as one does it, a sort of contemplation, or what Carter (1990, p. 301), in a review of studies of teacher work, refers to as "reflection-in-action." Another form is reflection-after-the-fact, a revisiting of what transpired, perhaps a reconstruction, or a comparative, as in comparing the mental record of what happened with the written guide or plan on which the actions were based, a lesson plan, for example. The purpose is ultimately to understand the actions in their particulars (i.e., the process engaged, outcomes sustained, reactions of those involved, etc.) and as the collective act. Metaphorically, it is like reviewing a performance, a play, for example. The actors, their actions, and each act of the play are the particulars; the experiencing of it renders it whole, and it can be revisited both as to its particulars and as a completed entity.

Summary and Conclusions

Curriculum and curriculum work are important in themselves, regardless of who does them and where they take place. Several points are important. Remember that curriculum is framed by a set of general work functions: knowledge making, policy making, planning, creating curriculum, managing, and monitoring. Second, those functions are performed in different ways in places as diverse as the local school, a state department of education, a publishing house, and national organizations such as the Council of Chief State School Officers or the National Governors Conference. The terminology "performed in different ways" is used deliberately to emphasize the tendency of work activities to be more specific, detailed, or defined by the workers and the situation or place in which they are doing the particular curriculum work. Curriculum work has a rhythmic quality. The various functions are clearly separate but related, each a contributor to the overall effort. Metaphorically, the functions are much like the distinctions between brass, string, and other orchestral sections that constitute the whole orchestra and work together separately to create music. The conductor, the oboist, each individual as a person and as a member of a group of musicians, has a perspective on the music that takes in his or her part as well as the total collective contribution. Curriculum workers, like musicians, build a professional perspective and are mindful of their own personal perspective, both elements in a critical perspective that illuminates the various practice, activation, communication, envisioning, and reflecting aspects of curriculum work as it is done.

Critical Perspective

1. What does the term *culture of work* mean? Can you identify examples from your own experience?

2. Using the curriculum work categories, identify examples from your experiences or that you know about that fit under the various categories. Are there any other general categories you would add?

3. How do you define *expertise*? Identify several teachers or persons you consider to be experts. What are the salient features of their expertise and do those match your definition?

4. Settings for curriculum work are many and varied. Can you identify other settings than those discussed in the text?

5. The text mentions several ways of classifying knowledge: declarative, procedural, informal, formal, nonpropositional, and so forth. What other ways of classifying knowledge can you identify?

6. Doing curriculum work encompasses at least four actions: activating, communicating, envisioning, and reflecting. Can you identify any other actions?

Resources for Curriculum Study

1. Local school-community-work relationships often drive configuration of the curriculum. Few studies make the connection. The famous Lynd study of Muncie, Indiana, *Middletown: A Study in Modern American Culture* (1929), and Allan Peshkin's *Growing Up American* (1978) offer interesting insights into vocational and college curriculum orientations that relate to the work life of a small town and farm community.

2. Authors Kantor and Lowe (2004) point out that any intellectual excitement about what is to be learned or about knowledge itself is often canceled by the manner of instruction. Memorization and question-answer methods, for example, tend to dull student interest. This presents an interesting curriculum problem for study: How does organizing the curriculum in different ways encourage student motivation? Check out the authors' references for further exploration of this issue.

3. The literature on policy making in education is relatively new but growing. Probably the best sampling of the early efforts in educational policy work is *History, Education, and Public Policy*, edited by Donald Warren (1978). Sandra Stein's *The Culture of Education Policy* (2004) is the best since Warren's and covers particular federal initiatives since 1965. Two insightful articles are "State Authority and the Politics of Educational Change" (1991), by Thomas James, and "Curriculum Policy," by Richard Elmore and Gary Sykes (1992). James offers a good analysis of the state of policy work and summarizes it in terms of the larger educational field. The Elmore and Sykes contribution is one of the few to explore the status of policy work specifically in curriculum. These works taken together document the evolution of policy making in general educational matters and the transition into more specialized studies such as curriculum.

4. Curriculum policy making is not limited to the United States or Western nations. UNESCO, the United Nations Educational, Scientific, and Cultural Organization, an arm of the United Nations, studies international approaches and trends. A specific publication, *Processes of Curriculum Policy Change,* which summarizes the centralization and decentralization approaches to policy making in selected nations, can be found at http://www2.unescobkk.org/ips/ebooks/documents/building curriculum/pt2.pdf

5. There is no uniformity across the 50 states about education; each state controls schooling in its own way. Using the Internet, sample state Web sites by region to find how they organize education. For example, you might go to the state sites of Idaho in the Rocky Mountain region, Virginia on the East Coast, Michigan in the upper Midwest, Oklahoma in the central Midwest, and perhaps Oregon on the

West Coast. At your selected sites, sample how individual states assign policy making in curriculum. Exploring what they are doing about policy to comply with the NCLB Act of 2001 is useful.

References

Alexander, P. A. (2003). The development of expertise: The journey from acclimation to proficiency. *Educational Researcher, 32*(8), 10–14.

Alexander, P. A., Schallert, D. L., & Hare, V. C. (1991). Coming to terms: How researchers in learning and literacy talk about knowledge. *Review of Educational Research, 61*(3), 315–343.

Bereiter, C., & Scardamalia, M. (1993). *Surpassing ourselves: An inquiry into the nature of and implications of expertise.* Chicago: Open Court.

Bobbitt, F. (1924). *How to make a curriculum.* Boston: Houghton Mifflin. (Reprinted 1972, New York: Arno Press)

Brint, S. (1994). *In an age of experts: The changing role of professionals in politics and public life.* Princeton, NJ: Princeton University Press.

Bruner, J. (1990). *Acts of meaning.* Cambridge, MA: Harvard University Press.

Carter, K. (1990). Teacher's knowledge and learning to teach. In W. R. Houston (Ed.), *Handbook of research on teacher education* (pp. 291–310). New York: Macmillan.

Charters, W. W. (1923). *Curriculum construction.* New York: Macmillan.

Clancey, W. J. (1997). The conceptual nature of knowledge, situations, and activity. In P. Feltovich, K. M. Ford, & R. R. Hoffman (Eds.), *Expertise in context: Human and machine.* Cambridge, MA: AAAI/MIT Press.

Coburn, C. E. (2001). Collective sense making about reading: How teachers mediate reading policy in their professional communities. *Educational Evaluation and Policy Analysis, 23*(2), 145–170.

Danielson, M. M. (2004). Theory of continuous socialization for organizational renewal. *Human Resource Development Review, 3*(4), 354–384.

Davenport, T. H., & Prusak, L. (1998). *Working knowledge: How organizations manage what they know.* Boston: Harvard Business School Press.

Doyle, W. (1992). Curriculum and pedagogy. In P. Jackson (Ed.), *Handbook of research on curriculum.* New York: Macmillan.

Elmore, R. F., & Sykes, G. (1992). Curriculum policy. In P. W. Jackson (Ed.), *Handbook of research on curriculum.* New York: Macmillan.

Gamoran, A. (1998). Curriculum change as a reform strategy: Lessons from the United States and Scotland. *Teachers College Record, 98*(4), 608–628.

Hutchison, D. (2004). *A natural history of place in education.* New York: Teachers College Press.

James, T. (1991). State authority and the politics of educational change. In C. Grant (Ed.), *Review of research in education* (pp. 169–224). Washington, DC: American Educational Research Association.

Kantor, H., & Lowe, R. (2004). Reflections on history and quality of education. *Educational Researcher, 33*(5), 6–10.

Kelly, A. V. (2004). *The curriculum: Theory and practice* (5th ed.). London: Sage.

Lévi-Strauss, C. (1966). *The savage mind.* Chicago: University of Chicago Press.

Lynd, R. S., & Lynd, H. M. (1929). *Middletown: A study in modern American culture.* New York: Harcourt, Brace & World.

National Commission on Excellence in Education. (1983). *A nation at risk.* Washington, DC: U.S. Department of Education.

Nuttall, A. D. (2003). Why scholarship matters. *Wilson Quarterly, 27*(4), 60–71.

Peshkin, A. (1978). *Growing up American.* Chicago: University of Chicago Press.

Polanyi, M. (1958). *Personal knowledge: Towards a post-critical philosophy.* Chicago: University of Chicago Press.

Schon, D. A. (1983). *The reflective practitioner.* New York: Basic Books.

Stein, S. J. (2004). *The culture of education policy.* New York: Teachers College Press.

Sternberg, R. J. (1990). *Metaphors of mind: Conceptions of the natural of intelligence.* New York: Cambridge University Press.

Sternberg, R. J. (2003). What is an expert student? *Educational Researcher, 32*(8), 5–9.

Teilhard de Chardin, P. (1975). *The phenomenon of man.* New York: Harper & Row/Harper Colophon/ Perennial Library.

Uneo, N. (2000). Ecologies of inscription: Technologies of making the social organization of work and the mass production of machine parts visible in collaborative activity. *Mind, Culture, and Activity, 7*(1 & 2), 59–80.

UNESCO. (n.d.). *Processes of curriculum policy change.* Retrieved February 2004 from http://www2.unescobkk.org/ips/ebooks/documents/buildingcurriculum/pt2.pdf

Vallance, E. (1999). Ways of knowing and curricular conceptions: Implications for program planning. In M. J. Early & K. J. Rehage (Eds.), *Issues in curriculum: Selected chapters from NSSE Yearbooks* (Ninety-Eighth Yearbook of the National Society for the Study of Education, Part II, pp. 49–70). Chicago: National Society for the Study of Education.

Warren, D. R. (Ed.). (1978). *History, education and public policy.* Berkley, CA: McCutchan.

Weick, K. E. (1995). *Sensemaking in organizations.* Thousand Oaks, CA: Sage.

Wood, M. (2003, December 18). What Henry knew. *London Review of Books, 25*(24), 21–25.

Wraga, W. (1997). Patterns of interdisciplinary curriculum organization and professional knowledge of the curriculum field. *Journal of Curriculum and Supervision, 12*(2), 98–117.

CREATING CURRICULUM

Textbooks, book bags, and backpacks are synonymous with school. Textbooks, what you lugged around, represented authority, the summarized versions of various kinds of knowledge. The teacher's knowledge, the textbook, and illuminating activities like videos, experiments, and field trips symbolize the live curriculum. For a curriculum to occur, it has to be wanted, thought out, and organized, and materials have to be produced. Curriculum has to be created.

ORIGINS OF CURRICULUM DEVELOPMENT AS CURRICULUM WORK

In 1918, Franklin Bobbitt's book *The Making of Curriculum* was published. This was an important event for several reasons. First was the use of the word *curriculum* as a common term subsuming such others as *courses of study, content,* and *subject matter* for referring to what was taught in schools. Second, it was the first book devoted specifically to creating curriculum. Earlier, others, like John Dewey (1902), had used the word *curriculum* in their publications but not in the same direct manner. Bobbitt cut straight to the heart of the matter in two important ways. First, curriculum was about schools, and making curriculum was for school use; he effectively connected curriculum with schools. His second influential idea was that curriculum could be created by those who used it, teachers and others who worked in schools and were concerned with schooling as a learning process. Those two key ideas came to characterize curriculum as a practical matter among practitioners in schools, a matter of making or developing curriculum. Almost imperceptibly, thinking about curriculum and curriculum work was acquiring an institutional face; it was being associated almost exclusively with schools as important institutions in the society at large. Simply put, the curriculum was schooling and schooling was the curriculum!

The Emergence of Curriculum Development

In the 1920s and 1930s, the main activities in curriculum were focused on curriculum theorizing and curriculum development. The former was most closely aligned with the academic community and its interest in curriculum. The latter, curriculum development, became the practical side of curriculum work, an important activity in diverse places. In cities such as Saint Louis and Denver and in small districts and rural settings in states as widely separated as California, Alabama, and Vermont, *curriculum development* meant just that, creating materials for actual use in the classroom. Much of the activity was an important part of the educational arm of the progressive movement and the popular belief that human progress was made through education (in its larger meaning), and this was possible through the schools as a common place of access. Probably the most important early documentation of thinking by curriculum scholars about curriculum development is found in the famous two-part Twenty-Sixth Yearbook of the National Society for the Study of Education, *Curriculum Making: Past and Present* and *The Foundation of Curriculum Making,* published in 1927 (Rugg, 1927a, 1927b).

In today's climate, it is difficult to appreciate the rather freewheeling nature of curriculum development. As Franklin Bobbitt had suggested, teachers and other school-based practitioners were quite capable of doing curriculum development. Alongside this workforce developed a parallel new cadre of consultants, the college- and university-based professors, the new faculties in the emerging departments, schools, and colleges of education. Those who weren't involved with the new specialty of curriculum theorizing were working in curriculum development, and some were doing both. Creating curriculum through curriculum development was becoming a mainstream type of curriculum work. While many others, including such luminaries as John Dewey (1915),

Boyd Bode (1921), W.W. Charters (1923), and George S. Counts (1926), made significant written contributions to curriculum thinking, it was Franklin Bobbitt's ideas about
curriculum that stimulated the elaboration of curriculum development as an important
kind of curriculum work.

Curriculum and Instruction

Usually, thinking about the order of curriculum development work links curriculum
with instruction. This tends to mask the singular importance of curriculum as the first-
order question, what is to be taught. Once that is decided, the second-order question is the
instructional one, how it should be taught. For example, a civics teacher preparing to teach
the American constitution has to decide how that bit of curriculum will be organized for
student learners. This may involve content considerations such as whether to begin with
basic concepts of government, for example, branches of government or separation of powers, before delving into their constitutional implications, or instead do an introductory
overview of kinds of constitutions so the uniqueness of the American one can be appreciated. In other words, the curriculum has to be set before instruction. Decisions about
using the textbook, overheads, a CD, a video, or discussion groups—the choice of instructional tools to engage the curriculum—can follow. Sometimes, in instructional design
work, you are admonished to consider them in tandem (Seel & Dijkstra, 2004). In preparing a lesson, any teacher does both, but try deciding the instructional question first—you
have no idea why you are using a particular tool because there is no reason to employ it;
imagine an overhead projector turned on with a blank transparency.

Instruction also follows curriculum in the sequence of activities that mark curriculum work. Recall from Chapter 2 that policy and planning tend to be the lead activities
before curriculum development. Those activities usually do not include decisions about
instructional tools. In the case of proposing a new curriculum, that would be an appropriate sequence. However, any curriculum work activity (policy making, development,
management, etc.) can be stand-alone work. There are essentially three traditional forms
of stand-alone curriculum development activities: First is the school-based informal
curriculum, ranging from development activities of a single teacher in a classroom, to
the collaborative work of many teachers in a school, to the development work carried
on by a school district, state, or other agent. A second is the commercial curriculum
development carried on by publishers and others, particularly the packaging of curriculum in a textbook and the production of supporting materials for classroom use. Third,
there is the academic side of curriculum development, not just the teaching of procedures or step-by-step ways to do development but the actual creation of proposals and
models of curriculum based on a curriculum theory with a detailed elaboration of the
curriculum. An excellent example of this academic development is Phillip Phenix's
Realms of Meaning (1964), blending curriculum theory and development together. The
key difference between Phenix's model and other scholarly theory-based proposals is

the full discussion and extensive elaboration that allows actual use of the model. One measure of the value of a curriculum development proposal or model such as Phoenix's is its potential use, whether it can be taken as it exists and implemented.

KEY FACTORS IN CURRICULUM DEVELOPMENT

In the same way textbooks have come to embody curriculum, curriculum development has come to stand for activities that actually create curriculum. Obviously, people, the participants, carry out those development activities in identifiable ways and in some particular location. Because curriculum development can take many forms, such as a textbook, a series of classroom science demonstrations, or a video about some historic event, there are some conditions that apply. First, the intended result, perhaps a textbook, can be made in different ways; there is no single development process. Second, for some materials that are constructed, their value, or worth, depends on two levels of expertise, the developer and the user. This highlights the importance of curriculum knowledge and practice, the knowledge capital, what the workers know about curriculum and what each person and the group bring to the developmental task. Each consideration reflects the degree to which developers have acquired basic curriculum knowledge and gained experience knowledge from the actual practice of doing curriculum development work.

The Participants

Often there is a presumption that only designated professionals get involved in curriculum development. The reality is that there are many possible participants in curriculum development, from teachers to school board members to publishers. What determines involvement is not always a matter of professional preparation having to do with schools and schooling. Further, it is not always a response to some policy initiative or formalized planning, or even an informal, in-house, teacher or district curriculum specialist response to an immediate curriculum need. A publishing house, for example, might act on opportunity, engaging in curriculum development based on its determination that the development of a particular textbook or text series is needed. That decision could be based on competitive market considerations, in response to some state or district school policy, or perhaps initiated by a scholar interested in writing a text. National organizations and interest groups also create curriculum materials that parallel areas of the curriculum in hopes that they will be used. Governments at all levels also create materials for curriculum use. A critical question, one you might have already noted, is who or what sanctions the use of these specialized materials. This is a matter you will return to later in this chapter and that will reappear frequently in other discussions throughout the text.

The Local Scene

Local curriculum development takes place at the classroom, school, and district level. Easily the most representative example is the preparation of daily lesson plans by the teacher. The *lesson plan* is not only the primary document in teaching, but it is also the basic operational curriculum document. How the curriculum embodied in a lesson plan plays out is a matter of moment-to-moment adjustment by the teacher. It is like making a tactical adjustment to a strategic plan, or orchestrating a piece of music in different ways but remaining true to the original music as the composer intended. Depending on their foundational knowledge about the curriculum content they are teaching, teachers have a significant opportunity to organize and, like the original music, orchestrate the curriculum in different ways while still retaining the intended message. Curriculum development may also occur at the grade and school level. It is not uncommon for teachers to carve out responsibilities for curriculum. Elementary teachers may choose to team up on curriculum responsibilities, each teacher being responsible for the preparation of lessons in a given area of the curriculum. In middle and high school, formal and informal departmentalization can mean teachers are assigned responsibility for preparing and coordinating particular curriculum content consistent with their training. A science teacher prepared in the physical sciences may be given the physics and chemistry curriculum whereas another with expertise in the biological sciences will be assigned to the curriculum in biology. Similar differentiations can apply all across the schooling spectrum. In larger school districts with an extensive central office support staff, curriculum supervisors also perform curriculum development work in addition to completing assignments as area specialists in mathematics or reading, for example. Persons in those roles also support classroom teacher curriculum requests through executing resource searches, securing current research reports on curriculum matters, and functioning as lead liaisons with teachers in different schools and appropriate state department of education personnel. Teachers also develop *curriculum units.* This is a process of chunking, or breaking, the total curriculum organization into manageable units for curriculum and teaching purposes. Units are then often further separated and organized into individual lessons. This in-school curriculum development work may also occur in-district as a combined effort of curriculum specialists and teachers.

The State Level

Most school personnel think intrastate schooling matters are exclusively handled by their state department of education. The appointed or elected state board of education and superintendent usually carry statutory authority for oversight of all schooling, public, private, and parochial. Keep in mind that all agents authorized to carry out functions of the state do so under that state's constitution and legislative enactment. Each is a creature of the state and subject to legislative direction or administrative action by the executive branch. Whereas the state board and superintendent have responsibility for schooling, the legislature may by law and the governor by grant of legislative authority direct them to do anything they wish regarding schools consistent with the state's constitution as amended. Pressure from special interests can also influence state-level actions and curriculum. If, for example, advocates of a different way to study science were successful in enacting a new policy to include teaching about intelligent design, the upshot would be a massive new orientation of the curriculum in science, with possible side effects to other content areas such as history and literature. The amount of curriculum realignment required could be formidable: preparing a new curriculum scope and sequence; calling a special textbook committee to prepare an approved state textbook list for districts to select texts for adoption; and developing guidelines for district curriculum development projects and for implementing the new curriculum. This hypothetical example underscores both the importance of curriculum and its control, and the varieties of curriculum work that such a policy change could entail; it would be no small decision and no small result.

The Nation and Regions

When considerations about schooling and schools telescope away from individual states to regional and national platforms, curriculum development work becomes different. Because things curricular are not tied to any specific constitutional authority as they are in the individual states, curriculum development work now occurs in a different realm, one characterized by regional and national activities and a variety of players, especially those that are commercial and for-profit. In national and regional curriculum development work, publishing houses and similar commercial agents are the largest producers of curriculum materials. There are also other publishers who specialize in more limited curriculum areas such as music, the arts, character education, and drug education. These are developers of *niche curriculum* areas and materials that have unconventional characteristics. One is the lack of universal applicability. For example, unlike a standard text in science that has a vast national market, materials for a drug education curriculum have to jockey for fit across a diverse collection of different curriculum expectations and controllers. A second matter is the often off-handed way that such niche curricula are assigned responsibility for inclusion in a local or state curriculum. For example, drug education and character education are often mandated but left to local curriculum specialists or teachers to decide what materials to use and where to place them in the organization of the total curriculum.

Nationally and locally, there are a variety of professional organizations that carry on curriculum development activities in addition to commercial venders. These organizations, the National Council for the Social Studies, National Council of Teachers of English, National Council of Teachers of Math, and Council on Basic Education, to suggest a few, are dedicated to supporting particular curriculum content interests. They prepare curriculum scope and sequence guides, develop supplementary curriculum materials for teacher classroom use, and carry on a variety of other professional activities, including journal and yearbook publications, a national conference, special member training institutes, and regional and state affiliate meetings. When questions about curriculum arise, matters of revising or creating new curriculum, for instance, these organizations are often in the role of the expert providing advice about scope, sequence, and other curriculum issues.

EXPANDING THE CONCEPTION OF CURRICULUM DEVELOPMENT

Actions often lead to unforeseen consequences and problems that have to be faced. The use of the atomic bomb in World War II and subsequent realizations about the long-term implications of radiation is one example. On the positive side, the development of antiviral medicines has enhanced life in ways that were unforeseen as well. Although certainly not of the same life quality importance, the unfolding of curriculum development work raised consciousness about the curriculum and its use. As in anything new, actually doing curriculum development unearthed new realities about the work itself and the materials that resulted from that work. One aspect was the seemingly dual nature of curriculum development as both a process and a product. Another aspect, that multiple producers of materials for potential use existed outside teachers and schools, raised questions about the process and product in other settings and how to judge those materials.

Curriculum Development as Process and Product

What does it mean to speak of curriculum development as a process and a product? It means a series of steps, a procedure, recipe, or formula that guides an activity from beginning to end, resulting in something useful. A recipe is a process, and the result is a cake, dish of food, or other tangible result. In curriculum development work, a *process* is an applied activity to guide creation of a curriculum or materials for a curriculum. In its *product* form, it is perhaps a curriculum guide, a textbook, or some material in some other medium useful for teachers in schools. The book you are reading is an American-style textbook. It is a product of a developmental process. A film or film series, Ken Burn's *The Civil War,* for example, is also a development product. The textbook was created to fit a particular curriculum; the videos were not. Yet, as a set of curriculum materials, those videos are extremely useful for a secondary United States history curriculum. It provides a superb visual amplification that takes the American history curriculum beyond the classroom text. These examples illustrate different developmental paths based on specific proposals developed in a process that took them from idea to product. Both are examples of commercial for-profit ventures in curriculum development. Commercial curriculum products include text series, supporting materials, and stand-alone curriculum packages for special curriculum like character education and drug education. You may be familiar with publishing houses such as Pearson Education (Merrill, Prentice Hall), Allyn and Bacon, and Silver Burdett from the textbooks you used in school. Lists of approved publishing resources are available from state departments of education, from curriculum specialists in district offices, and online via the Internet. *Approved* means publishers and their products that have been screened by the state—for example, published books sanctioned after vetting during a formal textbook review and selection process.

There are also noncommercial materials, those that are either free or have some minimum cost recovery purchase fee. These publications are produced by sources that wish to get their message into classrooms. The American Red Cross provides supplemental materials about health and medical issues that are of use in schools. Resources like those from the Red Cross or the American Medical Association about disease prevention carry a message that is value neutral—few persons would disagree with the message or consider it controversial except, of course, in matters related to sexual practices, which become value loaded. As noted earlier, the value nature of a message carried in curriculum materials can be a problem. Teachers and curricularists often find themselves in the cross fire of curriculum concerns where value-loaded materials are under scrutiny. It is important to know the message and the messenger when stepping outside approved materials. This intent to convey a message is also the most likely reason noncommercial materials are either free or at minimum cost, which, motives aside, usually reflects the cost of covering production, distribution expenses, or both.

Identifying Other Curriculum Materials

Obviously, commercial sources are easily identified and commonly known. In addition to publishing houses, there are television, radio, film, and other media production corporations. Disney, for example, and other conglomerate subsidiaries, also produce curriculum materials for sale. Elementary teachers often use *Sesame Street* materials or others like it for building skills in reading, listening, and working with numbers, time, and other curriculum basics.

Organizations providing noncommercial curriculum resources are easily accessible and range across a wide variety of agencies, organizations, and interest groups. For example, if you peruse the Internet, you will find federal agency resources from information about touring the White House to the latest list of terrorist organizations from the State Department. States offer similar individual Web sites with access to materials and other resources. And so it goes; there is something available from virtually every county, borough, parish, township, village, town, and city that is incorporated, and sometimes from others with names only.

In addition to materials from supposed value-neutral and government sources, there is another world of sources ranging from those that strive for value neutrality to those that are purposefully value loaded. In the first category are most professional organizations. The American Bar Association is one example. It provides very useful materials about the law, court systems, and the constitution that fit in any school history or civics curriculum. The American Political Science Association and other discipline-related academic professions offer materials for classrooms and the latest discipline knowledge so teachers can be current in their teaching. This is especially useful for teachers who have out-of-date texts and materials and need to supplement the curriculum. In the second category are organizations that create materials with a specific purpose and agenda in mind and that offer a fascinating array of opportunities. These include tax-exempt institutes, associations, and those incorporated as special interests. A sampling might include these:

- *Council on Basic Education.* An advocate for humanities and arts in the school curriculum, particularly concerned with balance across the curriculum and equal time with math, science, and the social studies.

- *The Sierra Club.* Just one of many conservation associations that seek to inform people about the environment and such issues as global warming and wilderness preservation.

- *Eagle Forum.* A national organization with state units, it scrutinizes the curriculum, particularly history, for accuracy and patriotic concerns. This is representative of a number of similar groups that have a range of special interests such as screening books and reading programs for appropriate themes and language or presenting alternate content views in science. Their materials run the gamut from simple watch lists of books or publications they consider inappropriate to materials for substituting or supplemental texts and other materials.

- *National Council of Teachers of Mathematics.* This is one example of professional organizations inclusive of schoolteachers, professors, and other persons with an interest in a particular curriculum area. There is some advocacy group for every area of the curriculum, from kindergarten readiness to physical education.

- *National Association of Manufacturers.* The NAM, as its name implies, is a trade organization for manufacturers. There are various organizations like this for pharmaceuticals, companies in various kinds of energy, banks, stockbrokers, and just about any area of business and commerce one can name. These associations produce materials that highlight interests of the membership.

Some Caveats

The diversity of organizations, interest groups, and various other constituencies points to a wide range of available information and materials in a variety of forms. Those materials portray what an organization does, why it is important, and the message it wants to convey. They issue reports, commission studies and books, and prepare position papers, the purpose of which is to weigh in on some issue and influence policy making. As they are special interest or advocacy organizations trying to get out the message, caution is the operative word for teachers and others who might wish to use the materials. Curriculum is, in this sense, a political cross-fire area, and teachers, curricularists in general, and administrators should entertain the use of materials with their collective eyes wide open. There is, after all, a difference between the sanctioned curriculum of the state and the unsanctioned curriculum created in using materials from the many organizations that provide them. Any organization's material may hold curricular value; the determinate is your professional judgment.

ESSENTIAL KNOWLEDGE FOR CURRICULUM DEVELOPMENT WORK

Summarizing what has been discussed so far, curriculum development can occur in a variety of places, it is a process, it results in both a product that is the curriculum and in materials that represent the curriculum, and it is an activity carried on by both school and nonschool participants. Curriculum development is not some difficult technical pursuit such as trying to understand and work with nanotechnology or grasping what string theory is all about. Curriculum development work is very practical, requiring a basic understanding of certain elements that are involved in working with it. Curriculum workers, when developing curriculum, need to know certain conceptual fundamentals and initial ideas before engaging in that curriculum work. For example, curriculum can't truly be discussed without considering scope, sequence, continuity, and balance, which can be collectively referred to as curriculum fundamentals. Similarly, you will find that scale and capacity are important considerations in other curriculum work such as policy making and planning, as well as curriculum development.

Developing and Monitoring a Perspective

One of the continuing encounters in all professions is the need to understand the importance of perspectives, the critical, the personal, and the professional. This is essential so each person can understand the subjectivity of his or her objectivity in forming a perspective. Briefly, recalling discussion from previous chapters, a perspective is the response given when you ask, "How do I view this?" or "What do I think about this?" It calls for reflection about self-knowledge and acquired formal knowledge (as in what is studied about curriculum), and accepting the tentative nature of all knowledge and its fragility in application. In a way, it is similar in intent to the analysis that a person seeking to become a professional psychoanalyst must undergo, the final step of undergoing personal psychoanalysis by another analyst. This is not to advocate that process; it is a statement about the importance of understanding subjectivity and being reflective about your perspective in practice. Understanding and creating a professional perspective is of singular importance in curriculum work because there is great potential for influencing curriculum in the development process quite aside from any policy or planning intent. Furthermore, if all workers attain a reflective mode toward their perspective, it enhances the possibility for cooperative dialogue and the potential for productive work.

Understanding Commonplaces

Commonplaces refer to general attributes of education that are always inherent in any deliberation about educational matters. These are presented in Figure 4.1. and trace their lineage to contributions by Joseph Schwab (1969) and John Goodlad (1985), who articulated them in curriculum terms. Goodlad's conceptualization includes instruction, curriculum, learning, and evaluation elements. Because it is important to treat curriculum as a distinct body of knowledge, the idea of commonplaces is recast in the figure as three commonplaces, the educational, teaching, and curriculum. The specification of curriculum commonplaces used here is based on an idea suggested by Decker Walker (1990). Each set identifies the basic foundational elements in which the idea of the

Figure 4.1   Commonplaces Reconsidered

The Educational Commonplaces

Teachers	Learners	Subject Matter	Milieu

Source: Schwab (1969); Walker (1990).

The Teaching Commonplaces

Goals and Objectives	Content	Materials	Learning Activities
Teaching Strategies	Evaluation	Grouping Practices	Time-Space Use

Source: Goodlad (1985).

The Curriculum Commonplaces

Goals, Objectives, Outcomes Documentation	Scale, Capacity	Process Choices	Fundamentals

Source: Hewitt (2004).

commonplace is grounded. The sets are different in two important ways. First, the scope of focus for each is different, broad in the sense of educational commonplaces and narrowing when considering teaching and curriculum, in that order. The second difference is one of complexity of details, from the general to the specific. The complexity at the broad educational level is less than that at the curriculum level. It is much like thinking about a map having a scale of one inch equaling 50,000 feet on the ground and another having one inch equaling 5000 miles on the ground. Which provides more detail and which one would you like to have if you were lost in the woods? I hope you would have the map with a representation of one to 5000 feet with you because it is more detailed. If you were planning curriculum, you would want to have the detailed curriculum commonplaces rather than the more general educational commonplaces, although you would probably think first from the educational to the curriculum commonplaces. These commonplaces have interesting uses in curriculum and schooling work. You will encounter them again in different contexts, such as the discussions on policy making in Chapter 9 and implementing curriculum in Chapter 11.

Scope and Sequence

Scope and sequence are curriculum concepts that illuminate the scale and shape of curriculum. *Scope* refers to what is included in the curriculum, what is covered, what it contains. *Sequence* means the order in which the curriculum is presented, how it is progressively organized. Both have micro and macro considerations, what can be called matters of small and large scale. Micro, or small, scale refers to the content and organization of curriculum in the smallest unit such as a textbook, teacher lesson plan, or, at the school organization level, the classroom and grade. Large, or macro, scale refers to the curriculum from kindergarten to twelfth grade, a statewide curriculum, or a specific curriculum area like science, either as K–12, districtwide, or statewide. There are also horizontal and vertical considerations in scope and sequence. Vertical can refer to the curriculum sequence going upward from kindergarten to Grade 12 or the curriculum sequence from the first to the last day of the school year. Horizontal sequence can refer to the curriculum at a grade level across several classrooms, schools, or districts. Similarly, vertical scope can refer to curriculum content across grades in a school or schools in a district, or across K–12 grades within a district, across districts, or within a state. The matter of scope and sequence can also affect thinking about evaluation in curriculum, a matter you will return to in Chapter 12.

Continuity and Balance

Continuity and balance are another set of fundamental curriculum terms. Consider the matter of *continuity* in the mathematics curriculum, the continuous way it is organized for teaching. For example, it is unlikely that curriculum sequence considerations in elementary arithmetic would put the study of subtraction before addition or, in teaching addition, would start with one-place addition and then jump to third-place addition while skipping second-place addition. What that also implies is a failure to consider curriculum *balance*, the relationship of a curriculum to learners. Here the concern is twofold, the match between the developmental level (age and capability) of the child and the sophistication and complexity of the curriculum. You would not expect a second grader to understand concepts from a high school physics course, but you might suppose that some basic concepts, gravity, for example, could be taught in second grade as introduction to the study of science that follows in succeeding grades.

Scale and Capacity

School size, determined by the number of students or classrooms, might seem to have little relationship to curriculum. Actually, size is an important consideration because school size affects curriculum in some interesting ways. The relationship between school size and curriculum is a matter of *scale*. As demands for curriculum increase or decrease, the curriculum usually expands or contracts accordingly. Essentially, this is a matter of the more students, the more the options for learning, and thus the increase in curriculum. The reverse is also true to the point where the base curriculum (not a minimum curriculum) is sufficient for the needs and expectations of a school or community. Scale is also reflected in curriculum development activities. Examples of small units of scale are the individual teacher making materials for classroom use and the student preparing an assigned report. Large-scale examples would include developing a national curriculum, as has been done in the United Kingdom, and publishers producing textbooks. Closely related to scale is *capacity*, or workers such as teachers and developers having the necessities to carry out curriculum work. Capacity includes considerations about material resources (pencils, paper, etc.), worker knowledge and expertise, time allotted, and authority to do the work assigned.

The details in doing successful curriculum work are in the degrees of complexity and scale encountered by the workers and their capacity to do the development work. Matters of scale and capacity affect the complexity of planning. Developing a curriculum in a small school, in a large school, or for an entire district or state is obviously a matter of the scale of the task and the capacity of the workers to accomplish their mission. Authority to do work as part of capacity is very important. For instance, if the responsibility is given to the state department of education, the planning has to take in all the schools and districts in the state. If the responsibility is with the district-level central office staff, it is contingent on the size of the staff and the number of schools in a district. If it is the responsibility of the principal and school, it may be keyed to the number of teachers and students involved. Although scale and responsibility are important framing factors in deciding who or what will conduct curriculum activities, planning in those different contexts will range in complexity and be determined by the capacity to plan and the expertise available in the staff and available as resources for planning. Simply put, it is a matter of whether the agent responsible can carry out the task, whether the size of the curriculum undertaking, the consideration of scale, and the capacity of the unit to do the work will result in successful implementation.

Alignment and Articulation

Interrelating scope, sequence, continuity, and balance is important in curriculum work. In curriculum development, *alignment* refers to the adjustment of a curriculum in the particulars of its scope, sequence, continuity, and balance. Alignment also has other implications. One is the relationship of the curriculum to what the teacher actually teaches, the taught curriculum. There is also the matter of curriculum and assessment, particularly the relationship of tests to the curriculum, what they measure and how that affects the curriculum. If there are standards, what should the curriculum-standards alignment be like? These are all alignment concerns, but each is distinct and different. Regarding curriculum alignment, the considerations are presented in Figure 4.2. Alignment depends on *articulation,* the careful specification of the elements in alignment. Keyed to the current reform movement, this means articulation of relationships involving content standards, performance standards, curriculum, and tests (Educational Testing Service, 2004). *Reflection,* concern for inclusion of critical *components, coherence,* and the *capacity* to do alignment work, all key considerations, are developed in Figure 4.2 as a set of threshold considerations for alignment.

The conversation here is simply an introductory one to begin building the concept of curriculum alignment. The related matters of assessment, standards, and alignment will be further developed in the discussion about curriculum adaptation and implementation in Chapter 10.

Figure 4.2   What to Consider Before Curriculum Alignment

- **Reflection:** These critical questions are asked and written responses prepared: Why is curriculum alignment needed? How is a process of alignment created?
- **Components:** Alignment requires four critical documents: a written curriculum, written standards, a written school-based curriculum, and a documented taught curriculum.
- **Coherence:** There is a congruence, or fit, of the written curriculum, the written standards, the school-based written curriculum, and the documented taught curriculum.
- **Capacity:** Planning, developing, and implementing curriculum alignment requires a commitment of resources; it is important that the unit (school, district, etc.) has the capacity to handle the initial needs and long-term management the commitment requires.

PERSPECTIVE INTO PRACTICE: How Selected Knowledge Essentials Apply to Elementary and Secondary Curriculum		
Knowledge Essentials	*Elementary Setting*	*Secondary Setting*
Commonplaces: The teacher, student, subject, milieu, and curriculum.	Teachers in any elementary grade are aware of curriculum and its compatibility with the students, their perspectives about the subject, and milieu factors such as the community and family, which can affect curriculum interpretation and delivery.	Teachers in a secondary school setting consider how the subject matter and knowledge about students will suggest options for engaging the curriculum. How, for example, would a physics requirement be framed for students that are not college bound? Milieu factors, such as the community, family, and student work, can also suggest how to tailor a subject to the audience.
Scope and Sequence: What the curriculum covers and how it is organized.	The elementary curriculum addresses first skills (e.g., learning to read numbers) and expands those as it also covers areas of knowledge (e.g., science, language arts). The curriculum in any subject is ordered across grades and topics for study in a natural progression.	The secondary school curriculum addresses what is to be learned by providing subject matter options (e.g., mathematics follows a required progression with options for specialized mathematics course needs keyed to special groups such as the college bound or vocational student).
Continuity and Balance: Curriculum is organized in a continuous manner so there are no unintended gaps. The curriculum options accommodate a variety of student learning styles so there is a possibility of fit between student and curriculum.	Entry readiness of students in elementary can vary greatly; and remedial or extending qualities of a curriculum are available to accommodate students' differences. This will require that students do not encounter unintended gaps in the curriculum.	Experience with curriculum in secondary schools is time intensive; there is little time to recover gaps. Curriculum-student match is more critical in some subjects than in others; the match of student capability to degree of curriculum difficulty greatly affects matters of curriculum balance.
Scale and Capacity: Size of unit to curriculum needs (the number of students-to-curriculum), number	Elementary schools usually are of a size that permits more contact and assistance so curriculum (particularly critical areas like basic reading,	Class size and student diversity are different scale factors in secondary school settings. Student numbers and differences in student goals

(Continued)

(Continued)

of teachers to teach and their expertise, and number of books (material and instructional resources) reflect the capacity to create and maintain the curriculum.	communication, and mathematics skills) is learned. Capacity should match the demands of scale; if there are five first-grade classes and three second-grade classes, the first-grade curriculum will require more capacity (materials, etc.) than the others because of scale (i.e., the number of students is greater).	(college, vocational, etc.) dictate scale of curriculum offerings. Although materials are important, the critical capacity element is teacher expertise in the subject matter to enhance curriculum quality.

Analyzing Curriculum Proposals

Curriculum doesn't just appear; it has to be invented, articulated, and presented. Sorting out various proposals takes time and human resources that are precious. Some economy of effort is required, and some procedure or set of protocols, a path of presentation, needs to be in place. The crucial part of that process is establishing criteria for judgments about the proposals. This is the threshold to development, and decisions have to be made about which and how many ideas will come to fruition. The important activity at this point is to make an initial analysis of what is being proposed. Analysis actions refer to considering something in terms of its parts and their relationships, the curriculum commonplaces, for example. Again, these are not absolutes to be implemented but things to think about, a first sizing up of the process. The analysis is a preliminary appraisal of the fit of the selected development process, perhaps an existing one or one specially created, to the development envisioned before the onset of actual activity.

- *Feasibility:* Knowing the curriculum development project, are the tasks and work assignments reasonable and doable?
- *Conformation:* What is the estimated degree of fit between the planned work and the developmental process selected? This is an early determination of appropriateness inclusive of the preceding considerations.
- *Installation:* Thinking about the development process and creating the features that will aid in making the resulting product both utilitarian and desirable to the users.
- *Standards:* The ultimate purpose of curriculum development work is a product for use by teacher and students. It is a significantly important product when it contributes to attaining some curriculum standard. This product-standard relationship needs early recognition.

If the analysis is favorable or at least the project is deemed worth trying, the project moves forward to consideration of ways to proceed with development. Keep in mind that these are some suggested elements that should be considered early on. You will learn about others as the complexity of creating curriculum is developed in succeeding chapters and particularly in Chapter 10.

Selecting a Development Model

A decision to move forward with a curriculum proposal leads to a critical decision about forming and using a process to guide the work, the actual framework for creating the curriculum. Among the choices are considering the use of an existing development model, modifying it, combining elements of several models, or creating a new one. Deciding to use an existing model then leads to a decision about which one and for what reasons. There are many models specific to curriculum and others that integrate curriculum, instruction, and other elements, and those can be found by exploring the literature on instructional design (see Reigeluth, 1999; Seel & Dijkstra, 2004) or curriculum books (see chapter references and the Recommended Readings section) oriented to curriculum as development. Categorizing or grouping models can be based on whether they are descriptive or prescriptive as suggested in Figure 4.3. A *descriptive* model does just that, it describes what you can do with it and leaves its use up to you, the worker. The *prescriptive* provides a detailed progression, a series of steps or some type of ordering that you are to follow more or less explicitly. The "more or less" qualification is necessary because some prescriptive models do allow for modifications. For example, the Tyler Rationale as a model is prescriptive, a series of steps in question form, but in thinking about and using one step, you open up considerations that expand the question. On the other hand, Walker's model describes a deliberation process that doesn't require a sequential movement but offers actions that should occur with the flexibility of their occurrence left to the situation or context of their use. The ideal in selecting a model is, of course, to match where you want to go in developing something, the characteristics of the model, and the characteristics of the proposal under consideration that you have previously analyzed. That effort may lead to another alternative, creating a process from scratch.

If it is beneficial to create a new developmental process, then the question is, what should it include? A sample developmental process is provided in Figure 4.4. This

Figure 4.3   Selected Models for Creating Curriculum

- Models with a specified process (prescriptive)
  - Tyler Rationale
  - Taba Model
  - Bruner Model

- Models that describe a process (descriptive)
  - Walker's Deliberative Model
  - Freire's Emancipatory Model
  - Hunter's Lesson Cycles

Figure 4.4   Considerations for a Model Curriculum Development Process

- Preliminary Resource Analysis Phase
  Analyze developing unit capacity needs, available workers and supporting resources, allocated time and authority, developmental perspectives; consider a possible model process.

- Conceptual Phase
  Identify specific goals/objectives; envision curriculum characteristics; articulate parallel assessment-evaluation-management framework.

- Design Phase
  Perform actual series of design-test-revision actions in pilot and field applications.

- Implementation Phase
  Produce curriculum materials and embed continuous production management and assessment evaluation elements.

four-phase process suggests how the creative process might proceed and summarizes what might be included in each phase. Created developmental processes like this one are subject to revision in use. As an untried new process, the model, when implemented, creates important experience knowledge that is useful in making adjustments to the model itself and altering curriculum development work. This is not as complex or abstract a process as it seems, and this first encounter with curriculum models is to introduce ideas you will develop about curriculum tools in Chapter 6. It is also intended to familiarize you with some classic models that have appeared and will reappear in discussing curriculum knowledge and work. How curriculum development work moves from this phase of a process to use will be discussed in Chapter 11, which is about adaptation and implementation in curriculum work.

Documenting the Development

Using models and doing development is nice in getting you from ideas to use. However, there is one more important aspect to consider along with selecting a model and preparing to use it in curriculum development work, and that is to know how you got from the idea to its use. It is important to be developmental in its fullest sense by creating a record of thinking and actions taken. All professional work depends on knowledge not only to be applied but also about what has occurred in the doing of some task. Too often, the outcome is evident but the events getting there go unrecorded. It is often important to be able to replicate events, particularly processes that are the path of development, what can be called *after-knowledge,* the lack of which can lead to wasteful duplication and sometimes unfortunate results. This after-knowledge is the knowledge of record, often described in narratives and case studies of actual curriculum work, the representation of individual and collective thinking in the developmental process

(Connelly & Clandinin, 1988, 1990). This special kind of knowledge should become part of the knowledge base available to all practitioners and especially those who are studying to specialize in curriculum. That kind of knowledge, the documented record, is also important for understanding how particular models work and ways the circumstances of their use affect developmental thinking. To create this after-knowledge, the record of what happened, you establish a recording process, perhaps using a curriculum document notation system (see Armstrong, 2003, pp. 234–240); an assessment procedure using checklists or other devices; or, particular to developmental projects, an account of the pilot testing and field testing that should be built into development work.

Summary and Conclusions

Curriculum work has many facets, creating curriculum through development activities being one of the oldest and most representative. Key factors in curriculum development include the variety of people who participate and its pervasiveness as an activity in schools, in districts, in states, nationally, and internationally. Development activities constitute a process, a way to do development that is practice, and the knowledge developed about that practice becomes curriculum knowledge. The perspectives that guide thinking about development and consideration of knowledge essentials such as commonplaces, scope, sequence, and so forth configure any development process.

Critical Perspective

1. A number of participants in curriculum development are identified, teachers being the most obvious. Students are also participants. Consider ways students and their classroom participation might influence curriculum creation.

2. Evaluating sources that contribute curriculum materials is important. Identify some sources other than those mentioned in the textbook and state the reasons care should be given in evaluating potential materials from those sources.

3. If you have participated in anything called curriculum development, describe the activity. Can you describe the guiding perspectives and the process on which the development was based?

4. If you have participated in a curriculum development activity, can you state if any of the knowledge essentials discussed in this chapter were evident in the activity?

5. Why are commonplaces important considerations in curriculum development?

6. Scope, sequence, continuity, and balance are sometimes referred to as curriculum fundamentals. What does that imply about their use in creating curriculum?

7. In the Perspective Into Practice section of this chapter, examples are not provided for *alignment* and *articulation*. Can you suggest ways each would apply in an elementary or secondary curriculum?

8. Some authorities advocate doing needs assessments before curriculum development activities. Given the requirements that standards create, is a needs assessment necessary? Why or why not?

9. Curriculum developers and teachers are often told to fit the curriculum to student needs and capabilities. Standards and testing suggest the important result is student scores, thus suggesting that curriculum should be adjusted to test demands. Are those two views compatible? Why or why not?

Resources for Curriculum Study

1. Visit the School Division of the Association of American Publishers at http://www.publishers.org/school/index.cfm. This site has useful information on text adoption, text and materials accuracy, and other issues.

2. For further study of the ideas, influential people, and projects in early curriculum development work, there are several good sources. Herbert Kliebard's *The Struggle for the American Curriculum, 1893–1958* (1986) is very reliable. *Curriculum Books: The First Hundred Years*, by William Schubert and others (Schubert, Schubert, Thomas, & Carroll, 2002), offers useful contextual discussions of the period from 1900 through the 1930s in several chapters, with a comprehensive listing of curriculum books published during those years.

3. In this text, the perspective on curriculum development is American. For a sampling of comparative perspectives, A. V. Kelly's *The Curriculum: Theory and Practice* (2004) is worth perusing for the United Kingdom. Interesting policy papers on Australian curriculum are accessible at http://www.acsa.edu.au, the Web site of the Australian Curriculum Studies Association.

References

Armstrong, D. G. (2003). *Curriculum today.* Upper Saddle River, NJ: Pearson Education / Merrill Prentice Hall.

Bobbitt, F. (1918). *The curriculum.* Boston: Houghton Mifflin. (Reprinted 1972, New York: Arno Press)

Bode, B. H. (1921). *Fundamentals of education.* New York: Macmillan.

Charters, W. W. (1923). *Curriculum construction.* New York: Macmillan.

Connelly, F. M., & Clandinin, D. J. (1988). *Teachers as curriculum planners: Narratives of experience.* New York: Teachers College Press.

Connelly, F. M., & Clandinin, D. J. (1990). Stories of experience and narrative inquiry. *Educational Researcher, 19*(5), 2–14.

Counts, G. S. (1926). *The senior high school curriculum.* Chicago: University of Chicago Press.

Dewey, J. (1902). *The child and the curriculum.* Chicago: University of Chicago Press.

Dewey, J. (1915). *The school and society.* Chicago: University of Chicago Press.

Educational Testing Service. (2004). *Unfinished business: More measured approaches in standards-based reform.* Retrieved January 2005 from www.ets.org

Goodlad, J. (1985). Curriculum as a field of study. In T. Husen & T. N. Postlethwaite (Eds.), *International encyclopedia of education* (pp. 1141–1143). Oxford, UK: Pergamon.

Hewitt, T. W. (2004). *Considering curriculum commonplaces.* Unpublished manuscript.

Kelly, A. V. (2004). *The curriculum: Theory and practice* (5th ed.). London: Sage.

Kliebard, H. M. (1986). *The struggle for the American curriculum, 1893–1958.* Boston: Routledge & Kegan Paul.

Phenix, P. H. (1964). *Realms of meaning.* New York: McGraw-Hill.

Reigeluth, C. (Ed.). (1999). *Instructional design theory and models: A new paradigm of instructional theory* (Vol. 2). Hillsdale, NJ: Lawrence Erlbaum.

Rugg, H. O. (Ed.). (1927a). *Curriculum making: Past and present* (Twenty-Sixth Yearbook of the National Society for the Study of Education, Part I). Bloomington, IL: Public School Publishing Company. (Reprinted 1969, New York: Arno Press)

Rugg, H. O. (Ed.). (1927b). *The foundation of curriculum making* (Twenty-Sixth Yearbook of the National Society for the Study of Education, Part II). Bloomington, IL: Public School Publishing Company. (Reprinted 1969, New York: Arno Press)

Schubert, W. H., Schubert, A. L. L., Thomas, T. P., & Carroll, W. M. (2002). *Curriculum books: The first hundred years* (2nd ed.). New York: Peter Lang.

Schwab, J. J. (1973). The practical 3: Translation into curriculum. *School Review, 81*(4), 501–522.

Schwab, J. J. (1983). The practical 4: Something for curriculum professors to do. *Curriculum Inquiry, 13*(3), 239–265.

Seel, N. M., & Dijkstra, S. (Eds.). (2004). *Curriculum, plans, and processes in* instructional design. Mahwah, NJ: Lawrence Erlbaum.

Walker, D. (1990). *Fundamentals of curriculum.* New York: Harcourt Brace Jovanovich.

Part II

Knowledge Bases That Serve Curriculum

Understanding something begins by engagement with the knowledge about it. Knowledge developed from the results of such scholarly inquiry is foundational in our lives. In Part I, two ideas central to building understandings were introduced. The first is that one way to come to know a thing is to determine how it is put together, its structure. Another way to understand something is to identify who does it and observe how they do it. The idea here is that there is a duality to work. It is both a process, a way of doing something, and an evolving product. An author, for example, creates a manuscript, which is the product; in doing so, he or she develops a process or set of actions in creating the manuscript. To understand authoring you have to know or study both the result and the process used to achieve the result. Both ideas help in understanding curriculum as knowledge and work, a practical profession that is an academic and practice-based pursuit, a dialectic, an interaction that informs curriculum knowledge and practice. In this Part II, you will be introduced to and study the extensive knowledge base that serves curriculum work and practice.

Chapter 5

KNOWLEDGE AND THEORIES ABOUT CURRICULUM

The textbook evaluations in the state department of education social studies curriculum review are complete. The state board of education has approved the textbook list and submitted it for school districts to use. Bay City School District and Shores Independent District 36 have decided to use different social studies texts for third grade. Selecting from the new approved list, Bay City decided on the text by Smith Publishing, whereas Shores ID 36 chose a social studies text issued by Jones Textbook Company. Two third-grade teachers, one in Bay City and the other in Shores, are teaching students about the importance of rivers in settling lands west of the Appalachian Mountains. Test questions used by the teachers are from the teachers' manual and keyed to specific pages in the textbook. Both teachers ask a similarly phrased question with the same possible responses. The question is, Which is the longest river in the United States west of the Appalachian Mountains? The choices for students are (a) the Ohio River, (b) the Mississippi River, (c) the Colorado River, and (d) the Missouri River. The knowledge about rivers the students learned is different in the two texts. The Jones text says it is the Missouri River, whereas the Smith text identifies the river as the Mississippi. Think of the possible implications. If a state standardized test asked a similar question with the Mississippi River as the response, all the students and teachers using the Jones text would give an incorrect answer; those students might also be in jeopardy of a failing grade because of one question based on knowledge assumed to be correct. All this could be repeated, but differently, if the situation were reversed.

What appears to be a simple issue of fact about the longest river in the United States west of the Appalachian Mountains depends on the validity of facts contained in a particular textbook resource. As you probably know, the answer is the Mississippi River. The upshot is that what is learned is wrong in one case and not the other. This creates dilemmas for students and teachers. Students are penalized because one text presents the wrong information. For the teachers, it is the subtle problem of having the knowledge expertise in geography to recognize a textbook error, a particular problem for elementary school teachers, who are more generalists than specialists in the discipline knowledge with which they work. What compounds the dilemma is the preemptive trust that schools and teachers must have in the accuracy of the textbook development and publishing process and thus in the authority of textbooks and other curriculum materials. That trust of teachers and students is framed in what they need to know and what knowledge will meet that need. Each needs a knowledge base to do his or her work.

THE CURRICULUM KNOWLEDGE BASE

All knowledge is fragile, and no person can know everything. What is known, the facts and certainties of knowledge, are organized into bodies of knowledge, like geography, that are constantly changing. Knowledge, what humans come to know, begins in vicariously created, scattered, discrete human consciousness. It is also social and culturally created because it is "human" knowledge. Psychologist Jerome Bruner points out in *Acts of Meaning* (1990) that individual human knowing of the world and self is culturally embedded. As a cumulative entity, knowledge is part of the cumulative overarching knowledge of all human social and cultural consciousness. Knowledge is held in common and shared, a synthesized knowledge that provides ways to understand and comprehend the world. Students in schools study knowledge that is packaged and ready to be learned. In colleges and universities, students invest extensive amounts of time in specialized chunks of it called majors or, more specifically, disciplines of knowledge. In studying a body of knowledge, they encounter the theories, philosophies, history, methods, perspectives, and inquiry traditions that form the core content of a discipline.

Like other disciplines, there is a core content knowledge, a foundational base of theories, philosophies, perspectives, and so forth, to study in learning about curriculum.

Knowledge can be generally categorized in different ways. As initially introduced to you in Chapter 3, dividing knowledge into the informal and the formal is one way. Informal knowledge is held personally, often without being verifiable or made credible in other ways. It is what you know and use to guide your thinking and behavior. It may not be proven or validated but it is useful because it works in satisfactory ways. Informal knowledge, personally held, is your own creation and not necessarily held to be the same by another person. Although two persons may share informal knowledge, each may know it differently. It can also be cooperatively known with others, such as the distinctive personal walk-about knowledge: ways to behave, rules, the ordinary social and culturally acquired things that guide our daily ways of living and participation in the public life. In schools, it is the classroom rules and the unspoken but assumed appropriate set of behaviors for walking about, going to the rest room and the library, and speaking to others. As a second, general kind of knowledge, formal knowledge is collectively organized and specialized, forming a sanctioned body of knowledge for anyone to acquire and use. Formal knowledge is proved, standardized, and useful because it is true and applicable under specifiable conditions. It has been proved or validated as formal knowledge through a consensual confirming process. That is why you could verify an answer from the knowledge base in geography. This formalizing is often referred to as *knowledge production and use* (Eraut, 1985) and represents a cycle of actions forming a process that certifies its use as suggested in the *knowledge cycle* (Rich, 1981; Short, 1973) in Figure 5.1 and exemplified in the companion Figure 5.2. It can be the formal applied knowledge of the electrician, the plumber, and the farmer, or the commercial knowledge of the shop owner and real estate agent, validated in applied activities. It can be technical knowledge used by the engineer, the draftsman, or the architect. It is also the academic and professional knowledge of the professor, researcher, and other scholars, a created body of facts, concepts, ideas, procedures, and multiform data held together by a system or systems of thought. In each case, the knowledge creation occurs in a culture of disciplined work. This is particularly important for the formal knowledge that underlies the work of teachers, medical personnel, lawyers, and others in the pursuit of science. Curriculum also exists as a body of formal disciplined knowledge in the field of education.

Fields and Disciplines of Knowledge

All that is or can be known, the totality of formal knowledge, has been organized so it is accessible and can be used in an economical way. You are familiar with formal knowledge in large chunks, the arts, sciences, and humanities. Organized fields of knowledge also relate to particular categories of work (e.g., the medical field, the

Figure 5.1   A Knowledge Cycle

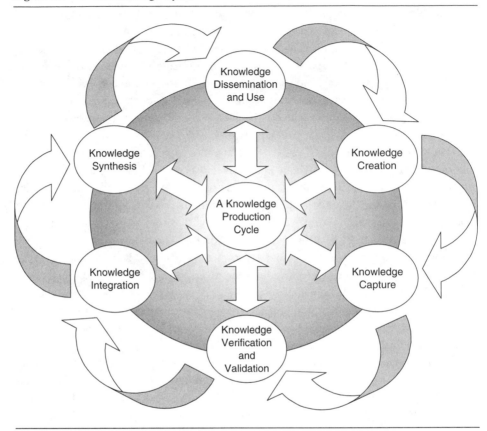

engineering field, and the education field). Each field has a cohort of workers performing different functions but gathered under the field's banner. In each field, the workers rely on smaller, more specialized areas of knowledge with familiar names such as physics, biology, history, and philosophy. These smaller collections of knowledge are referred to as academic disciplines, disciplines of knowledge, or just disciplines. Each discipline serves as both a repository of special knowledge and as a center for producing the specialized knowledge.

All disciplines evolve and have a history. The origins of biology, chemistry, and sociology can be traced to philosophy. Plate tectonics, as illustrated in Figure 5.2, is a new discipline created in the last 50 years as the study of the earth's surface plates and their movements that helps to understanding earthquakes and volcanic activities, the manifestations of the living earth. The new also includes cybernetics and the information

Figure 5.2   An Example of a Knowledge Cycle

Plate Tectonics

Creation: Nineteenth-century scientist puts forth an idea of movements of the earth as surface crusts engaging one another.

Capture: He writes a paper expressing the idea as a theory while pointing to some evidence suggesting its possibilities, but the paper results in no particular notice of the theory by others.

Verification: Scientists in geology and geography note growing evidence of continental rifts, volcanic activity, and seismic compatibility in dispersed areas of the earth.

Validation: American and international research projects in the 1950s to 1960s investigate the theory, and new data-gathering techniques allow for coring the ocean floor to test the idea of moving plates.

Integration: Based on research results confirming the basic elements of the theory, other scientists test findings to corroborate evidence and probe new applications. In the scientific communities, others develop next-level ideas and seek confirmation in the developing database.

Synthesis: Dissemination broadens understanding in other disciplines through articles in scholarly journals and among new researchers in graduate education. College science courses begin to include plate tectonics, particularly in geology and geography.

Dissemination and Use: Dissemination of plate tectonics knowledge includes school and college textbooks beginning in third grade, and it is the subject of TV programs on Nova and TLC (The Learning Channel).

sciences that Herbert Simon wrote about in *The Sciences of the Artificial* (1981). Some disciplines, phrenology for example, disappear to become historic footnotes. Some are the child of other disciplines; social psychology, for example, is formed from psychology and sociology. Political science, anthropology, sociology, geography, and economics trace from history and philosophy and now form a family of social sciences. The traditional wellspring of discipline and knowledge change has been the province of scholars, those designated to produce, organize, and disseminate formal knowledge. In the early civilizations of the Orient, the Middle East, and later, Greece and the Roman Empire, scholars served the interest of the state or rulers. During the European Medieval Age, knowledge functions were entrusted to monks or other church officers primarily because they could read Latin, the language of the privileged and scholars (Cahill, 1995). The rise of colleges and universities in Europe began the academic traditions of today in which knowledge creation and its keeping became the secular province of public institutions and their workers. There were several important effects of secularization. Materials began to be produced in the common language of the people rather than the Latin of the elite. There was a gradual inclusion of students and scholars from the general public and a lessening of control of knowledge by the church and royal court.

Universities such as Oxford and Cambridge in England were created by royal decree, and with the expansion of universities in Europe a cloak of legitimacy began to spread over pursuit of knowledge and especially new disciplines. Status for a new discipline usually was ensured when it was designated as an academic department or provided with a dedicated chair in a college or university, a tradition that continues in various forms to the present. Another indicator of a discipline's arrival is the initiation of scholarly publications, especially academic journals and scholarly books, in the new area of knowledge. Finally, there is the conferring of national stature under an umbrella organization to promote the discipline. The American Sociological Association and American Economic Association are examples. Curriculum also has these characteristics. There are dedicated chairs and professorships, departments carry curriculum in their titles, special journals and books are available, and there are several national curriculum organizations.

Communities of Discourse

A discipline is, in a sense, its own world, a thing to be understood in and of itself. Each is a community of discourse, a dialogue among practitioners about the discipline and knowledge (Burbules, 1993). Disciplinary discussions occur in a particular intellectual culture necessary for framing thought and work in a particular discipline or knowledge field. This knowledge work consists of a content core and one that is procedural. The content core is the body of fact, literature, and data, loosely referred to as the discipline's knowledge base. The procedural core exists as a mindset, a defined, embedded way of thinking *in* and *with* content knowledge. This is comparable to the historian thinking in historical terms with a historical perspective, a chemist thinking and working in chemistry, or a teacher working with curriculum. In every discipline, the process is essential for screening knowledge creation—created knowledge becomes "disciplined" by passing through that process. In this way, discipline practitioners operate under a shared culture of thought, what Kuhn (1970) has called a *paradigm*, a formalized perspective that is shared and guides work. The paradigm provides the parameters for personal and professional practitioner perspectives in the discipline (Margolis, 1994). Perspectives allow access to the reasoning processes that act as decoders, allowing you to see into the knowledge and make sense of it. For example, space exploration created a paradigmatic shift in terms of how humans view themselves and the earth. Entering space, the stepping outside the earth and looking back on it, has changed or added a perspective to human thinking based on new knowledge, not speculation, about earth and earth's place in space as a dynamic planet that is subject to forces yet to be found and understood. In the same way that Ptolemy's earth-centered paradigm gave way to the Copernican sun-centered paradigm and gradually changed thinking about the universe, paradigm shifts require important changes in prevailing perspectives or the invention of new ones. There may be one or several perspectives under a paradigm. In such cases, the perspectives may or may not complement each other, but in the work of the discipline, they form a vital tension that energizes thinking. In curriculum, there might be the perspective of the academic researcher, the teacher in the classroom, or the specialist at the district office. What connects each worker is a reliance on a common body of knowledge about curriculum that can be used in different contexts.

Discipline Dialectics

Disciplined knowledge is created knowledge resulting from scholarly interplay in the actions of knowledge creation. This process occurs under prescribed procedures by persons trained in those practices and accountable for the veracity of the knowledge that is produced. Mathematics, political science, and history—each exemplifies a body of formal disciplined knowledge. Each knowledge discipline stands as a collection of validated *information* (data in multiple forms), *processes* (research methods or modes of inquiry), *logics* (ways of thinking), and *networks* (reticules of associated interactions or linkages) particular to the area of study. Workers hold in common and adhere to practices that guide their work as scholars, researchers, and practitioners. Using existing knowledge, discipline-related problems are studied to create new knowledge. It is dialogue as dialogic inquiry between the discipline as an entity of inquiry and knowledge production and the discipline as a place of applied practice and knowledge production. It forms a dialectic embracing knowledge production, organization, and use, as well as work by research specialists and teachers (Wells, 1999). The work of producing and using knowledge by all kinds of practitioners powers the dialectic relationship. Initiates to a field or discipline study in a preparatory program, a process of being schooled in a common perspective to understand what the discipline is about (Schulman, 1998). Other perspectives can be developed as practitioners enter into and perform different aspects of curriculum work in locations and settings as diverse as the teacher in a classroom and the specialist in the department of education at the state capital. This tri-perspective of discipline, setting, and type of work creates a healthy dialectical tension within the discipline among different workers at different tasks, each in their own way contributing to the work of the discipline, a series of checks and balances, a collective sense making as knowledge is created and rendered useful (Davenport & Prusak, 1998). This is a process of knowledge production and use mentioned earlier that is dialectical in nature and represents the interaction of practice between the discipline and curriculum work. To illustrate this, consider the hypothetical case of a high school chemistry curriculum and two practitioners, one a university-based researcher and the other a high school teacher, both interested in how the atomic tables in chemistry can be organized in curriculum to facilitate learning. The teacher has been using a memorization approach while searching out other possibilities. The scholar's research about chemistry curriculum *x* and *y* appears in a refereed journal article. The teacher reads the article and develops materials for the two approaches and implements them in the chemistry classes. Based on evaluations, the teacher determines both are valuable for certain students whereas others still prefer materials keyed to memorization. There are now three optional ways to prepare the tables in the chemistry curriculum. Correspondence with the researcher could further inform the research venture and perhaps lead to extending the original research, replicating the teacher's experience in other settings, or further curriculum development for more options and another cycle of research as both the researcher and teacher continue exploring curricular possibilities. In the example is the interplay of the researcher as practitioner and the teacher as practitioner, a confluence of research and practice knowledge in the creation and use of new knowledge.

Discipline Structure

Because all formal knowledge is an evolving human creation, it can be known by how the creators of that knowledge initially organized it and how it has been ordered as changes occurred. Organization and ordering refer to the pattern or arrangement that gives the knowledge structure. To know a discipline of knowledge is to recognize and understand the structure (Schwab, 1962). A *discipline structure* allows entry into its knowledge and practice by illuminating what is to be learned—the discipline's content, its body of data, the ways of thinking in and with the content, and the perspectives used in the discipline's structural characteristics or idea architecture. A discipline's utility lies in its capacity to be learned, be shared, and produce knowledge. Exploring a discipline is a journey through layers of meaning and knowledge, to be immersed in contexts, processes, and content consistent with the depth of study undertaken in order to acquire the discipline and use it. Both Joseph Schwab (1962) and Jerome Bruner (1960) have suggested this as a way to understand and come to know a disciplined body of knowledge. Among scholars in any knowledge community, the conversation is often structural or paradigmatic, like the one generated in the sciences by Thomas Kuhn in *The Structure of Scientific Revolutions* (1970). In the earlier discussion of the paradigm, it was simply referenced as the umbrella way of thinking, the overarching idea structure or idea set that guides scholarly work. Framed in this way, a discipline, a body of specific knowledge, has a number of elements, perspectives, logics, inquiry, language, literature, and special tools. All disciplines will have these elements, but they will be constituted in different ways, as suggested in Figure 5.3.

Perspectives are specialized views held in common by workers in a discipline. Political scientists study politics and government from at least two perspectives: one is institutional and the other behavioral. The office of United States president is an

Figure 5.3   Knowledge Elements in a Discipline

Inquiry is a process that will differ across disciplines in a variety of qualitative, quantitative, historical, artistic, and literary forms.

Perspectives are schools of thought, sets of ways of looking at the discipline, usually with a dominant one and often several others vying for a central position and creating a vital tension important in a discipline.

Logics are the particular ways of thinking and doing the work of the discipline and are particular to it, as in how a mathematician or a historian go about thinking and doing things.

Language refers to the special terms, concepts, and expressions in the discourse of the discipline that differentiate it from other areas of knowledge.

Literature loosely refers to the body of publications or published works that is considered essential in the discipline; these can be books, formulas, and theories, numerical or textual in many forms.

Tools are those special materials, logics, instrumentations, and the like particular to use in a discipline and unlikely to be used in other disciplines.

institution with specified characteristics and powers. The office is also what the person as president does, how he or she behaves in office. In curriculum work, there is the perspective of the academic scholar, another of the school practitioner, and another of the student. *Logics* are ways of thinking in and with the discipline. The geographer thinks about the earth, humans, place, location, and the interactions of those elements. In curriculum, both the academic and school practitioner work with scope and sequence. The academic works with them as abstract ideas, whereas schoolteachers apply them in their curriculum work. *Inquiry* refers to the techniques and investigative methods commonly used in a discipline to solve problems and generate knowledge. Case studies, narratives, quasi-experimental, and experimental are familiar types of methods. Curriculum tends toward the use of interpretivist or qualitative traditions (case studies, narrative, evaluation, etc.) of the social sciences rather than positivist traditions (experimental, etc.) of the biological or physical sciences. *Language* refers to the special terms and concepts workers use in their daily discourse. Every discipline and field has a special language. Curricularists talk of scope, sequence, and other curriculum terms. Anthropologists use terms such as culture, enculturation, and ethnography. *Literature* is, as you might expect, a reference to all the publications in whatever form that constitute a specific body of knowledge. The literature is a record of how the knowledge evolved as a specialty and as work. Special *tools* emerge in doing the discipline's work. These are usually particular to the discipline or field and have no counterpart in other knowledge areas. For example, historians developed cliometrics, a statistical method for working with historical data. In curriculum work, there are the special tools like curriculum theory models and critiques.

PERSPECTIVE INTO PRACTICE:
Appling Discipline Knowledge in the Development of a Lesson in Geography

Discipline and Knowledge	Elementary Classroom	Secondary Classroom
Perspective: Importance of waterways in the United States and the world—a geography perspective.	Use maps to show the waterways and other topographic features in the United States. Use topographic, product, and political map examples to provide different data and perspectives of map use.	Identify main U.S. river systems by regions or geographic area and differences between a river as a specific entity and a river system as a complex waterway. Emphasize primary river systems such as Mississippi, Colorado, Ohio, and Missouri systems.
Logics: How a geographer thinks, the embedded perspectives of thinking in geography.	Introduce geographic thinking of earth-human and earth-space relationships, and logics of place and location applied to school and community. Use pictures and maps to represent those ways of thinking.	Explain comparative thinking in geography as physical geography, human geography, and spatial geography. Use maps, separating each to compare and contrast the different kinds of information each can give.
Language: Special concepts, ideas, and words particular to use in geography.	Explain kinds of maps (e.g., political, social, topographical) with examples and common names for waterways and bodies of water: gulf, ocean, bay, river, bayou, creek, stream, and so forth.	Introduce special geographic terms such as map projections, with examples; the concept of distortion in representing earth on flat surface of a map; and special words for bodies of water, and how they are different (ocean, gulf, sea, lake, strait, sound, etc.).
Literature: Appropriate examples of literature that are important in geography.	Direct students to National Geographic magazine, materials online, National Council on Geographic Education Web site, NASA, special atlases, and map collections.	Access online resources: NOAA, Weather Channel or equivalent, University of Michigan Weather site. Books of maps, or atlas, specific geography resources, and the National Geographic Society.
Inquiry: What are the problems to be investigated, the methods of inquiry to use.	Discuss problems a geographer studies in simple terms: human use of earth and how it changes the earth, dams on rivers, locks, and the introduction of species such as the lamprey eel in the Great Lakes and the effect on native species.	Give examples of human geography—land use and how it changes the topography—such as shopping malls in wetlands, docks, locks, and other intrusions on waterways or bodies of water. Discuss physical geography as the study of relationship of climate and water resources: weather and topography effects of hurricanes and tornados.

Tools: The special theories, critiques, processes, and materials used in geography.	Discuss maps as special geography tools, computer modeling and graphics, satellite resources, and other monitoring devices used by geographers. Emphasize mixed-inquiry methods using quantitative data gathering as well as observational data (e.g., pictures, field trips, etc.).	Use examples of various tools a geographer uses: cartography or mapmaking, satellite imaging, and sensors of the earth's surface. La Niña and the El Niño effects can be used as an example to study human and physical geography changes to the earth.

DISCIPLINE PERSPECTIVES

Your perspective, what you bring to a task, is important because how something is viewed, the particular take on it, is often a coalescing of different ways of seeing things. Analysis of perspectives involves development of what was called, in Chapter 1, the critical perspective. What is meant is that whereas there is a variety of kinds of perspectives, their confluence forms a metaperspective, a critical perspective in a discipline. Among the important aspects of a critical perspective are those that are personal, professional, and practical or practice-based and ones such as the scholarly and disciplinary that arise in the pursuit and acquiring of knowledge. To know your perspectives, that conversational sense of where you are coming from, is to understand and be able to declare the scholarly rationality behind your behavior. Concerns about perspective, the reasons and motivation, the ways things are perceived, are common in everyday life. They are of great importance in professional and scholarly work, especially in the pursuit of knowledge and truth.

Discipline and Scholarly Perspectives

Earlier in this chapter, two concepts, discipline and structure, were introduced in suggesting a particular perspective for exploring curriculum, a *discipline perspective.* The concept of structure illuminates the working of curriculum as a discipline and facilitates an understanding of its particulars. A *scholarly perspective* is a set of conditions about how to view something chosen for study. It is constructed through formal thought, a mental synthesis based on academic study, acquired knowledge, and reflective experience. A scholarly perspective is a scholar's rationale, knowingly constructed, not vicariously acquired. The process of building and understanding a perspective is important in disciplinary work because each perspective frames what each scholar will see, consider, and act on in the discipline. The scholar in curriculum uses that perspective to frame his or her work. The scholarly perspective represents a view of curriculum based on certain studied considerations about the technical, methodological, and moral-philosophical aspects of the discipline and what constitutes scholarship in a disciplined way. A scholarly perspective addresses questions about what constitutes knowledge, what does it mean to know, what is curriculum, and what purposes should it serve. In any discipline, the credibility of what results from the study of such questions is linked to the workers' acquired understanding about scholarship.

Education Perspectives

In the field of education, various philosophies of education cast a shadow over curricular perspectives. A philosophy of education is broader and affects education in all its particulars: curriculum, learning, instruction, evaluation, and research. A philosophy is comprehensive and forms a set of ideas that guide thought. What is meant by the philosophical refers to fundamental questions about what knowledge is and what it means to know; the nature of being human; and values, ethics, and moral behavior. Consider, for instance, the use of democratic or authoritarian management in a classroom. Is the purpose to achieve participation and thoughtful deliberation or to enforce and control? What would a matching democratic or authoritarian curriculum be like? Philosophies of education can help clarify responses to such issues. These philosophical positions are important considerations related to three important aspects of curriculum: (a) what should be taught, (b) to whom it should be taught, and (c) when and how it should be taught. Developing responses for those issues requires that you study in several knowledge bases that serve curriculum. At this point, it is only necessary to alert you to that need. Further study in the particular knowledge bases waits in Chapter 6, in the discussion of historical knowledge about curriculum in Chapter 7, and in the discussion of social, cultural, and intellectual foundations in Chapter 8. It is important now to consider some general ideas about orientations, theories, and inquiry that preface study in those knowledge bases for curriculum.

CURRICULUM ORIENTATIONS AND INTERESTS

Fields of knowledge have different traditions in describing the various ways people view the field. Sometimes it is straightforward, sometimes it is confusing. Often you encounter the reference to a particular "school" of something, usually designating a particular group or set of ideas. There was the famous Bauhaus school of the 1920s in building and architecture and the interdisciplinary Frankfurt School of the 1930s with its influential critical theory postmodern academic critique. In psychology, there are behavioral, cognitive, and humanistic schools, among others. Similar names for schools of thought can be found in the education field and in the realm of inquiry (note

Figure 5.4 Examples of Curriculum Orientations and Interests

Curriculum as a Historic Orientation	*Curriculum as Kinds of Knowledge Building*	*Curriculum as Knowledge and Meaning*

Humanistic
Postmodernist (Social)
Cognitive
Developmental
Technical
Academic
	Formal and Informal
	Procedural
	Impressionistic
	Personal & Self-
	   Regulatory
	Tacit
	Representational
	Artifact and Object
	Differentiated Perspective
		Symbolics (mathematics,
		   language)
		Empirics (sciences)
		Esthetics (arts)
		Synnoetics (personal)
		Ethics (moral)
		Synoptics (history, religions,
		   philosophy)

(Based on Figure 2.2)	(Based on Bereiter & Scardamalia, 1998)	(Based on Phenix, 1964)

them in Figure 5.4). Making the translation across disciplines is, however, perplexing. Does a developmentalist or humanist mean the same thing in curriculum, instruction, or learning? And, is it possible to be a developmentalist or behaviorist in assessment and evaluation in education? How does the school of thought designation play out in curriculum? Earlier in Chapter 2 (see Figure. 2.2), in framing the world of curriculum, these orientations were called frames of reference as used by particular curriculum scholars. They are recast in Figure 5.4 as a summary of orientations and interests that do not represent a specific philosophy but are relational to philosophy. They are particularly curricular as they are ways of considering curriculum itself. In the discussions about curriculum in Chapters 1 and 2 (see Figures 1.3 and 2.2), they were called frames of reference, and sometimes they are called philosophies or philosophical positions. Does the meaning of *humanist,* identified in Figure 5.4 as a historic orientation, really change if different curriculum scholars use different terms, *humanistic* and *humanist,* respectively? Not only the labels but also the groupings are often different. For example, Eisner and Vallance, writing in 1974, called their orderings "orientations." McNeil (1977) referred to "prevailing conceptions" and a somewhat different list of those conceptions. Kliebard (1986) called his categories " interest groups," and again there is variation in those selected. Others have differed from traditional interpretive categorizations as school of thought, philosophies, or orientations. Bereiter and Scardamalia (1998) suggest a different frame of reference, reinterpreted in the figure as "kinds of knowledge building," applied as in flowing from Gilbert Ryle's (1949) distinction between knowing "how" to do something, and knowing "that" or about something. By articulating the types of experiences, activities, and content that would develop at each level, you could plan, design, and develop a curriculum. That is much more direct than working through a particular school of thought to a curricular conclusion. The third example is an interesting one based on a "knowledge-as-meaning" orientation developed by Phillip Phenix (1964), which you will consider in Chapter 6. There are many other orientations and interests (see, for example, Bronfenbrenner, 1976; Eisner & Vallance, 1974; Smith, Stanley, & Shores, 1957) that have been put forward that could be explored as well. However, the point in citing these examples is fourfold: (a) to make you aware of the rich and varied knowledge available; (b) to suggest that the curriculum thinking you do will necessitate understanding the curriculum-philosophy connection (to come in chapter 8); (c) to think of orientations and interests rather than the philosophical as particular to thinking and working in curriculum; and (d) to introduce you to the idea that orientations and interests, both general and particular, lead to more complex considerations about what "knowledge" is important, the "social purposes" to be served, and the place of the "learner" in the scheme of things. At some point in developing a curriculum perspective, you will find one or more of these concerns entering into your thinking. Identifying and illustrating linkages between the three considerations and the orientations and interests can expand your understanding of their place in curriculum knowledge. Because that would go beyond the scope of this chapter, a more limited discussion follows using the historic orientations to curriculum.

Humanism

Easily the oldest and most classic orientation to curriculum is the humanistic. Often referred to as rational humanism, the emphasis is on the capabilities of the student to develop thinking (in the critical sense of it) through engaging in the wealth of literature (preferably Western thought) and emphasizing the original classics of antiquity, Plato, Shakespeare, and so forth. Assorted organizations like the Council on Basic Education and the National Endowment for the Humanities advocate for equal inclusion in the curriculum for literature and the arts. Humanism is the home of the educated person who is deeply and broadly schooled in the classics. Its goal is the preparation of people who will be rational citizens in a society ruled by reason. The curriculum is prescriptive; it already exists in the classics or those works that will be so designated by the leaders of the society. John Dewey's writings (1964) represent a quintessential American humanism, particularly about education as broadly conceived and the role of schools and schooling for the individual and learning. One of the more interesting writers on contemporary humanism in life and for the individual is Ken Plummer (2001), who has a wide-ranging concern on the humanistic turn in life.

Cognitive

The brain has always been referred to as the seat of human reason, the place of thought, or where thinking occurs (Fauconnier & Turner, 2002). Psychology has traditionally inferred mental operations by external observation; now the neurosciences of the brain study those as specific internal functions (Churchland, 2002). Like the variety of terms for humanism, there are a number of terms, such as cognition, cognitive pluralism, and cognitive science, that refer to the business of studying how human brains function and the relationship to thinking and the stuff of thinking, the knowledge that is thought about. You are probably familiar with Howard Gardner's *Frames of Mind* (1983) and his multiple intelligences theory, and perhaps Robert Sternberg's (1988) exploration of the triarchic mind. The message for curriculum workers is to put together that school curriculum that emphasizes all the intelligences as particular so that, as they are arranged in the individual, the curriculum can encourage development. The important question is what a curriculum would be like that has as its basis various kinds of symbol systems, and not just those you think of as mathematical or languages. In the relationship of the curricular trinity of purposes, the emphasis is on the human learner through schooling in various symbols that will yield a socially fit citizen.

Developmental

The emphasis among developmentalists is to essentially fit the curriculum to the students' needs and interests as they mature. The curriculum would emphasize personal development; the students' interests and development would cue the kinds of knowledge a curriculum might offer. This is a broad orientation that could include the contemporary interest in constructivism (see Phillips, 2002, for a discussion of constructivism) and older approaches such as self-actualization, which was addressed in the 1962 Association for Supervision and Curriculum Development (ASCD) yearbook, *Perceiving, Behaving, Becoming* (Combs, 1962). You can easily perceive that it would be very difficult to individualize the multiple kinds of curriculum needed, something like a maturational smorgasbord for learners. Although this orientation is on most lists, it is the least successful in influencing curriculum thinking in general.

Postmodernist

There are several dangers in using this term as an orientation to matters that are also of a sociocultural nature. First is the unintended possibility that it might be construed as political. Second, if you sample across a variety of writings and scholarly claims to postmodernism, it is difficult, as Carl Bereiter (2002) and others (Breisach, 2003; Constas, 1998; Detmer, 2003) point out, to get any sense of a commonly held meaning. Finally, although there is a certain emphasis on personal subjectivity and introspection, the term also carries some social and cultural implications that are significant. Topics such as gender issues, queer theory, critiques of institutional power, multiculturalism, and ethnic and cultural studies often claim an alignment with critical theory or postmodernist thinking. For curriculum workers, particularly developers and planners, there is the postmodernist obligation to be introspective and reveal their particular subjectivities. Beyond that, there is no clear agenda for curriculum except to critique texts and curriculum materials in general to eliminate bias such as sexist language, male gender dominance, and stereotypes that detract from individual and group dignity or depose their natural power. Postmodernism is used in a collective sense to refer to the reconceptualists like William Pinar (1975) and critical theorists like Michael Apple (1979) and Paulo Freire (1970).

Technological

At the turn of the 20th century, the early 1900s, Frederick Taylor and others (see Spring, 1986) birthed what has become known as the *social efficiency movement,* an emphasis on schooling and learning for economic benefits to the individual and society through specialization and building expertise. At the core was a reliance on technology in the mechanical form, a typewriter for example, that later included other developments such as computers. The curriculum was to be determined based on the needs of society, or as decided by those who presumed to speak for it. Schooling would prepare the individual for a particular life work or calling. Permutations off this basic idea would lead to the behavioral objectives movement, computer-assisted instruction, and the contemporary assessment-evaluation modes that emphasize measurement and accountability through testing technology, input-output analysis, and systems thinking. The clear implication is that technology eliminates or voids human subjectivity and ensures the objectivity of technologically driven work, an assumption, or claim, that is open to question. The curriculum to be employed would of course change with the perceived needs of the society and the workforce. James B. Conant (1967) perhaps had this orientation in mind when he advocated the comprehensive high school idea that is still with us today.

Academic

The general school curriculum you experienced included study in the sciences, social studies, and humanities. Those experiences, along with the famous three R's of the elementary school, constitute the knowledge in a traditional American school curriculum. The key point is that it is the curriculum essentially dictated by the academy, the colleges and universities. This academic orientation to curriculum could also be called academic rationalism or the academic knowledge curriculum; through knowledge, you come to think and know. The appeal of knowledge is as old as the classics. There are differences in the use of applied knowledge to organize the curriculum, as Bereiter (2002) suggests, and the interesting and unusual re-organization of basic knowledge that Phillip Phenix (1964) has done. When necessary, the academic knowledge orientation flexes to accommodate fads, trends, or the technology—postmodernist, developmental, or cognitive interests that come forward from time to time.

LEARNING THEORY AND CURRICULUM

Learning theories are about how humans learn. They are usually derived from theories in psychology and are important in a general way because any curriculum thinking or development has to take into consideration students and their learning processes. The theories discussed here are more in the mainstream of curriculum thinking and work. Theories are not curriculum orientations but could be addressed in a particular orientation. It is also possible that a particular learning theory might be named or labeled the same as a curriculum orientation, but that is not ensured. The important thing is to keep learning theories and curriculum orientations separate because they serve different purposes. Curriculum orientations are triangulations of knowledge, social, and learner purposes. Learning theory is first about learning and second about other things such as curriculum. You can consult any learning theory textbook for more detailed discussions or to explore other theories. In doing so, you will find other authors have different ways of organizing those theories depending on their purpose. The purpose here is to group learning theories that have some degree of importance for the curriculum worker.

Behaviorism

The emphasis in behaviorism is to find or create observable indicators that learning is taking place. Behaviorism accepts that the mental processes that cognitivists or neuroscientists study do exist but are unobservable. This is learning theory based on the conditioned response work of J. B. Watson (Todd, 1994) and, later, the operant conditioning made famous by B. F. Skinner (1961). The application in schooling is the use of direct instruction whereby the teacher provides knowledge to the students, usually directly or through rewards. The use of exams as measures of observable behavior of learning, computer-assisted instruction, and Robert Gagne's conditions of learning (1965), which translates into instructional design, are examples of behaviorism's influence in schooling, particularly in organizing instruction and assessment-evaluation. Its curricular importance lies in the emphasis on incremental content organization that is important in self-paced instruction and programmed learning.

Cognitivism

Cognitivism refers to a group of learning theories associated with understanding the brain as mind, a place where thinking occurs, and as a body organ. Probably the most familiar of the cognitive learning theories is constructivism (Phillips, 2002). Related to cognitive psychology and often referred to as either cognitive or social constructivism, this theory focuses on the learners' ability to mentally construct meaning in and of their own environment and to create their own learning processes. The instructional emphasis is discovery and problem solving oriented. The implications for curriculum are to anticipate and provision the learners' environment with whatever curriculum materials are needed and prepare the content to maximize the opportunity for creating mental learning processes as the students construct their knowledge. The curriculum should not be developed to guide but to facilitate mental construction. John Dewey and Jean Piaget are two of the more famous persons associated with constructivism. The multiple intelligences theory of Howard Gardner (1983) and Robert Sternberg's theory of the triarchic mind (1988) are also included under cognitivism.

Humanism

Theories that imply that human phenomena under study have a social and cultural origin or have causes that can be explained in social and cultural terms are often referred to as humanistic theories. Humanistic learning theories emphasize the individual and his or her development through reason and encounters with the knowledge of human culture. This is the learning theory of the self-actualization advocates, with holistic approaches sometimes incorporating religion and mysticism. In the humanist group, you will find reference to Sigmund Freud (see May, 1953), Abraham Maslow (1973), and Carl Rogers (1961), among others, who focused on the individual learner. Lev Vygotsky (1978) and Albert Bandura (1986) emphasized the social interaction aspects of learning, the social and cultural context in which the learner exists and in which and through which the learner moves. The implications for schooling are obvious, as the school and classroom are centers of social interactions. The subtle relationships to curriculum are several. One is the sociocultural background with which a learner comes to the curriculum that is possibly culturally and socially different than that of the classroom, school, other peers, and perhaps the teacher. Another has to do with that background and how the learner actually learns, what are his or her processes and do they parallel the learning pattern that the curriculum anticipates. Think also of what a learner might need that is not taught or the rules that are part of the hidden curriculum, and you can understand the humanistic awareness that pervades the perspective of this group of theories.

Technology

In his famous book *The Gutenberg Galaxy* (1962) and later in *Understanding Media* (1964), Marshall McLuhan provocatively laid out the importance of type and other media and the way they influence human learning. Whether to call this technological learning theory or a technological theory about learning is perhaps a significant issue. However, the purpose here is straightforward—how does technology affect curriculum thinking and work? It is an emerging arena of theory building where new ones are born, such as engagement theory (Kearsley & Shneiderman, 1999); theory about computer-supported collaborative learning and work; theory about human learning technology that envisions the Internet, cell phones, the iPod, and other technology extending human sensory capability and ways of thinking. This is perhaps an unparalleled freedom to learn on one's own or interact selectively with others over great distances, to access a wealth of knowledge via Internet sources and in networking contacts with others. It makes the advent of the so-called Information Age seem plausible (Dede, 2000). Learning-on-the-go, distance learning, and schooling literally without classrooms is here. It is not a supplanting of the school but perhaps an alteration of the teacher-dominated delivery system to a learner-controlled accessible curriculum. The potential importance of curriculum is magnified if you consider that the new means of accessing a central curriculum make it portable and accountable in new ways. The content probably won't change, but the medium that conveys and the setting in which it is engaged will (Jackson, Poole, & Kuhn, 2002). If curriculum workers have to change from curriculum in books for classroom students to a central curriculum source accessed by technology, it will mean a reorientation in thinking and imagining what schooling will be like and the purposes curriculum should serve.

INQUIRY TRADITIONS AND CURRICULUM

Disciplines are constantly producing new knowledge using what are generally known as research methods. Using those investigative procedures, scholars and researchers explore questions, issues, and problems particular to the discipline. Unfortunately, the world of research is complex, and it is not easy to make a simple declaration about what constitutes research in all disciplines and fields of knowledge. Sometimes this has to do with the nature of what is being studied; more often it has to do with whether the particular inquiry is scientific or not. What that implies is the researchers' perspective about the inquiry traditions under which they are doing their research. Earlier, the idea of an overriding culture of inquiry thought, a paradigm, was introduced. The paradigms that govern the two traditions of inquiry are the positivist and the interpretivist.

Positivist, Interpretive, and Eclectic Traditions

The word *tradition* is used to imply the same thing as a *paradigm,* discussed early in this chapter. Particular research methods are also associated with a particular tradition. The main inquiry traditions are positivist and interpretive, or interpretivist. Some scholars (Margolis, 1994) suggest that there is a third, interdisciplinary, or eclectic, tradition to accommodate both new research methods and the established ones that are sometimes used outside the two main traditions, including what Urie Bronfenbrenner (1976), Pence (1988), and others call ecological research methods. The positivist tradition characterizes the world as made up of what is empirical, those things that can be verified by observation and measurement. That tradition is associated with disciplines like biology, physics, and chemistry, and the methods are quantitative in nature. The interpretivist tradition is newer, and it portrays the world as complex, in flux realities, constructed by people in settings that are socially and culturally derived and with methods that are qualitative. That tradition is associated with disciplines such as anthropology and sociology. Among the research methods, there are some that cross over or find use in the other traditions, some historical methods, for example. That crossover characteristic gives some credence to the claim for an eclectic tradition. Across all three traditions are found different types of research methods, theory building, and other scholarly activities as part of disciplined inquiry.

You have most likely heard of or been introduced to research names such as historical, qualitative, quantitative, experimental, quasi-experimental, and philosophical, to suggest the most familiar. In the education field, researchers employ methods from both positivist and interpretive traditions and also evaluation. The relationship of evaluation to methodology or to a tradition placement of evaluation is problematic. Evaluation has no particular historic reference to any tradition but plays a prominent role as a method in studying educational programs. The matter of sorting out methods is often an esoteric discussion and important to students of research. What is important here is an introductory familiarity with inquiry and methods in general. That is the reason for the framework of methods and traditions presented in Figure 5.5. Educational inquiry might involve any of these methods, depending on the questions being asked, the task assigned, and what kind of curriculum work is being studied.

For example, in the positivist tradition, quantitative, quasi-experimental, and experimental methods are usually included. The historical, philosophical, and qualitative are in the interpretivist tradition. A simple distinction is that positivist methods usually incorporate statistical procedures and the research findings are in numerical form, whereas interpretivist methods use language and the research findings are descriptive, using words. The eclectic tradition would include both. While this is perhaps an oversimplification of a very complex matter, the intent is to offer a reasonable means of organizing and understanding an often confusing array of terms and categories that demarcates types of research within inquiry traditions. Second, at this level of understanding, you are not concerned with choosing among specific methods for a particular research venture; rather, you are concerned with establishing a basic awareness of the various methods within a tradition, as that might be generally useful in understanding the investigative approach taken in any research studies you are assigned or might

Figure 5.5   Inquiry Traditions and Examples

Tradition	Method Examples	General Features
Positivistic Inquiry: The Quantitative Tradition	Methods are often associated with the scientific and include the experimental, quasi-experimental, comparative, and qualitative descriptive	• Search for objective reality independent of human subjective contamination. • Data gathering is numerical rather than descriptive, and any interpretation is in objective terms. • Positivistic-empirical emphasis on methodological rigor.
Interpretivist Inquiry: The Qualitative Tradition	Methods that seek to reveal meaning in a situation, context, or setting include case studies, narratives, grounded theory, and the ethnographic	• Acknowledges the role of human subjectivity in inquiry. • Data are in words or other descriptive symbolic representations. • Naturalistic-experiential emphasis on interpretive rigor or construction of reality.
Eclectic Inquiry: The Mixed Tradition	Methods that are selected unmodified from the other traditions, hybridized in a mix of methods or mix of parts of methods	• Acknowledges the importance of the objective-subjective characteristics of the focus or purpose of inquiry. • Data could be a mix of numerical and descriptive symbols. • Empirical-experiential emphasis on both methodological and interpretive rigor.

encounter. Emphasizing a categorical exclusiveness also seems to suggest that all types of research and methods must be shoehorned into a specific research framework to be considered legitimate. Although this awareness of appropriateness and legitimacy is essential for any initiate in research methods, disciplined slavery to specific methods or traditions is ultimately fatal to robust inquiry. That doesn't mean anything goes; it does mean that it is appropriate to consider the use of various methods. There is no lock on the door to inquiry, and if a method works, so be it; the issue should not be the purity of what tradition it belongs to but how it will facilitate knowledge creation. More will be said about the inquiry-curriculum relationship in Chapter 12.

Inquiry, Research, and Curriculum

Questions about which method to use or whether a particular qualitative or quantitative research method is being discussed are, of course, legitimate concerns when planning or doing research in particular settings. For that reason, the concept of inquiry is used to avoid those often contentious, esoteric methodological issues. That is why the discussion of the research and curriculum relationship is gathered under the rubric of curriculum inquiry. This is also a useful distinction because, in curriculum work, there are some methods from other scholarly areas that don't fit neatly into an interpretivist-qualitative or positivist-quantitative scenario and seem more appropriate in the eclectic tradition. For example, curriculum can borrow from the tradition of criticism in literature and the arts in conceptualizing the critique as a scholarly form of curriculum inquiry. Curriculum is also a young discipline and a unique knowledge area that can benefit from alternative forms of investigation. Disciplines often develop and use different methods of investigation in creative responses to problems and circumstances for which available methods don't fit. For example, meta-analysis, developed by Gene V. Glass and colleagues (Glass, McCaw, & Smith, 1981) in educational research, has found a wider use in general social research. Meta-analysis was developed to create ways of analyzing a variety of studies that had been conducted using different methodologies but that addressed a related topic or problem. The nature of a discipline, the problems or interests it focuses on, also can dictate the choice of methods to employ. Anthropologists devised ethnographic methods to study primate animal and human groups. Those methods and ethnomethodology from sociology are proven tools in studying classrooms and focusing on the particular work of teachers in schools and schooling. The pioneering work by Barker and Gump in *Big School, Small School* (1964) was an early application. Other scholars followed in this vein. Phillip Jackson (1968) adapted similar techniques in his study of life in school classrooms. Lortie (1975) produced a sociological study of schoolteachers, and in the same decade, Peshkin (1978) studied the school-community link. Although these are not examples of research exclusive to curriculum, they are important early studies that blend aspects of schools, schooling, teaching, and curriculum. These are also some of the first studies to focus exclusively on the classroom and teacher practices as a center of research interest in the interpretivist inquiry tradition.

A research strategy or particular method that travels well across several disciplines is always of possible use. This interdisciplinary use is important in curriculum work, both for research and theory building. In studying the history of curriculum, scholars use methods borrowed from history. Ethnographic methods associated with sociology and anthropology have been used in public health, nursing, and medical studies. Case study and action research methods, widely used in studying classroom work and teacher decision making, actually were used first in business and law. Another example, an interdisciplinary application in a cross-cultural setting, is Dahllof's (1971) study of time-on-task related to grouping patterns and other factors influencing learning of a curriculum in Swedish classrooms. These examples characterize the broad methodological reach of inquiry in the educational field. They also suggest the range of method choices that are adaptable in school settings of such eclectic contexts and behavioral dynamics. In spite of the apparent strides in using methods appropriate to education, in curriculum the inquiry has been limited, particularly by the lack of a strong and long inquiry tradition that would develop a rich body of knowledge about inquiry in curriculum. In the discipline's early, formative years, theory building and curriculum development were emphasized. There is only a sketchy record of work to evaluate curriculum development activities or their use with learners in classrooms. John Dewey wrote about the University of Chicago laboratory experiences, and Franklin Bobbitt about working with curriculum development in Los Angeles. Both were descriptions, anecdotal narratives, about experiences in limited settings and without recourse to any evaluation or research activities. Examples such as those by two of the premiere early workers in curriculum suggest that evaluation and research activities were not of paramount importance early in the formation of curriculum and schooling. With the exception of Aikin's (1942) report of the Eight-Year Study in the 1930s and Lawrence Stenhouse's important volume *An Introduction to Curriculum Research and Development* (1975) in England, the literature on research in curriculum, the body of actual reports of curriculum research, is limited.

A second and related problem in curriculum inquiry and research relates to the type of curriculum issues investigated. There are what can be categorized as direct questions, those related to the specifics of curriculum such as research about sequence, scope, continuity, balance, and development of curriculum and materials. These are important topics for curriculum research projects. Another set of curriculum issues for investigation involves curriculum and the teacher, the curriculum-student relationship in the classroom, and the curriculum and the outcomes of schooling. Some examples of this type of collateral inquiry would be the relationship of curriculum and how learners learn a curriculum or what relationship there is between effectiveness of a particular instructional method and the scope and sequence in a particular curriculum subject. For whatever reason, research about such purely curriculum questions is difficult to find. Curriculum has a tradition of being indirectly related, a secondary or collateral issue or question as part of other research in education. For example, research has favored studies of instruction to find what methods (lecture, small group, etc.) are best, the contextual elements that influence learning (light, architecture, furnishings, etc.), and the learner and learning process itself. As a result of the reliance on theory building, curriculum development activities, and support for a purely curriculum research agenda, there are few studies exclusively dedicated to curriculum, and much of the knowledge about curriculum must be extrapolated from other studies.

Summary and Conclusions

Formal knowledge results from disciplined knowledge creation. Knowledge is arranged in fields and disciplines. Curriculum, for example, is a discipline in the field of education. The essential work of disciplines is to create and serve as a repository of knowledge that is useful for solving problems, creating more knowledge, and furthering the search for truth. This is the knowledge cycle of production and use. The concepts of paradigm and discipline structure offer a useful way to understand organized bodies of knowledge and the work of people in the process of creating knowledge. Those ideas and concepts form a foundational knowledge of perspectives, logics, literature, language, special tools, inquiry, and research. The concept of disciplinary structure also helps to understand the content of curriculum, such as the particular positions or perspectives and inquiry traditions that have evolved. That knowledge allows the student of curriculum to develop a critical perspective for working in the discipline, a knowledge base that prefaces other knowledge bases in curriculum study.

Critical Perspective

1. The history of human knowledge creation and preservation is fascinating. During the European Medieval period, roughly from the 5th to the 16th century, what existed as knowledge from the Greeks and other civilizations was saved by the Islamic societies of the Middle East and the Christian monks in Germany and Ireland. Two interesting books about how that human knowledge was saved are *The Middle East,* by Bernard Lewis (1997), and *How the Irish Saved Civilization,* by Thomas Cahill (1995). If that preservation had not occurred, what would the school curriculum be like today? What knowledge would have to be re-created?

2. You may already have or are working on a degree and certification in a particular field or discipline, general science or physics, for example. What are the particular questions that workers in that field or discipline consider important?

3. Using the structural elements discussed in this text (literature, logics, inquiry, etc.), try applying those and build a structure for the field or discipline in which you are majoring or seeking your degree.

4. Connecting curriculum orientations and personal thinking about curriculum is important to professional practice in curriculum work. Review the orientations provided in the text and consider how your thinking relates to them. Is yours a

mixed orientation involving two or more? Do you seem to fall into one particular orientation? Would you prefer inventing a new orientation? What would you call it and how would you describe it?

5. Learning theories are just that, theories; the problem is how such theories interrelate with curriculum, instruction, and learning. To check your thinking about learning and how it fits with teaching, go to http://www.cloudnet.com/~edrbsass/edlea.htm, and at the top of the page, select Your Emerging Theory/Philosophy of Teaching. How did your views relate to the theories/philosophies presented? What is your impression of the theory-to-teaching model applications without considering curriculum?

6. The idea of the knowledge cycle in Figure 5.1 can be applied to your own learning. Using the tectonic example as a model, can you create a learning cycle around something you have learned?

7. Many discussions about the two inquiry traditions, the positivist and interpretive, seem to suggest an either/or approach to their use. Do you think a more eclectic or mixed approach would be useful in curriculum inquiry? Why or why not?

Resources for Curriculum Study

1. The ideas of communities of discourse and dialectics may be unfamiliar. For background about discourse communities, refer to Wenger (1998) and Wenger, McDermett, and Snyder (2002). Dialectics is borrowed from philosophy and, for its contemporary dialogical use in educational conversation, a good source is N. C. Burbules's *Dialogue in Teaching: Theory and Practice* (1993). For further exploration of the dialogical self, see the articles by John Barresi and H. J. M. Hermans in the journal *Theory and Psychology* (2002). The whole issue is devoted to that topic.

2. The terms for curriculum orientations discussed in this chapter are mine; others may use different words for orientations and organize them differently. Two suggested readings to broaden your perspective are Eliot Eisner's *The Educational Imagination* (1994), particularly Chapter 3, and Herbert Kliebard's *The Struggle for the American Curriculum, 1893–1958* (1986).

3. How curriculum is viewed, the professional perspective taken, has been referred to in this textbook variously as orientations, traditions, positions, and frames of reference. The use of various terms to mean essentially the same thing is an inherent characteristic of new disciplines of knowledge. In the *Handbook of*

Research on Curriculum (Jackson, 1992), there are two extensive discussions of the various professional perspectives: Chapter 1, "Conceptions of Curriculum and Curriculum Specialists," by Philip W. Jackson, and Chapter 11, "Curriculum Ideologies," by Eliot Eisner.

4. The interaction of curriculum, technology, and learning is a new area of study. Under such new topics as computer-supported collaborative learning (CSCL), computer-supported collaborative work, and technology-supported collaborative learning, a broad interdisciplinary line of inquiry is emerging. The implications for schools, schooling, curriculum, and instruction are important. You can go online and refer to those topics to locate sites for further study. A useful discussion of the concepts and problems in CSCL as it is evolving is available at http://www.cis.drexel.edu/faculty/gerry/publications/journals/cscl2/cscl2.html (Stahl, n.d.). For a useful general introduction to CSCL and other accessible resources on the Web, http://www.edb.utexas.edu/csclstudent/Dhsiao/theories .html is worth visiting.

References

Aikin, W. M. (1942). *The story of the eight-year study.* New York: Harper.

Apple, M. W. (1979). *Ideology and curriculum.* London: Routledge.

Bandura, A. (1986). *Social foundations of thought and action.* Englewood Cliffs, NJ: Prentice Hall.

Barker, R., & Gump, P. (1964). *Big school, small school.* Palo Alto, CA: Stanford University Press.

Barresi, J. (2002). From the "thought is the thinker" to the "voice is the speaker": William James and the dialogical self. *Theory and Psychology, 12*(2), 237–250.

Bereiter, C. (2002). *Education and mind in the knowledge age.* Mahwah, NJ: Lawrence Erlbaum.

Bereiter, C., & Scardamalia, M. (1998). Beyond Bloom's Taxonomy: Rethinking knowledge for the knowledge age. In A. Hargreaves, A. Lieberman, M. Fullan, & D. Hopkins (Eds.), *International handbook of educational change* (pp. 675–692). Dorbrecht, NL: Kluwer.

Breisach, E. (2003). *On the future of history: The postmodern challenge and aftermath.* Chicago: University of Chicago Press.

Bronfenbrenner, U. (1976). The experimental ecology of education. *Educational Researcher, 5*(9), 5–15.

Bruner, J. (1960). *The process of education.* Cambridge, MA: Harvard University Press.

Bruner, J. (1990). *Acts of meaning.* Cambridge, MA: Harvard University Press.

Burbules, N. C. (1993). *Dialogue in teaching: Theory and practice.* New York: Teachers College Press.

Cahill, T. (1995). *How the Irish saved civilization.* New York: Doubleday.

Churchland, P. S. (2002). *Brain-wise: Studies in neurophilosophy.* Cambridge, MA: Harvard University Press.

Combs, A. W. (Ed.). (1962). *Perceiving, behaving, becoming: 1962 yearbook of the Association for Supervision and Curriculum Development.* Washington, DC: Association for Supervision and Curriculum Development.

Conant, J. B. (1967). *The comprehensive high school.* New York: McGraw-Hill.

Constas, M. A. (1998). Deciphering postmodern educational research. *Educational Researcher, 27*(9), 36–42.

Dahllof, U. (1971). *Ability grouping, content validity and curriculum process analysis.* New York: Teachers College, Columbia University.

Davenport, T. H., & Prusak, L. (1998). *Working knowledge: How organizations manage what they know.* Boston: Harvard Business School Press.

Dede, C. (2000). Emerging influence of information technology on school curriculum. *Journal of Curriculum Studies, 32*(2), 281–303.

Detmer, D. (2003). *Challenging postmodernism: Philosophy and the politics of truth.* Amherst, NY: Humanity Books / Prometheus.

Dewey, J. (1964). *John Dewey and education: Selected writings.* New York: Random House.

Eisner, E. (1994). *The educational imagination: On the design and evaluation of school programs* (3rd ed.). New York: Macmillan.

Eisner, E., & Vallance, E. (Eds.). (1974). *Conflicting conceptions of curriculum.* Berkeley, CA: McCutchan.

Eraut, M. (1985). Knowledge creation and knowledge use in professional contexts. *Studies in Higher Education, 10*(2), 117–133.

Fauconnier, G., & Turner, M. (2002). *The way we think: Conceptual blending and the mind's hidden complexities.* New York: Basic Books.

Freire, P. (1970). *Pedagogy of the oppressed.* New York: Herder & Herder.

Gagne, R. M. (1965). *The conditions of learning.* New York: Holt, Rinehart, & Winston.

Gardner, H. (1983). *Frames of mind.* New York: Basic Books.

Glass, G. V., McCaw, B., & Smith, M. L. (1981). *Meta-analysis in social research.* Beverly Hills, CA: Sage.

Hermans, H. J. M. (2002). The dialogical self as a society of mind: Introduction. *Theory and Psychology, 12*(2), 147–160.

Jackson, M. H., Poole, M. S., & Kuhn, T. (2002). The social construction of technology in studies of the work place. In L. A. Lievrouw & S. Livingstone (Eds.), *The handbook of new media.* London: Sage.

Jackson, P. W. (1968). *Life in classrooms.* Troy, OH: Holt, Rinehart, & Winston.

Jackson, P. W. (Ed.). (1992). *Handbook of research on curriculum.* New York: Macmillan.

Kearsley, G., & Shneiderman, B. (1999). Engagement theory: A framework for technology-based teaching and learning. Retrieved April 5, 1999, from http://home.sprynet.com/~gkearsley/engage.htm

Kliebard, H. M. (1986). *The struggle for the American curriculum,* 1893–1958. Boston: Routledge & Kegan Paul.

Kuhn, T. (1970). *The structure of scientific revolutions.* Chicago: University of Chicago Press.

Lewis, B. (1997). *The Middle East.* New York: Simon & Schuster.

Lortie, D. C. (1975). *Schoolteacher.* Chicago: University of Chicago Press.

Margolis, H. (1994). *Paradigms and barriers.* Chicago: University of Chicago Press.

Maslow, A. (1973). *The further reaches of human nature.* New York: Viking.

May, R. R. (1953). *Man's search for himself.* New York: Norton.

McLuhan, M. (1962). *The Gutenberg galaxy.* Toronto, Canada: University of Toronto Press.

McLuhan, M. (1964). *Understanding media.* New York: McGraw-Hill.

McNeil, J. (1977). *Curriculum: A comprehensive introduction.* Boston: Little, Brown.

Pence, A. R. (Ed.). (1988). *Ecological research with children and families.* New York: Teachers College Press.

Peshkin, A. (1978). *Growing up American.* Chicago: University of Chicago Press.

Phenix, P. H. (1964). *Realms of meaning.* New York: McGraw-Hill.

Phillips, D. C. (Ed.). (2002). *Constructivism in education* (Ninety-Ninth Yearbook of the National Society for the Study of Education, Part I). Chicago: National Society for the Study of Education.

Pinar, W. F. (1975). *Curriculum theorizing: The reconceptualists.* Berkeley. CA: McCutchan.

Plummer, K. (2001). *Documents of life 2: An invitation to a critical humanism.* London: Sage.

Rich, R. F. (1981). *The knowledge cycle.* Beverley Hills, CA: Sage.

Rogers, C. R. (1961). *On being a person.* Boston: Houghton Mifflin.

Ryle, G. (1949). *The concept of mind.* London: Hutchinson.

Scardamalia, M., & Bereiter, C. (1991). Higher levels of agency for children in knowledge building: A challenge of the design of new knowledge media. *Journal of the Learning Sciences, 1,* 37–38.

Schulman, L. S. (1998). Theory, practice, and the idea of professional. *Elementary School Journal, 98*(5), 511–526.

Schwab, J. J. (1962). The concept of the structure of a discipline. *Educational Record, 40,* 197–205.

Short, E. C. (1973). Knowledge production and utilization in curriculum: A special case of the general phenomenon. *Journal of Curriculum and Supervision, 9*(1), 77–86.

Simon, H. A. (1981). *The sciences of the artificial* (2nd ed.). Cambridge, MA: MIT Press.

Skinner, B. F. (1961). *Cumulative record.* New York: Appleton-Century-Croft.

Smith, B. O., Stanley, W. O, & Shores, J. H. (1957). *Fundamentals of curriculum development.* Yonkers-on-Hudson, NY: World Book.

Spring, J. (1986). *The American school 1642–1985.* New York: McGraw-Hill.

Stahl, G. (n.d.). *Rediscovering CSCL.* Retrieved February 2004 from http://www.cis.drexel.edu/faculty/gerry/publications/journals/cscl2/cscl2.html

Stenhouse, L. (1975). *An introduction to curriculum research and development.* London: Heineman.

Sternberg, R. J. (1988). *The triarchic mind.* New York: Viking.

Todd, J. T. (1994). *Modern perspectives on John B. Watson and classical behaviorism.* Westport, CT: Greenwood Press.

Vygotsky, L. (1978). *Mind in society: Development of higher psychological processes.* Cambridge, MA: Harvard University Press.

Wells, G. (1999). *Dialogic inquiry.* New York: Cambridge University Press.

Wenger, E. (1998). *Communities of practice.* New York: Cambridge University Press.

Wenger, E., McDermett, R., & Snyder, W. M. (2002). *Cultivating communities of practice.* Boston: Harvard Business School Publishing.

Chapter 6

METHODS AND TOOLS FOR CURRICULUM WORK

In 1707, four British Navy ships carrying troops were lost on uncharted rocks at the Scilly Islands on the southwestern coast of England. Why? They were off course because they lacked the appropriate navigation tools to determine their location. The event, as told in the book *Longitude* (1995) by Davia Sobel, prompted a search by the British Admiralty for a reliable way to determine longitude, the east-west positioning part of the latitude-longitude equation. It was a dogged British clockmaker, John Harrison, who finally succeeded with the chronometer. Navigation tools evolved, from compass to astrolabe to sextant, but it was the chronometer that ruled the waves until the advent of modern GPS, the global positioning system. The chronometer is an interesting example of a tool because it combines a "mind tool," Mr. Harrison's knowledge of clocks, with the development of a "mechanical tool," the chronometer. There are, of course, various classifications of tools. Screwdrivers and hammers, for example, represent "hand tools," whereas foundry presses that stamp out automobile parts are "industrial tools." Now, there are robots, lasers, satellites, and other kinds of "technological" and "cyber" tools.

KNOWLEDGE TOOLS AND CURRICULUM TOOLS

Humans are not the only toolmakers; apes, chimps, and birds have been observed using tools to facilitate food gathering. The video that captured the crow flying down to the street, dropping a nut on the pavement, waiting for a vehicle to run over it, and then retrieving the meat, is one you may have seen on various television programs. What humans have over other animals is the brain to develop mind tools, the kinds of thinking that produce other tools. To human advantage, those mind tools have been captured as kinds of *knowledge tools,* things to be learned in the formal knowledge of disciplines and fields where work is creating and validating useful knowledge. Discipline workers, the cadre of scholars, researchers, and practitioners, often talk about theory, models, and critiques, the knowledge and mind tools in their work. Tool use, even the tool itself, can vary across disciplines. Also, reading about the use of one tool or another can give the impression that each category is something unto itself rather than one tool of a set for workers to employ, each tool having a particular use or a range of applications. For any kind of tool, it is important to understand and respect its application in each discipline.

Curriculum, like any discipline, has a set of tools that is used by practitioners in different ways. Part of the foundational knowledge that is important in curriculum work involves understanding those tools and their use. The tools, as they are employed, acquire more specialized meaning modified by the particular work of the discipline. Theory in curriculum differs in meaning and use from theory in other disciplines such as economics or physics or history. In curriculum work, it is important to remember that tool use occurs in a curriculum frame of reference, a curriculum perspective. The tool set in curriculum work includes theory, models, and critiques.

CURRICULUM THEORY

Theory in curriculum work has a muddled history. Curriculum theory originated in the early 20th century primarily among progressive educational scholars as a formal way to present ideas and arguments to improve schools through curriculum. These proposals were made in a written format that usually detailed the purposes for the curriculum and the contents to be included. Tradition seems to suggest that what was claimed as theory was accepted as theory. From those early beginnings to the present, curriculum theory development has primarily been the province of university academics. George Beauchamp's *Curriculum Theory* (1961) and Mauritz Johnson's article "Definitions and Models in Curriculum Theory" (1967) are two examples of writings about curriculum theory that try to give it form by definition and substance by describing its features and use. Nearly thirty years later, Decker Walker provided this useful definition:

> A curriculum theory is a coherent and systematic body of ideas used to give meaning to curriculum phenomena and problems to guide people in deciding on appropriate, justifiable actions. (1990, p. 133)

Those important works and a definition aside, there appears to have been little consistent effort to gradually bridge between the curriculum theorizing of the early educational progressives and the contemporary context, the exception being William Pinar's book (2004) *What is Curriculum Theory?* Part of the problem was finding other ways than definitions to describe curriculum theory that acknowledged the nature of its use as it developed. Curriculum theory, being descriptive in form, will have, as Walker noted, a basic set of carefully articulated ideas intended to illuminate phenomena and problems or guide practice. Concomitantly, the definition for theory used in this text takes in that practice sense of theory; *curriculum theory* is a set of propositions, observations, facts, beliefs, policies, or procedures proposed or followed as a basis for curriculum action. Although definitions help, the use of curriculum theory usually gives it particular characteristics, often describing it better. Decker Walker provided useful thinking about that by articulating a set of criteria for curriculum theory, which is presented in Figure 6.1.

Figure 6.1   Walker's Criteria for Curriculum Theory

Validity

There is clarity in the exposition, definition, and presentation of the ideas. There is no apparent internal contradiction, and ideas are consistent with what is known.

Serviceability

The aim of theory is to assist practice, so it should address the conditions of practice; it should be realistic.

Power

The theory has promise for wide application in matters of practice and potential for prediction and control in matters affecting curriculum work.

Morality

The theory is grounded in acceptable values upon which judgments issuing from its use would be considered ethical and moral.

What are important in his formulation are the criteria. Because they move beyond definitional words to qualities that are observable, they can be used to make professional judgments about theory and its use in practice. They bridge between the "form" of theory, its format for presentation, to matters about what constitutes theory, its "substance."

Theory Form and Substance

Curriculum matters are often cast in theoretical terms, and curriculum theory has its own particular nature. Much of the theoretical conversation has been about improving schooling and education rather than about theory as a tool to understand curriculum, schooling, and other educational matters. Theory making in curriculum is descriptive, involving a particular format, or form, that addresses the manner of presentation within which is a discussion of the theory itself. These matters of form and substance in theory making are summarized in Figure 6.2 that follows.

The form of presentation evolved as a written set of ideas openly advocated and scientifically defensible. The use of the term *scientific* was intended to grace the work with a certain respectability. What scientific implied at the time was (a) a carefully constructed scholarly and philosophical discourse, (b) presentation of a thoroughly articulated set of logically consistent ideas or propositions, and (c) supporting arguments that were vigorous and pragmatic. Considering the appropriateness of theory, form was essentially a pro forma judgment similar to knowing the parts that constitute a book and looking to see if they are all there. Similarly, when considering a second aspect of theory, the matter of substance, the object and intent of theory, other characteristics of

Figure 6.2   Considerations in Curriculum Theory Making

Form of a Theory

The matter of format or how it is presented in writing.

- Is it a cogent, orderly, sequential set of ideas?
- Initial assessment of credibility; does it seem reasonable based on what is known?

Substance of a Theory

Addressing what the theory contains and if all the elements proposed hold together in a logical way, are complete in their illustrations, with special attention to whether

- *Commonplaces* are addressed appropriate to the theory.
- A *plan of curriculum* is provided so the purpose-to-practice sense of application can be assessed.
- There is a *logical explanation* or argument in support of the idea.
- The *power* of the theory is suggested by the discussion of potential use and suggested results the theory might produce in practice.

curriculum theory apply. As in reading a book, concern is for the thesis, and whether the discussion in support of the book's thesis holds together and is credible. In a curriculum theory, the expression of purpose should address the links between knowledge and practice. These links were introduced to you in Chapter 4 (see Figure 4.1) through what are referred to as the *commonplaces* in education: the student, or learner; the content, or what is to be learned; the context in which curriculum is offered; and the enabling agents present, such as the teacher. Because one purpose for curriculum theory is to guide practice, a theory must address those commonplaces.

Another aspect in curriculum theorizing is to present a *plan of curriculum,* what the curriculum should look like, a reference to the proposed scope and sequence. This plan is an important inclusion, what Vallance in discussing systems of curriculum (1999, p. 58) calls the building of conceptual maps. The use of theory among early pioneers in curriculum was more like critiques of curriculum, proposals about conditions surrounding curriculum or ones advocating a position on some curriculum matter. They suggested scope and sequence of content but lacked details. Books such as Franklin Bobbitt's *The Curriculum* (1918) represent ways of doing things, methods, a process approach to purposes for schools rather than the organization of a particular curriculum and its content. John Dewey, in his seminal work *The Child and the Curriculum* (1902), provided a vision of and details for determining and building a curriculum, something he was later to implement in his famous Laboratory School at the University of Chicago.

A third condition of theory is to have a *logical explanation.* A number of criteria apply. First, the theory must hold together; it must be logically consistent. Second, the particulars must be factually correct in light of current knowledge. The theory must also be justified on the merits of the argument put forth for it. It should also back up or be linked to some aspect of actual practice. Finally, the theory should have a quality of probability; it appears to be practical and doable. A logical explanation plus the other qualities would suggest a rational fit of theory into practice, a hallmark of good theory in early curriculum thinking. Today, having logical fit does not by itself satisfy the claim for a theory of curriculum.

A fourth consideration in curriculum theory making is what Decker Walker (1990, pp. 138–139) calls the *power* of a theory, referring to the prospect that a theory allows prediction and control, permitting efficient and effective action with curriculum in given situations. The theory should therefore identify indicators of and suggest possible effects the theory might produce, allowing the deduction of possible consequences from acting on or implementing the theory.

Judging and Using Curriculum Theory

Proposing a curriculum theory is one thing; substantiating it as theory is quite another. If it does not address the suggested framework elements—power, logical explanation, a plan, considering the commonplaces, and adherence to a formal style of presentation—then its acceptance as a theory is problematic. This is not to argue whether a proposed theory is good or bad but to establish some criteria for use in judging whether it should be considered as a curriculum theory in the first place. The difficulty is sorting out theory from proposals about making theory from those that are about theorizing itself, or from other tools like the critique. If a purported curriculum theory addresses most of or all the criteria, then it should be acceptable as a curriculum theory. Ultimately, the true test, the worth of a theory, will come in its use, whether it successfully guides practice, helps to solve problems, or leads to furthering new knowledge in curriculum work.

In new disciplines like curriculum, creating the conventions for theorizing is an important part of discipline work. To illuminate more about curriculum theory, sample some examples of theory work, and indicate the diversity of thought and theorizing, several examples are offered. The first is a summary of progressive theory making. The second is a consideration of Mortimer Adler's *The Paideia Proposal* (1982), and third is a discussion of *Realms of Meaning* (1964) by Philip Phenix.

Progressives

Curriculum theory, as has been noted, originated with participants in the progressive movement in education during the 1920s. These were essentially writings about ideas to improve schooling by creating and implementing new curriculum to replace the traditional one that predominated in schools. It was basically a conversation among college- and university-based professors writing to convince one another and the general public about curriculum matters. Franklin Bobbitt represents the manner of thinking and theorizing among progressives in these comments:

> The central theory [of curriculum] is simple. Human life, however varied, consists in the performance of specific activities. Education that prepares for life is one that prepares definitely and adequately for these specific activities. However numerous and diverse they can be for any social class they can be discovered. This requires only that one go out into the world of affairs and discover the particulars of which their affairs consist. These will show the abilities, attitudes, habits, appreciations and forms of knowledge that men need. These will be the objectives of the curriculum. They will be numerous, definite and particularized. The curriculum will then be that series of experiences which children and youth must have by way of obtaining those objectives. (1918, p. 42)

Another of the educational progressives, Harold Rugg, proposed a curriculum theory based on a new synthesis of knowledge for schools in which "the conventional barriers between the existing subjects must be ignored in curriculum making [and the new] *starting points* shall be the social institutions, or the political and economic problem, and the capacities of children" (1927a, p. 155). Note the emphasis in both examples of alternatives to traditional subjects. Theory and other ideas about curriculum usually appeared in the form of a published book to convey the theory, proposal, or idea and supporting arguments. Today, that is still the favored venue for advancing curriculum theory, probably because it is the easiest way to disseminate ideas to three essential audiences: others in the academic community; the general public; and the community of practitioners in the field, particularly teachers in schools. It is not easy to encapsulate the rich array of ideas in progressive theory making. At best, the progressives can be summarized as believing in opening up schooling to curriculum that addressed social, developmental, and other human needs in the practical and real world of daily life. Progressive theory making was about proposals on how to meet those needs by providing schooling for all people.

Adler

Theory making reflects the contesting of traditional, knowledge-centered ideas with the diverse ideas of the educational progressives. *The Paideia Proposal* (1982) of Mortimer Adler is representative of theories that counter the ideas of the progressives and offer an alternative based on traditional subject matter as the basis for school curriculum. The essentials of Adler's proposal are two: first, that American society must provide both a quality education for all and equal access to that education; and, second, that there should be one form of curriculum for all that prepares students for earning a living, citizenship, and personal development. The basic curriculum Adler proposed will sound familiar: fine arts, history, mathematics, natural science, geography, and social studies. All the subjects, mathematics and so forth, would be the curriculum for the middle and high school. The elementary curriculum would have the same subjects with the exception of substituting socials studies for history and geography. Adler proposes this as the basic curriculum but subject to individualization according to learner needs. He also advocates opportunities for limited vocational interests, physical exercise, and what amounts to basic human skills like typing as preparation for work. This is a basic meat and potatoes curriculum, a one-size-fits-all, common schooling as prelude to any later specialization through higher education opportunities offered by community colleges, technical schools, apprenticing or on-the-job-training, and, of course, the 4-year college or university.

Phenix

In curriculum theory, the degree to which the curriculum plan is spelled out varies. Usually they are no more than general descriptions with perhaps a listing of courses or content of whatever nature that issues from the theory. In *Realms of Meaning,* Philip Phenix provides an interesting and more detailed plan in support of his particular theory based on the ways of knowing. Knowledge in Phenix's perspective is not about subject

Figure 6.3   Phenix's Realms of Meaning

The thesis for the theory is that the fundamental human motivation is the search for meaning.

Realms	Related Knowledge
Symbolics	Language, mathematics, symbols
Empirics	The physical, social, natural sciences
Esthetics	The arts, literature, and drama
Synnoetics	Philosophy, literature, religion, psychology
Ethics	Ethics, morals values
Synoptics	History, religion, philosophy

matter itself but about "the power to experience *meanings*" (1964, p. 5). Starting first with his philosophical view of human understanding, he proceeds by "mapping . . . the realms of meaning . . . in which the various possibilities of significant experience are charted and the various domains of meaning are distinguished and correlated" (1964, p. 6). What emerge from his analysis are six patterns of human understanding he refers to as symbolic, empiric, esthetic, synnoetic, ethic, and synoptic meaning. Disciplines and the particular meanings with which they are associated, their particular knowledge sources, are summarized in Figure 6.3.

This is the framework of the plan, and the discussion that follows from it in his book details what each realm means before closing with chapters on the scope of the curriculum and the possibilities of inquiry and imagination as the pedagogy for engaging the curriculum.

CURRICULUM MODELS

Models in general are representations of objects, settings, or processes. Model building is important work in disciplines because models function as forms of knowledge that represent what something should be like. They subsume the characteristics of something into a pattern. Models can take many forms: a physical object, a generic formula for application, or a set of criteria for prediction. Model airplanes, cars, and such come to mind in referring to simple physical objects. During hurricane season, the National Hurricane Center often refers to possible storm paths based on prediction models in developing storm strike scenarios. Models in curriculum vary from detail about the scope and sequence of what is to be taught to those that lead you through a process for thinking about a curriculum. Classes of tools usually have a set of familiar characteristics; hammers, for example, come in different sizes and shapes and have different uses. Curriculum models also have particular sets of general features. They are usually *descriptive,* explaining a process, or *prescriptive,* a set of procedures or a sequence of steps about how to do something. A cooking recipe is an example. The recipe is the process, and the beginner will scrupulously follow it step by step whereas the knowledgeable chef will probably skip through it or modify its use based on his or her experience with it. Models in curriculum are also *practical;* they represent specifics of practice and arise from and are proved by use. The Tyler Rationale introduced in Chapter 2 is an example. Curriculum models can be *replicated;* they can be transported to and used in different settings or under different circumstances. Curriculum models can also serve *constructive* rather than predictive uses because the curriculum is a construction resulting from development activities based on a particular model, but its use or impact can't be predicted based on that model. For example, if you built model airplanes, the result, a construction, is a physical representation of that particular model. However, as hard as you tried to construct it according to the directions and as true to the model as the result might be, the model may or may not fly as you hope or as the information about the model suggests or predicts it will. A fifth quality, the model's *utility,* represents a confluence of a model's practicality, replication, and constructive and descriptive character. Models in curriculum work serve a certain purpose; they are useful in creating curriculum. Finally, curriculum models are not exclusive in their use. Although each separate model may describe a process or procedure, they are often interchangeable, depending on how they relate to or fit the qualities of the contemplated curriculum action. The models of Walker and Freire describe the elements of a deliberation process, that is, they do not follow a road map or set of steps. The models of Ralph Tyler and Hilda Taba present a set of procedures, a series of steps for doing curriculum work. Within Walker's or Freire's processes, it would seem feasible to insert or use a set of procedures, Tyler's or Taba's, for instance, without compromising the intent of the model as long as the decision to use the set of procedures emerged within the deliberative process. As to the issue about whether the models presented are exclusive, the response is probably no. However, for purposes of this text and discussion of particular tools, sets of qualities for different curriculum tools are established. The intent in this text is to categorize curriculum knowledge differently, as tools in curriculum work, for example, and give examples to clarify and differentiate the structural sense of curriculum as a discipline. If some piece of curriculum knowledge reflects the criteria for some structural element, then it has a fit within the structure. Part of the study of curriculum, the understanding of the discipline's logic, is to develop a worker's professional judgment; reflecting on how things fit or relate is part of that practice.

   If you were to survey the curriculum literature, you would find that curriculum models accommodate different purposes and uses. There are models for thinking about curriculum matters in a preliminary way, conceptualizing something, like "getting the picture" before formulating plans for action. Others are guides for doing particular types of curriculum work, such as reaching a consensus on the goals or purposes a curriculum should serve. There are models for solving particular curriculum tasks, like curriculum development. A few serve as a specific plan of curriculum, a model K–12 science curriculum, for example. Others combine aspects of several models and serve multiple curriculum purposes. In general, all curriculum models have the following characteristics: they are descriptive, they apply to specific aspects of curricular practice, they are utilitarian, they address most of the commonplaces, they arise from practice, and they are proven in use. The models chosen for discussion, those by Franklin Bobbitt, Ralph Tyler and Hilda Taba, Decker Walker, Paulo Freire, and Jerome Bruner, exhibit most of the characteristics just summarized.

Bobbitt's Scientific Schooling

The formal beginning of curriculum is often dated from 1918 with the publication of Franklin Bobbitt's book *The Curriculum.* That book, along with his 1924 publication, *How to Make a Curriculum,* is important for two reasons. First, Bobbitt's ideas on curriculum established a prevailing curriculum perspective—the focus of curriculum was the school and schooling. What schools should teach would be determined by studying society, a process of analyzing life in which the school would ameliorate the social problems for which there were no other institutional correctives. By a scientific process of inquiry, the particulars of those social needs—the abilities, attitudes, habits, and so forth necessary for their attainment—would be identified and a curriculum crafted around them. The school was the focus and the professionals to do curriculum work would be the teachers, administrators, and school boards. The emphasis was on local needs and local control. The second important aspect of Bobbitt's perspective was the presentation of a way to do the work, a model process presented in his 1924 text *How to Make a Curriculum.* Work was to proceed in two phases: first, to discover the objectives for the curriculum; and second, to devise experiences for obtaining the objectives. Given the fledgling state of curriculum as a field of academic interest, the political support of forces under the broad banner of the progressive movement, and public support to change the perceived social evils of the time, his ideas were influential because they were practical, portable, and doable.

Tyler and Taba: Evaluation Is Key

Ralph Tyler's early professional career began in school and program evaluation at Ohio State University and with the famous Eight-Year Study during the late 1930s. Out of those experiences, he developed a process for thinking about purposes for schools and how to develop the curriculum. In his famous post–World War II syllabus for a course at the University of Chicago (1949), he articulated the elements of that process.

This is the famous Tyler Rationale, to which you were introduced in Chapter 2 (see Figure 2.3). It is arguably the most pervasive model for doing curriculum work in the postwar years and influential because of its wide use in the training of graduate students as future professors of curriculum or directors of curriculum in school districts. Tyler posed a sequence of questions: (a) What educational purposes should the school seek to attain? (b) What educational experiences can be provided that are likely to attain these purposes? (c) How can these education experiences be effectively organized? and (d) How can we determine whether these purposes are being attained? The first question directs you to the *goals* that schooling and the curriculum should serve, and the second question deals with the *scope* of the curriculum, what should be included to meet those goals. The third question asks how the content would be organized, a *sequence* matter. The last question, how will we know if we achieve the intended, refers to the need for *evaluation.* It is the emphasis on evaluation that is perhaps Tyler's greatest contribution to curriculum thinking and work. From Bobbitt's time to Tyler's, the emphasis in curriculum was on theory building, what might be called an "anything goes" approach that critics derided for its lack of rigor and failure to either address whether or provide evidence that a particular curriculum theory actually worked. What Tyler advocated was evaluation as a way of validating curriculum work, a legacy of his work with the Eight-Year Study.

The Tyler Rationale was eminently useful. It was influential in establishing planning as an important policy action for setting goals from local school districts to a number of national organizations. Perhaps it achieved its most practical use as an applied process at the school and classroom level pioneered by Hilda Taba. Working exclusively with teachers in Contra Costa, California, Taba refined Tyler's model for practical use by teachers. In her book *Curriculum Development: Theory and Practice* (1962), she articulated a curriculum development process for general use by teachers and others at the classroom level. Although her model was for application in all content areas of the curriculum, the research on which it was based was done in the social studies. Taba's reworking of Tyler (see Figure 6.4) is important in several ways.

Figure 6.4   Tyler and Taba

Tyler Rationale		Taba Process
--------------------	☐	Diagnose needs
State purposes	☐	Formulate objectives
--------------------	☐	Organize objectives
Identify experiences	☐	Select experiences
Organize experiences	☐	Organize experiences
Evaluate	☐	Evaluate

First, instead of a general call for identifying objectives, Taba starts with a *diagnosis* of learner needs, creating a needs assessment, as the source for *formulating* objectives. Where Tyler calls for determining the means to attain the objectives, Taba is preemptive, referring to means as the selecting of content and the necessary *learning experiences.* In the classroom, the critical center of curriculum practice, and for the teacher, the critical practitioner, the Tyler-Taba model was a proven tool. It was not just another formula or gimmick; it was a legitimate way to do curriculum development based on research and experience rather than on theory and anecdote.

Walker's Deliberative Platform

Models that emerge based on research or as extractions from the research experience are important for a discipline and for practice. Like the Tyler and Taba models, Decker Walker's Deliberative Model (1971) is based on research experience. He studied groups doing curriculum development and the way they made curriculum decisions. The key feature was the deliberation process and, specifically, getting personal agendas on the table so value positions (perspectives) were articulated openly. He noted that ways of proceeding were not predetermined but negotiated and documented as participants worked their way into and through the task. Their individual and collective beliefs about schools, schooling, and related classroom concerns form what Walker calls a *deliberative platform.* Think of the idea of a platform as like that of a political party, a negotiated consensus consisting of a set of beliefs and principles that guide actions and that, in turn, become the things for which the party stands and is held responsible. It is this sense of reflective responsibility, the degree of matching between the planning as it was recorded and the implementation outcomes, that is unusual. In effect, it functions as a built-in self-evaluation where the scripted proceedings provide a record with which to compare the decisions in the deliberative process with the results of the curriculum implementation itself. It is also a corrective process that wants to find solutions or make adjustments to the process, not create or assign blame.

Freire's Liberation Model

The preceding models share two common qualities: they offer practical applications for doing curriculum work, and their formulation emerged from a research experience. As a group, they are free of preemptive embedded bias, prejudice, or politics that might raise questions about their use. That is not the case with Paulo Freire's work, which was born in the political struggles of oppressed peoples in Brazil. Freire's model centers on creating the structures of thought to empower the oppressed to understand themselves and their circumstances and create their own self, social, and cultural knowledge so they can emerge into a world of their own making and control. The centering idea is that freedom of self-determination is not the end but the means. Freire articulated this idea as a theory of emancipation or liberation. In his book *Pedagogy of the Oppressed* (1970), he explained this as a dialogue about emancipation through a process of developing critical consciousness. Based on his work with the poor and oppressed, he developed teams who worked in common with people at the local level. The process has an anthropological feel to it; the habits and ideas and the social, cultural, and work activities are studied and used as the data from which themes are developed to use in the dialogic interplay of locals and the assisting team. This process continues through the creation and implementation of a curriculum of the people that becomes the path to self-awareness and empowerment. It is a distinctive curriculum of the people and for the people created for special schooling in a unique context. Although Freire's work is politically controversial, it has demonstrated viability as a process. It is an example of a model based on a theory emerging from practice rather than a model emerging from practice based on a research experience.

Bruner's Spiral Curriculum

The last example for discussion is based on the ideas of Jerome Bruner. In the 1960s aftermath of Russia's successful Sputnik launch, the U.S. federal government developed a policy designed to close the gap in science-mathematics training that had purportedly resulted in our failure to meet the Soviet challenge. The ideas incorporated into various training and curriculum development activities were elegant and practical. There are two basic elements. First, from the perspective of learning psychology, content to be learned could be presented in such a way that any learner could learn it or, in different words, organized in an intellectually honest way, *intellectually* referring to the child's way of thinking. The second aspect has to do with how knowledge is itself organized. Simply summarized, his idea was that any body of distinct knowledge, a discipline, for example, had a structure, and that structure could be patterned (think scope and sequence) to fit the learner. The key to organizing the curriculum based on Bruner's ideas was the concept of the *spiral curriculum*. The curriculum would flow from simple to complex, concrete to abstract, and from year to year as schooling progressed. This plan for designing and developing curriculum is arguably the most influential model of its kind. The key is how it influenced the way textbooks were written and presented by publishers. Text selection was no longer a text for a course at a grade level; instead, curriculum workers selected a publisher's text series because it fit a specific scope and sequence spiral and could not be disrupted, like the series of books in learning to read. Its application in curriculum development was widespread. The new math, perhaps the most well known, was followed by similar ventures in physics, other sciences, and the social studies.

PERSPECTIVE INTO PRACTICE: Curriculum Models in a Language Arts Lesson		
Model	*Elementary Classroom*	*Secondary Classroom*
Bobbitt: Determine needs, stipulate objectives, and build experiences.	Students select a poem, story, newspaper article, or online article of choice representing personal interest. They then choose other imagery (e.g., picture, other sources) from various classroom or online resources that represent words used in the selected poem and create a collage-as-meaning effect.	Using library or online resources, students select two stories/poems in literature or a mix to illustrate a literary theme, then create a collage of media that represents the critical ideas/words/phrases in the literature selected and expands or extends the meanings the author intended.
Tyler/Taba: Determine purposes of schooling, develop a scope and sequence, and evaluate.	Given four poems, students select one and briefly state why that choice and not the others. They then rank order the four poems and give reasons for the placement of each in the rank order. In pairs, students compare rank ordering and reasons. The class develops the sets of rank order with rationales from the pairings data, then combines sets that are common into a new order based on categories of interest/personal choice. The last task is to build generalizations about choices/interests and consensus building in judging poetry.	Based on a study of thematic constructions in poetry, students use the library/Internet to identify poetry they want to read. Each selects one poem representing a theme and provides a rationale for that selection. In groups, they agree on some set of criteria and organize selections accordingly. They re-form as a class and again arrange a common set of criteria with a rationale for arranging a composite of all selections. Using the developed criteria, they identify a second set of poems and apply the criteria to identify the problems in making judgments about poetry and thematic construction common in literature.
Walker: Deliberate on beliefs and values, develop curriculum, and compare.	Students engage in teacher-led collaboration-cooperation teaching in a language arts class. Using stories selected from a book of readings, the students in groups decide what factors (ideas, likes, dislikes, etc.) they would use to re-create the selected readings into a	Ground rules for group work are reviewed, and student groups then identify, adjust, or create new rules as discussion proceeds in evaluating two selected poems. Each group identifies values/beliefs they find in the poems and uses the poems as evidence. They then produce

	book of reading. Each group maintains a log of the proceedings so the deliberations have a record. At the end, the class discusses each group of ideas and the ways to identify what role personal intent and belief played in the reading consensus built in the assignment.	a set of observations to define and use in creating a set of criteria to apply to other poetry.
Freire: Develop curriculum for self-awareness and empowerment of the learner.	Students are assigned a selected reading and make a list of words they consider important to the message of the story. Students pair off and decide how to consolidate/organize their lists. Students discuss experiences in negotiating the list in order to attain agreement on the array of words and consider other options for discussion.	The proposed literature course reading list is given to students to review and individually reorder according to personal interests. In pairs, they discuss-compare, note similarities and differences, create a plan or scheme of organization acceptable to both, and arrange a new list of readings. Each student keeps a notebook recording his or her observations of the interactions as a discussion record. Using composite reading lists and notebooks, the class develops a composite set of readings and a set of rules that they infer from the notebooks about the discourse. This will be used to guide future discussions and modified as the class and course proceed.
Bruner: Design curriculum from simple to complex, concrete to abstract, based on the way people learn.	Students are reading two assigned books. As they read, they identify and list words/ideas they think are important to the story, then individually rank order their importance. Periodically, the teacher collects the lists and a student team consolidates them into a master list rank ordered from simple to concrete kinds of word/ideas to those that are abstract/complex. This will be modified each time. After doing this with both books, the class	An American literature class is reading and discussing a selection of books by Mark Twain and Nathaniel Hawthorne. Individually, students identify key ideas/themes/words for the particular author/book they are reading and provide evidence keyed to the book. Students reading similar books form a team to periodically meet and discuss ideas/themes/words and how these interrelate to build the story. Using that discussion, they then build a story framework of

(Continued)

(Continued)

	compares both ordered master lists and compares words/ideas in relation to how words or ideas build in complexity from start to finish in the stories.	ideas/themes/words around two tasks: (a) Identify how those would be ordered and interrelated from simple ideas/themes/words to complex, giving concrete to abstract examples from the book; and (b) suggest what preparatory knowledge, or ways of thinking, a reader would need prior to reading the particular book. Based on that data, the class builds a composite characterization of the ideas/ themes of each author and rank orders the books as a suggested reading path for an interested reader.

CURRICULUM CRITIQUE

The critique is another useful curriculum tool. Each critique is a written, scholarly per-spective on some curriculum matter. They are not, in a political or social sense, pro forma criticisms of something. The main purpose is to invite conversation and further consideration about what is presented for discussion. Critiques have various uses and take different forms depending on the discipline. In the arts, music, drama, and litera-ture, for example, the critique or formal criticism is an important form of scholarly activity. Usually the writer identifies an issue, problem, or topic and develops a frame-work in which to discuss it. This usually includes situating the matter within the purview of other discipline practitioners by stating the perspective being used or pre-sented; identifying particulars, conditions, and criteria or qualities about the topic, prob-lem, or issue; or presenting the pluses and minuses about it. The critique is often a comparative analysis. In curriculum, critiques often are in the style of a written, rea-soned appraisal of some aspect of the state of the discipline, a proposal, trend, tradition, theory, or model, for example. Critiques as academic exercises should not be confused with criticism. The former sets up some criteria used as the points of discussion, a focused, restrained analysis or comparative. The criteria are formally set forth as one might establish propositions in support of an argument or position taken. Criticism is often a disguised polemic, an attack that does not necessarily require such declared for-malities or attempt to set itself up as a scholarly discussion; criticism does not have to be grounded, as does the critique. Critiques are useful because they often point out a corrective to or a caution about something that is widely accepted and used in curriculum work. A number of critiques have led to significant alterations in curriculum thinking and practice.

Issues of Theory Versus Practice

While curriculum work grows and changes both as academic and as school practice, there continues to be a tug of war between those who advocate for curriculum theory by academic scholars and those who consider that curriculum work should be practice and school based. The first set of critiques by Joseph Schwab, William Pinar, and William Wraga address the theory-practice issue.

Schwab

In a series of publications in the early 1970s, Joseph Schwab offered a critique of curriculum work. As he saw it, curriculum as a field of study and work was ailing, and the problem was one of an obsolete work focus. Two factors had produced this state of affairs. First was the fixation on curriculum theory, a legacy of theory building by educational progressives in the earlier part of the 20th century. Second was the hegemonic role of university-based academics. The result was the ignoring of curriculum practice as practical work carried out in schools. As you learned in Chapter 4, Schwab and others described the practical as dealing with four *commonplaces,* the *learners* or students, the *teachers,* the *subject matter* (the curriculum commonplace as what was to be taught), and the *milieu.* The corrective, as he saw it, was to return curriculum to the study of practice and involve practitioners, not just academics. Curriculum work, as he discussed in an article in *School Review* (1973), should be grounded in the real world of schooling, not in esoteric discussions about curriculum theory among academics. Schwab's commonplaces of practice were the criteria for appraising the state of curriculum and for setting forth the remedy. The upshot of Schwab's work was to open up the discussion about the academic-school relationships and the nature of practice and create an introspective about what was the appropriate work for curriculum professionals.

Pinar

If Joseph Schwab's critique about curriculum was a call for the practical in curriculum work, William Pinar's (1975) critique of curriculum was one for reconceptualizing curriculum theory. The thrust of Pinar's view is that theorizing was dominated by one mode of thought, the social behaviorist school, and was in a condition of conceptual imperialism. His critique of theory is important because it opened theorizing to other perspectives. As a focus on just theory work, it was liberating to academics but it does not seem to have affected the practical problems of curriculum that Schwab addressed. The reconceptualist resurrection of theory work has liberated theory in many directions, particularly among those who lay claim to the postmodernist perspective. In *Understanding Curriculum* (2002) and *What is Curriculum Theory?* (2004), his most recent discussion, Pinar and others present curriculum as historical and contemporary discourse. In their ordering of things, curriculum is understood as various forms of text, a sampling of which include curriculum as aesthetic text, theological text, poststructuralist text, deconstructed text, postmodern text, and political text. The main criticism of the Pinarian formulations echo Schwab's concern that it is not practice focused and fails to address the actual work of curriculum in schools (Wright, 2000; Wraga & Hlebowitsh, 2003).

Wraga

Conversations in disciplines are dialogic, an often-extended exchange of point and counterpoint. The critical issue of curricular relevance, its practicality, is one of those extended conversations. The main positions, represented by Joseph Schwab and William Pinar, have been already noted. William Wraga has expressed a third position on the practice-theory issue. In a series of articles (1998, 1999, 2002), he articulated a perspective that appears to reconcile theory and practice. The essential element in Wraga's perspective is reflected in his statement that "curriculum practice should inform curriculum theory—that the latter should be tested by the former" (2002, p. 17, referencing 1999, p. 11). This neatly encapsulates the problem in the practice-theory debate that has been primarily an either/or choice rather than a third, confluent, or middle way. Since the Wraga-Pinar exchange has prompted other comments, it remains to be seen if this third way will enjoy a serious discussion. There are questions such as how to design such a curriculum inquiry to explore how practice should inform theory rather than the reverse. Perhaps a dialogue among practitioner scholars and teachers would build a community of discourse. After all, if it doesn't get to that stage of discussion, the issue is still back in the same moribund state that Schwab described. Wraga's critique also highlights the lack of a standing practice-theory inquiry tradition, a long-standing lament in this discussion, a condition attributable to the historical dominance of theory rather than research and practice in curriculum inquiry.

Issues of Values, Culture, and Power

In the curriculum literature over the last three decades, a second issue has centered on values, culture, and power in particular institutions and processes such as schools and schooling. The institutional world is large, and the initial thrust was aimed at political institutions and how they suppress the natural empowerment of people and empower elites (Breisach, 2003; Wink, 2000). There is, in all instances of curriculum critique, some discussion of relationships about values, how they are determined and the roles they play, a cultural and multicultural dominance, and the exercise of institution power.

Kliebard

Herbert Kliebard's (1970) critique of the Tyler Rationale has a different, narrower focus. Tyler's Rationale, discussed previously, provides a series of questions to guide thinking about curriculum matters. In contrast to Schwab's critique of the whole field of curriculum work, Kliebard's critique is focused only on Tyler's model. His key point is that any theory, model, or other tool used in curriculum work is not value neutral; nor does its use necessarily lead to value-free results. He pointed out several concerns about embedded values. First was the matter of a person's own values in choosing to use Tyler's model. There should also be a consideration of the values held by others involved in the process. Third, in addition to those value considerations, there is the addition of a value inherent in the very choice to use Tyler rather than some other model, in that some value positions are being raised over others. The emphasis on values is important because it opened up an extended discussion about value orientations in all aspects of curriculum. Among curriculum workers, its legacy is to be introspective about personal values and reflective about assumed and embedded values as part of one's perspective and practice in curriculum work. Because Tyler's Rationale was widely used at various levels and places of curriculum work, this admonition to be careful about values was important for all users.

Ong

In contrast to issues about the direction of curriculum or particular theories or models, some critiques focus on the social and cultural dimensions of curriculum, the milieu of commonplaces. Usually, this directs one to consider a different perspective, to think outside the box, to step outside what is being looked at, and in a detached way, to see it differently. Walter Ong (1971, 1982) asks one to do that by pointing to the dominant mode of expression in a culture and how it affects curriculum. Oral traditions mean a curriculum with the study of forensics, debate, and oratory. In a print-oriented culture, the concentration is on language, spelling, writing, and composition. As humans progress into the age of information and visual technologies, new curriculum requirements will emerge. Computers and the Internet are new media of expression. Print knowledge is still important but, with new media, different curriculum needs may emerge. Oral and print cultures necessitate creating different ways to think in the particular tradition. It is probable that new ways of thinking are emerging.

Apple

Another useful critique, by Michael Apple (1986), focused on the subtle role of textbooks in schooling. Texts are commercially produced and subject to subtle political pressures about what content to include. One example is how the choice of presenting ideas such as evolutionary theory, creation theory, and intelligent design in science texts shape thought in one direction and not in another. This exemplifies the problems of compromise and presenting all sides in a discussion in a democracy, which Apple discusses in *Ideology and Curriculum* (1979) and *Cultural Politics and Education* (1996). In Apple's writings, matters of historical inclusiveness (whose side of history is being told) and settings of power that influence the control of curriculum, schools, and schooling are important themes. Apple's point is that curriculum has the subtle power to indoctrinate by virtue of what is put into texts and, perhaps more important, what is excluded or left out. School personnel, as Apple notes, can be powerful influences. The public schoolteacher who leads the class in prayer behind closed doors in full knowledge that this is illegal is exerting power and influence as well as assuming the unwarranted role of parent or guardian.

Summary and Conclusions

Doing curriculum work necessitates understanding the kinds of tools curriculum workers use. Curriculum tools have evolved as the discipline of curriculum has grown. The set of tools includes theory, models, and critiques. Theory began in the initial formation of curriculum with the early educational progressives who were looking for ways to change the curriculum. Curriculum theory is not like the scientific or other varieties of theory. It has particular characteristics and a set of criteria with which to judge theory work in curriculum. Models are available for planning, development, and just thinking about curriculum work. Curriculum critiques are valuable discussions about curriculum ideas, theory use, models, and work among all curriculum workers. These are basics in the curriculum knowledge base, and knowing about these tools is an important part in understanding curriculum practice.

Critical Perspective

1. Should sets of criteria for judging theory be weighted or valued equally? What considerations should enter into deciding what weights or values will apply? What is the basis for weighting?

2. Using the criteria in Figures 6.1 or 6.2, try applying them to the Phenix and Adler examples. How many of the criteria apply in each instance? Could you argue that one or the other or both are curriculum theories?

3. What do professionals in schools consider to be curriculum theory and how do they define or describe curriculum theory? Interview several teachers and ask

them what definition, criteria, or characteristics they attach to curriculum theory and if they can identify one that fits into their frame of reference.

4. Using the characteristics given for the critique, go to the Internet or library and select a curriculum-related article, apply the characteristics, and determine if the article qualifies as a critique.

5. The term *theory* is used quite freely in education; there is learning theory, instructional theory, and so forth, and some topics or ideas, like multiple intelligences and learning styles, are sometimes referred to as theories. How do those conceptions of theory differ from the one developed in this text for curriculum theory?

Resources for Curriculum Study

1. The term *curriculum theory* has been applied quite freely in curriculum. Using the Internet, library, or references and Recommended Readings sections in this book, look for books or articles by these curriculum scholars: Ted Aoki, Michael Apple, Ivor Goodson, Maxine Greene, A. V. Kelly, William Pinar, or Thomas Popkewitz.

2. For a more detailed discussion of the deliberation idea applied to curriculum, see Chapter 6 in Decker Walker's *Fundamentals of Curriculum* (1990).

3. Aspects of the Eight-Year Study, its purposes, methods, outcomes, and their importance, are discussed in various chapters of the *Handbook of Research on Curriculum* (Jackson, 1992). Wilford Aikin's *The Story of the Eight-Year Study* (1942) is the usual primary source. One recent revisit to the Eight-Year Study is the Kridel and Bullough (2002) article "Conceptions and Misperceptions of the Eight-Year Study."

4. In curriculum, most of the important literature not related to theory or curriculum development has been produced since the end of World War II. Reprising from comments made in this same section at the end of Chapter 1, a selection of the more enduringly useful would include arguably the single best reference in the literature, by Schubert, Schubert, Thomas, and Carroll (2002), *Curriculum Books: The First Hundred Years*, the synoptic textbooks published in curriculum. No list would be complete without the *Handbook on Curriculum Research*, edited by Phillip Jackson (1992), which is a portal to just about any subject in curriculum, the various important scholars who contributed to it, and a reflection of the structural aspects discussed in this chapter. A third book, *Understanding Curriculum* (Pinar, Reynolds, Slattery, & Taubman, 2002), is a postmodernist

view of curriculum that is really a comprehensive discussion of curriculum theory. It also covers a wealth of curriculum knowledge.

5. Among professional associations dedicated to curriculum matters, publications of the National Society for the Study of Education stand out. The yearbooks in particular reflect the thinking and perspectives developed about curriculum, schools, and schooling over a period of 100 years. One very significant yearbook about curriculum is the Twenty-Sixth Yearbook of the National Society for Studies in Education, under the chairmanship of Harold O. Rugg, published in two volumes, *Curriculum Making: Past and Present* and *The Foundation of Curriculum Making* (Rugg, 1927a, 1927b). It is a compilation of writings by educational progressives that marks the formation of curriculum as a new area of interest and scholarly work.

References

Adler, M. (1982). *The Paideia proposal.* New York: Macmillan.

Aikin, W. M. (1942). *The story of the Eight-Year Study.* New York: Harper.

Apple, M. W. (1979). *Ideology and curriculum.* New York: Routledge & Kegan Paul.

Apple, M. W. (1986). *Teachers and texts: A political economy of class and gender relations in education.* New York: Routledge & Kegan Paul.

Apple, M. W. (1996). *Cultural politics and education.* New York: Teachers College Press.

Beauchamp, G. A. (1961). *Curriculum theory.* Wilmette, IL: Kagg Press.

Bobbitt, F. (1918). *The curriculum.* Boston: Houghton Mifflin. (Reprinted 1972, New York: Arno Press)

Bobbitt, F. (1924). *How to make a curriculum.* Boston: Houghton Mifflin.

Breisach, E. (2003). *On the future of history: The postmodern challenge and aftermath.* Chicago: University of Chicago Press.

Dewey, J. (1902). *The child and the curriculum.* Chicago: University of Chicago Press.

Freire, P. (1970). *Pedagogy of the oppressed.* New York: Herder & Herder.

Jackson, P. W. (Ed.). (1992). *Handbook of research on curriculum.* New York: Macmillan.

Johnson, M. (1967). Definitions and models in curriculum theory. *Educational Theory, 17*(2), 127–140.

Kliebard, H. M. (1970). Reappraisal: The Tyler Rationale. *School Review, 78*(2), 259–272.

Kridel, C., & Bullough, R. V., Jr. (2002). Conceptions and misperceptions of the Eight-Year Study. *Journal of Curriculum and Supervision, 18*(1), 63–82.

Ong, W. J. (1971). *Rhetoric, romance, and technology.* Ithaca, NY: Cornell University Press.

Ong, W. J. (1982). *Orality and literacy: The technology of the word.* London: Methune.

Phenix, P. H. (1964). *Realms of meaning.* New York: McGraw-Hill.

Pinar, W. F. (1975). *Curriculum theorizing: The reconceptualists.* Berkeley, CA: McCutchan.

Pinar, W. F. (2004). *What is curriculum theory?* Mahwah, NJ: Lawrence Erlbaum.

Pinar, W. F., Reynolds, W. M., Slattery, P., & Taubman, P. M. (2002). *Understanding curriculum.* New York: Peter Lang.

Rugg, H. O. (Ed.). (1927a). *Curriculum making: Past and present* (Twenty-Sixth Yearbook of the National Society for the Study of Education, Part I). Bloomington, IL: Public School Publishing Company. (Reprinted 1969, New York: Arno Press)

Rugg, H. O. (Ed.). (1927b). *The foundation of curriculum making* (Twenty-Sixth Yearbook of the National Society for the Study of Education, Part II). Bloomington, IL: Public School Publishing Company. (Reprinted 1969, New York: Arno Press)

Schubert, W. H., Schubert, A. L. L., Thomas, T. P., & Carroll, W. M. (2002). *Curriculum books: The first hundred years* (2nd ed.). New York: Peter Lang.

Schwab, J. J. (1970). *The practical: Arts of the eclectic.* Washington, DC: National Education Association.

Sobel, D. (1995). *Longitude.* New York: Walker.

Taba, H. (1962). *Curriculum development: Theory and practice.* New York: Harcourt, Brace, & World.

Tyler, R. W. (1949). *Basic principles of curriculum and instruction.* Chicago: University of Chicago Press.

Vallance, E. (1999). Ways of knowing and curricular conceptions: Implications for program planning. In M. J. Early & K. J. Rehage (Eds.), *Issues in curriculum: Selected chapters from NSSE Yearbooks* (Ninety-Eighth Yearbook of the National Society for the Study of Education, Part II, pp. 49–70). Chicago: National Society for the Study of Education

Walker, D. F. (1971, November). The process of curriculum development: A naturalistic model. *School Review, 80,* 51–65.

Walker, D. F. (1990). *Fundamentals of curriculum.* New York: Harcourt Brace Jovanovich.

Wink, J. (2000). *Critical pedagogy: Notes from the real world* (2nd ed.). New York: Longman.

Wraga, W. G. (1998). Interesting, if true: Historical perspectives on the "reconceptualization" of curriculum studies. *Journal of Curriculum and Supervision, 14*(1), 5–8.

Wraga, W. G. (1999). Extricating sunbeams out of cucumbers: The retreat from practice in reconceptualized curriculum studies. *Educational Researcher, 28*(1), 4–13.

Wraga, W. G. (2002). Recovering curriculum practice: Continuing the conversation. *Educational Researcher, 31*(6), 17–19.

Wraga, W. G., & Hlebowitsh, P. S. (2003). Toward a renaissance in curriculum theory and development in the USA. *Journal of Curriculum Studies, 35*(4), 425–437.

Wright, H. K. (2000). Nailing Jell-O to the wall: Pinpointing aspects of state-of-the-art curriculum theorizing. *Educational Researcher, 28*(1), 4–13.

Chapter 7

HISTORICAL FOUNDATIONS OF CURRICULUM

Everything is connected. . . . None of us is untouched by the swirl and eddy of serendipity that drives human endeavors at all levels from quantum chromodynamics to painting your house. (Burke, 2003, pp. 1–2)

In his many books, author James Burke continuously makes the point about connectedness, that all knowledge is related and no body of knowledge, no discipline, exists in isolation. While every discipline has a critical core of knowledge and tools, there is always other related knowledge to be studied in understanding the discipline. One of those areas of knowledge that enlightens a discipline's connectedness is its history.

Curriculum, like other bodies of knowledge, has its own history. Studying that history gives an understanding of the ideas, trends, and practices as the discipline evolved. It allows for a timely comparison of new ideas and practices with the past or the retrieval of past ideas and practices as relevant for use in current contexts. Sometimes procedures and ideas thought to be new are only refurbished ones and can be dismissed, thus saving work or the pursuit of a valueless venture. In doing curriculum work, it is not necessary to be a curriculum historian, but it is necessary to know the significant stops along the historical curriculum trail and where to go to find historical knowledge of value. Curriculum history will be explored using two historical perspectives, the chronological and the episodic. Chronology, of course, refers to time and particular time frames of reference in the American experience. The episodic approach allows for a more selective focus on particular historical knowledge out of which the discipline was constructed. The approaches are intended to complement each other and enhance your understanding of curriculum.

ROOTS OF AMERICAN CURRICULUM

The American curriculum evolved based on a number of overarching ideas, several from Western civilization, others genuinely American. The ideas generally fall into two groups, the philosophical and the practical. Although neither categorization is exclusive, they are used for several reasons. First, using the categories makes it easier to differentiate and cluster ideas about the development of American curriculum. Second, education scholars and historians, Cremin (1970), Spring (1986), and Walker and Soltis (1997), for example, who have studied the development of American schools tend to stress a similar dialectic of the philosophical and practical. The views of Rousseau and Plato represent the emergence of certain early key ideas that become in their philosophy and practice fundamentally American in the development of schools and schooling from earliest European settlement to the present. They symbolize evolving strands of thought about the relationships surrounding certain historical commonplaces, "ideas" about *society,* the *state,* the *individual,* and *institutions,* or, in this particular case, schools. The ideas of Plato and Rousseau represent two enduring perspectives about the reasons for schooling and schools. In many ways, they are the necessary antecedents, the precursors, of our contemporary dialogue about schools, schooling, and curriculum.

Transatlantic Ideas

The Greeks and French, through the writings of Plato and Rousseau, respectively, reflect the philosophical discourse. Curriculum historians and other writers usually put these forward as antecedent formulations of curriculum thinking. Their relevance is that the ideas became part of the culture of thought in the European West and were transferred to the New World with the European colonists who settled in America. Whereas they present two philosophies extolling visions of the "Good," a path to achieving the ideal in human affairs, each enunciates a particular recurring theme embedded in American views of schools and in what knowledge the young should be schooled. In degree, both themes echo in the writings of all American educational and curriculum scholars, particularly Franklin Bobbitt and John Dewey.

Plato's (c. 428–328 B.C.) book *The Republic* is a political discussion about the just state and preparing young citizens to achieve or strive for it according to their talents and nature. The heart of the just state was a trinity of intelligent citizens each according to their life station. There are those who govern with compassion; a second group, the brave and strong who would, as necessary, provide for the common defense; and a third group of entrepreneurs, the provisioners of goods and services. In the Greek scheme of things, humans possessed a three-part psyche, or soul. This personal trinity consisted of an appetitive part, the source of desires and needs; a spiritual part for protection and survival; and a final part, rationality, the center of good judgment. The key to Plato's just state was keeping the social and personal trinities in balance, both separately and in union. The way to achieve this was through schooling provided by the state. The key elements that filtered into Western thought are the conceptions of justness involving the citizen and the state and the key role schooling would play in building the just state. Plato's ideas are, in my view, antecedent ideas to our modern American belief of progress through schooling provided by the state. In discussing the nature of the psyche, Plato also stands as an early explorer of how and what humans should learn.

Skipping to the 18th century, there is a second seminal influence in Western thought, Jean-Jacques Rousseau. Whereas Plato's concerns were with the state-citizen relationship, Rousseau was concerned with development of the individual person. He developed his ideas in his book *Emile*. For him, the important thing was the freeing up of the individual through an idiosyncratic self-learning. He seeks to redress the stultifying power of the state and society to create conforming citizens. Simply put, Rousseau believed the young person should develop freely and in nature so that the unique worth of the individual might unfold. This theme, the viability of human learning and its possibilities in teaching the young, would have a 20th-century educational reinvention. It would influence the developmental and cognitive curriculum orientations you will encounter in Chapter 8 and provide a social and intellectual rationale for many in the progressive movement (Aaron, 1951) at the turning of the 19th into the 20th century, particularly among those in progressive education seeking change through new curriculum.

The First Curricularists

You probably have heard the expression, "you can talk the talk or you can walk the talk," meaning that there are talkers and there are those who act on what they say. Being philosophical, talking the talk in the scholarly sense, is being thoughtful as a prelude to action. The thoughtful action is, of course, walking the talk. The basis for philosophical talk was the ideas of Rousseau, Plato, and, later, the flow of 19th-century ideas from Europe (e.g., the kindergarten, the gymnasium) mixed with the actualities of the American experience. From that blend came two important developments—a new idea, curriculum, and people to pursue that idea, those who would later be called curricularists. The interest in schools brought with it questions about what should be taught, the substance or content to be learned, that led to the use of curriculum to represent what schools taught (Wright, 1962). The second important development was the rise of curriculum specialization, college- and university-educated persons who did curriculum work and either entered schooling as teachers and administrators or became faculty in colleges and universities. The term curricularists became associated with these new specialists.

There are essentially two schools of thought about when curriculum as knowledge specialization and the anointing of those who would be charged with that work specialty occurred. Some curriculum scholars place the emergence of curriculum shortly after 1900, whereas others mark its emergence much earlier in the 19th century, prior to the American Civil War. Those who fix it in the early years of the 20th century usually base that on the publication of the very first texts on curriculum by Franklin Bobbitt, John Dewey, and others. The publication of the two volumes of the *1926 Yearbook of the National Society for the Study of Education* is also cited as a benchmark. Those publications signify that people located in universities and colleges, the first curricularists, were actively studying and writing about schools and schooling and using the term *curriculum* to mean what schools were teaching. They were creating a body of new literature about a new subject, the curriculum. The second view marks the emergence of curriculum much earlier, citing when the 19th-century British sociologist Herbert Spencer framed the issue by asking, What knowledge is of most worth? In a publication (Spencer, 1861) and on subsequent lecture tours, he discussed this original curriculum question. It is an inventive question because it became widely discussed as both a public and a formal academic consideration of what knowledge means and what part of knowledge is more important. It was also accepted in that time that what the young ought to learn was "knowledge," as it was understood at the time, and that would gradually be linked with ideas about curriculum. Spencer's question is the precursor of two trends in curriculum that persist to this day. First is the consideration of knowledge itself, what it is, how do we know, or can we know what it is. And, of all the knowledge known, which of it is the most important or, as Spencer put it, "of most worth," and why is some knowledge held to be of more significance than another? The second trend concerned what "purposes" would be served by learning and which knowledge would best serve those purposes. In these two trends are the core of curriculum matters, what humans need to know, the knowledge question, and why they need to know it, the question of purposes the knowledge should serve. Over time, out of those two basic questions, curriculum emerged as a specific body of knowledge and specialized practice.

18TH-CENTURY CURRICULUM IN AMERICA

Excluding the Native occupants of America, ideas about schooling were what the immigrants brought with them or what the particular colonial power would allow. These were European ideas. The initial concerns were about "basic literacy"—who should be able to read and write and why—and moral development. Among the primary colonizers, English, Swedish, Dutch, Spanish, and French, there were different views on the kind and amount of knowledge and literacy that was even allowable (Cremin, 1970; Wright, 1962). In some, the Spanish for example, there was an elitist view that clergy, governing members, and colonial leadership should be literate and be able to read whereas settlers and indigenous people should not. After all, there was the necessity of being consistent with the mission of the colonial grant or charter under which they served. The New England–area colonials wanted people to read and write in order to understand religious tracts and the Bible. In the colonies around Chesapeake Bay and southward into the Carolinas and Georgia, where the company charters were concerned with profits, concerns for literacy and learning were more benign. Learning for the purpose of inculcating appropriate moral behavior was mixed in the colonies. Those colonists here for religious reasons, the early 17th-century Puritans and the later 18th-century Calvinists, for example, emphasized learning in moral texts suited to their religious purposes. The colonials from Catholic countries such as Spain and France used literacy in limited ways. One of the goals of their colonial rule was to save and convert sinners to the faith. This meant the conversion of the indigenous peoples who were, at the same time, the object of conquest and exploitation for gold and other riches.

Curriculum in the English Colonies

It was in the English-speaking colonies that curriculum had its first manifestation in the modern sense. What would be called curriculum today was the curriculum of the colleges established primarily to prepare ministers and other clergy (Rudolph, 1967). They incidentally provided opportunities for study to the young of families who could afford to send them. It was an incentive to send colonial children to colonial colleges rather than incur the expense of study in England. What passed as schooling for the young, mostly males, was limited to reading, writing, and arithmetic, infused with patriotic themes, moral virtues, and religion. It was disconnected, with no sequencing from lower to higher as experienced today. It was also sporadic. Schooling was considered to be mainly the responsibility of the family and was available in many cases only if a family could afford it or if the community or colony established laws providing for schooling. The Old Deluder Satan Law of 1647 in Massachusetts is representative of such laws. Over the next hundred years, various laws were enacted throughout the colonies providing for various kinds of schools, some for reading and writing; others, like the common school, for the classics; and later the academy, incorporating a more practical, vocational content. Even then, the problem of finding a schoolmaster or schoolmistress was difficult. Candidates were variously prepared, some barely more literate than those they taught, others qualified in some subjects but not in all. Often the schoolmaster or schoolmistress's knowledge was uneven across the subjects, and what was learned was what knowledge the teacher possessed rather than what was equitable or comprehensive.

Mandates for Literacy

In the days when knowledge was developed by apprenticing, as Ben Franklin did, or by reading the law to become a lawyer, the opportunities for accessing knowledge in books or studying to enter some sort of trade or professional practice were often informal and limited. What made literacy and learning accessible to large numbers of people was the gradual availability of commercially published books (Cremin, 1970). While there are a number of early examples, the famous *New England Primer* (c. 1687) for one, it was the creation of reading books, the earliest being Noah Webster's *An American Selection of Lessons in Reading and Speaking,* published in 1789, that helped promote literacy and spread learning. These early forms of the familiar textbook were important for two reasons. First, they contained the basics for learning to read; in a sense they were self-instructional. Second, by focusing on literacy in the English language, these primers and books emphasized national identity (note Webster's use of the term *American*) and personal morality through a common language. As Carl Degler (1959) points out, this early effort to Americanize initiated a trend to use schools, schooling, and curriculum to build a national sense of unity, of being one. That use of the schools for political and social purposes continues to the present. Witness the contemporary controversy over language between those advocating English language immersion for migrant and immigrant children and those favoring the English as a second language (ESL) approach. Finally, portability and multiple usability and the ease with which a book could be distributed made such works ubiquitous. This was especially true in cities and other communities where libraries existed. This trend toward available, affordable schoolbooks was as important in the promotion of literacy and learning as Samuel Colt's process of interchangeable parts and the factory system would later be for the manufacture and production of goods. Books, dictionaries, and other publications were realistic. They contained all the basic arithmetic problems and vocabulary that adults and parents might encounter in their work. Very few students were college bound; most would farm or prepare for the trades and other occupations. The emphasis was on the practical, being able to read a manifest, read or prepare a bill of sale, count change, or write a letter. And, during the Revolution, it was patriotic to read the news and reports from the Committees of Correspondence that existed in every colony.

Schooling and Curriculum Perspectives

The colonies, through the Revolutionary period into independence, supported the establishment of schools in many communities. There was little curricular uniformity in those efforts. As post-Revolutionary independent states, former colonies in New England, Pennsylvania, New York, and Maryland, among others, began to expand access to schools and schooling by establishing school districts and collecting taxes for their support.

Although schooling in the various colonies was limited and schools differed as to type and purpose, most were dedicated to building literacy for religious reasons in a specific settlement. If you could read and write, you could read and study the moral lessons and lead the good life, at least as it might be defined by local religious leaders. As settlement moved the wilderness frontier ever westward, written communication tied dispersed communities together. There was, as historian Daniel Boorstin notes (1958, p. 340), no more important member of a community than the printer, who served also as journalist, postmaster, and conveyer of public information.

Across the scattered, small communities and towns of the colonial frontier and the westward migrations that came later, schooling was secular and limited, initially focusing on reading and grammar. As towns and villages arose behind the expanding boundaries of the new nation, different needs and conditions led to other types of schools. Most notable were the grammar and common schools that evolved. Gradually schools became distinguished by what they taught. Children and others who sought to be schooled were often sent to board at some distance from home or local community because what they wanted to learn was only available at that location. Clear distinctions arose between reading and writing schools, grammar schools, and places for apprenticing. Schools and their curriculum also began to evolve a hierarchy. Reading and writing schools were first-tier schools focusing on reading skills and the rudiments of arithmetic. They are what you might think of as primary-grade equivalents of the modern elementary school, focusing on the famous three Rs. In the colonial period, these were often local neighborhood schools called dame schools.

A second tier of schools, grammar schools, taught Latin, Greek, and the literary classics. Patterned after the British curriculum with which colonists were most familiar, grammar schools offered a classic curriculum. Influenced by Renaissance views of the public leader drawn from Greek and Roman sources, the grammar school suited the needs of those seeking preparation for religious or civic leadership. It is important to realize that the early differentiating of schools by type carried subtle social implications. Attending a grammar school and college conferred higher social status in a community than apprenticing or attending reading and writing schools. Grammar school also influenced what would be learned at which level of schooling. By later requiring entering students to be able to read and write, grammar schools were establishing several subtle features of schooling. The requirements for entrance are an early example of the prerequisite conventions of today. They are also the earliest example of the trend to regulate and order the curriculum. Finally, by establishing prerequisites for entry, they were exercising a form of social sorting of individuals according to knowledge and performance. These were not policy-making decisions on the grand scale of today affecting thousands of schools; rather, they were incidental, unconnected changes in a variety of places that, taken as a whole, represented emergent practices with long-term implications.

The Academy Movement

In addition to the development of those more widespread types of schools, the dame, common, and grammar forms, and the division of curricular responsibility among them, a third important type of American school and curriculum emerged. In 1749, Benjamin Franklin proposed his famous Philadelphia Academy, the prototype form for academies that followed and the later American high school. The academy curriculum included the traditional study of English, reading, and writing, with attention to grammatical construction, pronunciation, writing style, and correct speech. History was included as the vehicle for learning morality, and new subjects included geography, philosophy, oratory (forensics and debate), politics, and human affairs. What was innovative, even radical, was the inclusion of new, practical subjects for study. These curriculum additions proposed by Franklin were agriculture, technology, science, and inventions. The curriculum continued to evolve as a more practical one, balancing academic and vocational studies, a pattern associated with the modern comprehensive high school curriculum. The academy movement was widespread in the early 19th century and took various forms, public, private, and parochial. It declined in the post–Civil War period, tending to become private and elitist rather than public and democratic. The academy curriculum was important because as the new nation struggled to define itself, the teaching of history was used to develop a national identity and unity. The problem the academy movement solved was a curriculum one. Other schools, dame schools, for example, were limited to the three Rs, the classics, or narrower educational pursuits such as the preparation of civic and religious leaders. The academy curriculum served a broader population with a curriculum of knowledge more suited to the nascent industrial-technical revolution. New forms of production, manufacture, and trade required new knowledge, and ways to obtain that knowledge in serving a different kind of workforce emerged from 1800–1865. The academy school form was flexible; it could be shaped to local needs to suit a workforce in the wilderness or one in the growing cities. The curriculum could be arranged to wed three purposes: the basics of literacy, learning new knowledge for emerging technical-industrial work and trades, and continuing development of a national identity. Serving these three purposes in various forms would define the American curriculum into the early 20th century.

19TH-CENTURY CURRICULUM
IN THE UNITED STATES

The theme of nationhood was endemic and undifferentiated as to place and location, the frontier, farm, or city, or social status as a farmer, preacher, lawyer, or laborer. There is a tendency to forget that egalitarian tendencies in the post–American and French Revolutionary era emphasized commonness of opportunity, of experiences being available to all regardless of station, a movement away from elitism and social stratification. This democratic tendency, a defining American characteristic, acquired political importance with the ascendancy of Andrew Jackson to the presidency in 1828.

The Jacksonian era began a significant shift in the development of the American nation and ideals. On a wave of newly enfranchised voters, American politics changed dramatically. Political power shifted away from the older states and the traditional landed Eastern aristocracy to Americans from the frontier and the new states on the western side of the Appalachian Mountains. New leaders also emerged from this America of the West. American ideals now emphasized popular sovereignty, institutional flexibility in the name of the public good, and a continuing belief in personal and public progress. Central to this idea of progress was the belief that the way to attain the most good for the individual and society lay with schooling opportunities based on the new knowledge of science and the technical and industrial arts in addition to the traditional curriculum of the common school.

A key to progress was flexibility, experimenting with institutional things at the local level, not being tied to tradition or expectation. The exception was adherence to the rule of law, which was not, however, incompatible with flexibility. This was true of the new America before, during, and after the Revolution for independence. The idea of secular, not religious, origins of knowledge and law, products of the Enlightenment, particularly of the Scots, brought a detachment of knowledge from religious hegemony that influenced the development of schools and curriculum. Schools in very limited ways were creatures of the individual colonies and later the independent states.

The essential American idea is that public life is based on the rule of law, civil and secular. All institutions exist at the pleasure of the public through the instruments of government based on a constitution ordained and approved by the people who allow themselves to be governed under it. This was magnificently summarized in Mr. Lincoln's famous phrase, "government of the people, by the people, for the people." Then, as now, the exercise of that authority depends on political control. Schools are institutions created under the constitutions of the individual states; they are creatures of the state. In the period between declared independence and the Constitution, former colonies became individual free states, and control shifted from colonial administrators to Revolutionary leaders who were concerned with governing their particular state. Although opportunities for schooling had increased, schools remained under local community or private governance. Early revolutionary state governments were busy with affairs of the war, dealing with other states, the Continental Congress, and the inherent problems under the Articles of Confederation. With the exception of the academy movement and emerging entrepreneurial vocational and apprenticing-type institutions, concerns about schools, curriculum, and control were, by necessity, essentially benign.

Curriculum for a New Nation

The curriculum story has early beginnings in the development of particular American institutions during the colonial experience and in the years after achieving independence. These were the various schools and colleges serving a variety of instructional purposes in the different colonies and, later, states. It was a disconnected, separated hierarchy of units much like the colonies and states themselves. In governing and schooling, there was a common problem, how to make governments and schools that were American. A public mind had to be created, a process, as Garry Wills so aptly put it, of *Inventing America* (1978). This was forged through a series of documents, the Declaration of Independence, the United States Constitution, and the Federalist Papers, the collection of newspaper articles in defense of the Constitution penned by Alexander Hamilton, John Jay, and James Madison (Rossiter, 1961).

By the 1790s, ideas about democracy and republics were confirmed in the public mind with the adoption of the Constitution and the initiation of a federal system of governance. The primary concern was nation building, the development of economic, social, and political institutions and a sense of national unity that defined what it meant to be American. Under the new Constitution, the delegation of powers to the central government resolved former interstate conflicts over commerce, defense, and relationships with foreign nations. States could now focus on different problems, particular concerns, and new ideas in addressing the needs of their citizens. Virginia, New York, Pennsylvania, and Massachusetts, for example, began to examine the need for schools and what should be taught. Increasingly, the focus turned to schooling and a curriculum to encourage informed civic responsibility and promote commerce. Individual states could, in effect, become centers of experimentation. Because they were different in population, location, and institutional experience, each state had a different historical experience for approaching problems and needs. Where schools and schooling were concerns, purposes and organization could be considered more effectively on the smaller scale of a village, town, or county. As smaller units for decision making within states, they could more readily address such questions as the need for schools, what purposes should be served, how they should be financed, and what curriculum should be formed to reflect their purposes.

A concomitant issue was the matter of economic development. From the decade of the 1790s to 1860 and the Civil War, a confluence of forces commenced the American

Industrial Revolution and social changes that occurred in response. Commerce was growing, there was new industry based on new technology, the nature of the workforce was changing, and different skills and knowledge were needed. Westward movement and settlement, immigration, inventions, and the changing nature of work from agriculture to commerce and manufacturing occurred at an increased pace. The distilling idea of what it meant to be American was a belief in progress, a can-do spirit tied to learning and individualism.

Democracy and Progress

As schooling and curriculum underwent changes, they became linked with progress and democracy. The ideas of Benjamin Rush, Noah Webster, Thomas Jefferson, and Horace Mann are representative and instructive. All four were for progress and democracy and considered schools and schooling essential for a free, independent, and responsible citizenry. Jefferson emphasized schooling in the basics (reading, writing, etc.) as essential for free persons and the general social good while trusting in the people to rationally arrive at positions in public matters based on the marketplace of ideas. In various degrees, the other three represented a second perspective that became ascendant, one that established the idea of state responsibility rather than Jefferson's sense of individual responsibility. Their writings argued that the purpose of schools and schooling was to impart basic principles of government, citizenship, morality, and history, the essentials for national unity. Schools were creatures of society, and the state had an obligation to determine what would be the content of schooling. The ascendancy of the idea that it is the obligation of government to set the school agenda and curriculum is crucial because it became the guiding principle for controlling schooling in America. Although schools might be creatures of any state under its constitution, it set in place an idea, an expectation, that in the commonplaces of life, the county, township, and town levels of governance, schooling was under local control.

Rush and Franklin also advocated studying scientific and technical knowledge in schools. This emphasis on new, practical knowledge challenged the traditional, narrower emphasis on schooling for leadership. As the need for new and different knowledge matched advances in types of work, new subjects entered the school curriculum. In addition to geography and history, advocates pushed for inclusion of the new physical and biological sciences. The expanding curriculum caused other considerations: a longer school year; the placement of new subjects, or scope, of the curriculum; and how to order or sequence curriculum as the student moved through the additional levels. The inclusion of new subjects raised governance questions of how to provide continuity to what was being taught—how to make a curriculum scattered across diverse, growing communities more uniform and accessible.

Curriculum in the Common School

As the frontier moved west, cities like Cincinnati, St. Louis, and Philadelphia filled up with newcomers, a mix of migrants and immigrants, many with young children. The immigrants, predominantly from Asia and Europe, differentiated by language and culture, were a new and special problem. How do you deal with immigrants? How do you go about Americanizing them, eliminating former loyalties and creating a new one to the United States of America? How do you insulate against radical ideas and cultural customs that are perceived as different, threatening? Noah Webster supplied the answer: write and publish books (famous dictionaries, spellers, and readers) that were readily available and affordable and that promoted patriotism and a common language. Books, dictionaries, and ideas were fine, but what was needed was an institution, a form of school that would incorporate all these aspects. The answer was the common school. No American schoolman was more important in this movement than Horace Mann, common school advocate, author, publisher, former lawyer, Secretary of the Massachusetts Board of Education, and, later, a member of the United States House of Representatives. His work expanded ideas about free schooling, compulsory education, free libraries, normal and teacher-training institutions and curriculum, and public funding of schooling and curriculum development work. His writings seem to summarize the many views on achieving social and political progress in America. His main theme was that the ills of society could be addressed by inculcating right motives through a common school, with a common curriculum, for a common people. The means to accomplish this was a curriculum constructed around principles of political and social morality. As historian Daniel Boorstin points out in the first and second volumes of his study *The Americans* (1958, 1965), the themes may express an egalitarianism (albeit selectively intended), but the intent was to institutionalize values to be commonly held. Mann's work exemplifies two important trends. First is the idea of creating and using institutions, specifically schools, to shape society. Second is the use of the content to be learned in schools, what is now referred to as the curriculum, to instill specific values. Both these trends had been part of the colonial experience, were now enunciated in the catechism of a new nation, and would continue in some form to the present. As the school curriculum emerged as an important source of control shaping the nation, it became the focus for various public agendas.

New Knowledge of Most Worth

One of the more curious developments in 19th-century America was the concept of public edification through the development of educational opportunities for adults. In the pre–Civil War years, this adult education was through the Lyceum movement. This was followed in the post–Civil War years and into the 20th century by the Chautauqua movement. Through the Lyceum and Chautauqua, the public was introduced to the cutting-edge ideas of the day. You could hear the famous lecturers of the time in the smallest, remotest communities. Possibly the most important ideas emerged from 1830 through 1860, a period of robust scientific thought and significant invention. Ideas and proposals included advances in mathematics, sciences, and the emerging social sciences. For example, in 1829, Jacob Bigelow published a treatise, *The Elements of Technology.* This is the first cited use of the word technology in a publication in America, and it exemplifies both the expanding amount and new forms of knowledge. Here was the new technical knowledge of invention and science. From biology, anthropology, sociology, and other new social sciences, new ideas were emerging about the nature of man and society. Concomitantly, from the 1830s through the years of the Civil War, immigration, migration, and federal government policies supportive of commerce and transportation expanded the nation westward. With the peopling came settlement, towns, new cities, and institutions. What fired much of this change was a shift in the American mindset, a perception of abundant opportunities and the potential for individual progress. This optimism was attributable to a number of sources. One source was, of course, the public education movement and the widespread availability of newspapers carrying those messages. Another was economic and social change that created a shift away from labor-intensive to machine-assisted production in agriculture, commerce, and industry with an accompanying increase in choices about career or work options. Urban growth and the social aspects of individual lifestyles as cities and settlements grew and farm populations declined also influenced the public frame of mind. Much of the intellectual ferment is represented in the work of one person, Herbert Spencer, and an idea, Social Darwinism. Spencer was a British sociologist who began writing and speaking in the 1840s and continued on through the rest of the century. Historian and sociologist Robert Nisbet assesses his importance this way, "It is impossible to think of any single name more deeply respected, more widely read among social philosophers and scientists, and more influential, in a score of spheres, than was that of Herbert Spencer" (1980, p. 235). Spencer influenced American thought through his writing and lecture tours, especially the circuits of the Lyceum. His doctrine was simple and direct: Freedom is necessary to progress, and the goal of progress is the realization of freedom. During this same time frame, Charles Darwin published his work on evolution, *The Origin of the Species* (1859/1995), in which he cites and adopts Spencer's phrase, survival of the fittest, a coalescing of scientific and sociological thinking whose issue, Social Darwinism, would influence government policies and institutions in America into the 21st century. For curriculum and schooling, one important effect of this intellectual coupling of Spencer and Darwin was to advance the idea that knowledge based on science was the basis for personal and human progress.

Discipline Standards and Curriculum Principles

Herbert Spencer's interest in a score of spheres included the nature of knowledge, and it is in that realm that he posed the question, What knowledge is of most worth? In both his lectures and a famous 1859 publication of the same title, he responded that science was of most worth. He was arguing for the new knowledge of the sciences as the source for individual and, therefore, social betterment. The net effect was to challenge what was the traditional knowledge of the classics and enjoin the issue of what schools should teach by advocating the new knowledge of the sciences and the emerging social sciences. After the Civil War, an eventual debate over the worth of traditional or new knowledge was inevitable. Several things suggest this. First, Charles Darwin's evolutionary thesis was a direct challenge to widely held beliefs about biblical creation, the nature of human societies, and the knowledge supporting them. Second was the changing nature of American colleges and universities. The addition of courses and programs of study in the new disciplines of the sciences and social sciences and the creation of new American-style universities emphasizing graduate programs such as Cornell, Johns Hopkins, and the University of Chicago were changing the notion of worthy knowledge. Advancing through levels, or degrees, of knowledge has a spiraling effect, each level being preparatory to the next. The development of graduate work requires appropriate undergraduate knowledge, and successful college work depends on appropriate school knowledge. The crux of the matter was the manner of the fit between the knowledge students were getting in the schools and what colleges expected for entry. The debate over that issue played out in the work of the National Education Association (NEA).

Today, in the world of unions, there is often a failure to appreciate the impact of the NEA as *the* center of conversation about schooling and the larger realm of education. From the 1880s and into the early 20th century through committees, reports, and speeches, it served as a forum for deliberation and a clearinghouse for ideas. Its membership included college and university presidents, schoolmen, teachers, United States commissioners of education, governors, and others with interest in schools. One hallmark of this period is the formation of new organizations, national in scope, like the NEA, the American Association of School Administrators (AASA), and the American Economic Association. These organizations with national memberships were centers for the new emerging class of professionals, those obtaining college degrees, whose growing importance lay in the preparation of scholarly publications such as yearbooks of organizations like the NEA, the AASA, and various state education bureaus and occasional papers published by universities such as Teachers College, Columbia University. These publications and the scholarly journals that sprang up provided access to the important ideas and discussions of the time.

Over a period of 25 years, 1893 to 1918, three NEA committees wrestled with the knowledge-curriculum-school issue in various ways. The arguments after 1893 shifted away from a focus on content or specification of courses to those about perspectives that would dictate the content. The three-committee reports reflect a series of skirmishes in a war between a loosely aligned group of traditionalists and another group of reformers, the so-called progressives. Charles Eliot, President of Harvard University, and William Torrey Harris, U.S. Commissioner of Education, symbolized the traditionalist perspective. In the reformist group, a coalition of sorts held together by a mutual disdain for traditionalist views, the leadership centered at various times on G. Stanley Hall, David Snedden, and others such as John Dewey.

The NEA Committee of 10 report in 1893 recommended four separate courses of study for high schools, any of which would be accepted by colleges, each containing subjects much like those that make up contemporary curriculums. The Committee of 15 report of 1895, like its predecessor, was also prescriptive; it provided a specific list of things to study in the elementary school. The sea change would come with the committee report of 1918 (Figure 7.1). Instead of a prescriptive focus, a list of courses or specific content to include in courses, the committee stated a series of seven principles that the curriculum would address. Each principle seems to be a bridge between a purpose and existing curriculum as envisioned by the traditionalist, thus seeming to deflect criticism. "Worthy Home Membership," for example, means learning in the arts, social studies, and literature, which refers to subjects such as literature and history advocated by the traditionalists. As progressives were inclined to make clear, what had been done was to explain the curriculum in a different way not as a list of subjects but subjects connected to the realities of human living and basic needs. This was, of course, a different way of creating a relationship between purposes and the curriculum. Simply put, the ends were stated, the means were not. This is very important because how a curriculum would be constructed was left to professionals and the path could take many forms so long as the outcome was the attainment of the seven principles.

20TH-CENTURY CURRICULUM: THE PROGRESSIVE MOVEMENT AND AFTER

If there was one movement of importance from the old 19th to the new 20th century, it was American progressivism. This was truly a quest that touched all issues and institutions, political, social, economic, and educational. It also reverberated in the celebrating of industry and progress. The 1893 Chicago World Columbian Exhibition and the St. Louis Exhibition of 1904 seemed to affirm the goodness and enterprising nature of Americans and herald to the world the uniqueness of the American nation guided by scientific ways of thinking and new knowledge.

Progressivism in Education

The Committee Report of 1918 and its famous Seven Cardinal Principles, as they came to be known, stand as a manifesto of the progressive movement in education. As the centuries turned, those principles through school and curriculum would assist the

Figure 7.1   The 1918 Cardinal Principles of Secondary Education

Issued by the Commission on the Reorganization of Secondary Education of the National Education Association, the purpose was to form objectives for developing curriculum in secondary education. The commission set a precedent by forming goals before reforms and moving from prescriptive curriculum to describing outcomes for curriculum that would take into account individual student differences, goals, attitudes, and abilities. The focus on democracy was the integrating concept to guide education and curriculum in America.

Health

Good health habits are to be encouraged through curriculum that provides courses in health and appropriate physical activity. School-community health links should include planning activates for youth and education of the public at large about good health. Teachers and the school facility should exemplify good health and safety.

Command of Fundamental Processes

Reading, writing, math, and oral and written expression are fundamental processes in the curriculum that should be developed using newer forms of pedagogy.

Worthy Home Membership

The development of qualities that make the individual a worthy family member (both by contributing to the family and deriving benefit from it) should be taught through literature, music, social studies, and art curriculum, with an emphasis on both the past and the present.

Vocation

The object is development of the student's self-knowledge and exploration of a variety of careers for selecting one that is personally suitable. The student should seek to understand the vocational-community relationship and consider becoming one who teaches others in the school or community workplace.

Civic Education

The goal is development and awareness and concern for the community through knowledge of social organizations and commitment to civic morality. Curriculum emphasis is on social diversity, cooperation, democratic organization of the school, and group problem solving.

Worthy Use of Leisure

Education should give the students the skills to enrich the mind, body, spirit, and personality through their leisure activities and recreation, especially in the curriculum areas of music, fine and performing arts, literature, social issues, and science.

Ethical Character

Instilling in students the ideas of personal responsibility and initiative develops character and ethical behavior, especially when those are emphasized and exemplified in the selection of teaching methods and in the school organization.

Source: Based on the original report available at http://tmh.floonet.net/articles/cardprin.html

progressive education agenda. One commitment was to help assimilate millions of newly arriving immigrants for life in America by studying our history and language. The rest of the agenda for progress was large: women's suffrage, conservation, reining in corporate monopoly, ending abuse in industry, child safety, food and drugs, and sanitation. While there were no specific courses addressing a particular agenda item, curriculum changes did include new studies such as civics, health, and the social studies based on the new social sciences and courses in the sciences, all of which reflected the agenda and were intended to prepare students for life and effective citizenship. The only jolt to the idea of progress and the social, political agenda to achieve it was the coming of World War I and the failed peace that followed.

The Common Good Versus Local Control

The two seminal events of 1918 were the armistice that ended the Great War and the NEA's Committee on the Reorganization of Secondary Education report, the famous *Cardinal Principles of Secondary Education*. Both events signify an end and a beginning. Although the war had interrupted the flow of progressive ideas about social, economic, and political changes, it returned with renewed vigor in the years after the war and into the 1930s. The NEA report of 1918 is the beginning of the educational strain of progressivism, confirmed in 1919 with the formation of the Progressive Education Association (PEA). As at least the symbol of this reform movement in education and schooling, it would last until 1959, a casualty to another era of school reform (Graham, 1967).

The progressive episode is important for several reasons. It was a sharp clash of perspectives about the purposes for schools and the matter of control, two issues that would define the dialogue throughout the 20th century. However, embedded in all the rhetoric was the controlling and quintessential issue, the curriculum. Ultimately, the product that mattered was what was to be taught based on the particular, articulated perspective. Simply put, it was all about the curriculum! The key questions were curriculum questions: What specific curriculum was best? and How do you determine that? Recall from a previous discussion in this chapter that in very simple terms, the traditionalist saw curriculum as based on subject matter, the disciplines of knowledge. What was traditional in subject matter was of course contingent on the time. Remember that traditional-reform clashes in the early to mid–19th century were essentially over old versus new knowledge, the classics or the sciences. What was new then was now the old, the traditional, of the progressive debate. Progressives wanted to reform the particulars of schooling, teaching, instruction, and concern for the individual learners through the curriculum. This was a new emphasis. Centering on the individual and his or her needs meant a broadening of the curriculum to include new content. With the landmark Smith-Hughes Act of 1917 establishing vocational education and in the writings, journal articles, and reports issued through the PEA, NEA, and other organizations, there is an emphasis on the curriculum to serve the individual, to *fit* individual needs, to be comprehensive in content. By focusing on curriculum, traditionalists and progressives were also forced to consider the people who did curriculum work: teachers, other school persons, and the larger special interest community—professors, state and national leaders, and publishers.

Problems of Progressivism

The PEA was the center of all this ferment. Originally founded by teachers, the PEA also became a home for professors in the new world of schools or colleges and departments of education. A host of professorates in education at universities in the East and Midwest evolved in the years after 1890, those at Harvard; Teachers College, Columbia University; Michigan; and Wisconsin being among the most prominent. Arguably the greatest influence came from the professors at Teachers College, Columbia, a number of whom served as president of the PEA. They, along with others, also influenced thinking about schools and curriculum through articles in a number of university journals that were started after 1890. The more important of these early scholarly publications were the *School Review* (now the *American Journal of Education*), *Journal of Elementary Education,* both from the University of Chicago, and *Teachers College Record* from Teachers College, Columbia University. In addition, there were other outlets. The National Society for the Study of Education (NSSE) published influential yearbooks, and the PEA and the NEA had their own association journals and yearbooks. What is of interest is that for a movement begun by teachers and laypersons, it was soon taken over by college and university professors.

In addition to progressive leadership and dissemination of ideas through national publications, two other important developments emerged during the progressive years. First was the unfolding of a division between practitioners in schools and the professorate in the colleges. This was exemplified by the dominance of the latter in the journal writings and other publications and in the leadership of various organizations. This divide would continue to mark the debates about schools and curriculum to the present. The second was the development of curriculum theory. As noted in Chapter 6, theory in curriculum was of a particular form, and theorizing was considered important in describing a curriculum, especially if a curriculum were being constructed as means to the ends, those being, for example, the Cardinal Principles. The arrival of college and university faculty as the source of knowledge about curriculum and curriculum development, along with the reliance on theory, created problems for progressives because it drew attention away from the school, the place of practice, and the contribution teachers could make to curriculum knowledge (Popkewitz, 1987).

The problems of progressivism were not just within the movement; they were also external. From the late 1920s through the 1930s, the experience of the Great Depression and the specter of German and Japanese aggression in Europe and China distracted the public from reform. Unfortunately, this occurred as the PEA began the Eight-Year Study in 1935. The results, published in 1942, were in essence that a traditional curriculum was no better than the various progressive ones in determining success in colleges. Unfortunately, the published results were buried in the dark days of World War II and, with the dissipation of the progressive education movement, not influential after war's end in 1945.

The Progressive Legacy

The Eight-Year Study of the PEA in the 1930s stands as both the first major study about curriculum matters and the first example of a good research plan and methodology in the general field of curriculum and education. The study was important also to curriculum as an emerging area of scholarship and practice. The purpose of the study was to compare the effects of the progressive and standard curriculums being used in schools. The progressive curriculums were of many stripes, the standard curriculum you would recognize as math science, literature, and so forth. The complexity of the evaluation plan, its longitudinal intent (5 years), articulation of the standard (the familiar math, science, literature, etc.) and progressive curriculums (varied patterns) under study, and selection of schools and students to participate were without parallel to that time. The cadre of participants included a mix of academic and school practitioners. The findings summarized were two. First, there was no difference in the success of students from the progressive or standard curriculum. That may not seem significant, but what it meant was that the progressive curriculum was the equal of the traditional, or classic, curriculum. The arguments for the superiority of the classic, standard curriculum were now moot. A secondary finding was that students from the progressive experience were more apt to be social and civic minded as indicated by their adjustment to college and their collegiate extracurricular activities. The series of publications that tell the story were published in 1942 and 1943 (Aikin). And, after the war, the PEA dwindled, and the results did not receive attention or wide distribution. That monumental study aside, most research purely about curriculum withered or became collateral with studies about instruction or other matters educational. Fortunately, the legacy of the Eight-Year Study lived on in the work of Ralph Tyler and others in their work with graduate students.

The second important legacy of the progressives was curriculum development as key curriculum work. While inquiry into curriculum and curriculum work is sparse, some collections of early curriculum work, materials, lesson plans, teaching logs, records of classroom visits, and other incidental classroom-related materials, exist and provide valuable insights (see Davis, 2002; Schubert, Schubert, Thomas, & Carroll, 2002). They are materials that give form and describe what doing curriculum development was all about. This work took two forms: (a) the hatching of ideas and their expression as theories about how curriculum development should be done, mostly by college and university faculty; and (b) the actual creation of curriculum. This latter activity was often school or school district based and much the province of classroom teachers. In its earliest incarnation, curriculum development was not the extensive process you think of or encounter today. It was limited to the formulation of curriculum consistent with reform efforts of the time. The addition of science, art and manual work courses, kindergarten programs, and other reforms often required an organized creation of materials by teachers. In this very limited sense, some of the earliest curriculum development actions were recorded in the late 19th century in the St. Louis, Missouri schools under Superintendent William Torrey Harris and in Colonel Francis Parker's schools in Quincy, Massachusetts. Probably one of the best known of the later comprehensive curriculum development programs was the one established in Denver, Colorado, in the 1920s during the tenure of Superintendent Jesse Newlon. Cities were the primary locations of curriculum development (or curriculum construction, as it was sometimes called) activities from coast to coast, and it had the character of a national movement. From the late 1890s through the late 1920s, the confluence of efforts to improve life, the can-do American belief in progress, the surge of immigrants who had to be assimilated, and the leadership of Americans like Theodore Roosevelt and Jane Addams led to an era of spectacular political, social, and economic progress of which the educational part was centered in the PEA. The movement's significance lies in the more expansive meaning it gave to the practical side of curriculum work. In addition to teaching the curriculum, the development activities by teachers to create curriculum assumed new importance. Now, both teaching the curriculum and developing curriculum defined the practice and work of curriculum. Curriculum development activities also served as a crucial contact point between academic professors and school personnel. Collage and university faculty often served as consultants to school districts engaged in curriculum development projects. The school and classroom became the focus for applying theoretical ideas to curriculum matters. Curriculum development became a professional activity, a conjunction of academic ideas about curriculum, the certainties of teacher practice, and the realities of what curriculum changes were possible to achieve. The central progressive theme was that curriculum would be made useful by its practitioners. In the main, it was the teachers doing curriculum work at the level of practice, the classroom, which was different. With the emergence of curriculum development as an important form of curriculum work, there was and is a tendency to think of everything that is proposed in curriculum as new. Instead, what are encountered today are refrains of yesterday's discussions removed in time but little changed in substance. Curriculum development, the activity, remains an important part of curriculum work, and the historical record suggests there is still much to learn from those early pioneers.

Defense Education

World War II segued into the cold war, which lasted until the demise of the Soviet Union in 1991. The issue that dominated developments in America was national security. The interstate highway system was started not just to improve transportation but also to allow ease of military movement from one part of the nation to another. A defense department was created to coordinate the military branches. As justified under the doctrine of containment, communist expansion was to be held in check. The resulting wars in Korea, Vietnam, and various other skirmishes and confrontations dominated the last half of the 20th century. The effect of all this on schooling and curriculum was to reassert subject matter as the content but with new subject matter from the disciplines, the traditional sciences, mathematics, and emerging technological sciences.

The Sputnik Era

Perceived threats such as communism require development of a course or courses of action that ultimately result in policies designed to move institutions in a desired direction. As for the major political parties, agreement on the common enemy, communism, necessitated a consensus about educational goals, if not always about the means. Translated into policy, schools were to prepare students primarily for entrance into colleges or equivalent study. The curriculum would emphasize preparation in mathematics and sciences; students with science and mathematical potential would be especially encouraged. Early induction into scientific research would be developed through college and university grants and fellowships in undergraduate and graduate study. Policies developed along those lines were based on reports and papers developed by Vannevar Bush and the National Science Foundation (NSF). The NSF realized that for those initiatives to be successful, significant change would have to occur in the school curriculums throughout the United States at all levels from elementary through high school. It is important to remember that federal involvement in schools and schooling had always been minimal and indirect. It was minimal in that there was no cabinet-status department, only the U.S. Office of Education headed by a commissioner. It was indirect because, historically, authority for things such as schools and schooling was held to be at the local level under authority of a state and its constitution. The federal government had involved itself tangentially in supporting general public education through such legislation as the Land Ordinances of 1785 and 1789 and land grants to the railroads constructing the transcontinental railroads in the 1860s. By providing land, there was no further need to be involved with the type of schools or their curriculum. The matter of federal involvement remained benign because there was no U.S. department of education, only a Bureau of Education placed in the U.S. Department of the Interior in 1869. It was not until the designation of a U.S. commissioner of education in 1888 that the federal role began to take on importance. Even then, the role of the commissioner of education was limited to speaking about education rather than influencing policy development and legislation. With the exception of the 1917 Smith-Hughes Act supporting development of vocational schooling, there was no further significant federal involvement in national schooling and curriculum until after 1955.

On October 4, 1957, the Soviet Union sent Sputnik into space. That event was significant for two reasons. It was a stunning blow because the Russians were the first to send something into space. Why weren't we first? Second, because it was lifted into space via an intercontinental ballistic missile, which suggested both Russian missile superiority and the possibility that they could hit the American East Coast. What followed was a harsh introspection into why we were not prepared for this challenge. The spotlight fell on the schools and the curriculum. The national response was a dramatic change in federal policy that would change schooling, curriculum, and the control of both.

Science and Mathematics

Nearly fifty years removed, it is difficult to convey the fear that Sputnik generated and the bitter fault finding that ensued. Politicians, editorial pundits, and critics such as Admiral Hyman Rickover, father of the nuclear submarine program, and historian Arthur Bestor focused on the failure of the schools and curriculum. These critics charged that a general educational deterioration had occurred, resulting in a failure to achieve the scientific excellence necessary to meet the Russian threat. Two culprits were identified. First was the existence of a soft curriculum, one that did not require sufficient study in the sciences and mathematics. Second was the inadequate training of teachers in appropriate subject matter, specifically science and math. Theoretical approaches to curriculum, the emphasis on the learner and learning, and the need for learners to have a curriculum that fit their interests—all those things associated with progressivism— were now suspect. Critics claimed that the progressive approach to schooling and curriculum had undermined the need for scientists and engineers and the appropriate scientific training.

New Schoolbooks and Curriculum Workers

The federal government, based on policy ideas suggested by the NSF, led the response to the Soviet challenge. There were essentially two federal initiatives, one to influence curriculum change in schools and the other to train teachers in those curriculum changes. In 1958, the United States Congress passed and President Eisenhower signed into law the National Defense Education Act (NDEA). The provisions of the act implemented a new national policy. The federal government began to exercise a gradual influence over schooling and the curriculum on a national scale. Funding programs required adherence to federal guidelines; the carrot was the funding; the stick was the set of requirements that the school or district had to fulfill or adhere too. Over time, district budgets and, later, state budgets became dependent in varying degrees on both the need for the programs and the funding that came with them. Considering the overall curriculum, the initial impact of the NDEA was indirect. The NSF established a series of curriculum projects in critical sciences and math, resulting in the creation of advanced materials such as the then-new math and project physics. Along with the curriculum development projects went training for teachers funded by the NSF. The intent was to influence change through an infusion of new materials and teacher preparation in them. This was not a direct challenge to local control of curriculum or teaching. The effects were more subtle. The curriculum projects as they were extended into foreign languages and the social sciences required several new curriculum considerations. How should the new knowledge be integrated into the curriculum? What knowledge would have to be left out to accommodate what could be covered in the school year? These were questions about the scope of the curriculum. A second series of question arose when curriculum sequence was considered. How should the scope be organized so that the progression through it would be appropriate for each grade level as students passed upward from kindergarten to 12th grade? Was it necessary to give it a K–12 configuration or was it at an advanced level and appropriate only in a series for upper grades? If so, what prerequisites should be placed in which lower grades so that students were prepared for the new curriculum when they arrived? Progressives had wrestled with these same constraints but in a theoretical way and from a variety of perspectives, not from a single, common, traditional subject matter perspective, and not in the formalized setting of large-scale curriculum projects with teams of experts working together to resolve curriculum matters.

Out of all the work done under the NSF auspices and in spite of the failure to influence long-term changes in classroom practice, there were some residual curriculum effects. One was how the curriculum projects influenced schoolbook publishing. The curricular scope and sequence built into project materials meant publishers had to create textbooks in a series in each subject that moved up through the grades. For example, at the elementary school level, content designated in the fifth grade depended on preparation in content at the fourth grade, and that depended on the third-grade content. Textbooks in middle or high school also had to address the matter of scope and sequence. Text adoption meant a district or school would consider a sequence of texts, K–6, for example, rather than selecting a different publisher's text for each separate grade or subject. Selection among publisher texts depended on the district's consideration of the quality of scope and sequence in publisher's offerings. This scrutiny forced publishers to improve the quality of textbook content by obtaining up-to-date knowledge and using the services of both scholars in the various disciplines and curriculum experts in preparing the materials for teacher use. The result was materials containing current knowledge and produced in interesting, if not entertaining, formats with supporting pictures, films, and teacher kits. All this was intended to give the teacher useful resources, enhance instructional options, and complement teaching across a range of student differences in the individual classroom.

The emphasis on scope and sequence in developing new curriculum materials in the 1950s and 1960s suggests a formalizing and standardization of curriculum development. However, as you can recall from earlier discussion in this chapter, the story of curriculum is more often a result of unconnected, dispersed actions by scores of curriculum workers and the evolution of their roles. From its birth at the end of the 19th century and in the beginning of the 20th century, a number of roles and activities became associated with curriculum work. Initially, the association was indistinct from the more general notions about education, schools, and schooling. As noted before, curriculum did not have a separate significance as meaning what the schools taught. More often, the reference was to the subjects or to what schools should teach rather than separating schooling into curriculum, instruction, assessment, and evaluation, as is the tendency today. Those working with schools in the early period of curriculum formation can be formed into roughly two groups. One group worked either in the school or in direct support; they were teachers and other school or district employees. The second group of workers was involved in a more general way. They were not employees but worked to support schools and, more specifically, the schooling process itself.

Obviously, teachers were at the center of schooling and most closely associated with curriculum work. The curriculum, as stated in syllabi or other written documents, absolutely depended on how the teacher organized the curriculum and engaged it. Larry Cuban has ably portrayed this in his book *How Teachers Taught* (1984). There were three curriculum sources. One was the teacher and what he or she knew about the various subjects under his or her responsibility. Another was the textbook and other material available to convey the curriculum content: maps and other curriculum materials, such as sticks for counting. Third was whatever the students knew and could contribute. This latter source was useful in the Lancastrian instructional system and in rural schools. In both, there was often a mix of different-aged students where the teacher used older students to tutor and instruct younger students either one-on-one or in small groups.

Schoolmen was a term for another role and type of work. Although the term is no longer in general use, it usually referred to principals, superintendents, and others charged with the responsibility of overseeing and managing schools. Women were predominant in teaching and men in administration, thus the emphasis on school*men*. Another role, that of the specialist at the school district level, evolved in the 1920s as curriculum development activities became important in the more innovative school districts. As work differentiation in curriculum, instruction, evaluation, and other types of work grew in importance, roles in those areas of work assumed more specialized meaning, and reference to a curriculum, instructional, or evaluation specialist became more customary. With the growth of administrative structures and bureaucracy, it became common to have directors or assistant superintendent levels of specialization.

The expression *school patron* seems foreign today but it was a designation often used in the early years of the 20th century into the 1920s. Patrons were the general public, the people who supported schools and worked for them as laypersons doing their civic duty. Many were involved in the progressive movement and worked tirelessly in support of social improvements such as sanitation, schools, housing, family assistance services, food and drug safety, child labor laws, prison reform, and women's rights, particularly the vote. As public oversight of schooling increased, publicly elected school boards grew in popularity. This experiment in public accountability and support made the patron's role important and influential. Accountability shifted from appointed or elected superintendents toward elected school boards made up of local citizens. This democratizing, the opening up to citizen involvement, meant that schooling and attendant policy decisions about curriculum, instruction, personnel, and financial matters was shifting toward the shared lay public-professional responsibility for schools that exists today.

Academics, the college and university professorial variety, were another distinct group of outsiders drawn to the study of schools and schooling. From their academic settings, college and university faculty engaged in many aspects of schooling: initiating early evaluative activities, theorizing about learning and curriculum, and engaging teachers in the construction of classroom curriculum materials. The creation of academic departments, schools, and colleges of education began the professionalization of teaching, administration, and other roles. The day had arrived for credentialing teaching, the entry to practice, as the threshold into other school roles and work.

The Comprehensive High School

The general thrust of the post-Sputnik reaction was twofold: a concern about curriculum per se, and the kind of school that would fit the curriculum. The curriculum discussion evoked three considerations. First was the matter of curriculum reform, the anchoring of subject matter firmly in the curriculum. Given the apparent resolution of that curriculum matter, attention turned to a second concern: which students would be the beneficiaries of the curriculum. Third was how the school curriculum should be organized for those students. If the curriculum was to be effectively delivered, a general standardized model was needed so that implementation in rural, suburban, or city locations would provide for uniform delivery and access to the curriculum. What evolved was, like the popular 3-D movies of the time, a three-dimensional curriculum robust enough to address the general college preparatory and vocational interests of students. This new curriculum proposal did not mesh with the existing architectural configurations; something new was needed. As Benjamin Franklin, in an earlier time, had proposed the academy in response to comparable concerns, James Bryant Conant, former president of Harvard University and supporter of the NSF, similarly advanced a new approach to schooling. Conant's model for democratic public schooling was the comprehensive high school. With the support of the American Association of Secondary School Principals, Conant published two reports, *The American High School Today* in 1959 and *The Comprehensive High School* in 1967. The recommendations in these reports were widely disseminated and implemented. Although the emphasis was on the high school, the elementary and middle or junior high school curriculums would, of necessity, also have to be changed.

Figure 7.2   The Comprehensive High School

After two years of studying high schools in the United States, James B. Conant put forward a set of proposals for reforming the high school in America. The proposals were widely disseminated and became an influential blueprint for reforming high school services and curriculum.

Rationale

Too many small schools with uneven provision of curriculum and services hinder national progress. It is more economical and efficient to have fewer high schools offering a comprehensive set of services and curriculum to a larger number of students. Providing more options and services provides more opportunity and promotes democracy.

Recommendations for Services

All students need counseling and guidance services, but it is especially important for the academically able students who will go to college. Students who have special academic or other needs should be provided with appropriate services.

Curriculum Recommendations

The *academically able student* (college bound) should have 4 years each of English, mathematics (one course in calculus), and foreign languages, and 3 years each of science, social studies (with a government-economics course in Grade 12), physical education, and art and music. The school organization and year should be adjusted so students could take the courses necessary in each year to complete diploma requirements.

Other students should have access to tracks leading to life work choices. Females should have access to courses in typing, stenography, the use of clerical machines, and home economics, and males should have access to courses in distributive education, vocational work (farming emphasis), trades, and industrial, as befits the local community.

Source: Conant (1959).

The elements in Conant's model (see Figure 7.2) conveniently complemented the new subject-based emphasis in curriculum and other recommendations of the NSF and paralleled suggestions given in the Harvard report of 1945. The comprehensive high school model and the 3-D curriculum would remain, with minor tinkering, the standard for American high schools into the 1980s. The high school curriculum scope and sequence would also be the measure in setting the scope and sequence for elementary and middle or junior high school curriculum.

INTO THE 21ST CENTURY: NEW POLICY INITIATIVES AND THE CURRICULUM

The history of curriculum is not necessarily the same as the history of American education or of schools. Schools and schooling could be affected in ways that did not force major changes in the scope, sequence, or content of curriculum. There were, however, in the last 50 years of the 20th century and the beginning of the 21st, a number of significant actions and events that dramatically affected education and schooling and, less dramatically but more important, curriculum.

Curriculum for Equality

Two of the most decorated units in World War II were made up of African American and Japanese American men. The total war experience had been fought to preserve freedom and access to the good life. After the war, even with the availability of the GI Bill of Rights, neither of those was immediately achievable for African American, Japanese American, or other historic immigrant minorities often referred to as "hyphenated Americans." Returning to a de facto segregated society, GIs, especially minority veterans, would not accept second-class citizenship. The time was ripe for change. The 1954 United States Supreme Court decision in the case of Brown v. The Board of Education of Topeka is one of those watershed historic events that mark critical, compelling change in all institutions in a society. With that case and a series of others that followed, the Court in effect ended all forms of segregation in the United States. The focus was, of course, on social reconstruction through legal means; through schooling, and, more subtly, through changes in the curriculum.

The civil rights movement and the "War on Poverty" that began after the Brown decision made essential use of schooling to desegregate America and to attack poverty. The Civil Rights Act of 1964 and the Elementary and Secondary Education Act of 1965 stand historically as a confirmation of the federal role to effect social and cultural change on a national basis. Two parallel movements, one directed at early childhood and the other at learners with special needs, established national policy and federal responsibility in new areas. The Head Start program, enacted under Title I of ESEA; the Education for All Handicapped Children Act of 1974; and Title IX on gender equity extended the federal role in education. With expanding federal leadership and financial support sprinkled throughout the various titles of each act, these programs in effect created a dependency further aligning local and state participation in federal programs for schools with federal policy initiatives in Washington. Keep in mind that participation carried with it a legal requirement to meet any federal mandates or standards attached to the funds. Each program also created a constituency whose main interest was the continuation of its program and appropriate funding. These were the new entitlements that signified a permanent role for the federal government in coordinating a national agenda on schools, schooling, and curriculum. Politics and schooling were enjoined nationally, as symbolized in the creation of the United States Department of Education in 1979.

Curriculum for Diversity

The change in curriculum was additive and incremental. First it was changes in the textbooks: pictures and stories were used to reflect the cultural and ethnic diversity, an expression of human capital and worth as well. Later it was addition of black history and other locally significant ethnic histories: Hispanic, Native American, Croatian American, and so forth, each adding something new to an increasingly diverse American population. As television fare became varied, so did the materials available for schools: new books told new stories, and access to the mix of the young provided the conversational glue that gives credence to relationships and sociocultural understanding through the Internet, music, and other technology. The changes in schools and schooling included class size; length of school day and year; instructional time allocated for teaching; multicultural emphasis in classroom materials, assessment, and evaluation; and broadened direct-to-school compensatory and support services. Curriculum was also affected, but in a more cosmetic sense. For example, a longer day and year might provide more time for curriculum engagement or a need to add to the available materials, but it did not require a marshaling of resources and a major commitment to make those adjustments. The critical point is that the expansion of federal programs affected curriculum in minor rather than major ways—not in any deeper sense of removing components but in the tinkering with what was there. The addition of more algebra requirements only changes the mathematics curriculum, as does requiring three more courses in biological-physical sciences. Neither example is a direct result of desegregation, civil rights laws, or antipoverty legislation, but either might be a response to some need for equity and equality, as in providing females with such courses. The points of impact where movements and actions cause change is like politics, always local, because blanket policy such as Title IX, civil rights, or similar laws achieve their particular importance in the minds and lives of the people in the elementary school, the middle school, and the high school through which they pass.

Political Control of Schooling and Curriculum

In the 20 plus years since the 1983 publication *A Nation At Risk* called for change, schooling in America has seen one wave of reform after another, many continuing as another begins. As depicted in Figure 7.3, the waves of reform have ranged from cosmetic change or quick fixes, taking action for action's sake, to thoughtful concerns for long-term monitoring of learning: the National Assessment of Educational Progress (NAEP), instituting both a tradition of research and a database; and the latest embodiment of reform, the 2001 No Child Left Behind Act signed into law in 2002. If there is a phrase marking all this reform, it is political control for accountability. Political control refers to the desire of political parties, interest groups, and others to have particular issues addressed through schools and the curriculum. The more familiar issues are those about charter schooling and vouchers, a different take on entitlements. A second set of interests has to do with control. One aspect of control is the jockeying for leadership reminiscent of the progressive versus traditionalist give-and-take in the

Figure 7.3   Waves of Reform in American Schooling, 1983–2005

Wave 1: Cosmetic Changes

This includes modest increases in diploma requirements, lengthening school day and year, and teacher certification upgrades, particularly in elementary mathematics and science course requirements and secondary subject majors.

Wave 2: Restructuring

The restructuring includes the impetus to study school effects and do research to determine what makes an effective school. Important research emerges in Goodlad's *A Place Called School* (1984) and from the National Assessment of Educational Progress. Periodic national conferences on school reform (1998, 2000) emphasize planning for reform and accountability. Charter school and voucher concepts emerge. No Child Left Behind enunciates a new federal strategy.

Wave 3: Curriculum Reform

Emphasis is given to basic skills development and remediation in elementary curriculum and increased requirements for science and math in secondary schools. An increase in school time is provided for curriculum teaching. Linking of curriculum-instruction-assessment emerges as a critical part of the movement toward standards. Added course work is required in teacher education programs.

Wave 4. Teacher Education Reform

There is a redefining of research in education with emphasis on the scientific base of research. Revision of requirements in teacher certification through optional certification tracks challenge college, university, school, or department of education control of teacher education. No Child Left Behind requires schools to certify that qualified teachers are in assigned teaching positions.

20th century. The second is about controlling curriculum decision making, particularly the policy-making function and especially where that affects the content of textbooks and other school materials.

Entitlements

Entitlements are benefits for which people automatically qualify as defined by some entity such as a government. You have a birthright of guarantees under your state and United States constitutions. They can be political (right to vote), economic (social security), social (civil rights), and educational (special education). Entitlements are controversial, and it is important to make clear the kind of entitlement being discussed. Issues about economic entitlements such as welfare and price supports are often contentious. Until recently, entitlements involving schooling and curriculum have not been troublesome because the issues have been about *inclusion* rather than *exclusion*. For example, historically, support for public schools and curriculum has remained stable over time; if citizens wanted to opt out to private or parochial schools, they could do so. Public education, after all, had a long-standing tradition and served the *public* interest, which included all citizens so defined. Taxes paid by all citizens paid for an entitlement for all citizens. Proponents of recent reform proposals, charter schools and vouchers, for example, argue for a different kind of entitlement, one for exclusion from the general welfare to special welfare inclusive of a particular interest or philosophy. For curriculum, this might mean the development of very special curriculum different from that in public schools. Vouchers would mean choosing other nonpublic schools, private, parochial, or some other option. These are complex matters to be explored further in Chapter 13.

Curriculum Wars

The so-called curriculum wars refer to contemporary issues about the content of curriculum. In *The Twentieth-Century Textbook Wars* (2003), Gerard Giordano traces the various conflicts and the particular groups and their agendas. Textbooks are at the heart of the controversy because they represent the point at which curriculum can be controlled that directly affects the classroom. Every state has some textbook and curriculum materials review process for each area of the curriculum. Books and student reading lists are favorite targets in literature courses. Inclusion or exclusion of evolution and replacement or equal time with intelligent design is a continuing issue in science. Content in the history and civics curriculum is controversial as are the contents of health and physical education courses. In addition, there are writers, journalists, and commentators in the general public who publish books, articles, and reviews on educational matters. As Michael Apple points out in several of his books (1979, 1991), much of the discussion is driven by ideology. Governors, presidents, and their affiliate political parties weigh in with publications and pronouncements about curriculum ideas, issues, and content, especially as part of political party platforms in election years.

Standards and No Child Left Behind

It is the rise of the accountability movement, the reporting of test results and the inevitable explaining of differences, which has led to the reemergence of curriculum as a central concern. This increased accountability (see Stotsky, 2000) and continued growth of federal control is evident in the provisions of the 2001 No Child Left Behind legislation signed into law in 2002. The movement of authority and responsibility from local districts to state and federal levels is one important change. The development of standards is another. Whereas the current emphasis is on states developing their own standards, this will not, as Squires (2004) points out, create the necessary alignment for national comparisons because there is no single set of standards that gives a measure of common equivalency. As required testing proceeds, several results are possible. It is likely that local control of the curriculum will be ceded to external authorities, and not necessarily to those who are responsible to the public. It is also likely that the idea of curriculum balance, the matching of curriculum and learner, will recede and the knowledge-to-performance relationship will ascend as the matter of testing rises in importance. Regardless of what is proposed, whether it embraces multiple teaching agents or plans to reorganize the schooling pattern, curriculum balance must address the curriculum question first and in the broadest, most interpretive way reprise Spencer's original question about what knowledge is of most worth as that relates to the purposes schooling serves in a democratic republic. This is a continuing issue of great importance and is a topic for further exploration in Chapter 13, Interpreting Contemporary Curriculum Issues.

PERSPECTIVE INTO PRACTICE:
Examples From the History of Curriculum Change

Curriculum Change	Elementary School	Secondary School
Colonial	The three Rs in a moral–religion context with an emphasis on reading and basic arithmetic numbers and counting.	The classic curriculum of the seven liberal arts—grammar, rhetoric, dialect, arithmetic, geometry, astronomy, and music.
18th and 19th Century	Dame and common schools curriculum of the three Rs with additional history, geography, and some general science.	Modification of the classic curriculum includes biological and physical sciences.
Progressivism	Emphasis on early childhood learning and activity curriculum with kindergarten and increasing the curriculum to include more years of the three Rs into six grades, with introduction of the social studies K–6, art, and music studies.	Multiple curriculum options and desegregated gender learning, physical education, gymnasium, and studied activities added. Lengthening of grades to 12th grade and introduction of balanced curriculum with math, science, social sciences, physical and health, and language to anticipate diverse learning interests.

(Continued)

(Continued)

Defense Education	Renewal of math and science and latest scholarship into textbooks. Increase in mathematic and science requirements. Language study emphasis.	Revised and expanded mathematics and science curriculums with more requirements for graduation. Lengthening of the school year and days to accommodate increased curriculum demands. Comprehensive high school model offers more vocational college options and curriculum.
Federal Policy Initiatives, 1980–2005	Reemphasis on science and mathematics needs and increased emphasis on elementary curriculum. Multicultural recognition of diversity in text materials with the addition of minorities in history and social studies, and in stories in language arts; and diversified English as a second language and special education programs.	Experiments with secondary school remedial programs in basic science and mathematics. Focus on diversity through English as a second language, special learning programs to promote competence in basic skills, questioning of content in school texts, and increase in curriculum requirements keyed to testing and standards.

Summary and Conclusions

From colonial times to the present, questions about schools and schooling have ultimately been about the curriculum: what kind and for whom. Curriculum issues have often been buried in other discussions, but they have always required answers in whatever context. Spencer's question about what knowledge is of most worth is still viable today. The struggles to use curriculum and schools as change agents are basic to understanding American social and institutional history. From the colonial era, through the 19th century expansion of knowledge and the progressive challenge, to the present, curriculum has steadily become a key to understanding the social-political affairs of the nation. What the curriculum has been and meant at any particular time is a reflection of the nation itself, both an expression of the thinking about the future and a reflection on the past. The history of curriculum suggests that responses to Spencer's question, whether made today or tomorrow, will continue to be contingent on the prevailing ideas about progress, the role of schooling, and the nature of the social, cultural, economic, and political milieu as the nation evolves.

Critical Perspective

1. Schools are often said to be key institutions in creating social change. Can you identify examples that suggest schools were directly responsible for changes? If you can't, does that suggest that perhaps that claim is more myth than reality?

2. Compare and contrast curriculum ideas of the progressives with those of reformers in the Sputnik era.

3. It has been suggested that a key factor in the great expansion of public schooling from the 1880s to the 1930s was the development of American cities. How would urban growth affect schooling and cause changes in the curriculum?

4. From your personal experience, can you identify ways Title IX or the War on Poverty or desegregation after the Brown decision directly affected your school curriculum?

5. Using Figures 7.1 and 7.2, compare and contrast the curriculum proposals of the NEA committee and James B. Conant. Are there any comparisons with those proposals and the No Child Left Behind Act? The Iowa Department of Education has a useful summary of the No Child Left Behind Act and its predecessors at http://www.state.ia.us/educate/ecese/nclb/

6. Gender, equity, and multicultural issues have surrounded curriculum deliberations from the colonial period. What is the contemporary meaning of each word? How are the three related?

7. Select a local or national daily newspaper and find articles about educational reform. What positions are being represented and to what degree are organizations or spokespersons expressing an ideological, special interest, or partisan view?

Resources for Curriculum Study

1. The story of schooling in the colonial period can be found in any number of educational histories such as Joel Spring's *The American School, 1642–1985* (1986) or in general histories such as Daniel Boorstin's *The Americans: The Colonial Experience* (1958). Lawrence Cremin's *American Education: The Colonial Experience, 1607–1783* (1970) and Merle Curti's *The Social Ideas of American Educators* (1959) are still definitive sources. Lewis B. Wright's *The Cultural Life*

of the American Colonies (1957) is an excellent source on the social and cultural life of the colonies.

2. It is important to make clear that what is known about early curriculum is inferred from more general discussions about what teachers taught, an emphasis on instructional methods, and what classrooms were like in terms of their physical layout and materials. To understand what the curriculum was like is a matter of dipping into the teacher accounts, syllabi, courses of study, and other documents that give a picture of curriculum and who worked with it. Three excellent sources for locating primary accounts are David Tyack's *The One Best System* (1974), Larry Cuban's *How Teachers Taught* (1984), and Schubert et al. *Curriculum Books* (2003). All three also offer a clarifying synthesis that places each particular discussion of curriculum in a timely context.

3. For those interested in the stirring of ideas that began the march toward a conception of curriculum, several sources are recommended. Herbert Kliebard's *The Struggle for the American Curriculum, 1893–1958* (1986) is excellent on the rise of curriculum in that period. For the importance of Herbert Spencer in the development of modern knowledge and on the issue of what knowledge is of most worth, see Robert Nisbet's most useful *History of the Idea of Progress* (1980) and Herbert Kliebard's chapter, "The Effort to Reconstruct the Modern Curriculum," in Beyer and Apple's book *The Curriculum* (1998).

4. The curriculum struggles of the past 20-plus years are a part of what has been dubbed the culture wars. A wealth of sources can be found on the Internet. In addition, this cross section of books may be useful in building a context for understanding the diversity of issues and participants: M. Duberman, *Left Out* (1999); and H. L. Gates, Jr., *Loose Cannon: Notes on the Culture Wars* (1995).

References

Aaron, D. (1951). *Men of good hope.* New York: Oxford University Press.

Aikin, W. M. (1942). *The story of the eight-year study.* New York: Harper.

Apple, M. W. (1979). *Ideology and curriculum.* London: Routledge.

Apple, M. W. (1991). Conservative agendas and progressive possibilities: Understanding the wider politics of curriculum and teaching. *Education and Urban Society, 23*(3), 279–291.

Beyer, L., & Apple, M. W. (Eds.). (1998). *The curriculum: Problems, politics, and possibilities.* Albany: State University of New York Press.

Bigelow, J. (1829). *The elements of technology.* Boston: Boston Press.

Boorstin, D. (1958). *The Americans: The colonial experience.* New York: Random House.

Boorstin, D. (1965). *The Americans: The national experience.* New York: Random House.

Burke J. (2003). *Twin tracks.* New York: Simon & Schuster.

Conant, J. B. (1959). *The American high school today.* New York: McGraw-Hill.

Conant, J. B. (1967). *The comprehensive high school.* New York: McGraw-Hill.

Cremin, L. A. (1970). *American education: The colonial experience, 1607–1783.* New York: Harper & Row.

Cuban, L. (1984). *How teachers taught: Constancy and change in American classrooms, 1890–1980.* White Plains, NY: Longman.

Curti, M. (1959). *The social ideas of American educators.* Paterson, NJ: Pageant Books.

Darwin, C. (1995). *On the origin of species.* New York: Gramercy Books/Random House. (Original work published 1859)

Davis, O. L., Jr. (2002). Prelude to professional identity and organization: American public school curriculum workers and their annual meetings, 1927–1929. *Journal of Curriculum and Supervision, 17*(2), 171–183.

Degler, C. N. (1959). *Out of our past.* New York: Harper & Row.

Duberman, M. (1999). *Left out: The politics of exclusion.* New York: Basic Books.

Gates, H. L., Jr. (1995). *Loose cannon: Notes on the culture wars.* New York: Oxford University Press.

Giordano, G. (2003). *Twentieth-century textbook wars.* New York: Peter Lang.

Goodlad, J. (1984). *A place called school.* New York: McGraw-Hill.

Graham, P. A. (1967). *Progressive education from Arcady to academe: A history of the Progressive Education Association.* New York: Teachers College Press

Kliebard, H. M. (1986). *The struggle for the American curriculum 1893–1958.* Boston: Routledge & Kegan Paul.

Nisbet, R. (1980). *The history of the idea of progress.* New York: Basic Books.

Popkewitz, T. S. (Ed.). (1987). *The formation of the school subjects.* New York: Falmer Press.

Rossiter, C. (Ed.). (1961). *The Federalist papers.* New York: Mentor Books, New American Library.

Rudolph, F. (1967). *Curriculum* (Carnegie Council series). San Francisco: Jossey-Bass.

Schubert, W. H., Schubert, A. L. L., Thomas, T. P., & Carroll, W. M. (2002). *Curriculum books: The first hundred years* (2nd ed.). New York: Peter Lang.

Spencer, H. (1861). *Education: Intellectual, moral, and physical.* New York: D. Appleton.

Spring, J. (1986). *The American school, 1642–1985.* New York: McGraw-Hill.

Squires, D. A. (2004). *Aligning and balancing the standards-based curriculum.* Thousand Oaks, CA: Corwin.

Stotsky, S. (Ed.). (2000). *What's at stake in the K-12 standards wars.* New York: Peter Lang.

Tyack, D. B. (1974). *The one best system: A history of American urban education.* Cambridge, MA: Harvard University Press.

Walker, D. F., & Soltis, J. F. (1997). *Curriculum and aims.* New York: Teachers College Press.

Wills, G. (1978). *Inventing America.* Garden City, NY: Doubleday.

Wright, L. B. (1962). *The cultural life of the American colonies.* New York: Harper & Row.

Chapter 8

SOCIAL, CULTURAL, AND INTELLECTUAL FOUNDATIONS OF CURRICULUM

The very moment a teacher initiates a lesson symbolizes a confluence of knowledge and thought from many different sources. At the least, that action represents knowledge of the subject or skill being taught, planning, the curriculum, instruction, evaluation, and the diversity of learning styles, as well as self-knowledge. Teaching draws together both formal knowledge and experience knowledge from practice. Knowledge about curriculum also benefits from knowledge in other disciplines and fields of knowledge, primarily from the humanities and social sciences. Knowledge from those

Figure 8.1   The Impulse for Democracy in America

- **American Revolution** and the ideals expressed in the Declaration of Independence, the United States Constitution, the Bill of Rights, and the Federalist papers
- **Jeffersonian Ideals** about the common man, equality, the important role of schools and schooling, and the advancement of society through science
- **Jacksonian Democracy** and expanding the right to vote as part of the popular sovereignty idea for entrepreneurial freedom and access to schooling for commerce and the trades
- **Civil War and Reconstruction** brought at least a legal end to slavery, and established the potential authority of the federal Constitution over states in matters affecting the Bill of Rights and particularly civil rights through the 14th Amendment
- **Progressive Movement** reaffirmed the idea of America as the land of hope and opportunity regardless of social or ancestral status or country and articulated the new role of schools and schooling for all as the path to success, with government's role to provide for the general welfare, particularly with support for schools
- **Civil Rights Movement** posits the idea that equality before the law applies to all persons and that a new interpretation of government's role is the protection and extension of individual rights through services and programs, particularly as those needs affect access to education and advancement

discipline sources is usually either work related (a method or tool, perhaps) or knowledge in the form of facts or concepts that attach to some knowledge in curriculum in a supporting or clarifying way. Some methods or tools in work, a theory from another discipline, for instance, could be useful in curriculum development. Perhaps a particular learning theory that originated in psychology has promise when coupled with a particular curriculum model or theory. Speculatively, constructivist learning theory might be wedded to, perhaps, a Taba model in developing a curriculum. In the case of a particular concept or fact from a discipline outside curriculum, the anthropological concept of culture is essential for thinking about diversity in learning related to curriculum and in developing curriculum materials that reflect the diversity in a society. All this supporting knowledge took form as either an intellectual, social, or cultural contribution to curriculum.

Another source of knowledge for curriculum comes from the periodic uprisings of democratic spirit that have created and shaped certain American expectations about curriculum and schooling. Examples of these democratic episodes are presented in Figure 8.1.

The turn-of-the-20th-century progressive education movement discussed in Chapter 7 is an example of how the emergence of new ideas of social and cultural democracy become intellectually held expectations for schooling and curriculum and have enduring influence. For example, three trends from that episode have implications for schools and schooling that are worth noting. First, for better or worse, it set the form and content of the school curriculum pretty much as it is today. Second, specialization became important. The curriculum specialist, or curricularists, represented a new role and form of work in schooling. Also, the school curriculum expansion—new subjects in the sciences, advanced mathematics, and the socials studies, for example—demanded that teachers specialize in particular parts of the curriculum. Third was the expansion of colleges and universities and formal kinds of knowledge, the emergence of the social sciences being of particular importance to the education field (Goldin & Katz, 1999). The popular interest in society, culture, government, and democracy in general lent a certain importance to the work of social scientists. From that era forward, reforms and social changes would be argued and justified with knowledge from the social sciences, particularly the theories coming from psychology and philosophy as they were applied by academics to the world of schooling and curriculum.

CURRICULUM AND EPISODES OF SOCIAL AND CULTURAL CHANGE

The years 1890 to 1920 represent one example of the recurring American penchant for self-renewal, a sense of pragmatic progressivism reflected in particular episodes and themes of reform in society, particularly with the conditions of life. The expansion of new universities and graduate education and the association of faculty with reformers gave academics new stature and access to society. This new stature of scholarly activity and expertise lent respectability to whatever was being studied by them, especially in matters of schooling and curriculum. The rise of the professions in general, such as dentistry, medicine, law, and academic professors, plays a central role in reform; the social science professional is a case in point. In sociology, for example, the exploration of social dynamics brought theories and structural schemes to explain human social organization in general and in smaller units such as the family. The case was similar in anthropology, especially the popularizing of culture by Franz Boas and his students at Columbia University. The growing importance of the academy and the new social sciences occurred in tandem with social changes in America. As the 19th century gave way to the 20th century, the American social, economic, and political milieu was in flux. Growth in industry and commerce created a need for labor, more than the nation itself could supply, and cities were initially magnets for immigrants from English-speaking nations and those who followed from other countries in southern and eastern Europe. The life conditions for indigent American poor and the immigrants in the cities were terrible by any measure. People of conscience sought to redress these matters through charitable and philanthropic organizations. It was in the work of social reformers and workers in the settlement house movement at the turn of the century that the applied, practical side of a new social democracy emerged.

Curriculum for Immigrants and the Poor

In contrast to the academic pursuit of grand social science theories and universal laws with which to understand and shape society, early reformers—in reality, early social workers—focused on the immigrant settlement houses in cities such as Chicago, Baltimore, and New York as laboratories for their ideas. Genuine human needs forced workers into a theory-practice dialectic in creating knowledge about social conditions and their amelioration. A consistent theme in those collaborative reform efforts was the belief in schooling and new curriculum to create hope and a path to a better life. Formally organized learning was important in places like Jane Addams Hull House in Chicago as a component in charitable and philanthropic activities. These places provided organized care for infants, programs for young children, new neighborhood schools, physical and recreational programs for youth and adults, and classes about health and hygiene, either within or around the settlement houses and neighborhoods. The curriculum, while by no measure standardized or well furbished with materials, emphasized practical essentials for the socialization and acculturation of immigrants. Children, youth, and adults had access to classes for basic literacy, reading, writing, arithmetic, and citizenship. Being practical, settlement houses held sessions at various times, including evenings. Volunteers were recruited from various social strata in the city; many of these people experienced the reality of the slums while staying and working in the settlement houses. If democracy, the ideal, was to be a reality, it must be for all, and that meant inclusion of the immigrant population and assistance to them and the poor in getting a piece of the American dream.

Curriculum for Teachers and Professionals

Reform eras in America always seem connected to scholars and knowledge. As both McKelvey (1963) and Kahn (1998) note, such episodes of change are usually grassroots affairs for the poorest and lowest economic levels of society by educated people in the middle and upper echelons of American society. When there is an expansion of services and creation of new kinds of work, it often creates a need to organize knowledge in ways that are specific to those emerging professions and work roles. For those wanting to teach, it meant opportunity to pursue a college degree and specialization. As teacher preparation became formalized, 2-year and certificate programs turned into college degree programs and 4 years of study. The curriculum expanded, and there was core course work in instruction, learning, and organizing to teach, the last a legacy of Herbartian methods. Teaching specialization required one to have majors and minors by taking courses in the college disciplines of the school subjects one was going to teach. School administration roles changed. It was no longer just school superintendents and principals; now midlevel curriculum and supervision roles began to be needed as the number of schools grew to meet the requirements of a burgeoning urban population. New service needs emerged in charity and philanthropic work, what would be classified today as social or human services. The colleges and universities essentially established the threshold for entry into the emerging professions and clothed them in degrees and formal study. In many of these institutions, both established and new, students received lectures from and studied under new faculty members from the social sciences, many trained in sociology. Education faculty appointments were often in departments with other designations; philosophy departments were home to many, and others found appointments in university departments with such diverse titles as home administration (Chicago), science and art of teaching (Michigan), pedagogy (Wisconsin), and social ethics (Harvard). Concomitant with the development of professions and formalized study was the entry of women into professional work. The suffrage movement not only got women the right to vote through the passage of the 19th Amendment but also opened up a new world of work mainly in the human service areas of teaching, charity, and philanthropic work. College preparation, especially for women, occurred in normal schools; colleges for women, such as Wellesley; or church-affiliated liberal arts colleges. Some of the better known examples are Jane Addams and Ellen Gates Starr, cofounders of Hull House, the famous settlement house in Chicago, who both graduated from Rockford College in Illinois, which at that time was called Rockford Female Seminary; and Sophonisba Breckenridge, who was instrumental in creating the school of social work at the University of Chicago. The knowledge about society and culture that reform workers brought with them from their college, university, or normal school studies was tested in the reality of the social problems they encountered. Practice knowledge often informed academic knowledge. Under the sponsorship of various charity and philanthropic organizations, special training programs evolved for specific tasks such as teaching, community organization, family, and child care. University departments and faculty often provided the lectures, sharing the platform with experienced practitioners. That spirit of shared practice in preparing teachers and other professionals did not prevail. The demise of progressivism in the early 1950s called for changes in the preparation of teachers and other school professionals. In the 1980s, John Goodlad's study *A Place Called School* (1984) made important suggestions for reframing teacher professional preparation. The creation of the Holmes Group in 1987 (see end-of-chapter resources) furthered the call for reform, emphasizing schools–teacher training institution partnerships called professional development schools. Much as you would expect a doctor to have hospital training, the expectation is that a teacher entering professional service would have an extensive internship in the schools.

Curriculum for Diversity and Equality

E pluribus unum should be a familiar phrase. Taken literally as "one out of many," it refers to the traditional and very American idea of the melting pot and diverse origins of the American people. It is also reflective of the traditional American creed inclusive of equality, justice, and the pursuit of happiness. As noted in Chapter 1, that theme of building nationhood and serving the common good is a continuing one in American schooling and curriculum. Particular episodes have highlighted the struggle to understand and give meaning to the concept of one out of many. Sometimes reform eras provide a confluence of understanding that bring new knowledge into the school curriculum and a search for different forms of schooling. Early 20th-century reformers such as Jane Addams and John Dewey promoted the school as the new social and learning center of the community. Their social conception of schools included the kindergarten; vacation, extended-day, and after-school programs; recreational centers; and night schools for adults. The school curriculum expanded with new subjects such as health; physical and vocational education; and social studies emphasizing civics, citizenship, and naturalization procedures. The urban school evolved as a new kind of institution, a system of schooling from kindergarten through high school, what James Bryant Conant would some fifty years later celebrate as comprehensive in a different wave of school reform. Those early 20th-century changes reflect the democratic American ideal to embrace all those who want to be included and provide the opportunities for successful life and citizenship. That was the dream but not the reality that played out.

In 1966, James Coleman, Earnest Campbell, and others published a study of schooling, *Equality of Educational Opportunity,* which brought into stark relief that access to the pursuit of those ideals was not available to all Americans equally. The ideals of the Declaration of Independence, the Preamble of the United States Constitution, and the Bill of Rights were not being practiced in the most fundamental of institutions, the schools and their curriculum. The Coleman Report (as it has come to be called), along with the Civil Rights Act of 1965, signaled an emerging awareness of the changing American social mixture in American life and institutions, particularly schools and schooling. At issue was the fundamental promise and fulfillment of life for all Americans, the right of the individual to be included in the society and institutions regardless of station or other characteristics. It was a recentering around *e pluribus unum,* a return to the reality of diversity. Issues that began to emerge concerning schooling and curriculum will be familiar to you: gender discrimination; needs of special learners, such as students who are gifted and those with disabilities; access to educational opportunities; and understanding what services or other support any learner might need to attain access and sustain the attainment of their goals. The concerns about diversity attempt to square the fact of inequality with the pursuit of common ideals through adjusting or reforming the appropriate institutions and practices. For schooling, this means making schools responsive to the needs of society and learners through continuous introspection, a dialogue about purposes, context, and the character of learners, as well as the cultural milieus they represent—all aspects of the schooling commonplaces. Certainly the implications for curriculum were clear. Diversity and different learner needs would mean differentiated curriculum, not in the way of setting up tracks but of providing staged curriculum or curriculum-within-a-curriculum or multiple minicurriculums from which a learning path for the individual could be constructed. It would mean a need to create the capacity in state governments, schools, and districts to do curriculum work—the policy making, planning, development, evaluation, and management that would be necessary. The Coleman and Campbell study marks the beginning of a critical episode in American society and institutions that continues into the present. The intellectual explication of diversity that followed led to significant cultural and social awareness of the schooling process and the role of curriculum in the ideology of public life, particularly the search for ideas and policies that would make the pursuit of American ideals available and accessible for each person consistent with their own personal choice to do so.

IMPACT OF THE SOCIAL SCIENCES ON CURRICULUM

Social science, an important collection of disciplines and sources of new knowledge, is the product of the 19th century. The social sciences, referring to the disciplines of psychology, sociology, anthropology, geography, economics, and political science, are also important in the study of American education, schooling, and curriculum. First, they are useful in studying an array of national political and social institutions, including schools and schooling. Second, the bulk of content in the social studies that is part of the school curriculum comes from social science. Third, social science knowledge is used to buttress arguments for particular ideas and proposed policies as different as vouchers and equal opportunity. Fourth, knowledge resources found in those various social science disciplines are useful in curriculum work. A great deal of the knowledge about things social and cultural, about institutions, comes from two particular disciplines, sociology and anthropology. Any discussion of society, culture, and institutions, such as schools, for example, will draw on applicable knowledge from those sources. Although the connections to political science, economics, and geography may initially seem tenuous, they, too, provide insights into curriculum and schooling.

Economics, Politics, and Curriculum

A typical person does not immediately think of a relationship between political science and curriculum. Political science is usually associated with the study of government, political theory, politics, law, public administration, and international relations. Wong (1992) suggests that this perception results from a tradition of viewing schools and school systems as existing in a world of political neutrality. In this world, schools are characterized as being outside politics, possessed of few political power mechanisms, and cocooned in an administrative professionalism that is benign as to external political influences. Given contemporary partisan politics over vouchers, school choice, and control of schooling, that, as Wong points out, is a questionable view. Michael Apple (1991) has corrected, if not destroyed, the perception of the school, schooling, and the curriculum as politically neutral. Political scientists, as they study the politics of power, especially institutional and leadership power, provide a body of knowledge about those political relationships that are relevant to schools and curriculum. Knowledge about tax resources and their allocation, the role of governmental units other than school boards, and, indeed, the total manner in which schools are supported and operated can give insights into curriculum as a product: what is to be taught, and the process of how, by whom, and under what influences it is created. Political science knowledge can help in understanding curriculum as both an instrument of politics and a political instrument.

A particular use of a political science method in education is the development of polling. In the field of education, polls, such as the well-known Phi Delta Kappa annual survey, provide data about the public's views of schools and schooling issues. Over the years, the polling results can offer insights into what the public considers are the purposes schools should serve, certainly a curriculum-related matter because longitudinal research data about public attitudes is very useful in thinking about the relevance of existing curriculum, the purposes it serves, and whether changes are needed. An often overlooked part of the curriculum and political science relationship is the use of curriculum to serve the interests of society through the legal avenues of the state. The state is a political concept, and knowledge about this political science concept is central to understanding the relationship of the state and political activity to education. In the United States, political parties all have some plank in their platform about education, often with specific proposals affecting things from preschool through graduate study. Platform promises may range from proposals for a general increase in funding to selective financing for perceived needs such as Pell grants for the college bound, resources for special education, or new curriculum-based reading initiatives. These appeals serve to illuminate public issues pertaining to schools and schooling—vouchers, home schooling, or charter schooling, to cite a few examples. Ultimately, the political party gaining control of the state political apparatus, the legislature, the executive branch, or both, sets the broader educational agenda. This may affect social and political control over curriculum and policies put in place to give direction to what will be included in a school's curriculum. Schools are instruments of the state (see Chapter 2) and commonly agreed-on or, at least, accepted public beliefs are the glue that holds a society together through curriculum that represents goals of universal national identity, literacy conceived broadly, civic responsibility, and access to academic knowledge. Safeguards to make sure schools serve the society in acceptable, popularly approved ways include our national ideologies and conceptions of democracy, the rule of law, and the checks and balances present in governing through a constitutional republic. Those plus an essential creed consisting of democratic ideals about freedom, equality, and opportunity are foundational areas of study in political science. So is the study of governmental institutions and the political behavior not just of citizens but also of those appointed or elected to office, such as mayors, senators, judges, and presidents. Carlos Torres, in an extended discussion of the state and the governed, notes that "[the] different notions of the state . . . involve different views of what . . . governance of societies should entail, including notions of power, participation, representation, and democratic decision making" (1995, p. 264). Interestingly, that constant working out of governance, ideas of power, and public issues all play out in curriculum and schooling. That also pertains to persistent issues like school reform that have been part of the political discussion in the United States since the publication of *A Nation at Risk* in 1983 (National Commission on Excellence in Education, 1983). The idea of reform is to make schools the best they can be, a noble goal that has led to actions by governments at all levels: local, state, and national. On the surface, school reform movements have the appearance of a public dialogue about standards and accountability. It is about that, but it is also, among other things, a political struggle over whether the individual states or the federal government will control schooling and curriculum. At its core, the matter of control is one about ideas. It is also fundamentally political. Curriculum standards, even those about mathematics or science, are an expression of the idea of what an American citizen needs to know. The curriculum and standards represent the interpreted particulars about how much national culture American society needs and how the essentials of the American experience are to be attained by the citizenry. W. M. McClay refers to this as "the hard fact that there seems to be a core of Americanness to which all immigrants and children must be trained if we are to have reliably loyal and competent citizens" (2003, p. 77). Knowledge from political science about the state, the civic culture, the political system, the instruments of government, and how those intertwine with decisions made about schooling and curriculum can help school leaders and curriculum workers understand the political dynamics. Although the student of curriculum is not expected to be a political scientist, given the highly political nature of schooling and curriculum, awareness of the discipline's pertinent resources and their possible use can inform the study of curriculum.

Paralleling school curriculum requirements for courses in government and the political system are mandates for economic education. As the former rely on political science for knowledge, so the latter draw on knowledge from the discipline of economics. While the political science curriculum–government association can be easily understood as preparation for citizenship, the relationship of economics to an economic education curriculum seems more tenuous. There are two aspects of this that bear discussion. First is the relationship between economics the discipline and economic education as a school curriculum requirement. The second has to do with the relationship between economic knowledge, accountability, schooling, and curriculum.

The purpose of economic education is to create a savvy consumer and decision maker who can effectively participate in the workforce and the economy. Economic concepts like macro- and microeconomics, supply side theory, and cost-benefit analysis seem far removed from life, particularly everyday decisions about groceries, clothing, housing, transportation, and planning for retirement. Much of that reflects matters of value and allocation of personal resources according to what is valued. Such concerns parallel decisions about the economies of life in the same way that schooling and other institutions of a society require public decisions about the allocation of resources for buildings, maintenance, salaries, benefits, transportation, equipment, supplies, and curriculum. Schooling, from childhood through graduate work, absorbs huge amounts of tax monies dedicated to an enterprise that has no saleable product and whose outcome is based on the graduate's potential to be an employed, contributing citizen. To that end, society and government have begun demanding some form of accountability by creating some value indicators that link schooling to functional citizenship. Economists, as E. A. Hanushek (1997) and S. E Meyers and P. E Peterson (1999) point out, have tried valiantly to establish a value for schooling by looking at the allocation of resources and at particular cost items, salaries and benefits, for example, to establish some baseline data that would allow some interpretation or determination about the economics of schooling and the benefits it provides compared to its cost.

Why is it important to place an economic value on schooling? Resources for all the services that a society expects or demands are finite, and the support for schooling requires an extensive commitment of funds. As long ago as the 1890s, efforts were made to tie the amount of time spent on certain curriculum subjects to schooling costs. Funding allocations for such important purposes as schooling are matters of policy. Add to that the matter of accountability, determining the cost of schooling by placing an economic value on schooling as a social service or good. A unit of value will be applied to provide an analysis of cost and benefit for any service or part of it. It should follow, then, that curriculum also has an economic value determined by the cost to provide materials such as texts, films, and related representations of the curriculum used in schools. Wages and benefits of curriculum workers also have to be included in the economic calculation of curriculum. A third aspect of cost, accountability, has to do with requirements placed on school curriculum by law. Consider the matter of economic courses in high school that are required for graduation. Although standards for economic education and a model titled "Economics American Program" are available from the National Council on Economic Education (see the end-of-chapter section Resources for Curriculum Study), the translation into economic knowledge of the discipline, the school curriculum, curriculum materials, and the realities of economic life has its critics (Baumol, 1988; Keen, 2001), who suggest that the discipline-based economics taught in the school has little relevance to realities of economics in life. There is no reflection of real personal and family economic decision making. Yet, decisions made by parents and the people in a community are reflective of economic choice, the selection among options about schooling and curriculum. Consider, for example, the parents or guardians making a decision about sending their children to a public, private, or parochial school. Public resources are allocated primarily for public schools, so choosing private or parochial school means spending their own funds. The intent of those kinds of decisions aside, they are making important economic choices that have other implications. In choosing a particular school, they are selecting a specific and possibly different curriculum that may not have to follow state curriculum policy; choosing a school is an economic choice that can influence what curriculum is learned and possibly the degree of national uniformity and social cohesion, as some studies of politics and ideology suggest (Apple, 1979; Giordano, 2004). If social cohesion through some standardized curriculum is important, then the economic-value school choice is important for the production and purchase of texts and other materials that are meant to meet *required* standards in curriculum guides. When the cost of producing curriculum materials and tests in all their variety is coupled with other applicable curriculum-related costs of schooling, considerations about the allocation of financial resources loom large. Add other curriculum and school-related issues such as vouchers and charter schools, and the need for understanding economics through economic education looms large in social importance. Economics has useful modes of inquiry, a knowledge base, and applied experience to explain and explore the relationship of economics to schooling and curriculum through economic education.

Geography and Curriculum

Geography has held an important place in the school curriculum. Places, locations, and geographical features are content in the school curriculum remembered from elementary school social studies or a specific geography course in high school. Contemporary geography still deals with much the same topics, now framed in five themes around which a set of geography curriculum standards have been written (see Gregg & Leinhardt, 1994, or Hardwick & Holtgrieve, 1996). In summary form, these are location, place, human-environment interaction, movement, and regions. Several of these themes have curriculum relevance other than as subject matter in the school curriculum. Location refers to a position on the earth's surface as given by degrees of latitude and longitude. A place can be located, but it is more fully understood in terms of its human and physical characteristics, the place relationship being defined by the human-environment interaction and the personalized perceptions students and parents have of their school and their community. A school has a location; it can be mundanely described as at 504 Johnston Avenue in your city, town, or community. It is a place as well, Johnston Elementary, a brick building with lots of trees around it; you know it very well because it has been committed to memory and defined by your experiences there and the interactions of students, teachers, other school personnel, and the community in which it is embedded. In that place and location, curriculum is also modified by the nature of the place, its geographic location, physical and landscape features, and the composite of students and teachers who think about and work with it. Imagine an eighth-grade United States history course taught in a small Arizona town along the

Mexico–United States border. Consider another place and location on Maine's Atlantic seaboard. Assume they are teaching toward the same objectives set down in the same set of standards and using the same textbook. All things being hypothetically equal, place and location can be influential. Contemplate the manner of life in each place: one very dry; the other moderately wet; one a place of sagebrush, cactus, and usually high temperatures; the other a place of woodlands, rocky coastlines, and colder climate. The requirements for living, the way of life, differ, as do the possibilities for work. The teacher in Maine and the teacher in Arizona each work separately with a required curriculum unit on the 19th-century conflicts between the United States and Mexico in the Southwest. The students in Arizona more easily understand the nature of the conflicts in the sense of the geographic features of the land and the lifestyle of the Southwest, because those things are associated with their life and experience. Another scenario is also possible. Because of the location, place knowledge, and artifacts at hand, the teacher in Arizona might opt to extend the study whereas the teacher in Maine would lack that comparable place knowledge and spend only the necessary or required time in study.

Place, location, and human-environment interaction leave their mark on schooling and curriculum in other ways. For example, in any given place, the nature of available work and the range of knowledge needed for the work may place different demands on curriculum. The degree of knowledge or workforce differentiation necessary for employment in an auto manufacturing plant or one in the chemical industry may shift curriculum emphasis as the community anticipates employee requirements for one type of work or another. Workforce needs in rural and urban place locations often require different degrees of curriculum coverage. Students and teachers are always place and location bound, participants in the human-environment interaction that gives a local slant to what knowledge is of most worth. Geography, with its key concepts, is useful to curriculum work in general and at the school level in particular, especially as it helps to understand the whys of local curriculum organization and give insights into doing curriculum work in a specific location and place.

Educational Psychology

Schools are designated as centers for learning. The discipline of psychology has traditionally been the knowledge base of reference in understanding learning as a process, and that knowledge has crossed over as educational psychology. Educational and psychological studies attempt to illuminate not only the learning process but also its relationship to curriculum, instruction, assessment, evaluation, and, indeed, all aspects of schooling. Teaching methods like the *Models of Teaching* by Bruce Joyce and others (Joyce, Weill, & Showers, 1992) were developed and used to approximate various models of learning. With the possible exception of Jerome Bruner's spiral curriculum concept, models of learning from psychology and educational psychology have had few enduring applications in curriculum work. The problem is the difficulty of inferring from the outside what kind of activity is going on inside the student's brain and how that characterizes learning that can lead to models, theories, and the conceptualizing of learning itself. Laboratory experiments to understand the learning process—for example, Pavlov's work with dogs and Skinner's work with operant conditioning—can provide a basis for theory development about instruction or suggest how to structure a particular scope and sequence for a curriculum. Aside from some useful theory and model building, educational psychology research has thus far been of limited use in understanding the learning-curriculum links or the complexities of the curriculum-instruction-assessment continuum in learning. Yet, curriculum work, at least according to most textbooks in education and curriculum, acknowledges the importance of several schools of thought in psychology that contribute to curriculum thinking and work. Keep in mind that these schools in psychology also reflect the orientations discussed in Chapter 5, the difference being the particular application here to learning as a focus of research.

Faculty Psychology

In the mid- to late 19th century, phrenology and faculty psychology dominated scholarly and scientific thinking about learning. Phrenology was the scientific study of the skull's conformation based on the belief that it represented mental characteristics. *Faculty psychology,* its handmaiden, was the emphasis on achieving mental discipline that would exercise the mind's faculties. The idea of faculties and *mental discipline* was based on an assertion in the Yale report of 1828 that the purpose of a college education was to discipline the mind. Various subject areas were then matched with a mental faculty; for example, the physical sciences were in the curriculum because they disciplined factual use and inductive and problem reasoning. Although those beliefs and pursuits in the name of science seem archaic today, mental discipline still influenced thinking about teaching, learning, and curriculum into the mid–20th century. Consider how the school and college curriculum is organized, and you will find a vestige of mentalist faculty psychology, including the use of the term *faculty* for those who teach in those settings.

Cognitive Psychology

Psychology and educational psychology still tend to inform the understanding of learning through inferences drawn from behavioral observation. Recent developments in a range of subjects such as cognition, brain science, and neuroscience are gathered under the banner of *cognitive psychology,* a concept that rather loosely defines the study of the brain and its functions using technology such as imaging to observe the brain in action. In *Mapping the Mind* (1999), Rita Carter lays out the interplay of the brain, behavior, and culture as they represent the biological mechanisms and chemistry under-lying thought and actions. New configurations of cognition and the psychology of human learning can have important implications for schooling, curriculum, and teach-ing. These new frontiers are not without their perils. As Patricia Churchland points out in her book *Brain-Wise* (2002), aspects of cognitive psychology, particularly the rela-tionship between neuroscience and philosophy, raise moral and ethical questions about the sense of being human, who and what you are, as that is changed by knowledge about our biological and chemical nature. Cognitive psychology as a broad concept has possibilities for understanding such issues as (a) whether humans are reactive rather than proactive in that the brain might be chemically driven and (b) what are the impli-cations for schooling and curriculum in that no two brains are shaped or organized the same. These are the frontiers of cognitive psychology in its several forms, and particu-larly among those working in neuroscience. It is a new world of different possibilities beyond the old boundaries of psychology. At some future point, cognitive psychology, as the confluence of knowledge from cognitive science, neural science, and psychology, may yield a vision of learning in ways that enable the meshing of curriculum and all aspects of teaching.

Behavioral Psychology

How does the mind work? How do we learn? There are two (at least) perspectives on seeking answers to those important questions, one by inference, and the other by direct observation. The first, by inference, might be like Freud's interpretation of dreams; the other seeks to manipulate actions to induce observable behavior, as Pavlov did with dogs and Skinner later did with human subjects. Both examples represent a school of psychology called behaviorism. The thrust of *behavioral psychology* is to move away from concerns about causes and work on increasing the frequency of appro-priate behaviors. Behaviorism has been an experimental rather than applied psychology, with apparently limited general value in schooling and curriculum except as findings might suggest individual or group applications, as in therapeutic situations. Applications in programming and computer-assisted learning suggest some potential for individual-izing and stylizing curriculum that might be useful in promoting particular behavior. The eternal question with behaviorism is, of course, who—what person, persons, body, or agent decides what behaviors ought to be important and to whom should they apply or be applied?

Humanistic Psychology

Until the mid–20th century, there were two main schools in American psychology, behaviorism and psychoanalysis. In the decade of the 1950s, an important new branch, *humanistic psychology,* developed in America. Much of the foundational ideas and

Figure 8.2   Basic Ideas About Schooling From Humanistic Psychology

- Focus is on the whole person, and each student is a unique, developmentally different individual
- Understanding behavior is a function of the views of that behavior by both the observer and the person doing the behavior
- The person is not solely a product of the environment but also of the context in which the behavior occurs and the person who is doing the behaving
- Humans grow through experience, thoughtful actions, and teaching and learning
- All humans share common characteristics of love, grief, caring, self-worth, and esteem

practices in humanistic psychology came from the work of Rollo May (1953), Carl Rogers (1951), and Abraham Maslow (1954). The essence of humanistic psychology is a focus on the whole person. Moving away from behaviorism and psychoanalysis, humanistic psychology expanded into the study of motivation, emotion, self-actualization, creativity, sensory awareness through movement, and encounter groups. New forms of therapy—rational-emotional, reality therapy, psycho-synthesis, for example—emerged and expanded the range of psychological practice. Although no particular school in educational psychology has dominated or dramatically changed the practice of teachers in schools, the learner centeredness in humanistic psychology has had a sustaining influence, especially as practitioners might interpret the views of humanistic psychology suggested in Figure 8.2 in their teaching. Particular aspects of the humanistic approach suggest that humanistic psychology has had an important influence in schooling, especially as it has meant helping students as individuals and understanding the person-environment (i.e., student-classroom) relationships. Other influences of the humanistic view on schooling and curriculum can be found in the open school and classroom movement, student-centered learning with its emphasis on student choices in what is to be learned, the encouragement of personal curiosity and interests, preference for a variety of curriculum materials for learning rather than a single textbook, and emphasis on cooperative learning forms of group work. It would be remiss not to mention the influence of humanistic psychology in the training of school counselors as well as the learner-centered emphasis given to instruction techniques in teacher education colleges.

CURRICULUM CONTENT AND THE HUMANITIES

The celebrated microbiologist René Dubois once made the comment that "the human species has the power to choose among the conflicting traits which constitute its complex nature, and it has made the right choices often enough to have kept civilization so far on a forward and upward course" (1974, p. 79). He celebrates the human ability to think and change the world about us and ourselves; that which can be known and sensed is summed up in the concept of humanity. As you can discern, the humanities, in their various disciplinary forms, shed light on what it means to be a human being. Humans are curious and seek to give meaning to things they perceive and experience, to create knowledge that is useful in negotiating a way in the world. Schools became the special place, the repository of formal knowledge about how to negotiate and understand the world. In antiquity, this collected knowledge was known as the seven liberal arts, the earliest curriculum. That is a far cry from the idea of the humanities found in the school curriculum today. From then to now, the humanities represent the wisdom of the ages compacted in the school curriculum to provide an economizing access to humanistic ideals and knowledge.

Humanistic Ideals

A famous social studies curriculum project of the 1960s, "Man: A Course of Study" (1968; see Dow, 1991) inquired into the nature of humanness by posing three questions: What is human about humans? How did humans get that way? How can humans be made more human? The thrust and purpose of the project and the comments by microbiologist René Dubois noted in the previous paragraph both inquire into the nature of man. Though from different perspectives and disciplines of knowledge, they come together in that each seeks a basic understanding of what it means to think, know, feel, and be human. Other aspects of the humanities, literature, the arts, and philosophy, also prompt thought about the human qualities of being, knowledge, morality, ethics, and the like. The study of the arts, especially when considered in the broader sense of aesthetic knowing rather than just as forms of art, painting, dance, and so forth, illuminates the creative, expressive nature of our humanness. Knowledge found in philosophy and in the aesthetics of the arts, language, and literature has in some form always been part of curriculum. For example, the seven liberal arts of the European Middle Ages included rhetoric and grammar, which were keyed to the study of great literary works as well as music. You have at various points in your schooling encountered art, literature, and writing, and perhaps participated in theater, band, or chorus, each an example of the place the humanities hold in contemporary schooling. Additionally, the humanities contribute a particular way of knowing, a mode of thinking called judgment that makes valuation possible when there are no standardized measures. This mode of thought, what Elliot Eisner refers to as "our powers of critical appraisal" (1999, p. 286), requires an acute encounter. This implies awareness of the context in which something is embedded, its subtle qualities or nuances; personal reflection about the characteristics of the lens, the mind's eye, through which things are viewed; and how both personal reflectivity and the lens have been culturally shaped. The humanities offer us certain ways to know among a number of what Vallance (1999) has called the modes of knowing, the forms of thinking as in the manner of logic and judgment that, as acquired, open individual perspectives and are an entrée to knowledge about how to see the world and ourselves as human beings. The issues raised in "Man: A Course of Study," what it means to be human and how to become more so, are eternal and basic issues that never have a static meaning; rather, they must be continually addressed as the fundamental issues of life personally defined in the individual sense of personhood, yet collectively in the realm of social interactions. Issues about humanity are timeless yet immediate in the practice and work of professionals who confront an often unspoken but real curriculum about the nature of knowledge and knowing, being, and values, and the decisions about which reflect the purposes for schooling and determine what should be in the school curriculum.

Language and Curriculum

The humanities are home to language. A useful definition of language is a process of symbolic interaction, a deceptively simple explanation of human interacting using conforming symbols of sound and sight or utterances by tongue and voice. Languages such as Spanish, English, and Japanese come to mind, perhaps as part of your curriculum experience. Languages are formed of alphabetic symbols arranged in patterns. Understanding that patterning is called *linguistics,* or the study of the way that any language is structured, the elements that make it up, and their functions. Think of the familiar alphabet you are using, which is essential for most Western languages. Range further over the language landscape and you find different alphabets and different languages, the Cyrillic alphabet of Russian, the Arabic alphabet of Middle Eastern languages, and alphabets for languages in China and Japan. There is another side to language, and that is language of movement: body posture; a gesture; voice intonation; and culturally expected movement, as in a bow or diverting of the eyes, which, with an utterance or other movement, convey unspoken social and cultural meaning as part of the language of interactions. Classrooms are places of language as symbolic interactions, alphabetic patterns, enriched by movement such as a look given by a learner, body posture, or a particular intonation or utterance. In the classroom and curriculum materials, symbols are encoded in pictures, images, and spoken or illustrative representations as well as printed language. Language gives expression to love, grief, caring, and other emotions; it is not just formalized language but the social and cultural dimensions that make language so important in being human.

Literature and the Arts

Unfortunately for the arts in all their forms, they receive second, often third, consideration in the school curriculum. Sciences and mathematics share first notice, social studies and English, second. Yet, the case has been made for the value in general of the arts and for the development of the affective and expressive side of human behavior.

Imagine being without theater, music, or dance. The skills and sensory perceptions developed or experienced in the study of the arts contribute a discerning quality, a special perspective on life, an acquired literacy of approach to the world of things around us. This literacy of approach is what Gilbert Ryle (1949) discussed as the mind's capacity of *knowing how* to do something in addition to *knowing that* in the manner of logic and fact. The literacy of approach is an aesthetic repertoire of senses translated into symbolic forms for thinking about and expressing encounters with the world around us. An example could be the attentive process of studying a painting or picture and developing an interpretive sense of the painter's or photographer's intent. Awareness of individual powers of perception, the intensity of attending to something, is part of learning this aesthetic literacy. Engaging in public or academic discussions about the artistic, whether one likes or dislikes something or agrees with another on its qualities, forces us to converse in symbols that equate to what is sensed. This is a translation transformed into judgments, spoken or written, much like deciding if you do or do not like something. In the humanities and arts, this is the province of the critic. The meaning of criticism used here is that of an informed conversation usually associated with literary works and art forms. Criticism is the critic's view of something. The idea in curriculum and professional work is that of the critical perspective which was developed in Chapter 1. Criticism as a form of critique in curriculum work also has similarities with critical social theory (Leonardo, 2004). Unfortunately, criticism gets tangled up in notions of anger, put-downs, and other negatives. It actually is a way to enlighten, to enrich and illuminate, to enable others to hone their aesthetic understanding. Elliot Eisner refers to this perception-based process of thoughtful judgment as "the ability to see, to perceive what is subtle, complex, and important . . . [and] . . . to know how to look, to see, and to appreciate" (1994, p. 215). This art of appreciation is a private act he refers to as connoisseurship, a mental constructing like Ryle's literacy of approach. It is a state of being, a prelude to criticism, which is the public act of disclosure. Criticism in the manner of the arts is an act of providing a judgment through interpretation or explanation. It is a qualitative tool for thinking about things and, as discussed in Chapter 6, characterized as a critique used in curriculum discourse. The forms and examples of criticism available for study in literature and the arts provide a knowledge base for critique in curriculum.

PHILOSOPHY AND CURRICULUM KNOWLEDGE

Philosophy, from the Greek *philosophia,* literally means the love of wisdom. As an ancient discipline of Western culture, it is associated with philosophers like Socrates, Plato, and Aristotle, and in modern times with philosophers such as Europeans Teilhard de Chardin and Ludwig Wittgenstein and American John Dewey. It is also considered a body of first knowledge from which other disciplines of knowledge, such as physics, economics, and sociology, emerged. Today, philosophy follows from that idea of a search for wisdom in a more limited way for humans to give meaning to existence. Logic, aesthetics, ethics, metaphysics, and epistemology are the core conceptual areas of study.

Problems in philosophy generally fall into three broad categories: *ontology*, or problems of being; *epistemology*, or problems of knowing; and *axiology*, or problems of value. Matters related to those three categories are studied to develop a logical and consistent system that proposes answers. The conceptual areas (logic, ethics, etc.) may be used in building the system.

Philosophy of Science

In the field of education, there are periodic calls to create a science of education. To understand the emphasis on giving education in all its aspects (curricular, instructional, etc.), a scientific grounding requires a short excursion into the philosophy of science. Science is an undertaking to obtain knowledge of the natural world. A *philosophy of science* is the systematic study of its (science's) structure and components (data, theories, guiding principles), techniques, assumptions, and limitations. The scientific method, the way of doing science, has been at various times associated with fashionable thinkers such as Francis Bacon (inductive) and Isaac Newton (deductive) and their particular systems of reasoning, both of which espoused empiricism, or verification by observation and experiment. The problem with all schools of scientific thought, as Thomas Kuhn points out in *The Structure of Scientific Revolutions* (1970), is that none have proven satisfactory in solving *all* problems. This is, of course, due to discovering new problems that current procedures and theories can't solve and the perennial realization that it is impossible to conclusively falsify or prove theories by empirical means. The upshot is that periodically the meaning of science changes as the dominant school of thought (or paradigm, as Kuhn calls it) gives way to a new conception. The connection to educational inquiry would be the application of a particular school of science to define and articulate theory and experimentation in aspects of education such as curriculum, instruction, and learning, as scientifically researchable entities. That, as the history of education and the study of schooling suggest, is no easy task.

Philosophy of Knowledge

The school curriculum is in one sense a collection of content from various areas of formal knowledge. In another sense, it is the result of how humans and particularly philosophers have solved questions about how humans come to know and what is knowledge. Mathematics, literature, biology, and so forth represent different ways to know (how a mathematician does math) and knowledge as the result of different ways of knowing (mathematics itself). In philosophy, this is known as the study of episte-mology, or the task of logically analyzing knowledge. Think of that knowledge as what you studied in the school curriculum, the passed-on repository of human wisdom. As a teacher, you will encounter inquisitive learners who will ask disturbing questions such as how do we know anything, what is knowledge, or why do we have to learn this? You will need to develop answers, and that means engaging in very difficult philosophical study about knowledge and knowing. More will be said about this in later discussions about educational philosophy in this chapter.

Philosophy and Western Discourse Traditions

A fundamental element in Western societies is the belief in robust, public discussion about the nature and direction of the particular society. The intellectual traditions in any society are formed from the philosophical discourse, or continuing conversation anchored in knowledgeable disputation relying on disciplined knowledge from academic communities. The flow of development in Western thought has run through different phases that now carry a particular name and that are usually referred to as traditions. Think of a tradition's name or label as a term representing a collection of ideas and images, much like jazz, pop, or new age in the world of music. These intellectual and philosophical heirs, both present and past, represent evolving summations of human social, cultural, and intellectual development. Four intellectual traditions are important in Western philosophy. Prior to the 18th-century, what was taken for knowledge and approved for use was based on a *theological* tradition. That was, of course, a belief that all that is or could be known or was appropriate to know came from God and would be revealed in a theological context. The 18th-century *Enlightenment* tradition ushered in a secular philosophic and scientific approach. Employing the philosophy of science meant being logical and empirical in one's method of inquiry. In that sense, science was a dis-ciplined form of philosophy and often used as representing the same as philosophy. Over time, science took on its own meaning and the association with the discipline of philos-ophy waned. A third tradition, *modernism,* is associated with a scientific, logical, posi-tivist discourse with its emphasis on quantitative methods of inquiry. A fourth discourse, the *postmodern,* evolved from European roots in the 20th century during the years between World Wars I and II. In the early years of the cold war era, it gained influence among international scholars in the academic scene and in the United States. Probably its most significant American thinker was Herbert Marcuse, whose writings were influ-ential in the student protest movements of the 1960s and 1970s. Those were turbulent times; events seemed out of control, and the particular uses of modernist discourse appeared to fail in helping to understand and solve social problems. Scholars searched for other perspectives in thinking about society and exploring solutions to seemingly intractable problems. A new intellectual movement, a philosophy of *postmodernism,* emerged that offered new perspectives and ways to study contemporary problems. In

Kuhn's terms, the modernism paradigm and its philosophical base were being challenged.

Modernist to Postmodernist

If one characteristic of modernism was its acceptance of the quantitative and experimental forms of inquiry, then possibly the advent of qualitative inquiry methods mark the beginning of a postmodernist tradition. This is not to suggest that the modern discourse is giving way to the postmodern; it is too early to know if that is indeed what is happening. However, from the standpoint of discussing schooling and curriculum, postmodernism has exhibited some uses. A different type of discourse, it is grounded in a philosophical discourse that promotes an array of new perspectives from which to approach the study of society and culture. Postmodernism is an integration of knowledge different from the traditions of modernism. It welcomes theory and methods of inquiry from diverse disciplines. For example, discourse analysis is from communication; figurative language analysis is from literature; ethnography is from anthropology, a social science; and case studies have been used in law and business. Methods in this qualitative family provide new ways to study not only the larger societal context with its cultural, political, and economic aspects, but also embedded processes such as curriculum and schooling. They are also methods and theories that provide different ways to study society, culture, institutions, and organizations through the lens of participants in smaller units such as social groups and school classrooms.

The social sciences bridge the traditions from the modern to the postmodern. It is in the modernist tradition that the social sciences were formed and in which knowledge from the social sciences proved useful in curriculum work (Mazlish, 1998). Modernist discourse defined social science content for society through the social studies as an important part of the school curriculum. In the postmodern discourse, the social science disciplines, especially sociology, have oriented more toward understanding social processes as against the modern discourse with its emphasis on institutions and behavior. Where quantitative inquiry was a mark of modernism, qualitative inquiry denotes the postmodern.

Ideology and Critical Theory

Postmodern thought is centered in what is called critical theory. Two important figures in its development are Jürgen Habermas and Michel Foucault, whose works have been cited internationally in philosophy, political science, sociology, and other disciplines. Critical theory is not easy to describe; there is a risk of oversimplification and misrepresentation, so the purpose here is twofold—first, to briefly detail its particulars and second, to consider its importance for schooling, curriculum, and curriculum work.

Briefly put, *critical theory* is about ideologies, the way culture and history influence the construction of reality, personality, and identity under different social conditions. It is emancipatory in that it is a way to uncover and abolish social injustices that are hidden but abide in things of everyday existence. It is a way to explore the quality of our social and cultural environment and institutions to uncover the subtle forces that hold authority over us and to use that knowledge to revert power in whatever form to the individual. Probably the most significant and understandable example of critical theory in use is found in Paulo Freire's account of his work with Brazilian peasants, the *Pedagogy of the Oppressed* (1970). Freire's discussion illuminates the concept by associating the elements of theory in terms of the realities of application. What is also interesting is that the process of empowerment to emancipate is curriculum work, the creation of a curriculum by and specific to the needs of the indigenous population. Curriculum, in this instance, becomes the power to empower. However, a caveat is in order. Another characteristic of critical theory is that it is not a system, and it opposes attempts to make it one. In reading Freire, then, one must grasp two additional things about critical theory. First, it is situation or place specific; it is Freire's interpretive use of critical theory in particular circumstances. Second, because according to critical theorists it is not a system, a model, or a set of standardized procedures or way to see things, critical theory is fluid and may take on different forms depending on the nature of the thing to which it is applied. In that sense, it is amoeboid—it has the amoeba-like quality to move and change shape within the bounds of its environment. It is protean but retains its form, possessing the quality of changing or shaping itself in the context or setting by which it is bounded but which is itself changing. The form that critical theory assumes is, in Marshall McLuhan's turn of a phrase, the medium and the message.

The focus of critical theorists is on society, culture, and history. Within that purview are a number of distinct threads of inquiry. There is the usual neo-Marxist contingent; a genealogical approach represented by Foucault; the poststructuralist/deconstructionist French connection, Jacques Derrida being its best-known practitioner; and a fourth perspective that is epistemological. This last form of inquiry, associated specifically with Jürgen Habermas, is of particular interest because Habermas's work has been principally important in the thinking of persons concerned with schooling and curriculum, especially those engaged in theory building. As it is used here, critical theory is an umbrella term, enabling each perspective to remain distinct but associated under a general meaning. This will allow a focus on the use of critical theory as a particular perspective employed in the study of schooling and curriculum.

As you will recall from previous discussion, modern discourse essentially treats schools and schooling as neutral or at least benign from the standpoint of social science theory with its emphasis on grand theory development and structural-institutional functioning. The development of a late–20th-century behaviorism in various social sciences was an important transition, allowing a more speculative turn in thinking about society, culture, and human development. This turn was, of course, a new focus on human behavior and its causal effect on how society and institutions develop. An example, as Carl Degler suggests in his excellent study *In Search of Human Nature* (1991), is the transition in social science from institutional studies to the role of human intervention based on a revival of Darwinism, at least in the United States. This is a shift in the focus of what is to be studied from modernisms *objects* to postmodern *subjects*. For both, the context, the setting or environment in which they exist, remains important to the inquiry about them. Modernist discourse would seek to understand curriculum as part of an institutional structure, the school, within the larger social and cultural traditions, whereas postmodern discourse would look for the grounding ideas from which the curriculum as what is to be learned emerges. Cast in that way, curriculum is revealed as subtly constituted power, the engagement of which disposes participants to acquire some ways to see the world, but not others; to act consistent with a set of prescribed behaviors, but not others; and to construct a self within acceptable parameters, without knowing others. The curriculum and school experience massage the participants in controlling ways. A curriculum is more than just a written text, it is also social and cultural knowledge reconstituted through the teacher and students as actions with effects.

EDUCATIONAL PHILOSOPHIES AND CURRICULUM

In Chapter 5, you were introduced to various ways of thinking about curriculum that are found in the curriculum knowledge base. These were referred to as curriculum orientations. In Chapter 2, you were introduced to the idea of perspective building and the importance of the critical perspective. Another way to reflect on orientations and perspectives in curriculum is through their relationship with philosophy and education. There are some important distinctions to consider about the use of the term philosophy. First, keep in mind that philosophy is foremost a body of knowledge, a discipline. Second, be aware that using the term philosophy in an associative way, to talk about educational philosophy, for example, places the word philosophy in a different contextual usage outside the discipline—it doesn't carry the same meaning that philosophy as a discipline does. References to a personal philosophy or to being philosophical often imply a connectedness to logics or ways of thinking that are particular to philosophy the discipline. Consider *educational philosophy,* like educational psychology, as simply referring to particular schools of thought that have developed in education that, to a degree, mimic philosophy in its general way of addressing basic questions of life and existence, particularly about the nature of knowledge and the process of knowing. Also keep in mind that philosophical positions in education may or may not be parallel to orientations or other curriculum perspectives. Further comments about philosophy-curriculum relationships are provided in Figure 8.3.

Figure 8.3   Philosophy-Curriculum Relationships

Philosophy	Curricular Emphases
Progressivism	Content and experiences involve students in problem solving and reflection. There should be opportunities for students to learn in situations that do not isolate them from the world beyond the school. Content drawn from the social sciences often has relevance for programs associated with progressivism.
Essentialism	All students should be taught a common core of knowledge that they will need to function as productive, contributing members of society. Serious knowledge is particularly likely to be found in the sciences and technical fields. Content from the arts and humanities should be de-emphasized because it fails to prepare students in the ways science and technical knowledge does.
Perennialism	The emphasis on scientific experimentation and technology has resulted in neglect of knowledge about quality living found in the humanities and the world's great literature. That is what should be emphasized, not vocational programs and other subjects that clearly do not serve intellectual development.
Reconstructionism	Society as it exists has come under the sway of narrow groups with selfish interests who have imposed values that are contrary to American experience. Values such as fairness, equity, and humanity have been compromised. School programs should prepare students to study these social inequities and actively seek to reconstruct society through curriculum and schools to build a just society. Knowledge from the social and behavioral sciences should be emphasized in the school curriculum and activities.

It is standard practice in educational discussions to put forth a set of traditional educational philosophies so you, the student, can compare those with your own and find some approximation. The essence of any philosophical exercise for the curriculum worker is to be able to know what you think and why you think that way about particular aspects of schooling and curriculum. As a professional, your own particular philosophical set in your professional perspective is important because it becomes the lens through which you see schooling and curriculum as well as the larger world of education.

Idealism and Realism

Traditional discussions of Western philosophy begin with the Greek philosophers, particularly Plato and idealism, and Aristotle and realism. Both philosophies are concerned with the nature of knowledge and how humans come to know, the making of knowledge. Each also represents a position about whether the senses or the intellect is fallible as sources of how humans come to know. Obviously, the matter of how any human comes to know or create knowledge is an important issue for schooling and curriculum. The philosophy of *idealism* posits that reality, or what you can come to know, exists only in the mental world of ideas rather than through the senses. Schooling should be an intellectual search to identify abstract ideas and bring them to a conscious level of understanding. Key to this is an understanding of the past and how humans have developed ways of understanding and specifics of what has come to be known that are the truths to guide lives. The liberal arts tradition in schooling complements the idealism philosophy. Aristotelian *realism* holds that truths or knowledge exist and can be found in the real world. There is a high priority on rationality and teaching students to develop their thinking abilities, particularly through science and mathematics. This is the philosophy behind traditional views of curriculum and the idea of understanding a discipline such as biology for its own sake rather than in relationship to other areas of knowledge.

Pragmatism and Existentialism

Philosophies like idealism and realism often seem like discussions about abstractions rather than tangible aspects of life. Pragmatism and existentialism, on the other hand, seem more worldly, concerned with the practical, the reality of existence, and the grittiness of life. Indeed, *pragmatism* might be labeled as a philosophy of the practical where the concern is on the individual and learning problem-solving strategies that transfer across and are useful in different contexts. Content such as biology or history is not in itself useful but as it serves to develop thinking skills that would allow persons to adapt to change. American philosopher John Dewy was influential in promoting a form of pragmatism that emphasized personal experiences and understanding the learner's own time and culture while honing ways of thinking in adapting to and influencing the changing circumstances of life. If pragmatism is the reality of dealing with what is and possibly influencing what will be, then *existentialism* is the acceptance that there is no such thing as objective reality, at least in the search for principles or truths that apply to people or life. The ultimate reality for humans is to make sense of personal life and live it as best one can with the understanding that it will end in death. It is a philosophy of deadly practicality. The implications for schooling and curriculum are uncertain. The problem is finding much in the existentialist literature that directly addresses schooling or curriculum in the same way that John Dewey and others advocated and explained pragmatism. Existentialism is marginally related to curriculum in that, as A. V. Kelly points out, it is "warning us against the effects of imposing a universal curriculum on all pupils, particularly when the curriculum is regarded or presented, as non-problematic, rather than offering scope for personal exploration and the development of individual values and perspectives" (2004, p. 29).

Perennialism and Essentialism

Both perennialism and essentialism advocate the use of the traditional disciplines of formal knowledge in shaping the curriculum and as the basis for schooling. However, they differ about what in that knowledge should be used. *Essentialism* is, as the name suggests, an insistence that in schooling students should have "essential" academic knowledge. The meaning of what is essential rests on two important assumptions. The first is that in the present, the institutions of the society along with the economic and political climate are acceptable and benefiting citizens. The second has to do with that familiar philosophical issue about what is reality. For the essentialists, it is what is sensed or physically experienced through the senses. For curriculum, this would mean an emphasis on sciences, technology, and basic academics like mathematics, history, languages, and literature. Obviously, that emphasis would fill the curriculum and probably exclude music, art, and other humanistic studies, which are not of high priority. Essentialism is perhaps more of an American philosophical curiosity that owes much to the writings of William Bagley (see the end-of-chapter Resources for Curriculum Study). The pedigree of *perennialism* is also very American and relies on a selective interpretation of what knowledge is of most importance. In this case, it is that knowledge that has been authenticated over the centuries and handed down as the collective wisdom of what the educated person should know. Through exposure to this trove of wisdom, the citizen gains knowledge that will serve him or her in life and acquires reasoning or thinking powers that have historically led good thinkers to right actions and the moral life. The usual implication for curriculum is to study the great books or literature so deemed. Through this kind of curriculum, the student has access to traditions of thinking and resources in understanding how to live a thoughtful and effective life where change is a reality. Among others, Mortimer Adler (1982) and the Council on Basic Education have been consistent advocates for perennialism.

Progressivism and Reconstructionism

Reconstructionism is a particular philosophical position that holds that contemporary conditions, particularly the social, economic, and political features, of a society are inherently unfair. The task of schools and schooling is to prepare students for change as a natural life process and to be in the vanguard of that change in order to promote and attain a just society. Obviously, the curriculum would incorporate the knowledge, thinking skills, and experiences to promote the individual and collective understanding of change and ways to work for the just society. The progressive movement in America during the early 20th century reflected the social and political aims of using institutions to change or reconstruct society in pursuing policies for a just life for all citizens. The educational arm of that movement, progressivism, reflected the ideas of John Dewey's pragmatic philosophy and reconstructionism. George S. Counts's provocative essay and book *Dare the Schools Build a New Social Order?* (1932) captures the ideological challenge of the time and symbolizes an interesting coming together of pragmatism-progressivism as educational reconstructionism.

PERSPECTIVE INTO PRACTICE: Ideas From the Social Sciences and the Humanities, and Their Application in Elementary and Secondary Curriculum		
Ideas	*Elementary School Curriculum*	*Secondary School Curriculum*
Diversity and Curriculum	Teachers should check materials to assure that pictures, stories, and so forth reflect human diversity and use a variety of stories or experiences to depict variety of life and living, especially in the local school community.	All curriculum and especially literature and the arts should exemplify human and cultural diversity, especially as that diversity is expressed in the lives of students and their future as citizens and workers.
Politics and Curriculum	The curriculum should constantly illuminate ideas about fairness, thoughtful deliberation, listening, majority rule, protection of the minority, and all other aspects of citizenship in a democracy and constitutional republic.	Across the curriculum and in civics classes, the idea of constitutional neutrality, that it is racially, ethnically, culturally, and gender neutral, should be emphasized to highlight that no privilege or advantage attaches to any of those characteristics.
Philosophical Traditions and Curriculum	Rationalism, empiricism, and pragmatism as philosophies are subtly introduced in curriculum: rationalism as arithmetic; empiricism in science, like finding how a whole egg can be inserted through the neck of a bottle; and pragmatism in experimental applications that apply something to determine consequences.	Rationalism is represented in curriculum through all branches of mathematics; empiricism in the working of science, such as biology and chemistry; and pragmatism in applied ways, perhaps as in using different media in art to see what occurs or applying different tempos or scales musically to experiment with results.
Educational Psychology and Curriculum	Elementary curriculum tends to stress acquisition of basic skill such as reading through individualized sequences that expand from simple to complex and from concrete to abstract. Seemingly, this is a mix emphasizing the humanistic and cognitive approaches to mind and person.	Secondary curriculum is a contested philosophical ground between cognitive and humanistic approach. The former is knowledge centered in curriculum areas such as mathematics and sciences, the latter in literature and the arts. The major premise is cognitive in the development of thinking skills.

Summary and Conclusions

Grounding in the knowledge of and about curriculum is indispensable in curriculum work. It provides a common knowledge for discourse and helps frame the boundaries of work. Curriculum has connections to other knowledge. Intellectual, cultural, philosophical, and social associations with curriculum come from the social sciences and the humanities. Transcending ideas from particular historical episodes also contribute specific knowledge by influencing practices; creating trends; and introducing new ideas, concepts, and experiences that support curriculum work. As a collectivity, this collateral or adjunctive curriculum knowledge base offers ways to enhance and amplify the curriculum discipline itself and empower curriculum work. Philosophical positions have a particular importance as the philosophy that practitioners identify as theirs can set a particular direction in their work and form a foundation of values and perspectives through which they engage the curriculum as professionals.

Critical Perspective

1. Episodes of social and cultural ferment prompt change in curriculum. Identify a recent social or cultural issue or event that is or will soon be affecting schools and suggest what changes that might bring to curriculum.

2. The more often used reference characterizing the American social mix is that of the great melting pot. Another is that of America as a big bowl of salad. Are these metaphors the same or are there subtle nuances in meaning? What implications does each have for curriculum and schooling?

3. Differentiation means to set things apart so they can be considered individually; curriculum or instructional differentiation are examples. Can you give a separate example of curriculum and instructional differentiation? Are there any examples you can identify that serve both curriculum and instruction simultaneously?

4. Often, the importance of an era or particular time is not appreciated until the look back. Today, the discussion is often about a shift from modernism to postmodernism. What do those terms mean? What characterization of schools and schooling does each represent?

5. Multiple intelligences theory has interest and appeal for schooling, especially as it applies to building alternative curriculum keyed to the various intelligences. However, there is scant research to back it up. Despite that problem, some teachers and schools have used it. This raises an important philosophical question about the ethical and moral right of a teacher or others to implement such

theories in teaching and specifically to use any theory to adjust curriculum to fit the theory's requirements. What is your position? What evidence or argument would you marshal for or against the use of multiple intelligences theory?

6. If research in cognitive psychology findings suggests the uniqueness of each brain, what are the implications for individualizing the curriculum and the instructional modes of receiving it; should curriculum be individually tailored for each learner?

Resources for Curriculum Study

1. The work of teachers and what schools and curriculum are like at any given time provide snapshots of change in practices and thinking. Larry Cuban's *How Teachers Taught* (1984) captures what teaching and schooling were like from 1900 through 1980. The Ninety-Ninth Yearbook of the National Society for the Study of Education, *American Education: Yesterday, Today, and Tomorrow* (Good, 2000), contains several useful chapters about education over the past 100 years. S. L. Nichols and T. L. Good offer insights into society and education. Of particular interest are discussions about diversity and equality. D. A. Spencer comments on various factors such as social characteristics, working conditions, and the impact of reform movements on teacher work.

2. Democratic impulses as they play out in America usually have some residual effect. The impulses presented in Figure 8.1 all left some enduring idea or process in curriculum and schooling. Each represents a movement with an intellectual quality, an idea or a set of ideas that enter into public discourse; are sustained in the popular conscience; and, as they play out, insert themselves into the national ideology or become embedded in institutional life. Carl Degler's old but excellent work *Out of Our Past* (1959) is representative and offers a number of insights and examples. The three volumes in Daniel Boorstin's *The Americans* (1958, 1965, 1973) capture aspects of America's rising popular democracy and the particular boosterism that is a social and lived expression of democratic ideals. There is a sense of these democratic tendencies and how they find expression in the local scene in Alan Peshkin's *Growing Up American* (1978), which is an excellent study of a community and its schools.

3. Philosophy and its subset, educational philosophy, are addressed in just about any discussion in higher education, either in a department of philosophy or educational foundations. As one of the oldest disciplines, philosophy proper has references that are easily accessed just by going online or to any library. For philosophy of education (or educational philosophy, if you prefer), there are some useful volumes in the yearbooks of the National Society for the Study of

Education, particularly the 1981 volume, *Philosophy and Education,* edited by Jonas Soltis. A very good online source about philosophy and education is http://www.en.wikipedia.org/wiki/Philososphy_of_education. This Web site covers the historical evolution of various schools of thought and provides a list of suggested books and articles to consult.

4. Teacher education has often been viewed as too theoretical, impractical, and deficient in real-time school practice. The Holmes Group, created in the mid-1990s, a consortium of some sixty-plus colleges with school district partners, has sought to be a force for change. It, too, became a changed organization in 1997 and is now known as the Holmes Partnership. Various publications and information about the group can be found at http://www.holmespartnership.org. Archived articles at the online newspaper www.edweek.org provide the most useful information about the evolution and impact of this organization. An excellent recent overview of teacher preparation ideas and problems is the National Society for the Study of Education's 103rd Yearbook, Part I, *Developing the Teacher Workforce*, edited by Mark A. Smylie and Debra Miretzky (2004).

5. Out of any particular school of philosophy or psychology in education, new ideas will emerge. Constructivism is a new idea about learning that has links to both philosophical progressivism and to cognitive and humanistic psychology. Constructivism in schooling means that learners create or construct what they learn. As a philosophical or psychological concept, it has multiple implications. An excellent source for understanding the complexities of what seems simple is the National Society for the Study of Education Ninety-Ninth Yearbook, Part I, *Constructivism in Education,* edited by D. C. Phillips (2000). There are also many articles and books available online.

6. The many disciplines of the social sciences enter the curriculum at different levels and through different courses. A very good resource for standards and discussion about social sciences in the school curriculum is the National Council for the Social Studies, which is available online at http://www.ncss.org. This is also a good link to particular discipline-affiliated associations that have Web sites; for example, the National Council for Economic Education Web site is http://www.ncee.org.

References

Adler, M. (1982). *The Paideia proposal.* New York: Macmillan.

Apple, M. W. (1979). *Ideology and curriculum.* London: Routledge.

Apple, M. W. (1991). Conservative agendas and progressive possibilities: Understanding the wider politics of curriculum and teaching. *Education and Urban Society, 23*(3), 279–291.

Baumol, W. (1988). Economic education and the critics of mainstream economics. *Journal of Economic Education, 19*(4), 323–330.

Boorstin, D. (1958). *The Americans: The colonial experience.* New York: Random House.

Boorstin, D. (1965). *The Americans: The national experience.* New York: Random House.

Boorstin, D. (1973). *The Americans: The democratic experience.* New York: Random House.

Carter, R. (1999). *Mapping the mind.* Berkeley, CA: University of California Press.

Churchland, P. S. (2002). *Brain-wise: Studies in neurophilosophy.* Cambridge, MA: Bradford Books/MIT Press.

Coleman, J. S., Campbell, E. Q., Hobson, E. J., McPartland, J., Mood, A. M., Weinfeld, F. D., & York, R. L. (1966). *Equality of educational opportunity.* Washington, DC: U.S. Government Printing Office.

Counts, G. S. (1932). *Dare the schools build a new social order?* New York: John Day.

Cuban, L. (1984). *How teachers taught: Constancy and change in American classrooms, 1890–1980.* White Plains, NY: Longman.

Degler, C. N. (1959). *Out of our past.* New York: Harper & Row.

Degler, C. N. (1991). *In search of human nature: The decline and revival of Darwinism in American thought.* New York: Oxford University Press.

Dow, P. B. (1991). *Schoolhouse politics: Lessons from the Sputnik era.* Cambridge, MA: Harvard University Press.

Dubois, R. (1974, December 14). The humanizing of humans. *Saturday Review / World,* 76–80.

Eisner, F. (1994). *The educational imagination: On the design and evaluation of school programs* (3rd ed.). New York: Macmillan.

Eisner, E. (1999). Can humanities be taught in American public schools? In M. J. Early & K. J. Rehage (Eds.), *Issues in curriculum: A selection of chapters from past NSSE yearbooks* (Ninety-Eighth Yearbook of the National Society for the Study of Education, Part II, pp. 281–300). Chicago: National Society for the Study of Education.

Freire, P. (1970). *Pedagogy of the oppressed.* New York: Herder & Herder.

Giordano, G. (2004). *Wartime schools.* New York: Peter Lang.

Goldin, C., & Katz, L. F. (1999). The shaping of higher education: The formative years in the United States, 1890–1940. *Journal of Economic Perspectives, 13*(1), 37–62.

Good, T. L. (Ed.). (2000). *American education: Yesterday, today, and yomorrow* (Ninety-Ninth Yearbook of the National Society for the Study of Education, Part II). Chicago: National Society for the Study of Education.

Goodlad, J. (1984). *A place called school.* New York: McGraw-Hill.

Gregg, M., & Leinhardt, G. (1994). Mapping out geography: An example of epistemology and education. *Review of Educational Research, 64*(2), 311–361.

Hanushek, E. A. (1997). Outcomes, incentives, and benefits: Reflections on analysis of the economics of schools. *Educational Evaluation and Policy Analysis, 19*(4), 301–308.

Hardwick, S. W., & Holtgrieve, D. G. (1996). *Geography for educators* (2nd ed.). Upper Saddle River, NJ: Prentice Hall.

Joyce, B., Weill, M., & Showers, B. (1992). *Models of teaching* (4th ed.). Needham Heights, MA: Allyn & Bacon/Simon & Schuster.

Kahn, A. J. (1998, June 12). *Themes for a history: The first hundred years of the Columbia University School of Social Work.* Paper presented at the Plenary Session I, Centennial

Celebration, New York City. Retrieved July 30, 2003, from http://www.columbia.edu/cu/ssw/welcome/ajkahn/

Keen, S. (2001). *Debunking economics.* New York: St. Martin's Press.

Kelly, A. V. (2004). *The curriculum: Theory and practice* (5th ed.). London: Sage.

Kuhn, T. (1970). *The structure of scientific revolutions.* Chicago: University of Chicago Press.

Leonardo, Z. (2004). Critical social theory and transformative knowledge: The function of criticism in quality education. *Educational Researcher, 33*(6), 11–18.

Maslow, A. (1954). *Motivation and personality.* New York: Harper & Row.

May, R. R. (1953). *Man's search for himself.* New York: Norton.

Mazlish, B. (1998). *The uncertain sciences.* New Haven, CT: Yale University Press.

McClay, W. M. (2003). Do ideas matter in America? *The Wilson Quarterly, 27*(3), 66–84.

McKelvey, B. (1963). *The urbanization of America, 1860–1915.* New Brunswick, NJ: Rutgers University Press.

Meyers, S. J., & Peterson, P. E. (1999). *Earning and learning.* Washington, DC: Brookings Institute.

National Commission on Excellence in Education. (1983). *A nation at risk.* Washington, DC: U.S. Department of Education.

Peshkin, A. (1978). *Growing up American.* Chicago: University of Chicago Press.

Phillips, D. C. (Ed.). (2000). *Constructivism in education* (Ninety-Ninth Yearbook of the National Society for Studies in Education, Part I). Chicago: National Society for the Study of Education.

Rogers, C. R. (1951). *Client-centered therapy.* Boston: Houghton Mifflin.

Ryle, G. (1949). *The concept of mind.* London: Hutchinson.

Smylie, M. A., & Miretzky, D. (2004). Developing the teacher workforce (103rd Yearbook of the National Society for the Study of Education, Part I). Chicago: National Society for the Study of Education.

Soltis, J. F. (Ed.). (1981). *Philosophy and education* (Eightieth Yearbook of the National Society for the Study of Education, Part I). Chicago: National Society for the Study of Education.

Torres, C. A. (1995). State and education revisited: Why educational researchers should think politically about education. In M. Apple (Ed.), *Review of research in education* (pp. 21, 255–331). Washington, DC: American Educational Research Association.

Vallance, E. (1999). Ways of knowing and curricular conceptions: Implications for program planning. In M. J. Early & K. J. Rehage (Eds.), *Issues in curriculum: Selected chapters from NSSE yearbooks* (Ninety-Eighth Yearbook of the National Society for the Study of Education, Part II, pp. 49–71). Chicago: National Society for the Study of Education.

Wong, K. (1992). The politics of education as a field of study: An interpretive analysis. In J. G. Cibulka, R. J. Reed, & K. K. Wong (Eds.), *The politics of education in the United States.* Washington, DC: Falmer Press.

Part III

WHAT CURRICULUM PRACTITIONERS DO

Curriculum, as a discipline, is constantly refreshing its foundational knowledge. It does this mainly with knowledge produced by academic and school-based workers. Collectively, those practitioners and others engage in various kinds of curriculum work. Understanding curriculum work, the forms it takes, who does It, and where they do it, is part of curriculum knowledge that practitioners need, and that is the focus of Part III.

Chapter 9

POLICY MAKING AND PLANNING IN CURRICULUM

Thomas James, commenting more than a decade ago about authority and politics in educational change, observed that "education is a contested public good in American society [in which] agreements forged . . . through social conflict and political consensus become embedded, tacitly or explicitly, in law and policy" (1991, pp. 169–170). In the secular world, human actions emanate from and are justified under some authority. In the Western tradition, institutions of a society derive their character and importance from a source that has authorized them into existence and given them responsibility for particular functions on behalf of the people. In America, that authority has traditionally been the people, through law based on a written constitution. Important functions such as governance and education, and specific institutions like schools and courts of law reflect constitutionally intended purposes. What makes the intended purpose real is the actual behavior of the human actors, the workers who give the ideas and activities life. Central to that work are policy making and planning activities. The former, *policy making,* is really the process of interpreting what institutions and the people in them should do and then stating what it is that they will do while giving them the tools to do it. *Planning* can be thought of as the process of creating an image, graphic, or textual representation of how the intent of the policy will be carried out and how the tools will be used. In American education and schooling, the tradition has been for policy making and planning to occur at the local level of the township, county, town, and city. As Claudia Goldin and Lawrence Katz (1999a, 1999b) suggest in their studies, this tradition existed until World War II, and that power has since been gradually ceded to the state and federal governments. The purpose here is not to revisit that historical change but to discuss policy making and planning as kinds of work in curriculum.

POLICY MAKING IN CURRICULUM WORK

Schools in America are traditionally the responsibility of the individual state for the education of its citizens. This responsibility can be thought of in two ways, structural and functional. The structural refers to the arrangement of elements, such as when a state legislature authorizes the setting up of local school districts and the executive branch of government is authorized to administer or exercise control over the schools, usually by a state board of education. The functional side of creating schools is the delineation of what it is they are to do, the curriculum they will teach and other matters related to what you think of as schooling. Think of this creative process as involving two grants of authority, one enabling the constitution (legislative), the other being delegated, as in assigning administrative responsibility, with the executive branch, state, and district sharing different degrees of authority. This structural arrangement is depicted in Figure 9.1 in relation to the policy-making function and at what level this is shared. Certain caveats are in order. First remember that there are 50 different states, and the authority–policy-making relationship establishing responsibility and organization will vary according to each state constitution. Second, keep in mind that the usual pattern has been to cede to the local school district the authority and responsibility under some state board of education umbrella. At any time, that can be altered, and, since World War II, the states have tended toward centralized policy and planning functions or have at least moved toward a more shared responsibility with local districts. This tendency will probably accelerate as more schools are designated to be in some degree of jeopardy according to the No Child Left Behind (NCLB) Act and state expectations in meeting those requirements. Third, there is the realm of lawsuits and litigation over authority and responsibility not only under NCLB but regarding funding and other perceived

Figure 9.1   Policy-Making Authority, Responsibility, and Roles

Responsible Unit	Authority	Policy Role
State	A constitution usually gives general authority to the legislature for schools and specifies enabling authority, but it can be more detailed, specifying organizational details, responsibilities, and lines of authority.	Usually authorizes the legislature to create enabling laws that set up an organization plan.
Legislature Branch	Usually makes enabling laws that specify executive branch responsibility for education while retaining oversight through legislative committees and budgetary controls.	Enables laws essentially establishing policy, but the legislature can pass laws about policy as necessary.
Executive Branch	Governor is usually an ex officio member of the state board and, in some instances, hires the state superintendent.	Houses the department of education and can establish policy for state schools and districts through the department and board.
State Board	Either elected or appointed, it is the body delegated the authority for administration of the state system of schools.	The primary day-to-day operational policymaker exercising control through the state department and superintendent.
State Department	Follows board policy and promulgates and issues directives to carry out policy as the superintendent may direct. Depending on the specificity of a policy, the board may have discretion to interpret and implement through directives.	The most important operational role in state policy making. Usually has flexibility to delegate some discretionary operational authority for policy making to the local school districts depending on the constitutional arrangements.
School District	Local board and superintendent have administrative responsibility for schools consistent with state department policies and directives. Often given flexibility in implementing policy initiatives and directives.	Has important grants of authority to make policy in areas designated by the state board and as authorized under directives from the state department of education.

inequities that have to be interpreted and with which our traditional third branch of government, the courts, gets involved. Finally, what looks like a top-down relationship of delegated authority into layers of responsibility is really a bottom-up and top-down mix where policy initiatives, the basic ideas, can begin anyplace even though they ultimately require legislative enactment through law and or executive action for implementation.

Although these structural-functional relationships are important in prefacing the matter of authority and empowerment, they also serve as a necessary prelude to understanding the critical activities of policy making and planning in schooling and curriculum work.

Law and Policy

Reiterating a crucial point, governance in American society begins with laws made under a constitution, and any authority and responsibility for doing something is assigned to some existing or created governmental agent or institution. The shared power to make laws involves specified grants of authority to do so. Laws are made at levels of authority such as the state legislature and a parish or town council, each having delegated authority in their sphere of interest. The relationship of law and policy is often likened to the chicken-egg question, which came first. Make no mistake, policy making follows from law as a grant of authority to create more laws or policy within a specified area of authority; school districts make policy for schools and schooling. You might think of this as primary and secondary lawmaking authority, such as the legislature's primary authority specified in the constitution and the secondary authority as what the legislature might grant to another agent. A second simple but important and often overlooked observation is that a legal grant of authority is essentially a piece of paper, inert until it is activated. The enabling or activation process, the act of putting something into effect, is always related to some expressed intent. What follows from enabling are the directives, usually written, that spell out the scope of authority and responsibility. In America, this has been traditionally referred to as establishing a policy, or policy making. As noted earlier, a policy has two faces: (a) as an idea prior to being enabled and (b) as a result of being enabled or made into a policy. This can be fraught with difficulties. In making policy, those responsible sometimes find they are unsure of what is intended, and they proceed to do things that were not intended. A reality sets in, the operative directive or order was faulty, vague, or both, perhaps a failure to clarify the intent implied in the directive or order, and often resources are not adequate to carry out responsibilities and organizational needs. This involves matters of scale and capacity, two ideas you will revisit later in this chapter. These interpretive voids can lead to mistakes and misinterpretations that have long-term consequences. In one notorious example, the infamous Supreme Court decision in the 1896 case of Plessy v. Ferguson in effect allowed the creation of two separate and unequal societies based on race and allowed the states to pursue policies of discrimination, particularly in regard to schools, that were not remedied until the Supreme Court reversed that ruling in 1954 in the case of Brown v. Board of Education of Topeka. This example highlights the realities of creating policy and the unexpected legal and social implications that derive from a grant of authority under law that is subject to interpretation. Your local school board, for example, has a prescribed grant of authority to enact policy in specified areas such as locating schools, reviewing approved lists of texts for selection, deciding on more general things like dress and conduct codes, hiring personnel, and approving special-purpose curriculum such as character education and drug education for use in schools. There is, of course, a very real difference between U.S. Supreme Court decisions about policy and local school board dress code policy. However, to those affected, it is still a matter of policy with its effects.

What Is Policy Making?

An observation about policy work in general is that a policy is not necessarily a law, nor is derived from one, nor becomes a direct reality by the authority of some regulation or as promulgated in a specific document. Seem confusing? This points to an interesting subtlety. When considering what a policy requires, there is an important distinction to keep in mind—it can exist in two forms, as a statement or as an enactment. Ripley (1985), in an early study of policy analysis, refers to a *policy statement* as an expression of intent by some agent or agency and differentiates it from a *policy enactment,* where the agent or agency sets up the actions it will implement. A policy-making process begins in a statement about the policy desired, the enactment occurring either through a mix of further directives or legislation in pursuit of it by the policy-making agent or agency, or by a grant of authority to some other actor.

Policy making is a priority undertaking. From the creation of a policy movement, the super idea, flows the laws and regulations that govern all activity undertaken in pursuit of that policy. It begins with the floating of ideas into the public domain, a primary activity of interest groups, political parties, and other organized entities and individuals. The contemporary scene has numerous ideas seeking to become policy items. The movements for vouchers and charter schools are examples of ideas that groups are seeking to implement by influencing policy-making bodies, particularly state legislatures and the Congress of the United States. Probably the most important current policy initiative is the NCLB legislation, which is essentially a law putting into force a policy of accountability. In Figure 9.2, the policy-making process is suggested in relation to the development of the NCLB legislation in 2001. This is, of course, a very limited rendering of a far more time-consuming and complex deliberative process in promulgating the law. The effect of that policy has been alluded to in various preceding chapters and will occupy an important place in Chapter 13 and 14 discussions about issues and trends in curriculum and schooling.

Characteristics of Effective Policy Making

The world of policy making encompasses a variety of activities, from policy initiation to statements and enactments. Andrew Porter (1994) has studied policy matters and

Figure 9.2   A Policy-Making Example

Policy Idea	In order to have a competitive, world-class educational system, there is a need for some centralized systematic accountability to evaluate school performance.
Policy Making	A law, the No Child Left Behind Act of 2001, is created by the United States Congress and signed by the president in 2002. The law is now national policy.
Policy Statement	The law as published (the official and primary statement) authorizes the U.S. Department of Education to establish regulations (secondary policy statements) as necessary to carry out the congressional intent, establishing among other things a process for evaluating schooling.
Policy Enactment	The U.S. Department of Education implements the law through directives that apply to any recipient/participant in a federally funded program and exercises authority as the official interpreter of the act.

Figure 9.3   General Policy and Curriculum Policy Characteristics

General Policy Characteristics	*Curriculum Policy Characteristics*
• It must be *coherent*, as in being logical, orderly, and perhaps even aesthetic, in the relationships of its parts.	• It must be *articulate* and specify clearly what the curriculum is to be and how it is to be organized.
• It must have *authority* specified so responsibility for executing the policy is clear.	• The policy is self-*explanatory;* it addresses itself so that participants or stakeholders understand what it is and how it will affect them operationally.
• It is *empowered* in itself, meaning it is not dependent on other agents to assist it and has sufficient resources to carry out its responsibilities.	• An articulate and explanatory policy earns *acceptance,* which enhances the possibility for successful implementation.
• It is *stable* in that it is coherent, has the requisite authority, and is empowered.	• *Stability* depends on it being *replicable* and *feasible;* it can be applied in various school settings with a likelihood of success.

formulated a set of four characteristics that frame policy development and implementation. These general characteristics are summarized in Figure 9.3.

One characteristic is *coherence;* a policy makes sense as an entity unto itself and doesn't contradict other policies. It has to have *authority,* as in being legitimate through or under law. A third quality is *power;* a policy has to have some incentive system that compels or inclines participants to support and become directly involved in the policy. Last is *stability,* the idea that a policy must be consistent over time, retaining support and a seamless existence. As with most formulations of elements or characteristics that are used to shape a frame of reference, there is no particular order to their consideration. This sense of random path building was suggested some years ago in Decker Walker's (1971) study of real-world curriculum work. Think of these elements as frames around a window: if you look left, down, up, or right, you encounter one of the frames that bound the window, but you ultimately have to encounter or consider all frames. Often, how you address the frames is a function of your own thinking or perceptual style, and, as suggested in Chapter 8, a reflection of your social-cultural understanding and your philosophy. In Figure 9.3, these are recast as characteristics in curriculum work and the formulation is a little different. In curriculum it requires *articulation,* formulating and confirming its intent, and *explication,* making it understandable to others. It has to be *acceptable,* as in suggesting how it will apply, in what cases, and with what result. Additionally, two other conditions seem warranted, it has to be *replicable* and *realizable* in application, meaning what applies in one place will be the same as another, and those using or implementing the curriculum believe it will work. For example, any educational policy must have stability. If it is a policy about curriculum, that stability factors into characteristics of being replicable and feasible. To get some idea of how policy making relates to schooling and curriculum, consider the case for comprehensive schooling made after World War II when returning veterans came home, marriage boomed, and so did the numbers of children soon to enter school. The upshot was a need to develop some way of schooling for the diverse needs of that burgeoning population, a challenge taken up by the National Education Association (NEA) and James Bryant Conant, respected president of Harvard and influential advisor on science education matters. The NEA was at that time not the labor union of today but the national forum for discussing all things educational. In two 1947 reports issued under the auspices of the NEA and two later books by James Conant, *The American High School Today* (1959) and *The Comprehensive High School* (1967), the movement to reinvent schools and particularly secondary schooling prompted policy initiatives in the form of reports and books outlining what curriculum should be like, initiated new functions such as guidance and counseling, and influenced thinking to mesh architectural form with curricular intentions. The policy initiatives that became laws were primarily in states like California and New York. At the federal level, the most important event was the enactment of the National Defense Education Act in 1958 and related federal legislation that followed over the next decade. The carrot was the money being offered at the federal level, which led schools and teachers to participate in the new math and science curriculums under the National Defense Education Act. The stick was that to authorize participation, the states in varying degrees were to imitate comprehensive school ideas by enacting their own laws: financing school construction and developing curriculum and related services in line with the reports and Conant's recommendations. Using the comprehensive high school movement as an example and applying the characteristics of curriculum policy making helps to illustrate how policy making works.

Articulation

The formulation of a comprehensive school policy began with the reports of the NEA and its affiliates, the Association for Supervision and Curriculum Development and the National Association of Secondary School Principals. The specific curriculum ideas emerged as ways to expand the curriculum to serve vocational, college preparatory, and general job or business (as it was referred to at the time) interests as appropriate to individual and community needs. It was a set of policy proposals to achieve a standard curriculum and make it equally available to all students with supporting services to enhance learner success. Whereas the primary aim was the high school and secondary education, curriculum scope and sequence led to considerations about K–12 schooling as well. As noted in Chapter 7, the history of change in schooling has been predominately a top-down affair, with colleges dictating curriculum to high schools and they to middle/junior high schools, who in turn influence elementary schools; schooling is a flow-through process. The idea of schooling being a flow-through process seems rather simplistic, but it has very important implications for articulating curriculum. First, the idea of flow-through made it acceptable to consider curriculum from top to bottom. It made it easier for the National Science Foundation and academic discipline experts to suggest a curriculum structure for science and mathematics. Second, because they were the experts, their views were acceptable and they were able to articulate a K–12 science and mathematics curriculum scope and sequence. Third, the legitimacy gained in science and mathematics articulation carried over into social studies, arts, and other areas of the curriculum. This was not, of course, in the same vein as contemporary efforts to articulate standards and assessments, but it created the possibility for that. What was and is still missing is the joining of standards with a clearly articulated curriculum scope and sequence. That is an issue that will be discussed further in Chapter 13.

Explanation

The set of proposals under the comprehensive school banner was made easily understandable in Conant's books. With Carnegie Foundation support, the book received free distribution to all NEA members and a wider circulation to political, business, and community leaders. Reading either of Conant's books, one is struck by the careful marshaling of evidence and the direct connection to a curriculum recommendation—elegant simplicity followed by a clear discussion, relevant to and in the language of the public. Parallel to Conant's ideas, other elements in support were being marshaled. The cold war was reality, and a well-educated citizenry would enhance national defense.

More subtly argued to influence the federal government was the point that American success against communism was dependent on engineers and scientists that were well schooled in sciences and mathematics. America's international leadership role and political power necessitated development of a cadre of experts with knowledge of other parts of the world. There followed an expansion of curriculum projects into languages and socials sciences because language and knowledge experts in such areas as Chinese, Russian, and Slavic studies were needed. It is interesting to note that studies focusing on the nations of the Middle East, Mexico, and the Americas were not considered as important, a lack of foresight and balance that would later lead to a serious lack of such experts, particularly those with fluency in the languages and knowledge of the Middle East.

Acceptance

Gaining acceptance for a proposed policy involves perceptions about needs and wants, and the transparency of intentions by advocates. Acceptance is sought at two levels at least. The first is the public the policy would serve, and the second is the participants: teachers, administrators, and scholars whose work the policy will most directly affect. For the public, acceptability may mean simply the legitimacy of who says it is needed and the level of trust that provides. For the participant crowd, it is a matter of reasonable proof, the development of assessments with evaluation that give weight to arguments for or against a policy. Matters of assessment and evaluation are a particular kind of curriculum work and await discussion in Chapter 12. For the audiences at either level, there are several key considerations. Is the problem or the perception of a need evident in the target audience or the public in general? And, if so, is it wanted—is there a perception that the proposal fits the need? The condition of American schooling in the immediate postwar years was one of benign neglect. There was a general public sense of the need to refurbish schools because materials for civilian use had been committed to the war effort, school building had languished, books and materials were old, and teachers had entered military service so that few were in the teacher education process. The effects of the inevitable neglect of the war years, such as old curriculum materials and aging schools, along with the immediate need to expand public schooling to accommodate the new wave of children entering kindergartens and who would in a few years overwhelm high school capabilities, were compelling evidence. It was a time when an articulate, explicated proposal was saleable and acceptable, especially for curriculum and particularly for what would be called the new mathematics and sciences. There was a generally observed public need energized by the end of war and a feeling that it was time to get on with life! Reading in the newspapers and the editorials of the day, you get a sense of the public trust for authorities and experts to run things in the best interests of the people. Selling America on America was not an issue in 1946 or during the Korean War in the early 1950s. The skeptical times would come later.

Replicability

The matter of replicating a proposal is more tenuous than other characteristics because replication is synonymous with duplication and copy. Applied to curriculum policy making, replication does not refer to replication of images, that associated with the machine process of duplicating or copying a whole thing like this page you are reading. Rather, replication refers to application, as in a conceptualization that is dependent on the inclusion of proposal particulars as they fit the situation or circumstance. Think of second-grade teachers Archer and Smith who are implementing the nine-step Fictitious Reading Process. The process is nine steps and has to be used that way. However, each will use it consistent with considerations of and knowledge about the classroom setting, the children as individuals and readers, the complexity of the process, and the framework or guidelines for implementation. If you were to observe their work, you would probably note how each teacher maintains the integrity of purpose for the process while modifying the implementation based on the factors noted. The integrity of the process in this example is maintained, but the process is adjusted to fit the context in which it is placed—that's replication. Obviously, in some curriculum policy work, the integrity of the policy is important, but it is also important to remember that the proposal must form a fit with other considerations that will vary across settings and sociocultural concerns. Proposals for the comprehensive school curriculum would of necessity need to fit the local setting and conditions and be modifiable as they were implemented. A model for an urban or suburban setting might not fit in a rural setting or the reverse. There is also the local reception to curriculum change. People in rural areas living farm lives might not perceive the new math or science curriculum as essential to work and life in the countryside. Those in a community with high-tech opportunities or who expect their children to enter college might think otherwise. Articulation is about implementation itself, not about whether it is selectively or universally applied. There is sometimes the specter of eliteness: which group gets the new curriculum, which doesn't, and how and by whom those decisions are made. In the mix of characteristics, matters of replication can often highlight the failures to articulate, explain, and gain acceptance of a policy and what follows from it.

Feasibility

A proposal may fulfill all the preceding conditions and still not be feasible. You are probably familiar with the term *feasibility study,* referring to making a determination about whether something is workable. The literature on contemporary school and curriculum reform proposals since 1983 (e.g., Cohen & Hill, 2001; Gamoran, 1998) suggests that for a proposed policy to be feasible or tangible (e.g., the creation of a curriculum), it must be seen as matching the intent of the policy statement and that it can be accomplished. When the NCLB of 2001 was passed, the United States Congress and the president were declaring that act to be feasible. In the few years since its inception, state experiences with its implementation suggest, however, that there are problems that bring the assumptions underlying feasibility into question, a point Benjamin Levin raised in an earlier 1998 study. Problems with the workability of such a law are not uncommon and can result from different perceptions of whether a policy result reflects the policy as intended and as written into the laws and acts to carry out a policy. Policy makers may see it one way, participants or observers another, for any number of reasons: The intended may not occur, what was replicable fails to fit, what was acceptable may lose support over the time it takes to implement, or replication may not prove viable with the conditions of implementation. All these factors suggest the fragility inherent in policy making. A policy flourishes to the degree each of its constituent elements is implemented and fulfilled as it was intended.

In applying those measures of success to the proposals for a comprehensive high school and its new curriculum, there was an overall effectiveness in creating a standard of curriculum that was variously implemented across states and communities. One measure of success would seem to be whether a person could move from one place to another, from one curriculum to another, and fit into that new curriculum without personal penalty. The historical record suggests that test was met. A second measure, one also initially as subjective, was whether there would be a residual curriculum impact— that is to say, would the new approaches in curriculum result in improved learning? The failure to implement evaluations for most aspects of the policy is a notorious deficiency. However, the need to answer the second question led to another significant policy, the development of the National Assessment of Educational Progress (NAEP). Over time, the historical trail of events and results from that assessment program suggest that the policy decision for the NAEP was a step forward, and at least anecdotal evidence suggests the reforms were a success in their time and place. Possibly the most important residual effect of the comprehensive school movement and subsequent curriculum changes was the growing role and clout of the federal government in Washington in all matters educational, especially in schooling and increasingly in curriculum.

PERSPECTIVE INTO PRACTICE:
Policy, Curriculum, and Implications at the Elementary and Secondary Level

Policy-Making Level	*Elementary Application*	*Secondary Application*
At the **national level, in the NAEP,** certain curriculum knowledge area discrepancies are found from last year's scores.	NAEP results indicate fourth-grade science learning has slipped nationally but unevenly by state, suggesting individual states need to study the problem.	NAEP science scores at the 10th-grade level have not changed compared to last year's results. However, analysis suggests certain weaknesses in knowledge about biology in some state scores.

(Continued)

(Continued)

The **State Board of Education**, based on a comparative review of state and NAEP data by the State Department of Education, develops a policy to review key curriculum areas.	The state has required each district to review results across affected schools and, as applicable, submit a plan of corrective action for the district and/or identified schools, submitted in a report with material resource, curriculum, and personnel needs.	State data suggest 14 school districts with deficiencies. State department science specialists and State Science Advisory Board experts meet with identified districts' curriculum specialists and biology teachers to develop responses to a State Board policy directive to address problems.
The **local school board** directs the district curriculum staff to prepare recommendations for the board to approve and send to the state, including a plan of action, materials, staffing, and assistance needs the district can supply, together with a request for any additional assistance in those areas where district capacity is inadequate.	Assistance is needed in reading in two low-performing elementary schools. The district temporarily reassigns three specialists and requests matching assistance in personnel or funds to hire the same.	The district board creates a science advisory panel coordinated by the science curriculum specialist, with biology experts from the local college, a scientist provided by a local biomedical company, and the biology/science secondary faculty to study discrepancies and make recommendations, immediate and long range, for biology and then for other sciences, such as chemistry and physics, commensurate with the state test data.

PLANNING IN CURRICULUM WORK

In discussing policy making and policy-related elements, one element in particular, planning, has been alluded to but touched on lightly. Policy does not just fall into place, it requires thinking about how to implement it, what course or courses of action to take. In a word, it needs a plan. Simply put, a *plan* segues from policy to implementation. Planning can be a random exercise, such as children planning to build a tree house and proceeding while adjusting activities as they learn along the way. In the adult, academic sense of it, planning should take on a robustness that adheres to certain practices found to be useful or proven useful as part of a particular vocation, profession, or practice. Teachers, for example, have lesson plans. These are usually composed of goals or objectives, a series of steps to implement them, identification of curriculum to be taught, instructional tools to use, and some immediate feedback loop for evaluation of the experience. That is the general sense of planning and a plan. Having been introduced to the matter of policy and policy making as part of the world of curriculum work, now consider what comes next: the formality of planning that follows in curriculum work once policy has been established.

Characteristics of Effective Planning

Planning, like policy making, is characterized by certain conditions. There is an old adage in the military that "proper planning prevents poor performance," the so-called 5 Ps of success. In curriculum, the planning focus is also on proper planning so that a developed curriculum will perform satisfactorily in the actual living of it in schools. The word "proper" unfortunately conveys the idea that there is a particular way of doing planning; you need to keep in mind that there is no single model but many models, a veritable menu of models, and they often differentiate by the profession or kinds of tasks for which they are formulated. A planning model in engineering or one in mathematics is distinguished by the knowledge area, purpose, and context of its use. The differences in planning a mission to the moon and a 30-minute lesson plan for curriculum engagement in an elementary classroom might seem extreme; however, each in its own way is important and leads to consequence of scale, specific results, and long-term effects. Inherent in each is a planning process and, as some studies (Boostrom, Jackson, & Hanson, 1993; Connelly & Clandinin, 1988) seem to suggest, there are at least four qualities that are important in planning as a work activity in curriculum: outlining or creating a *perspective,* establishing a *framework,* identifying a *design,* and creating *documentation* that serves as a record of the activities and a body of data that can be revisited.

Planning Perspective

A perspective (see earlier discussions in Chapters 1 and 3) refers to the cognitive or intellectual angle from which you look at and distill the critical elements from a policy that must be followed or included if the policy is to be implemented as intended. It forms a formal, shared understanding about how to commonly think about the work to be undertaken. Two aspects of planning are important here. One, perhaps the most important, is to uncover the embedded perspective the policy makers used and agree upon its implied intent. Second, and consonant with the first, is to focus on the purposes or goals for which the curriculum change is intended. Keeping those in mind is important if the results of the policy, which flow from planning, are to attain what was intended. A consensus on the perspective does not mean workers must all think the same way; rather, the importance is to raise a common consciousness about the policy's interpretive, operational frame of reference and applicable policy directives. Differing perceptions that appear can suggest and point to a working group's professional knowledge needs that will encourage and enhance the composite of personal-professional philosophical points of view that participants bring to the work. As discussed in

Chapters 5 and 8, the foundational professional beliefs formulated by you frame your perspective and are always at the front of your involvement. That philosophical personalization is embedded in two points that are important here. First, it is essential to remember that the planning function should provide the framework for curriculum development and other work under the policy umbrella. Second, planning reflects multiple perspectives, the personal professional ones of each worker, and the shared formal perspective developed to guide planning. Inherent in a professional perspective is recognition that it is one among other possible perspectives that might be constructed. A perspective developed to guide work is similar to the formation of what Decker Walker (1990) refers to as the "deliberative platform" in his model of curriculum work. Simply stated, the perspective is what is created when one responds to the thought, "Now how am I going to do this?" and comes up with a way to proceed. It is the creating of a frame of reference, a construction for thinking about and doing curriculum planning work.

Framework

Central to curriculum planning is the creation of a framework that serves two essential purposes. First, it has to function as a frame of reference, a guide for thinking about curriculum based on an articulated perspective. Second, the framework should identify and set up the actions that take place in preparation for segueing into other types of curriculum work: development, management/maintenance, and assessment-evaluation activities, for example. The framework becomes a mental picture, like a blueprint that is preparatory and guides building construction, a map that allows one to traverse a landscape, or a recipe as in cooking. Blueprints, maps, and recipes are preliminary guides that frame the range of thinking about actions to be taken. The frame-of-reference-as-framework allows for creative changes in the doing of other curriculum work that follows from it. Teachers in contemporary classrooms are responding in various ways to the NCLB as interpreted and extended to classroom matters. An individual teacher and his or her colleagues have to "react" and possibly interpret what is expected of them. They already possess a professional perspective and may be concerned and reticent about the unknowns where accountability is the byword. In short, they have a framework but it may not fit; they may not have been provided an opportunity to conform or convert to policy that has been sent down to them but not explained to them at the school and classroom level (Swanson & Stevenson, 2002).

Design

The framework bounds another aspect of planning, creating an image, a form, of what the curriculum might look like, as in something imagined but not developed. This is the scheme of things, the heart of the framework, a design of something. The problem is that among curriculum writers and scholars, there is no precise, consistent use of design. Some consider the whole matter of planning that is included in curriculum development as, for example, a "design" (Armstrong, 2003) phase or as creating an "organizational pattern" (Walker, 1990). The term *design* is used here not as "curriculum design" but in the larger meaning of design as a creative process of representing something before it is articulated in its details, as in a house design before it is drawn architecturally in its details. Designs occur after a plan has been formulated, and they are based on the particulars set forth in a plan. This gives the process of design a pliable rather than fixed quality that is important and allows reference to the activities of policy making as the foundation for plans and then designs. The design function in planning is part of the planning process, not necessarily a result. The better-known references to design are adaptive ones; those cited most often in curriculum books (see Pinar, Reynolds, Slattery, & Taubman, 2002; Schubert, Schubert, Thomas, & Carroll, 2002) carry titles such as fusion, broad-fields, core, and subject matter curriculum, which will be discussed in Chapter 10 (or you can consult the Glossary). Each represents a planning process based on a particular design but not necessarily a specified way of actually creating a curriculum from a design, as in thinking about the transition of making a dress or suit from design to pattern to product.

Documentation

Often what is missing in curriculum work is a record of proceedings: in short, a record in written or other data form that confirms (documents) what has occurred. Think of the minutes of a meeting that as nearly as possible represent an accurate report of what went on. It is essential to have a recorded history of deliberations, a calendar of work and notations of how something was planned, designed, and managed. Documentation simply refers to the need to create a record that mirrors what was done, when, and by whom. Documentation already exists at the policy-making level because the policy itself is in some written form (see the discussion in Chapter 4). Even so, it may lack notational details that help one understand the policy-making process out of which the document arose. Documenting the planning function that issues from policy provides a record of work and if, for example, a curriculum is to be developed based on the planning, it helps to have rich documentation so the planning process holds as faithfully to policy as possible. School board meetings, for example, have official records that are usually both written and voice recorded so there is a redundancy in verifying the decisions and discussions that occur. In curriculum and schooling, documentation takes many forms, such as assessments, evaluations, notes, written papers, and anecdotal compilations, and is found at all levels of curriculum work. Several examples of methods or formats for documenting work are also management tools; curriculum-mapping, for example, discussed in Chapter 11, and assessment and evaluation tools, discussed in Chapter 12, can be documentation tools as well.

Factors Affecting the Complexity of Planning

Planning in curriculum work is very much a process of elaboration. Often it is the proceeding from something simply understood through degrees of complexity, a layering that builds up or adds to what is meant originally. There are several factors affecting elaboration and the degree to which it is needed; these aspects refer to the matters of scale, responsibility and capacity in planning and, as you will encounter in the next several chapters, other curriculum work. The simplicity or complexity of the planning work being undertaken will determine the degree of significance each factor assumes in the planning activity.

Scale and Capacity

The creation of a policy does not mean that a single, specific, common plan will necessarily follow from it. Much depends on scale and capacity, two terms previously discussed in Chapter 4. Suppose a school board establishes policy X and directs administrators to implement it. Several scenarios are possible. The superintendent could direct the central administrative staff to create a plan. Another option is to direct each school principal to come up with his or her own plan. Those considerations about the units to be involved represent the scale of effect, the numbers and inclusive settings affected by the policy. In a centralized approach, there is one plan for all. When the planning task is decentralized, there could be as many plans as there are schools; obviously the scale will vary. The characteristics in planning, the perspective, framework, design, and documentation, would all be affected in different ways. The capacity of a unit such as a school is what it is capable of doing, the capital consisting of people, resources, funds, and so forth that allow it to do its mission. For example, it is difficult for a school to provide an up-to-date curriculum if the materials are out of date or if the teaching faculty doesn't keep up with what is going on in their particular knowledge area or doesn't have the special support to retain that capability.

Variation in Standards

One of the problems with current curriculum standards reform, such as the NCLB, is the variation in standards both across state standards and within content areas such as mathematics and history. The efforts to change curriculum as part of the larger school reform movement are often interpreted as based on a "one size fits all" perspective, whereas each state and the various curriculum content experts tend to see standards and planning as state or discipline specific. The matter of the perspective from which these issues are viewed looms large in these debates. The Council on Basic Education has, for example, historically been an advocate of liberal arts curriculum, particularly the arts and humanities, and a watchdog for curricular imbalance, that is to say, less time devoted to the study of that part of the school curriculum. Their survey of school principals in the United States (Council on Basic Education, 2004) suggests that the humanities, arts, and social studies curriculums are receiving less instructional time than other curriculum areas. One inference is that this is due to the emphasis on meeting standards in math and science curriculum. A second implication, the matter of the perspective taken, is that the scope and sequence of the total curriculum are out of balance, with not enough time devoted to those curriculums. Of course, if you were of the perspective that math and science are more important, then it is unlikely you would see an imbalance. The heart of those issues is the curriculum. It is partly a contemporary concern about policy and planning for curriculum standards, an almost eerie reprise of Herbert Spencer's question, "What knowledge is of most worth?" It is also partially a struggle over what agent or agency will have policy responsibility for deciding curriculum issues. In choosing one agent over another, there is also the problem of settling on one particular framework for planning over another, perhaps without knowing the particulars of either framework that will guide planning or design decisions. If either the Council on Basic Education or the National Science Foundation were given master control over the curriculum, you could surmise in what direction curriculum policy and planning would take.

Responsibility and Control

Central to any policy-planning discussion is the matter of responsibility and who will control the process. As noted earlier in this chapter, policy making and the planning that may issue rely on clear statements of assigned responsibility and having the capacity to carry out the work. If there are several agents under consideration, will control be outright or shared? For example, under the NCLB, it is very murky as to whether federal or state authorities have responsibility for some aspects of planning or making further policy at the state level to implement mandates, an important and as yet unresolved matter of legal standing in the federal relationship. Given that you know the constitutional divides in America, what would and should be the role of the federal government and individual states? What part should local districts, nationally influential lobbies, interest groups, and professional organizations play? As Meredith Honig (2004) suggests in her studies of the role of such intermediary organizations in educational policy, at the present time, the matter of control over curriculum and other aspects of schooling is still contested. Matters of policy and planning in curriculum work that affect American schooling hinge on these legal mechanisms and the power influence of those various forces. With a federal rather than centralized arrangement of authority, it will continue to be that way. Those, however, are issues ripe for a more extended discussion in Chapter 13.

STATE AND LOCAL POLICY AND PLANNING

Who are other players in curriculum policy and planning work? The parties already mentioned include the key federal and state agencies such as the U.S. Department of Education and state departments of education or instruction, as they are variously titled. The general public in the local context is aware of most policy making and associated planning. That's because stories about it appear in the local papers, it is the subject of local TV reports, or an announcement about it comes home from school with the family students in some form, perhaps a newsletter. Policy in the broad sense is the responsibility of the school board, most often based on policy initiatives either given to or requested by the board from the school superintendent and staff. Again, keep in mind that this will vary by states and sometimes by local tradition and law. Policy aside, curriculum planning usually is the province of the district central office and usually handled by a curriculum supervisor or someone in a similar midmanagement position. Because there are a range of policy and planning possibilities and a variety of contributors, a look at the impetus for policy and planning, the relationships that direct those activities at the state and local levels, is in order.

State Mandates

The primary locations for all kinds of policy and planning work about schools and schooling are the individual states. As suggested earlier, the granting of policy-making authority in a state usually begins with legislative action. A state constitution may also direct that the authority be vested in a particular body or department such as a state board of education but gives the legislature statutory authority to create that body and specify its powers. The key point to keep in mind is that legislatures usually delegate responsibility to another body. They may attach strings, but the work is done elsewhere. The legislature at times effects curriculum change through legislation that tells the state board or some other authority to do a certain thing. It is not uncommon for state legislatures to do that, especially establishing special mandates like those for economic education, character education, or some other addition to the curriculum or school program. They can also establish policy about instructional time, days in the school year, and other schooling matters that can impact curriculum and teaching. Usually the manner of implementing policy, how it will be planned and carried out, and who will bear the responsibility, is left to the state board's discretion. In that case, curriculum-planning work assumes a central work importance. One recent extension of state mandates has been in the area of policy development in response to NCLB of 2001. That law can be seen as either suggesting or requiring intrusion (Elmore, 2002; Kohn, 2001) into schools in a state if assessment-evaluation results indicate a school is failing according to some measure, either a federal one or one that the state has set up. Keep in mind that the concept of failure or of a failing school is tied to tests and attendance and does not take into account cultural, ethnic, historical, or social factors at the local school community level. Identifying failing schools as far as states are concerned has to do with student performance on tests, not what they may or may not know, or other factors previously mentioned. State remediation responses have ranged from taking over a failed school, providing money to employ staff or experts in an effort to build on-site or school or district capacity to remediate, reconstituting school boards, closing schools permanently or reopening with all new staff, transferring students, opting for alternative schools such as charters, and, in some citywide school districts, turning the matter over to the mayor or a specific group of experts set up to run the district. A casual reading of *Education Week* offers a continuous presentation of such examples. Some studies (James, 1991; Loveless, 1998) of this new mandating role suggest that the crucial factor is the capacity of the state department of education to plan and implement such activities and that, with a few exceptions, state-level departments have not been up to the task.

The Textbook Review Process

At the state level of government, one of the most important curriculum work functions related to policy and planning is the process of reviewing and selecting textbooks. Whereas other curriculum work matters seem routine (e.g., creating scope and sequence documents or directives about reading and subject matter areas), planning for text selection is often the most notorious and interesting. Although it varies, each state has some procedure for approving curriculum materials for use by school districts. Some allow districts to set up their own publisher solicitation and approval procedure. Others do it through the state department of education, which then creates textbook review committees. Committee participants are usually chosen according to some politically agreed -on formula to include laypersons (prominent citizens, for example); appointees by the governor, appointees by key legislative leaders, curriculum experts, particularly college or university faculty; and schooling representatives such as school teachers, administrators, and staff. Whether it is a state- or district-established approval process, it is often a contested one.

The planning process for selecting texts usually proceeds according to curriculum areas, social studies, mathematics, and so forth. It is usually cyclical—mathematics one year, language arts the next—giving the process a rhythmic quality. The distance in years between reviews varies by state but a curriculum text is often in use for up to 6 or 8 years before it is replaced, and sometimes legislatures extend that when there is a budget crisis. There is also a related obsolescence issue. After several years of use, the content is not current in conveying the latest knowledge or scope and sequence changes. Even a new textbook takes 2 years to develop, though the evolution through editions after that does allow for keeping the contents somewhat current. State boards and the state department of education often must do additional planning in curriculum areas where text obsolescence creates obvious knowledge gaps. Teachers are often aware of this with regards to history and science texts that are outdated. In most states, planning for text selection includes developing content specifications for textbooks so that publisher submissions have met some preliminary set of criteria. The committee's task is to review and recommend which texts should be approved, that is to say, those that in the judgment of the committee most closely "fit" the state course of study for the curriculum or other criteria being used. Following a series of meetings that may take most of a year, the state department of education takes the committee-approved recommendations to the state board for its consideration and approval. The crucial point is reached during the series of public meetings where any interested citizen can ask to speak. These can be contentious sessions, especially when advocates for sensitive issues offer comments about curriculum materials. In Texas, California, and other volume text-purchasing states, the stakes are obviously high and legislative approval is important. Publishers often have to meet special requirements such as ensuring accuracy and including changes and modifications to content. In some cases, the state itself may take action in the form of disclaimers in texts or the issuance of specially constructed curriculum materials in place of some offending text content or as a supplement to some perceived content deficiency.

The whole textbook selection process, regardless of the state in which it occurs, is a reflection of how curriculum planning works at the state level. And, to a degree, what happens there affects how and what planning occurs at the local district level. The degrees of freedom allowed in selecting textbooks and other curriculum materials, the range of vendors and choices, and the number of texts approved can affect local curriculum planning options. Another problem is that districts may be confined to text choices they don't think are the best academically for their students and communities. Or special interests at the local level may complain about the content in the same way they did at the state level and require some form of compromise. In states where it is a more decentralized process and districts evaluate texts, textbook committee composition may also involve similar political considerations about what is selected.

Aside from the charged process of text approval, most curriculum planning functions are fairly mundane and noncontroversial. States, particularly the state department of education, maintain a capacity for continuous planning because they need to serve the state board, the state superintendent, and legislative committees dealing with K–12 educational matters, all of whom request research information, ask for testimony, and make other demands that require considered responses. Governors often sit as ex officio heads of the state boards and in some instances appoint the members. As head of the executive branch, governors also influence planning by creating agendas for the state, which can in some cases be carried out by executive order. The dual legislative and executive influence further reinforces the need for a responsive planning capability that in turn gives guidance by creating plans that provide a framework for school district implementation.

Mandates and Expectations in the School District

School districts have the authority to establish policy within the constraints established under the state constitution and powers exercised by the legislative and executive branches of government. What follows in terms of planning responsibilities will vary from state to state. However, several comments about planning do apply in a general way. Often, the state makes mandates on what schools are to do both operationally and with curriculum. These affect the kinds of curriculum issues with which school districts have to deal, their responsibilities and capabilities in regard to them, and the expectations that accompany them in the community they serve. Policy and planning matters usually don't appear on the radar screen unless they are controversial. What's controversial? Check out your local newspaper and the school board reports and you will get some hint. Most of it is routine but important, such as developing policies about school bus routes, appropriate dress (an example of the hidden curriculum), budget matters, food services, and related operational issues.

Outside of increasing taxes, sports, and dress issues, few things matter more or become more controversial than what affects what is to be learned, the curriculum. A requirement to teach economic education or character education can require extra time and unexpected expenditures for materials to the detriment of some other curriculum. An increase in state graduation requirements, more mathematics and science, for example, means something else has to give, usually something in the arts and social studies curriculum. That may not sit well with local parents and students because it may be seen as a threat to students' career desires or even to their graduation. Public acceptance of changes in schooling is premised on the expectation that curriculum requirements will remain consistent and adjustments will not unduly threaten their students' successful passage through the schooling process. The general tendency of the public is to understand that as times change, so does knowledge and thus the curriculum, but radical departures must be justified; what you remember about your curriculum experience prefaces in a general way what you think students should be learning moderated by the changes in knowledge that have occurred since your time in school. Possible clashes between parent and school are likely when there is a parental perception of messing with a child's schooling, sometimes attributable to the mismatch between a parent's expectations and perceptions and the reality of school life, curriculum, and policies pursued.

Beyond the individual school problems with curriculum, there is also the pressure on schools, administrators, and local boards from interest groups. Certainly, one of the most vocal and demanding groups are parents of children with special needs. The push-pull effect of different federal policy initiatives from one administration to another often results in confusing policy changes. One year, special needs children are pulled out of regular classrooms to receive assistance; the next year, special teachers are embedded in the classroom. And so it goes as policy changes. Think of the changes in planning that are needed to accommodate such policy shifts and remember the attendant start-up costs that attach to planning and implementing a new policy. The financial capacity to provide not just a meat-and-potatoes curriculum but one with salad and dessert translates into money for supplemental texts; the latest in laboratory and support materials, such as maps and software programs; and advanced placement and honors curriculum courses. The differences in district financial capacity is a problem across the nation—what basic level of curriculum is necessary to ensure equity is the question now headed to the courts in a number of states.

Local Responsibilities and Capabilities

Suppose a state board of education under its policy authority directs the state department and superintendent to review elementary reading programs in the state. After the review, the state board of education recommends that there are too many different programs and the state should focus on one approach, either whole language or phonics. Sidestepping this polemical issue, the state board establishes a policy letting local districts decide the matter. Responsibility for policy and planning has been set; the state board has passed the matter to the local level. Establishing a reading policy and planning for it are now the obligation of the local board and district. Given this speculative situation, what options are there? At least two options are possible. They can choose one or the other reading approach and proceed to provide the relevant curriculum. A second choice might be to provide curriculum for both options so the teacher can adapt a flexible approach based on what works with individual students. The net effect in choice two is that the decision is made at the classroom level. Any of these choices carries with it important capability considerations. Proposals for curriculum change also entail new responsibilities. Consider the following aspects that need to be included in curriculum planning where the curriculum is being changed by adoption of a new text or textbook series.

Funding. A new curriculum requires new books and other materials. Where will funds come from? The state? The district? Does the local district budget have funding set aside? If there is no contingency for this new curriculum, where will adjustments be made in the district budget and will that be at the expense of some other area of the curriculum? Funding will also be needed for professional development work and other needs.

Training. Every new curriculum entails some professional development/in-service time. Central office staffs, usually the appropriate curriculum specialist, prepare to lead the implementation. They must become the district's curriculum authority, conducting curriculum workshops, giving presentations, and being generally ready to assist teachers with the curriculum and the range of materials with which they will work. If there is no in-district training capability, where does it come from? Publishing houses often provide consultant service for training district personnel according to the cost of the purchase package. These services may include training appropriate in-district curriculum specialists or conducting familiarization sessions for teachers for on-site training. The amount of training or consulting assistance accessible is usually scaled according to the amount of money spent. Take the example of adopting an American history text for high school. If it is a text-only purchase, the assistance package will be limited in comparison to a text-plus-supplementary-materials package.

Resources. In addition to funding and training issues, curriculum planning work may entail other resource needs. Training or provision of explanatory materials may mean the copying or printing of reproducible materials that accompany the text. Videos, CDs, or other training media will require appropriate supporting technology that must also be accessible. Districts with limited technical capabilities, portable or fixed, or with limited funds for such equipment will be at a disadvantage in planning.

Support. A fourth and often overlooked factor in planning is considering after-adoption support needs. Sustaining the curriculum after implementation means planning for the long term. Texts and other curriculum materials have an obsolescence factor. Content in new materials is usually out of date at publication and obviously becomes more so as the years of use increase. Texts are usually in use from 6 to 8 years. Support is needed in updating materials or developing strategies such as using the Internet or in some other way updating curriculum materials for classroom use. Curriculum planning at the local level should be long-term.

NATIONAL AND REGIONAL POLICY AND PLANNING

Policy and planning outside state jurisdictions have historically taken on a cooperative character. There being no specific grant of constitutional authority to the federal government, the national policy has traditionally been one of encouraging and supporting the larger realm of education in addition to K–12 schooling. As noted at other points in this book, federal laws, like those establishing the land grant colleges in 1863 or setting aside land in territories for schools or supporting vocational schooling, were not meant to specify what the curriculum should be but to encourage schooling in a general way. What has evolved is an informal but influential set of collaborative relationships involving both governmental units and quasi-governmental and other agencies and organizations that are national in their interests and influence. These various categories of organizations and entities play important roles in the national and regional arena. They serve as important forums for discussing national policy matters, particularly where a common national policy rather than 50 different state variations is needed. National stages are essential in societies that consider themselves democratic. National and regional organizations serve as forums where issues are raised and ideas about social progress can be aired for public consideration. Recall that prior to its recasting as a union some 50 years ago, the NEA served such a purpose. Today it falls into a role as a union that serves teachers nationally and, along with the American Federation of Teachers, forms an important group of advocacy organizations concerned with schools and schooling issues. The various roles and activities of the federal government have already been mentioned in discussing some aspects of curriculum work at the national level. The exceptions to all this harmonious history are the current movement to establish standards for schooling and the implied but unspoken creation of a national curriculum. The former, standards, is mentioned here because it breaks new ground in the relationships among governmental units and those that are not governmental. The parties to this contentiousness are important, a point to be discussed more extensively later in this chapter.

The changing dynamics of policy making make it increasingly important for curriculum workers at all levels to be aware of the kinds of organizations, their purposes, and what they seek to influence. There are many important and interesting players who can influence curriculum work, educational policy making, and planning in general. These can be generally grouped into three categories. One is the more easily identifiable quasi-governmental organization with interests in educational matters and that has some purpose and affiliation with government. The second, interstate education agents, is a collection of various associations with primarily regional and national educational interests that include curriculum. This categorization also includes usually nonprofit educational entities including foundations and institutes. Last are the nongovernmental organizations (NGOs) that may have regional, national, and sometimes international interests and affiliations and are often found in a special relationship to government and other institutions in a society (Stromquist, 2002). The NGOs' interest in education or curriculum is usually secondary to their charter or mandates.

It is not always easy to place an organization neatly in any particular category; they sometimes seem to have charters or stated purposes that bridge from one category to another. Nonetheless, it is useful to consider such categorizations, and where an organization falls can be usefully differentiated in these ways: (a) the degree to which they are involved with educational and schooling matters either as stated in their organizational purpose or exhibited by their activities or possibly both; (b) where the payment for the membership comes from, either through an institutional membership, through an institutional reimbursement for the membership, or by some subsidy, grant, or contract; (c) the organization's particular focus and opportunity to influence issues regionally, nationally, and transnationally, because of its affiliation with a particular cause, program, or educational purpose; and (d) the status of the organization as a professional or nonprofessional entity aside from having advocacy interests in schooling and curriculum matters. Consider these four characteristics as indicators for screening the schooling or curriculum interests or broader educational claims of organizations. The most problematic category and one that is engaging scholarly attention across disciplines (Ginsburg, 1998) is that of the NGO. Nellie Stromquist (2002), in her book *Education in a Globalized World,* offers some useful and cutting-edge views. Meredith Honig's (2004) studies of what she calls "intermediate organizations" and their effect on policy making and planning seem a parallel conceptualization. The practical matter of how this categorical conception might help you decipher claims and categorize organizations yourself is illustrated in Figure 9.4, where the indicators have been used to

Figure 9.4   Profiling Organizational Categories and Characteristics

Category and Example	Characteristics[a]
Quasi-Governmental: Council of Chief State School Officers	1. Stated educational curriculum purposes 2. State funding provided directly 3. State and national influence 4. Professional and political closed membership
Interstate Education Agents: Association for Supervision and Curriculum Development	1. Stated educational purposes with special interests as the name implies 2. Varied funding, some personal and some paid for as work related among midlevel management people in school districts and state departments of education 3. National originally as a division of the NEA but now a stand-alone organization 4. Professional emphasis but open membership
Nongovernmental Organizations: American Red Cross	1. Educational interests are peripheral to its disaster and relief missions 2. Congressional charter and some financial grant/contract support but not for membership 3. Transnational, national, state, and local affiliates 4. Nonprofessional orientation with its own workforce

a. 1. Purposes, 2. Membership funding, 3. Levels of interest, 4. Professional status characterize several well-known organizations. The NGO category is the most unsettled because it has been used mostly to describe transnational entities and only recently to include regional and national organizations (Ginsburg, 1998). Considering the examples and the indicators should help you to home in on and assess organizations as to their curriculum and schooling interests.

Quasi-Governmental Organizations

Quasi-governmental entities are organizations that take their membership from those who are elected to or employed by governments. You may recall earlier references to the National Governors Association or the Council of Chief State School Officers. The former is an organization of governors of the various states who meet yearly to discuss problems of mutual interest, educational issues being among the most significant. The Council of Chief State School Officers is a national organization for state superintendents of education or their equivalent. Obviously, they are concerned with schools and schooling. There are also other organizations for representatives of state legislatures, judges in state court systems, and other governmental workers. Funding for their organizational membership is usually provided by the state and viewed as a legitimate function in support of the office they hold or the state work they do. These organizations maintain permanent staff headed by an executive director and perform valuable services for the membership, including performing research, collecting and maintaining a database, and conducting liaison activities. For example, the National Governors Organization has been very influential in developing and supporting the National Assessment of Educational Progress and coordinating with the various national standards projects in the continuing school reform movement. The U.S. Secretary of Education and often the president of the United States attend the annual sessions of the National Governors Organization. At the meeting in 2004, many governors expressed concerns about the impact of national policies on the states, particularly the costs and application of stringent regulations encountered under the 2001 NCLB law. These sessions afford governors an opportunity to express their particular partisan views and obtain national exposure on critical schooling issues; both are powerful incentives for membership.

Interstate Education Agents and NGOs

The designation *Interstate Education Agent (IEA)* is a neutral term used to refer to other organizations outside specific government or quasi-governmental standing that can be either regional or national in their scope of activity and their memberships. This also differentiates those national agents and agencies from others called *NGOs*; the term is often used to refer to noneducational and humanitarian agencies such as the American

Red Cross in the larger national and international scene and sometimes to educational organizations like UNESCO, the United Nations Educational, Scientific, and Cultural organization, that also operate at that level. Using either term, IEA or NGO, suggests the organization's purpose is to act on behalf of the membership in the realm of activities related to the organization's stated purposes, particularly those having some educational component as part of their overall mission. Many of the IEA organizations are nonprofit and professional. The International Reading Association is, as its title suggests, an affiliation of various international reading association professionals in a variety of countries. The National Society for the Study of Education is another example, one that is strictly a national entity. As a national American organization of academics and related scholars, its interests are in the various aspects of education, particularly what happens in schools. These IEAs and NGOs provide important publications about things educational and are not particularly advocates for any cause, their interests being in presenting various scholarly viewpoints or reviews of research, the many sides of a topic, about some issue or activity. Other organizations, like the Association for Supervision and Curriculum Development (ASCD), are national organizations of a more specific professional focus that draw membership from a variety of groups (e.g., midlevel district curriculum specialists, academics with curriculum and supervision interests, and state department administrators). This does not mean the organizations are exclusive in their purpose or membership; they are interested in anything that affects schooling but view issues from the organization's particular perspective. The American Association of School Administrators, for example, might have a position statement on improving science curriculum in schools. So will the ASCD and the National Science Teachers Association. Each organization's statement will reflect and advocate the concerns of their constituency, as the American Civil Liberties Union and the National Rifle Association might about gun control. If the organization's purposes are studied, the particular perspective on schooling and educational matters should be evident.

Membership funding sources also vary with the interstate education agents. Although some members might be from governmental agencies, others might be corporate, personal, business, religious, or some combination of those. Funding for a membership will also come from diverse sources, sometimes personal, often corporate or business related, sometimes from for-profit organizations, and sometimes from nonprofits. School districts often provide memberships for specific administrators but usually not for teachers. The latter may receive financial support to attend conferences related to specific curriculum interests that the district can justify for meeting specific curriculum needs. Another characteristic of these IEA and NGO agents is their common interest in or an advocacy for schools and schooling, curriculum, and higher education, or something else educational. Their interest is not fleeting but sustaining; they are interested in the long term, in monitoring the curriculum in general as the ASCD might, or in particular, as the Council on Basic Education has in arts and humanities or as the International Reading Association might in reading. Each school curriculum area is represented by a national organization. The National Council of Teachers of Math, National Council for the Social Studies, and National Science Teachers Association are examples. Each agent monitors national, state, and regional policy initiatives, development of textbooks, resource materials, and the particular controversies about what the curriculum should contain related to their particular interests. They provide monographs, journals, summaries of research, and other publications for their members and engage in lobbying activities with other like-minded organizations seeking to influence policy making and planning. They have traditionally offered model curriculum plans, the ideal curriculum of lofty aims, purposes, and cutting-edge content. Today, these plans include suggestions and rubrics for creating the path between classroom curriculum and the standards the curriculum is planned to meet.

Standards and the Bully Pulpit

One of the interesting features of the federal involvement in education in general and schooling in particular is the role of the president. Few presidents have been more closely tied with the use of the office of President to promote a national agenda than Theodore and Franklin Delano Roosevelt. The term *bully pulpit* represents the use of the office as a pulpit to "preach" a message to the people and "bully" the congress into accepting a policy idea of the president and passing laws to authorize further policy making and planning in the executive branch or other designated agents (see, e.g., Glantz, 2004). As you will recall from Chapter 7, much of the discussions about educational matters in the 19th and 20th centuries took place inside and around the various bureaus and affiliates of the NEA. The demise of the NEA as a national forum has forced presidents to find different paths, such as convening a national forum to highlight and energize a presidential agenda. Theodore Roosevelt used this kind of forum to convene a study of the "economy of time" in the early 20th century. The current standards movement is the result of presidential use of the bully pulpit to convene a national conference and promote an agenda. In 1989, President George Herbert Walker Bush joined with the nation's governors to convene the first meeting out of which the standards movement sprung. With an invitational list of politicians and business and labor leaders, and a sprinkling of academics, college presidents, and school leaders, including such luminaries as Louis Gerstner, the CEO of IBM as its titular chair, that meeting was the jump-start for the standards movement that today permeates the national, state, and local district agenda and garners a vast allocation of resources. The offspring of that meeting include the quasi-governmental National Educational Goals Panel and the National Council on Education Standards and Testing. In 1994, Congress passed the Goals 2000 legislation establishing the National Education Standards and Improvement Council, all steps toward establishing a national policy that culminated in the NCLB of 2001. Parallel with those developments were the gradual involvement of the 50 different states as designated standards agents, and standards promulgated by or influenced by various academic and curriculum content organizations such as the National Council of Teachers of Math and the American Historical Association. Diane Ravitch developed a public-user-friendly guide, *National Standards in American Education: A Citizen's Guide* (1995), to help popularize and build support for the movement. As Stotsky's book *What's at Stake in the K-12 Standards Wars* (2000) suggests, the matter of standards is contentious, and agreeing on a unified course is difficult at best. One of the few studies of the standards-based reforms is Swanson and Stevenson's article, "Standards-Based Reform in Practice: Evidence on State Policy and Classroom Instruction From the NAEP State Assessments" (2002). As the title suggests, the standards-curriculum-instruction-assessment relationship is at the heart of the standards discussions, and progress toward standards-based curriculum work is subject to contesting views and diverse expert opinions.

Summary and Conclusions

All curriculum work, regardless of the kind of activities carried on or the level at which they occur, ultimately is a response to or impetus for some policy-making and planning actions. Various actors are involved, ranging from specific people in particular roles to important state, regional, national, and international organizations and groups. These agents may include state workers such as legislators, state board of education members, and governors, and organizations dedicated to both general and particular curriculum interests like the American Enterprise Institute, the American Educational Research Association, and the National Science Foundation. Forming policy and giving it expression in a plan precede and frame the activities creating curriculum. Even though those activities about curriculum will be dispersed, the results will ultimately be found in the classroom. The linking of policy making and planning to classroom teacher use suggests the next aspect of exploring curriculum, the matter of creating and managing the curriculum that follows from curriculum policy and planning work. In curriculum, curriculum policy making and planning work might seem to loom large in the national and regional arena, and less so in the local district, school, and classroom. It may seem that way, but the political realities of policy making (e.g., standards), especially where money follows, suggest it is otherwise. Policy making for schools and curriculum may well be primarily the province of the individual state, but the presence of and pressure from the multitude of quasi-governmental, interstate educational, and nongovernmental agents exerts a powerful influence on what controls what the teachers teach, the curriculum.

Critical Perspective

1. Control through authorized policy making is often portrayed as being under local control, that is to say, operationally local in and subject to the will of the community. Does this mean the state grants or cedes power to a local school board to make policy? Or, is the range of authorized policy making controlled by the state, usually the legislature? What is the meaning of "local control" in your state?

2. Probably the most important recent law creating policy and prompting policy-making actions is the No Child Left Behind Act of 2001. What law preceded the NCLB? What differences are there between the old law and policy and the new?

3. What are the key provisions of the NCLB? What policy-making activities were incurred at the federal level? Were the states required to formulate any policy or do any policy making?

4. Given the information developed in 1 and 2 above, consider each of the characteristics of effective policy making and briefly formulate a statement of how and in what way each characteristic was addressed.

5. It often seems that school reform and standards go hand in hand. That is not always the case. School reform has included separate elements such as improving reading programs and urban high school reform. What other kinds of programs or issues are there under the school reform umbrella?

6. Not all forces for reform are governmental. Various kinds of quasi-governmental and interstate agents are also working in reform. Identify some of those organizations and agents that can be found in your locale, state, and region.

7. In your state, what is the law concerning the role of the legislature and state department of education in curriculum and reform efforts? Select another state and identify the roles of each. Are there similarities and differences? Are responsibilities or restrictions spelled out about roles?

8. One of the complaints raised about the standards movement is the increase in paperwork required of teachers on the one hand and the lack of input from the classroom and school level on the other. If you are a practicing teacher, what are your views? It might be useful to casually sample others teaching in different schools and at different levels to find out what they think of standards and what positive or negative views they hold. You might form a small group, develop a simple set of questions, and use them for interviewing other teachers or non-school individuals.

Resources for Curriculum Study

1. The concept of local control of schooling is often cited in arguing power relationships between local, state, and federal authority. Among education historians, Joel Spring in *American Education* (2004) provides a useful discussion. Students interested in this very American idea of local control should read two articles by Goldin and Katz in the *Journal of Interdisciplinary History* (1999a) and the *Journal of Economic Perspectives* (1999b) that provide interesting insights into the idea and offer factual evidence of it in practice through interpretation of rather than clear and specific grants of authority.

2. Reforms often take unplanned paths, even when a pattern seems evident to follow. D. A. Squires, in *Aligning and Balancing the Standards-Based Curriculum* (2004), offers some insights into the policy-planning mix.

3. Collections of policy development and planning studies, the linkages between national assessments and policy making, for example, are slow to develop because the studies are mainly underway and unreported. One example of those kinds of studies is Swanson and Stevenson's article (2002) "Standards-Based Reform in Practice: Evidence on State Policy and Classroom Instruction From the NAEP State Assessments." While of more interest to the technical professional and academics, this article and others can be found in the American Educational Research Association journal, *Educational Evaluation and Policy Analysis,* an excellent resource and avenue to other studies and materials.

4. Reform that leads to policy making, planning, and implementation of activities in the name of reform is often interpreted in different ways. M. R. Berube (1994) offers an interesting account of reform from 1883 to 1983. Diane Ravitch, in her book *Left Behind: A Century of Battles on School Reform* (2000), covers much the same ground but from a different perspective.

5. One of the marks of the thoughtful scholar is the persistence in studying a topic and exploring it from different perspectives. Michael Fullan (2001) is an excellent example in the study of leadership. In studies of school reform, Andrew Porter's work is always worthy of consideration. His article "National Standards and School Improvement in the 1990s: Issues and Promise," in the *American Journal of Education* (1994), is some 10 years distant yet prescient in anticipating current discussions of school reform and curriculum.

6. Articles and books that specifically address curriculum reform are few. One thoughtful exception is S. T. Hopmann's article "On the Evaluation of Curriculum Reforms" (2003) in the *Journal of Curriculum Studies.* This journal is an excellent

resource for articles, and the table of contents can be accessed online by typing in the name of the journal.

7. *Culture* is perhaps an overused word that has lost the precision that anthropologist Franz Boaz intended. Today you find it used in different ways, such as the culture of poverty, the culture of war, or the culture of policy making. What culture implies both in anthropology and its other applications is a bounded set of particulars, ideals, manners, modes of thought, costumes, and the like that configure a way of behaving. Applied to policy making, it frames the activities and behaviors of policy makers in both a collective and individual sense; culture mirrors the context in policy making and planning. In *The Culture of Education Policy*, S. J. Stein (2004) captures the context and range of behaviors in policy work. Policy-making culture in context, the urban school reform one, is the subject of F. M. Hess's book *Spinning Wheels* (1998).

8. The tentacles of reform spread wide in the school-state-federal relationship. Whether it is school reform per se or standards, or a mix of the two, the relationships it spawns are tenuous and contentious. There are many angles to explore, and F. M. Hess's *The Economics of Schooling and School Quality* (2004), Cohen and Hill's *Learning Policy* (2001), and Tom Loveless's article "Uneasy Allies: The Evolving Relationship of School and State" (1998) are useful starting points.

9. Among the quasi-governmental agents, several offer excellent materials about various aspects of school reform and development of standards. The Internet sites for the National Governors Association and the Council of Chief State School Officers are both outstanding. Each tries to be nonpartisan and provide leads to other agencies and organizations. Both are readily accessible by typing in their respective titles.

10. The standards movement is in many ways as Engel's title suggests, *The Struggle for Control of Public Education: Market Ideology Vs. Democratic Values* (2000), a matter of power and control—school governance and who governs sets the agenda and approach to standards. A good resource on governance is D. Conley's *Who Governs Our Schools?* (2003).

References

Armstrong, D. G. (2003). *Curriculum today.* Upper Saddle River, NJ: Pearson Education / Merrill Prentice Hall.

Berube, M. R. (1994). *American school reform: Progressive, equity, and excellence movements, 1883–1983.* Westport, CT: Praeger.

Boostrom, R., Jackson, P., & Hansen, D. (1993). Coming together and staying apart: How a group of teachers and researchers sought to bridge the "research/practice gap." *Teachers College Record, 95*(1), 35–44.

Cohen, D., & Hill, H. (2001). *Learning policy: When state education reform works.* New Haven, CT: Yale University Press.

Conant, J. B. (1959). *The American high school today.* New York: McGraw-Hill.

Conant, J. B. (1967). *The comprehensive high school.* New York: McGraw-Hill.

Conley, D. (2003). *Who governs our schools?* New York: Teachers College Press.

Connelly, F. M., & Clandinin, D. J. (1988). *Teachers as curriculum planners: Narratives of experience.* New York: Teachers College Press.

Council on Basic Education. (2004). *Academic atrophy: The conditions of the liberal arts in public schools.* Washington, DC: Council on Basic Education. Retreived October 26, 2005, from http://www.music-for-all.org/documents/cbe_principal_Report.pdf

Elmore, R. F. (2002). Unwarranted intrusion. *Education Next, 2*(1), 30.

Engel, M. (2000). *The struggle for control of public education: Market ideology vs. democratic values.* Philadelphia: Temple University Press.

Fullan, M. (2001). *Leadership in a culture of change.* San Francisco: Jossey-Bass.

Gamoran, A. (1998). Curriculum change as a reform strategy: Lessons from the United States and Scotland. *Teachers College Record, 98*(4), 608–628.

Ginsburg, M. B. (1998). What's in an acronym? *Current Issues in Contemporary Education.* Retrieved June 5, 2005, from http://www.tc.columbia.edu/cice/v011nr1/a1152.htm

Glantz, D. M. (2004). *The bully pulpit and the melting pot: American presidents and the immigrant, 1897–1943.* Lawrence: University Press of Kansas.

Goldin, C., & Katz, L. F. (1999a). Human capital and social capital: The rise of secondary schooling in America, 1980–1940. *Journal of Interdisciplinary History, 29*(4), 683–723.

Goldin, C., & Katz, L. F. (1999b). The shaping of higher education: The formative years in the United States, 1890–1940. *Journal of Economic Perspectives, 13*(1), 37–62.

Hess, F. M. (1998). *Spinning wheels: The politics of urban school reform.* Washington, DC: Brookings Institute.

Hess, F. M. (2004). *The economics of schooling and school quality.* London: Edward Elgar.

Honig, M. I. (2004). The new middle management: Intermediary organizations in educational policy implementation. *Educational Evaluation and Policy Analysis, 26*(1), 65–87.

Hopmann, S. T. (2003). On the evaluation of curriculum reforms. *Journal of Curriculum Studies, 35*(4), 459–478.

James, T. (1991). State authority and the politics of educational change. In C. Grant (Ed.), *Review of research in education* (pp. 17, 169–224). Washington, DC: American Educational Research Association.

Kohn, A. (2001). Fighting the tests: A practical guide to rescuing our schools. *Phi Delta Kappan, 82*(5), 348–357.

Levin, B. (1998). An epidemic of education policy: What (What) can we learn from each other? *Comparative Education 34*(2), 131–141.

Loveless, T. (1998) Uneasy allies: The evolving relationship of school and state. *Educational Evaluation and Policy Analysis, 20*(1), 1–8.

Pinar, W. F., Reynolds, W. M., Slattery, P., & Taubman, P. M. (2002). *Understanding curriculum.* New York: Peter Lang.

Porter, A. C. (1994). National standards and school improvement in the 1990s: Issues and promise. *American Journal of Education, 102*(2), 421–449.

Ravitch, D. (1995). *National standards in American education: A citizen's guide.* Washington, DC: Brookings Institute.

Ravitch, D. (2000). *Left behind: A century of battles on school reform.* New York: Touchstone/ Simon & Schuster.

Ripley, R. (1985). *Policy analysis and political science.* Chicago: Nelson Hall.

Schubert, W. H., Schubert, A. L. L., Thomas, T. P., & Carroll, W. M. (2002). *Curriculum books: The first hundred years* (2nd ed.). New York: Peter Lang.

Spring, J. (2004). *American education* (11th ed.). New York: McGraw-Hill.

Squires, D. A. (2004). *Aligning and balancing the standards-based curriculum.* Thousand Oaks, CA: Corwin.

Stein, S. J. (2004). *The culture of education policy.* New York: Teachers College Press.

Stotsky, S. (Ed.). (2000). *What's at stake in the K-12 standards wars.* New York: Peter Lang.

Stromquist, N. P. (2002). *Education in a globalized world: The connectivity of economic power, technology, and knowledge.* Lanham, MD: Rowman & Littlefield.

Swanson, C. B., & Stevenson, D. L. (2002). Standards-based reform in practice: Evidence on state policy and classroom instruction from the NAEP state assessments. *Educational Evaluation and Policy Analysis, 24*(1), 1–27.

Walker, D. F. (1971, November). The process of curriculum development: A naturalistic model. *School Review, 80,* 51–65.

Walker, D. F. (1990). *Fundamentals of curriculum.* New York: Harcourt Brace Jovanovich.

Chapter 10

DEVELOPING AND ADAPTING CURRICULUM

*C*urriculum development and curriculum are terms often used in ways that make them appear to be the same thing. Witness the number of curriculum textbooks that carry the words curriculum development in their title or articles in which the terms are used interchangeably. They are not one and the same, nor should they carry the same meaning. Curriculum is a discipline of knowledge whereas curriculum development is a type of curriculum work contributing to that knowledge. Both are closely associated with schools and schooling. Chapter 4, "Creating Curriculum," introduced you to the idea of curriculum not just as a body of knowledge but also as a creative process that involves a particular kind of work called curriculum development. This textbook, or those in any classroom, and other media associated with something being learned are the products resulting from a collection of conceptual and production activities subsumed under the general idea of curriculum development.

CREATING CURRICULUM DEVELOPMENT

Curriculum development is a mainstream type of curriculum work comprising several different kinds of activities. Obviously, most curriculum work occurs in relation to schools and schooling, in different locations, and with different degrees of activity, from the local district to the national arena. Matters of scale, complexity, and tempo also differentiate those activities. Most curriculum development work can be classified generally as either development or adaptation. *Curriculum development* involves the creating of curriculum according to specified purposes, using a designated process, having an intended distribution beyond a single use, and having a large and varied cadre of personnel involved. It is development in two distinct forms. First, it can be development of a scope and sequence in the way that the curriculum is created across the K–12 continuum as represented in a curriculum guide. The second form of development is the actual production of materials, such as a textbook for the curriculum, the conceptualizing and production of materials that represent the curriculum from scratch. *Curriculum adaptation* is just that, using already developed, existing curriculum and materials and "adapting" them to fit a specific curriculum purpose. Some development and adaptation examples are given in Figure 10.1. There are no hard-and-fast rules or principles to differentiate whether an activity is purely one or the other; some activities might involve both developmental and adaptive actions. The factors suggested here, time or tempo,

Figure 10.1   Examples of Development and Adaptation

National Curriculum Development Project	National in scale, development process is specific and activities are complex, extensive time frame and target dates for completion and publication, involves varied participants
Textbook Development and Publishing	Targets either national or regional publishing, set process is followed, time frame is critical for development and marketing, involves corporate participants and consultants
School District Development Project	Local district schools (or a specific school), smaller in scale and targeted users, development process is stated but may be homegrown/ad hoc rather than a particular model, time frame is driven by district calendar, involves local participants
School Adaptation Project	Single location, personnel limited to participating teachers in the school, activities may or may not be coordinated, materials are cannibalized to fit specific classroom or grade level needs, time is not critical because adaptation is an insertion as needed, factors keep it a simple rather than a complex activity
Classroom Adaptation Activity	Teacher controls the activity in a single location, no other personnel, time is not a factor, simple rather than a complex activity

personnel, scale, and complexity, allow you to make the determination as to whether an activity might be developmental, adaptive, or some degree of both.

- **Complexity** refers to the details of the activity, for example, the mission, scope, planning, and resources that are needed or accrue as the work is undertaken.
- **Time** is an important factor because it expresses long- or short-term activity and commitment of personnel and resources. In schools and school districts, the curriculum has to flow with the calendar year, publishers have to consider timely marketing, and homegrown projects have to be ready for insertion in a timely manner.
- **Scale** of the activity reflects the scope of the mission. If it is local, it could range from all schools in the district to teachers in one school at one grade level or even, in the smallest scale, one teacher developing materials specific to a classroom.
- **Personnel**. The greater the number of people involved in a curriculum activity, the greater the need for controls and careful planning so the result is consistent with a mission. Personnel involved can vary from a single teacher to hundreds, as in publishing house operations or national activities like standards development.

Those characteristics and other considerations in creating curriculum discussed in Chapter 4 (commonplaces, alignment, etc.,) suggest the scope of work and what has to be taken into consideration in any development or adaptation work. Development work could follow specific models like the spiral curriculum of Bruner (1960) or that of Tyler (1949) and Taba (1962; see Chapter 4, Figure 4.3), or some might be created from scratch to fit the uniqueness of a curriculum mission. Consider developmental purposes to be similar to a recipe in preparing a pot of soup—it's fairly standard but changed by the kind of soup desired and the particular ingredients needed (consider making a gazpacho vs. a potato soup). It is important to remember that there are many models for creating curriculum, either as a new development or as an adaptive one. Given the choice of using an existing model, using a prototype process, or starting from scratch, what might a curriculum development process look like?

A SAMPLE CURRICULUM DEVELOPMENT PROCESS

Building a development process begins in thinking about the preliminaries, the perspective elements that frame the considerations about how to proceed. The next effort should be a conjuring one, setting up a development process. As noted previously, there is the option to choose a process (e.g., follow the Taba model) or to start from scratch to create one. For illustrative purposes, a sample "from scratch" process will be created so the various elements that are really generic in thinking and doing curriculum development and adaptation can be identified and discussed. The process envisioned here is neither fixed nor exclusive; it is a series of activities including conceptualizing, designing and creating prototypes, testing activities, validating, and monitoring.

Conceptualizing a Curriculum

Conceptualizing begins with a thought or some assigned task, a thing you have in mind and want to complete. It proceeds through thinking about what has to be done to achieve it, perhaps a procedure or series of steps that can be acted out to achieve an end. Think of conceptualizing in curriculum development as a way of responding to this series of very simple questions:

- Why are we doing this? (goals and purposes)
- What results do we want to achieve? (proposed outcomes)
- How will we go about doing this? (the process)
- How will we know we got there? (management and assessment)

Goals and Purposes

First, the general goals or overarching reasons for the curriculum should be made explicit. Second, the purposes toward which the development is directed should be identified. Last, the quality characteristics of the curriculum should be described. A statement of purpose(s) presents a rationale for why the curriculum project is being undertaken. This is usually in response to some policy, such as to meet a standard, and often falls under some comprehensive plan, a blueprint, if you will, formulated to execute a policy. Goals are the ends to be attained in achieving the purposes. It is important in doing comprehensive curriculum development to have a clear policy-plan-curriculum development linkage. As noted earlier in this discussion, comprehensive developments like national curriculum projects and textbook publishing tend to be large scale. That doesn't mean ad hoc curriculum development projects such as those a teacher might vicariously institute in a classroom are unimportant; the concern even for them is the matter of justification, and how responses are made to those very simple questions posed in summarizing conceptualization.

Audience and Use

A curriculum product resulting from curriculum development work has an intended audience and use. For example, a mathematics curriculum articulated in a state curriculum guide is specific about what is to be taught, the articulation of content scope and sequence, and with whom it is to be used, the grade level and students. A scope and sequence guide often contains other supporting information, such as references to useful information, other curriculum materials, directives for implementing the curriculum, and other sources of assistance. You may be familiar with textbook teacher editions that provide such information. Consider the detailing of such characteristics as a way for developers to be inclusive up front about the curriculum and its use.

Often, there is a presumption that only designated professionals get involved in curriculum development. The reality is that there are many possible participants in curriculum development, from teachers to school board members to publishers. What determines involvement is not always a matter of professional preparation having to do with schools and schooling. Further, curriculum development is not always a response to some policy initiative or formalized planning, or even an informal, in-house, teacher or district curriculum specialist response to an immediate curriculum need. A publishing house, for example, often acts on opportunity, engaging in curriculum development based on its assessment that the development of a particular textbook or text series is needed. That decision is made on competitive market considerations rather than in response to some state or district school policy.

Easily the most representative example of audience and in-use curriculum development is the preparation of daily lesson plans by the teacher for students in the classroom. The lesson plan is not only the primary document in teaching, it is the basic operational curriculum document. How the curriculum embodied in a lesson plan plays out is a matter of moment-to-moment adjustment by students and the teacher. It is like making a tactical adjustment to a strategic plan, or orchestrating a piece of music in different ways while remaining true to the original music. Depending on their foundational knowledge about the curriculum content they are teaching, teachers have a significant opportunity to organize, or "orchestrate," the curriculum in different ways and still, like the original music, retain the intended message. Teachers also develop curriculum units. This is a process of *chunking,* or breaking the total curriculum scope and sequence up into manageable units for curriculum and teaching purposes. Units are then often further separated into a scope and sequence of individual lessons. This in-school curriculum development work may also occur in-district as a combined effort of curriculum specialists and teachers.

Curriculum development may also occur at grade and school level according to interests, expertise, or efficiency. It is not uncommon for teachers to carve out responsibilities for curriculum because of personal interests. For example, elementary teachers may choose to team up on curriculum responsibilities, each teacher being responsible for the preparation of lessons and possibly materials in a given area of the curriculum. In some states and districts where a curriculum concentration is required for elementary certification, the faculty consists of teachers who have an expertise in a curriculum area. In middle and high school, formal and informal departmentalization can mean teachers are assigned responsibility for preparing and coordinating particular curriculum content consistent with their training. A science teacher prepared in the physical sciences may be given the physics and chemistry curriculum while another with expertise in biological science will be assigned to the curriculum in biology. Similar differentiations can apply across the schooling spectrum. In larger school districts having an extensive central office support staff, curriculum supervisors also perform curriculum development work in addition to assignments as area specialists in mathematics or reading, for example. Persons in those roles also support classroom teacher curriculum requests through performing resource searches, securing current research reports on curriculum matters, and functioning as lead liaisons with teachers in different schools and appropriate state department of education personnel. Most school personnel think that intrastate schooling matters are exclusively under the direction of their state department of education. The appointed or elected state board of education and superintendent usually carry statutory authority for oversight of all schooling, public, private, and parochial. Any legislature may, by law, and the governor may, by grant of legislative authority, direct the staff to order schools to do anything it wishes consistent with the state's constitution as amended. As noted in the previous discussion about policy making in Chapter 9, special interest groups with concerns about issues like scientific theory versus intelligent design or creationism can pressure the state department and state board of education to establish a policy for their position (Dow, 1991; Zimmerman, 1999). If, for example, they were successful in having a new policy established to include teaching about intelligent design, the upshot would be a massive new orientation of the curriculum in science with possible side effects on other content areas such as history and literature. The amount of curriculum change required could be formidable: preparing a new curriculum scope and sequence; calling a special textbook committee to prepare an approved state textbook list; developing guidelines for district curriculum development projects and for implementing the new curriculum; and providing new staff development/in-service to help teachers and others prepare for and implement the new curriculum. This hypothetical example underscores both the importance of curriculum (especially its control) and the varieties of curriculum work that it could entail; it would be no small decision and no small result.

When considerations about schooling and schools telescope away from individual states to regional and national platforms, curriculum development work becomes different. Because things curricular are not tied to any specific constitutional authority as they are in the individual states, curriculum development work now occurs in a different realm, one characterized by regional and national activities with a variety of participants, particularly those who are entrepreneurial, commercial, for profit. Publishing houses do the largest segment of national and regional curriculum development work. These familiar school textbook names, Allyn & Bacon, Merrill, Prentice Hall, and Silver Burdett, carry on the development and production that constitutes real-life large-scale curriculum development work. There are also specialized and smaller regional publishing houses. Regional publishers, such as West Publishers and Interstate Books, market specialized texts in state history and geography keyed to the different individual state requirements. Specialized publishers develop curriculum materials in niche curriculum areas such as music, the arts, character education, and drug education. Nationally and locally, there are a variety of professional organizations that carry on curriculum development activities in addition to commercial venders. These organizations—the National Council for the Social Studies, the National Council of Teachers of English, the National Council of Teachers of Math, and the Council on Basic Education, to suggest a few—are dedicated to supporting particular curriculum content interests. They prepare curriculum scope and sequence guides and develop supplementary curriculum materials for teacher classroom use, as well as carry on a variety of other professional activities including journal and yearbook publications, a national conference, special member training institutes, and regional and state affiliate meetings. When questions about curriculum arise, matters of revising or creating new curriculum, for instance, they are often in the role of the expert providing advice about scope, sequence, and other curriculum issues.

Designing a Curriculum

One of the perennial problems in schooling and teaching is designing any curriculum to meet the diverse expectations of teachers, learners, the community, and policy makers. This problem speaks to a desire that a curriculum be sound, that it does what is expected of it for learners. The vagueness of soundness is obvious, yet it is an issue that constantly presses on curriculum developers. It is impossible to anticipate and establish the qualities of soundness definitively, and design work must proceed in view of what is discernable about expectations. This is why the perspective (inclusive of the philosophy discussed in Chapter 8) is important, because it subsumes all the previously noted preliminary elements so design can evolve in a justifiably professional way. As developers identify content for inclusion in the curriculum, they can choose to use existing materials containing the content elements, create new content and materials, or combine existing and new materials. Whatever the choice, they will proceed to design according to the scope, sequence, continuity, and balance concepts that are fundamental in curriculum thinking. In addition to those fundamentals, a sample set of what might be called additional design consideration factors is presented in Figure 10.2. These address such familiar teaching and schooling topics as developmental levels, learning and cognition, the importance of experience, and curriculum instructional matching.

Prototype Design

The primary purpose of creating a curriculum prototype is to make what is envisioned real. What is made physically present can then be compared to what has been conceptualized and all the proposed characteristics can be accounted for. Developmental outputs are materials that represent the curriculum and can be tried out in a real

Figure 10.2   Design Consideration Factors

Cultural Diversity

The array of cultural and ethnic traditions in American society suggests that schools and class-rooms will also be diverse, and curriculum development should respect and reflect that diversity in developing materials.

Cognitive Development

Curriculum and the materials that represent it should be as closely matched to the anticipated cognitive development levels of the target student population and designed to expand or contract to the setting-specific character of the learners.

Multisensory Learning

Curriculum materials should offer different sense mode options for understanding content, especially media options in curriculum content with a dominant reading emphasis.

User Friendly

Curriculum materials should present curriculum in a format for ease of engagement by the students and use by the teacher.

Teaching Options

Curriculum materials should suggest instructional options that provide for flexible engagement by students and enhance teacher implementation choices in the learning setting.

---

setting, the classroom. A parallel to this is what automakers do when they conceptualize a car, create a prototype and then a concept car, and then operate it so they can, using a naval metaphor, "shake it down." The developmental effort in creating a curriculum prototype is often makeshift and trial and error, with a concern for order, sequence, and content range that is dependent on the scale of the curriculum development project and work requirements. The curriculum product will be in various parts, what will be called curriculum components, each like the human gene, carrying a part of the message of the envisioned whole. At this point in the postconceptual work, it is important to find out how the curriculum components, collectively known as a prototype, will hold up in use and square with the conceptual design. This subprocess is referred to as testing out the prototype.

Prototype Testing and Revision

Nothing is particularly complicated here; prototype testing is the first "hands-on" application to find out at an early, first level of development what works according to script and expectations, what does not, and what needs revising. This is often referred to as *piloting,* and it is real; it occurs in actual classrooms with live students and teachers. Selection of settings is important, especially with regard to the premise factors and the design characteristics. Piloting a curriculum and its material representations, either in total or in parts, should occur across several classrooms with different teachers so there is a reasonable preliminary sense of its accuracy about intended audience, settings, and flexibility in use. What is important and demonstrates the multiple manipulations of different curriculum components is to have set up and implemented the actual monitoring process so the indicators for appraising the curriculum are embedded in or applied as part of the piloting process. The monitoring devices could range from a readability analysis of the materials, a pre- and postassessment, a teacher checklist or anecdotal follow-up questionnaire, the use of trained observers who monitor implementation for consistency with design characteristics and impact on the student users, or these techniques in combination. Results should lead to several further possible courses of action:

- *Proceed:* Going forward without any changes, as indicators are positive based on the pilot experience.
- *Revise:* Revision options might include revising one or more components followed by repiloting in total or in part (only the affected components), or performing continued small-scale piloting and revision to see if original problems arise with other populations and then revising in total or only those components affected.
- *Redesign:* Extensive reconceptualization and component modification usually implies a fresh start and creation of new components, then another piloting and revising cycle.
- *Expand Piloting:* Based on initial pilot monitoring data, it may be appropriate to add other pilot sites. Factors such as student cultural backgrounds or language and reading traditions may prompt this.

Field Testing and Revision

After piloting and any revision or redesign work has been completed, the curriculum and materials are made ready for expanded testing in multiple setting beyond the few classrooms used in the pilot study. Field testing refers to the widespread use of the curriculum in multiple schools and classrooms in a systematic way. Again, the monitoring is very important, especially teacher responses as to how the curriculum feels to them in use with learners. There should also be other forms of feedback, results of learning assessments, implementation checklists, and other instrumentations, so an adequate database is established consistent with the conceptualization and the final design used for formal production of the curriculum and materials. Data from the pilot/revision process and the monitoring system developed for it can be useful as a comparative to data in the field process or in suggesting that certain kinds of instrumentation may be useful in the field study. Successful completion of field testing revision is a signal that the curriculum has been standardized and is now ready for production. However, one more set of activities needs to be completed before the curriculum is ready for formal production and distribution.

Validation and Contextual Analysis

What determines whether a curriculum meets intended outcomes? Is it measured against the purposes and goals toward which it is aimed? Is it the performance of teachers and students, those who use the curriculum? Are there other considerations that apply? Those questions suggest the tentativeness inherent in any developmental undertaking and reflect concerns that seem rather straightforward, particularly whether the results—the curriculum and/or materials representing it—warrant acceptance. To that observation, there are two qualifiers: one, validity, is a matter of data and interpretation; the other, the nature of the curriculum implementation process, is a contextual concern.

The idea that something is valid because it does what it is supposed to do is seductively simple. The truth it is far more complex; whether there is a match between performance and expectations is a professional determination that is a matter of interpretation. The issue is how to get from personal subjectivity to an acceptable state of objectivity knowing that it can never be completely so. The periodic clashes between advocates for phonics and whole-language approaches in reading and the "validity" of the research is an excellent case in point (Lemann, 1997). The idea of *validation* in curriculum work is to determine the degree to which expectations in the form of outcomes and the curriculum or curriculum materials that manifest those outcomes match performance, represented in some form of data. In managing the curriculum, monitoring-process activities should provide a continuous flow of data during the various developmental episodes. These data are about each episode and form a composite of information from start to finish or as the time frame dictates. That composite is the basis for decision making about the validity of the curriculum development work and the curriculum. To repeat, validity simply means did the curriculum do what it was supposed to do.

Put a little differently, what factors in the context of doing the work and trying it out were important in the degree to which success or failure is understood? What is involved is interpretation and judgment. Now things begin to get more complex. Such questions suggest the range of factors or causes that could be identified, necessitating a determination about which ones are more important than others. Establishing first causes might, for example, have it that learner performance with the curriculum is the most important indicator. That decision would in turn lead to other insights affecting the starting point in ranking and ordering actions. For example, if learner performance is the measure there is a qualifier. The teacher is the intercessor, and variations in implementation (among other factors) can affect learner performance on a selective basis, necessitating an interpretation of the degree of influence on results and whether it is

Figure 10.3   Examples of Contextual Influences on Validation

Internal Influences	External Influences
• Materials are faulty—they don't represent the material effectively • Misalignment exists in the scope and sequence • Materials were designed for a different student developmental level • Materials lack options for accommodating diversity among students	• Instructional approach used is least appropriate • Extremes exist in learner audience ability • Classroom setting-climate distractions hinder learning opportunities • Time-on-task allocation is insufficient

important to the overall determination of curriculum validity. These are judgments about data made with the expectation that variations will occur. Such decisions are also a practical recognition of contextual matters, that in curriculum work not all variables are controllable and that classrooms settings have fluid rather than stable states and conditions. In such circumstances, the professional curriculum practitioner's decision making must rely on the basic curriculum knowledge foundation, traditions of practice, and the data available. The question is the degree of variation that will be allowed a matter of practical and professional judgment in identifying and analyzing the framework of factors involved in creating a picture of the context or setting, such as a classroom in which the curriculum was put to work. This *contextual analysis* creates an array of data about factors that seem indirectly involved but that may be exerting very subtle and important influences on the eventual determination of validity. Some of these are suggested in Figure 10.3, where you will note a further delineation of contextual influences as to internal, or within the curriculum, materials and external, as in the contextual factors outside the curriculum materials themselves that might influence it. Consider a teacher working a lesson who becomes suddenly aware that students are giving blank looks because the curriculum material is predicated on something they have not received, some prerequisite knowledge supposedly learned and now needed but absent. Was it something in last year's curriculum? Perhaps it is a flaw in the scope and sequence? Maybe the problem lies in the shift to a new textbook? You can guess at the multiple contextual possibilities that are possible and real to teachers in the classroom and to the curriculum development people.

CURRICULUM ADAPTATION

In traditional schooling, the focus was on the middle ground in curriculum and instruction, identifying and assisting those students who were deemed to be capable and could learn. Over the last 40 or so years, there has been a shift away from that premise, a realization that striving for the middle ground ignored a wide range of needs in students, especially the gifted and those with disabilities. It is now accepted knowledge that you are a unique individual, your brain is one of a kind, and your learning is individually differentiated as to your curriculum needs and what forms of instruction help you to best engage the curriculum. This has meant growth in adaptive practices in curriculum development work.

Adapting curriculum to particular settings, situations, or conditions usually implies actions at the classroom, school, and teacher level. It might mean an English as a second language (ESL) class, *curriculum differentiation* within a classroom to accommodate special cognitive modalities, or some as yet to be identified condition requiring specialized curriculum. Sometimes in curriculum development, *adaptation* is confused with *adoption*. Be clear in understanding that *curriculum adoption* is to take curriculum as it is, unmodified, and use it, whereas *curriculum adaptation* is to take curriculum and adjust it to fit the need or to modify and use existing materials for insertion in a regular curriculum for very specialized reasons. Adaptation as a process is not tied to a particular pattern or model. As you learned in Chapter 4 about the origin and characteristics of curriculum creation and in Chapter 6 about particular tools, there are many applications that can be used in developing and adapting curriculum. Distinguishing between the need for development or adaptation will depend on the special purpose to be served within the overall curriculum mission, particularly as adaptation serves a special need.

Learning Modalities

The basic concern in schooling is to find the way, or pathways, to effective learning. In the new emphasis on differentiated curriculum and instruction, the key ideas are about learning styles or modalities and the way curriculum can be adjusted to match the individuals' learning modalities or styles. This could be development envisioned as a capability to produce curriculum-on-demand in the virtual curriculum world and deliver to the student directly in the virtual classroom (Zucher, Kozma, Yarnell, & Morder, 2004). It can be the teacher's adaptation of curriculum for an individual student in the classroom. Depending on the authority consulted, style/modality can refer to the range of visual, motor, and auditory senses of a person, or it can be construed more generally to imply any cognitive-sensory way a person learns or the repertoire of capabilities and how they are applied by the individual. The problem is, do you infer modalities by studying the brain and its functions that produce behavior or do you observe behavior and infer modalities from it? Currently, the field of brain studies and the neurosciences are attempting to build models about modalities that are based on the brain functions (Bereiter, 2002; Carter, 1999). Most efforts in the education field have been to infer from behavior such things as structures of intellect (Meeker, 1969) or build a classification system, a taxonomy, with which to create progressive curriculum or instructional order that reflects thinking, skill development, and affective dispositions. The *Taxonomy of Educational Objectives* (Bloom & Krathwohl, 1956) is the best known of those efforts. In *Frames of Mind* (1983), Howard Gardner first suggested a multiple intelligences approach that now recognizes eight modalities of style in all learners. Compared to the hierarchical and seemingly lockstep way curriculum would have to be developed in the taxonomic approach, the seduction of Gardner's approach is its apparent flexibility in developing or adapting curriculum according to the intelligence modalities of the individual. In Figure 10.4, Gardner's modalities are shown along with Briggs and Sommefeldt's (2002) interpretation of MacGilchrist, Meyers, and Reed's (1997) reconstruction of Gardner's ideas into modalities that could guide schooling and support individualization. Keep in mind that multiple intelligences is a theory and, like all theory, is conditional depending on proof. Even with that caveat, its wide acceptance and application in schooling has to be noted, much of that owing to certain perceptions about it: (a) It is universal, and each person has these intelligences in some degree; (b) it provides a rationale for working personal intellectual capabilities, curriculum, and instruction together in schooling; (c) unlike hierarchical taxonomic approaches to learning, it is pliable and allows for flexible engagement with different curricula and instructional approaches that appeal to different learning styles; and (d) it is a positive approach to learning and reinforces the idea that all students can learn. In the Briggs and Sommefeldt school intelligence approach based on MacGilchrist's intelligences, the idea is that there is an institutional intelligence, a community's sense of itself. What might strike you in looking at it in Figure 10.4 is how mutually supportive the school could be with the learners' potential multiple intelligences development with school intelligence of the school and classroom. Imagine, for example, the possibilities if contextual school intelligence and spatial personal intelligence were the focus of curriculum development, or how the inter- and intrapersonal intelligences relate to the collegiality of the school. Think of the possibilities for curriculum development or adaptation in either example.

Students With Special Needs

One of the largest areas for curriculum adaptation in schools is for students with special needs. The variations make it unlikely any single curriculum or mix of curriculum materials could encompass any set of specialties. For example, it is possible that a student who is gifted in mathematics yet emotionally disturbed would require special curriculum for each of those and have to fit into the regular curriculum. Multiply that by the number of special needs and you can see the difficulty in having one standard curriculum. In reality, there is no one-size curriculum to fit all students.

Figure 10.4   Personal and Schooling Applications of Multiple Intelligences Ideas

Gardner (1993)	Personal Applications	Briggs & Sommefeldt (2002)	Schooling Applications
Linguistic/Language	Ability to use words and language, to think and express in words rather than pictures whether as a writer or speaker	Ethical	Intelligence that concerns itself with equity and equality in accessing and sharing resources in a school as an ultimate learning community
Logical/ Mathematical	Reasoning with numbers, ordering, sequential, geometric, progressive, problem solving	Academic	Intelligence that values engagement of learning for all students, teachers, parents, and others in the school community
Musical	Thinking in sounds, rhythms, patterns	Contextual	A self/other relational intelligence in which the school community sees both itself and the relationship to the wider local and world communities
Intrapersonal	Self-reflection, inner-state awareness, self-evaluative in strengths/weaknesses, presentation of self and social roles	Strategic	Intelligence about the present, past, and future intersection and direction of schooling, goals, and stakeholders
Interpersonal	Able to analyze self-to-others relationships, the other's point of view, sense feelings and social distance, and encourage cooperation	Reflective	Ability to interpret, apply, and evaluate knowledge and information in ongoing development
Bodily/Kinesthetic	Control and skill in body movement, balance, and spatial movement, and awareness of body-space relationship and coordination	Pedagogical	School viewing itself as a learning organization that applies other intelligences
Naturalist	Outdoors intelligence; recognition of plants, animals, and the artifacts in nature; space and location reckoning	Collegial	A practice intelligence where the school community works together to constantly improve practice

Spatial	Visual ability, thinking in images and pictures, interpreting visuals, conceptual imagery	Emotional/ Spiritual	Intelligence that recognizes need for valuing, self-expression, and consideration of the ways schooling affects every stakeholder/person

All curricula, to a degree, will be adaptations for the individual student based on and aligned with a standard curriculum. What brought that realization into curriculum work was the special education movement. The appearance of special education as a national movement came with the first Individuals With Disabilities Education Act or, as it is more familiarly known, PL 94–142. First passed in 1975 and subsequently reauthorized in 1990 and 2004 with amendments and name changes, this law affected schooling for individuals with talents and those with a host of personal challenges created by impairments or disabilities. In effect, the laws necessitated development of special and often individualized curriculum and instruction for each disability and also for teacher specialization in that curriculum. Sometimes that meant development of curriculum subsets matching the individual difference in the disability itself. Given the range of specialties suggested in Figure 10.5, these might be inserted into the curriculum as specialized packages or adapted to individual classroom and learner needs, sometimes on a daily basis. A regular teacher might need to use particular curriculum materials specifically developed for insertion in the curriculum for special needs learners, or he or she may have assistance from a specialist. Policies have varied from the "pullout," where students were taken out of class to work with a special teacher, to having that teacher come into the classroom during the time allocated to that curriculum area. Individualized instructional plans, or IEPs, specified the curriculum and instructional path for each student. Contracts were also used to individualize curriculum (Winebrenner, 1992). For those identified as gifted and talented, curriculum compacting was used to synthesize and accelerate what could be learned (Reis & Renzulli, 1992). How those kinds of ideas were used and what policies are currently in place for adapting curriculum depends on the latest 2004 IDEA reauthorization, measures related to specialties under the NCLB, and what your particular state is doing. Using the categories in Figure 10.5, curriculum adaptation might occur in the following ways.

- **Students With Disabilities.** Depending on the disability or mix of disabilities and the severity, curriculum adaptation might be through IEPs, special curriculum packages designed by special education and curriculum experts for students in

Figure 10.5   Categories and Examples of Special Needs

Students With Disabilities		
Physical disabilities	Speech impairment	Orthopedic impairment
Hearing impairment	Emotionally disturbed	Mental impairment
Learning disabilities	Visual impairment	Behaviorally disturbed
Gifted Students		
Intellectually gifted	Performance talented	Skill talented
Learning Adaptations		
Language needs	Basic skills (e.g., reading)	Sociocultural needs

special settings, or adaptive curriculum materials for classroom use, such as modular curriculum.

- **Gifted Students.** The curriculum challenge for the gifted and talented is accelerating the curriculum to match interests and motivation. Individual states have created and specially funded new schools for the talented and gifted, particularly in math and science and sometimes in the performing arts. Alabama, for example, has a school for each. In particular districts, some schools are set aside with emphasis in particular knowledge. These are often considered to be magnet schools. Where those options don't exist, special advance placement (AP) and honors courses cater to the curriculum needs of the gifted and talented. When there are only a few such students in a classroom or school, individualized curriculum contracts are useful. In other instances, special clubs (science, mathematics, etc.) provide ways to enhance individual talents and interests beyond the classroom.

- **Learning Adaptations.** Some students have temporary discrepancies in their repertoire that impede learning but can be remediated or bypassed to permit the students to participate effectively in school. Basic to learning is the capability to read, speak, and work in the common language and be aware of and develop personal behavior that accommodates social and cultural differences. Packaged curriculum can be adapted to those kinds of discrepancies, often at the entry point in schooling. ESL curriculum can, for example, help the student to learn English while learning to read and can offer materials that deal with social-cultural issues affecting the particular student or group.

Multicultural Curriculum

Two phrases, *curriculum that is multicultural* and *multicultural curriculum,* seem at first glance to be similar in meaning and approach to multicultural concerns in curriculum work. A multicultural curriculum is just that, a curriculum dedicated to the study of cultures and those particular to a specific society. A curriculum that is multicultural is one in which the emphasis is on representation of various ethnic and cultural groups in a society through the pictures, examples, and so forth in the materials such as textbooks and videos regardless of what content is being discussed. A curriculum can therefore be both, but the emphasis should be on curriculum that is multicultural in all areas of content. Adaptation usually means to review content materials for cultural representation, for example, making sure Native American contributions are presented in an American literature curriculum or in the arts. Of particular importance is having story problems in mathematics or experiments in the sciences in ethnic or cultural settings whenever possible so that a multicultural balance is considered.

Alternative Adaptations

In the evolution of curriculum and curriculum work, there have been proposals for alternative ways to organize the curriculum. These proposals have one thing in common: they do not essentially move away from or replace the traditional academic subject or content base or propose a radical new curriculum. They function more as designs for alternate adaptation in curriculum. These alternative adaptations were introduced in Chapter 4 and are historic curriculum development and adaptation artifacts that reappear in curriculum work. It is important for a curriculum worker to be aware of the particular configuration because they are often what practitioners discuss in school, particularly high schools with teachers who want to bridge between separate subjects and classes. For example, teachers in middle and high school often implement the correlation idea informally because it makes sense to integrate subjects; the knowledge gained in one can help learning in another. (See the Perspective Into Practice example at chapter's end). Often these are implemented without any particular awareness that these adaptation ideas have existed for a long time—that is why the term "informal" was used previously. These alternative adaptations, when they were originally proposed, were for more ambitious "formal" use, perhaps on a districtwide basis or as recommended in a general plan or for particular interdisciplinary purposes by curriculum or teacher associations or organizations. They are presented here because these or very similar ideas can appear naturally and spontaneously among workers in curriculum development and adaptation, and it is important to realize they have existed for a long time and it is not really necessary to reinvent them.

- **Structure-of-the-Discipline.** Based on the work of Joseph Schwab (1962), the idea was to emulate work in the disciplines of knowledge by emphasizing how the discipline knowledge was organized, what kinds of questions scholars asked, how they went about their work, and what evidence constituted truth. The new science and mathematics programs of the 1960s were an adaptation of this idea.
- **Correlation.** The emphasis is on articulation, meaning the identification of relationships among different subjects or areas of the curriculum. A favorite method was to link historical periods and events with literature of the time and developments in science. Disciplines remain intact but bridged by the content relationships.
- **Fusion.** This is similar to correlation in intent and design but different in that the lines between disciplines become blurred and the focus is on the emergent topic or subject. An example might be the study of globalization emerging from the study of history, economics, sociology, and political science.
- **Broad-Fields**. This is a fusion-correlation hybrid of new subjects of study (not disciplines) that emerge from two or more disciplines. One of the most familiar is the social studies curriculum when it is taught as such and not as discrete courses in history, government, and so forth.

CURRICULUM ALIGNMENT

Curriculum development and adaptation are important kinds of work in schools. They make curriculum real and viable as the centerpiece in schooling. As suggested throughout this text, curriculum work is a mix of activities that have to relate to each other in order for curriculum to be consistently effective. Although different work activities can occur simultaneously, they are still related because they are about curriculum. That relatedness is expressed in the idea of alignment. Whether the work is developmental or adaptive, or occurs in a district, school, or state, ultimately the matter of alignment has to be addressed.

The Alignment Idea

Rails on a railroad bed are a specific distance apart so the train's wheels will move effectively and efficiently; any separation or deviation and the consequence is obvious. This is a very simple example of alignment and why it is important. Alignment affects your life in a variety of ways, from alignment of your car wheels to placing a picture on the wall. Alignment also has more complex and abstract meanings and applications in fields of knowledge. It is an important one in curriculum work.

PERSPECTIVE INTO PRACTICE: **Classroom Adaptations of Elementary and Secondary Curriculum**		
Curriculum Adaptations	*Elementary Classroom*	*Secondary Classroom*
Modalities	Accepting that different learners have different modes of learning and the critical importance of these modes of learning in elementary schools, the district wants to emphasize curriculum embedded and organized in different ways (e.g., the same content on a video or CD, or in a text) to assist different visual-cognitive styles and enhance redundancy of the curriculum so it enhances possibilities for learning.	In the general science class, some students are having a difficult time with some basic concepts. The teacher notes that the more text-visual learners seem to get the ideas but others don't. A decision is made to use some new CDs with programmed conceptualizations of the concepts, some computer simulations, and hands-on demonstrations in the classroom to optimize the ways a student could develop the concepts.
Special Learners	The second-grade teacher is working with students in reading. The special education teacher has two students in the class with speech impairments and provides those students with reading material during regular reading time. To diffuse comparison with other readers, different readings with the same content are given to other students during reading discussion.	A student excels in music, especially improvisation with the clarinet, and performs well in mathematics but not in textbook-dominated courses such as science, history, and literature. Cooperation among the teachers in Special Education and teachers in those areas where the student has difficulties provides optional learning modes such as taped lessons, use of music as background, singing passages, and CDs and videos to enhance the students' grasp of knowledge in other curriculum content.
Multicultural	Students have arrived from the new Hmong community of Vietnamese people. The school has prepared by arranging for English-speaking Hmong leaders to visit, and is infusing materials about their community in reading, language arts, and social	As part of understanding different cultural life and the confluence of history, context, and place, students in the U.S. history classes are using materials adapted from studies of the Lakota Sioux and their art and literature to understand the

(Continued)

(Continued)

	studies to help the school community understand Hmong culture and life. Materials have been adapted from U.S. Department of State materials and resources provided by the state university's Center for Cultural Exchange.	conflict between the Sioux people and settlers and the U.S. Army during the 1870 to 1890 period.
Alternative Adaptations	The school board decides to change the K–3 elementary curriculum from the current historical studies in charting America's development to a social studies (broad-fields) format of historical-sociological-geographical emphasis that focuses on the complexities and variations in lifestyles, cultures, and place of early colonists and indigenous Americans.	Results on state assessments indicate that students aren't making connections between areas of knowledge in the state curriculum. The secondary program is revamped from discrete studies (history, literature, etc.) to include bridging projects that make connections, or correlations, between the areas of knowledge.

Curriculum Alignment

In Chapter 4, curriculum fundamentals were introduced. Although it was not emphasized at that time, it was your introduction to some initial thoughts about curriculum alignment. Although each has separate functional qualities, the four concepts—scope, sequence, continuity, and balance—share an operational symmetry through the idea of alignment. For example, sequence in an elementary mathematics program would have students learning addition by working from one place, to two places, and so on in an ordered fashion. They would not jump from one place to four places because that would disrupt curriculum continuity by breaking the curriculum sequence. *Curriculum alignment* means the relationship of scope, sequence, continuity, and balance in two respects. One is about alignment in the existing curriculum, as in the day-to-day working with it, as would a teacher or a curriculum specialist. The other is about alignment when you do curriculum development and adaptation work. For example, developing an adaptation for the curriculum would entail alignment considerations in these four ways:

1. *Scope:* It is important to identify what is covered where the adaptation is to occur. You obviously don't want an adaptation project in the wrong curriculum.

2. *Sequence:* The adaptation will have to be inserted so the overall content order of the curriculum is maintained.

3. *Continuity:* The adaptation will effectively fit into the curriculum at the intended point in the sequence so the order of learning is maintained.

4. *Balance:* The curriculum adaptation is appropriate for the expected level of learning and the students who will be doing the learning; it might be for third grade but does it fit the particular learners?

Other Considerations

Alignment is also often used in educational conversation in other ways, and it is important to specify the concept or perhaps activity to which alignment is being applied. This clarification is important because, although it implies a relational quality, it may also convey other meanings. For example, speaking of instructional alignment or alignment of instruction and assessment is different because the particulars or qualities are different. Instruction, for example, is not about scope in the curricular sense, but it could be about sequence if that were to mean the order of instructional engagement, such as moving between or alternating among group, student-directed, or teacher-led techniques. The concern is always to know what the particulars in a conception are and how they make one discussion using similar terms different from another. For instance, you would want clarification if someone started discussing "educational alignment." Does the individual mean curriculum, instruction, evaluation, or something entirely different?

Curriculum and Standards

One of the more interesting developments in schooling has been the movement toward standards, a topic entertained in Chapters 7 and 9 and that will be discussed again in Chapter 13.

Standards-based education refers to educational practices that have (a) stated measurable descriptions of what students should know and be able to do that results from school learning and (b) accompanying assessments that measure student achievement. Boiled down, that means specifying the curriculum content or knowledge in three ways, the processes, basic information, and specific knowledge and skills defined by the context of their use that are be mastered. Marzano and Kendall (1997) refer to those as *procedural* standards (processes), *declarative* standards (information), and *contextual* standards (special skills or knowledge defined by the context of their use). In essence, the curriculum, or what is to be learned, consists of knowledge represented in three kinds of standards under the standards-based education banner. Of course, the expectation is that assessments in the form of tests will establish some measure of how strong or weak is the relationship between the expectations as stated in the standard and what the students demonstrate they know. That expectation in the standards movement will depend on the *alignment* among the standard, the curriculum, and instruction as both planned and what is delivered; engagement, or what the student actually gets from instruction; and the assessment in test form, and how the results are valued or what value system is put in place to give them meaning. Obviously, alignment in any of the particulars, curriculum, for example, and among them all is a complex undertaking that is still evolving.

ASSESSING CURRICULUM DEVELOPMENT AND ADAPTATION

The ultimate question in curriculum development is, "How do we know this is doing what it is supposed to do?" Two kinds of work, curriculum management and curriculum assessment-evaluation, come into brief consideration here; the discussion is brief because each is discussed more extensively in Chapter 11 and Chapter 12, respectively. A management process is needed to make sure curriculum development proceeds with consistency and monitors both itself and the flow of development activities. Assessment requires some tests, checklists, or other procedures or tools to keep things on track, to create data for determining if specifications, design, and the materials created match or fit as planned and how they work with the intended users. It is formative in the way that the piloting and field tests discussed earlier in this chapter give initial data about development as it proceeds. Summative assessment in curriculum development is gathering data on how and if the curriculum actually works in use with the intended audience. The formative is quite straightforward and is only concerned with immediate development or adaptive effects so the process or product can be modified before being put into use. On the other hand, the summative effort has to have some value attached to it. For example, if a decision is being made to develop some material and adapt it in the curriculum and a similar commercial package is available, what are the criteria in making a decision about the value of using one or the other?

Assigning Value

Because the possible curriculum development activities have such a range, from formal large-scale projects to very limited adaptations, it is not easy to place a value on curriculum development that is either new development or adaptation. Another qualifier in valuing is that curriculum development is a process resulting in a product that can take many forms, a textbook, a series of classroom science demonstrations, a video about some historic event, or a single-page handout prepared by a teacher. It can, as a process, also be composed or put together in various ways. In sum, valuing to establish a benchmark of success is relative to the characteristics of the process and product, the expectations for the process and product, the contextual properties in which the process is implemented and the product is used, the caprices inherent in implementation of the process and in the use of the product, and the summative results. The value of the process and the product of development and adaptation will also depend on the perspective and knowledge of curriculum, the professional practice that workers bring to the tasks. This latter concern is, of course, an intangible one depending on the quality of personnel given the tasks to develop or adapt curriculum. These considerations point to the overall subjectivity inherent in valuing any process.

Assessing the Process

Previously, you encountered a sample curriculum development process, a series of steps or procedures for creating a new curriculum or producing a set of curriculum materials. As you may recall, at several points (piloting and field testing), data are gathered on the product in use and there is a double check going on when that occurs. The obvious purpose is to get data on how the product is working with the sample of users and make corrections or adjustments as appropriate to the findings. There is also a second purpose, to check on the process itself by looking at the data-gathering procedure and the data to see if what has resulted accords with the way the procedure was structured and if the procedure led to the collection of appropriate data. If there were problems in either case, the process has to be revised. This refers to an interesting parallel review of the development or adaptation and of the process creating the development or adaptation. Simply put, the process has a built-in self-check, a self-assessing characteristic that establishes an effectiveness value as the process is worked through.

Assessing the Product

In curriculum development and adaptation activities, there is a tangible product or service outcome. A product valuation is also subjective, but it is less so because there is some possibility for measuring it in the long term. For example, a curriculum development that is useful to teachers and is liked by them will probably be used extensively, or a textbook they like will have greater sales, thus giving a certain "use" value to the product. At least the sales numbers should decrease the subjectivity in making that valuation. This suggests that the valuation of a product can be less subjective because it is tangible and data about its use can provide a more accurate interpretation. A book, CD, or other curriculum product is tangible and complete and does not depend on the contextual factors of use to complicate making a judgment about it. This initial sizing up of the product and identifying considerations to apply places great reliance on the professional practitioners' role and their grasp of knowledge essentials such as knowing about and being able to do an analysis of the development project and its resulting product. Although those considerations apply to most development/adaptation efforts, some kinds of work have special considerations and characteristics. Niche curriculum areas and materials have unconventional characteristics. One is the lack of universal applicability. For example, unlike a standard text in science that has a vast national market, materials for a drug education curriculum have to jockey for fit across a diverse collection of different curriculum expectations and controllers. A second matter is the often offhanded way that such niche curriculum is assigned responsibility for inclusion in a local or state curriculum. For example, drug education and character education are often mandated, but it is left to local curriculum specialists or teachers to decide what materials to use and where to place the new content in the scope and sequence of the total curriculum. Obviously, assessing the product and assigning value in such special cases is just as important, especially for the potential user who wants the best in curriculum.

Summary and Conclusions

Curriculum development is one of the oldest and most important kinds of curriculum work. In the early years of curriculum development, the focus was on creating new materials for the classroom. As curriculum activity grew, it still meant creating materials for schools but expanded to include development work by those such as publishers outside schools. Knowledge about the various aspects of doing development work is part of the larger encompassing curriculum knowledge base that curriculum workers need to master. As knowledge-contributing work, curriculum developmental work exemplifies the curriculum dialectic, the creation of knowledge about curriculum development by doing it and the return of that knowledge into the foundational knowledge of curriculum. Curriculum development activities essentially fall into several kinds of work: the creating of new curriculum, the adaptation of existing curriculum, or some combination of both. In any of the three, alignment and assessment are important considerations because they must be addressed in the process that guides the work and in the use of the product resulting from the process. Additionally, student modalities, multiculturalism, students with special needs, and some alternative adaptation formats need to be considered.

Critical Perspective

1. The sample curriculum development process in this chapter offers a framework for new curriculum development from scratch. Select a grade level and a curriculum area of choice, and apply the process to develop a mock curriculum. Document your effort as you proceed.

2. Curriculum development work usually involves new or adaptation work. Have you ever done or experienced any new curriculum development work? Adaptation work?

3. In the classic satire *The Saber-Tooth Curriculum*, Harold Benjamin, writing under the pseudonym J. D. Peddiwell (1939/1959), pointed out several possible fallacies that could affect curriculum development. Using a copy of the book or typing in the book title and accessing several available sites, identify the fallacies about which the author was warning curriculum workers.

4. In Figure 10.3, Gardner's multiple intelligences theory and its reconceptualization for schooling by Briggs and Sommefeldt (2002) based on MacGilchrist et al. (1997) are presented. Both are about learning modalities as representations of school and personal styles. Are they comparable? For example, what in multiple intelligences theory relates to school intelligence? Is a synthesis possible? If so, what sort of synthesis emerges? What implications for curriculum adaptation do you see?

5. In the discussion about curriculum adaptations for disabilities, a number of examples are given. In addition to those (e.g., IEPs, contracts) are you aware of any other kinds of adaptations?

6. Traditionally, assessments are equated with objectively produced data, such as tests. In curriculum development/adaptation, there is a strong valuation consideration. Can you identify any school or classroom activities involving placing a subjective value on curriculum development or adaptation? What about the importance of one content area over others?

Resources for Curriculum Study

1. There are any number of textbooks that offer ideas on how to do curriculum development (Armstrong, 2003; Sowell, 1996). An old but excellent resource is Hilda Taba's *Curriculum Development: Theory and Practice* (1962). You can also go online and type in Taba's name to find other information about her work.

2. Two newer taxonomic efforts are Anderson and Krathwohl's *A Taxonomy for Learning, Teaching, and Assessing: A Revision of Bloom's Taxonomy of Educational Objectives* (2001) and Richard Marzano's *Designing a New Taxonomy of Educational Objectives* (2001).

3. Studies of adoption/adaptation grew out of the 1960s interests in reform and how reforms get implemented or adopted/adapted and what are the factors driving those processes. Some of the foundational work was done by Gene Hall

and associates at the University of Texas with the Concerns Based Adoption Model. Hall and Hord explore and update their work in *Implementing Change* (2001).

4. For a perspective on the topic of alignment in standards-based education, see Rothman's article on linking standards and instruction in *Educational Leadership* (1996) and the book *Measuring Up* (1995). *From the Capitol to the Classroom: Standards-Based Reform in the States* (2001), edited by Susan Fuhrman, is also useful.

5. Alignment, articulation, and coherence all refer to how educational elements are linked in a harmonious relationship. Armstrong (2003) and Oliver (1977) use the term *articulation.* This text uses the term *alignment.* Another term being used is *coherence.* A good resource for exploring contemporary meanings and applications of those terms is the volume *Towards Coherence Between Classroom Assessment and Accountability* (2004), edited by Mark Wilson.

References

Anderson, L. W., & Krathwohl, D. R. (2001). *A taxonomy for learning, teaching, and assessing: A revision of Bloom's taxonomy of educational objectives.* New York: Longman.

Armstrong, D. G. (2003). *Curriculum today.* Upper Saddle River, NJ: Merrill Prentice Hall.

Bereiter, C. (2002). *Education and mind in the knowledge age.* Mahwah, NJ: Lawrence Erlbaum.

Bloom, B. J., & Krathwohl, D. (1956). *Taxonomy of educational objectives: Handbook I: Cognitive domain.* New York: Longman Green.

Briggs, A. R. J., & Sommefeldt, D. (2002). *Managing effective learning and teaching.* London: Sage.

Bruner, J. (1960). *The process of education.* Cambridge, MA: Harvard University Press.

Carter, R. (1999). *Mapping the mind.* Berkeley: University of California Press.

Dow, P. B. (1991). *Schoolhouse politics: Lessons from the Sputnik era.* Cambridge, MA: Harvard University Press.

Fuhrman, S. H. (Ed.). (2001). *Towards coherence between classroom assessment and accountability* (100th Yearbook of the National Society for the Study of Education, Part II). Chicago: National Society for the Study of Education.

Gardner, H. (1983). *Frames of mind.* New York: Basic Books.

Hall, G. E., & Hord, S. M. (2001). *Implementing change: Patterns, principles, potholes.* New York: Allyn & Bacon.

Lemann, N. (1997, November). The reading wars. *Atlantic Monthly, 280*(5), 128–134.

MacGilchrist, B., Meyers, K., & Reed, J. (1997). *The intelligent school.* London: Paul Chapman/Sage.

Marzano, R. J. (2001). *Designing a new taxonomy of educational objectives.* Thousand Oaks, CA: Corwin.

Marzano, R. J., & Kendall, J. S. (1997). *The fall and rise of standards-based education.* Alexandria, VA: National Association of State School Boards.

Meeker, M. N. (1969). *The structure of intellect.* Columbus, OH: Merrill.

Oliver, A. I. (1977). *Curriculum improvement: A guide to problems, principles, and process.* New York: Harper & Row.

Peddiwell, J. A. (1959). *The saber-tooth curriculum.* New York: McGraw-Hill. (Original work published 1939)

Reis, S., & Renzulli, J. (1992). Using curriculum compacting to challenge the above average. *Educational Leadership, 50*(2), 51–57.

Rothman, R. (1995). *Measuring up: Standards, assessment, and school reform.* San Francisco: Jossey-Bass.

Rothman, R. (1996). Linking standards and instruction: HELP is on the way. *Educational Leadership, 53*(8), 44 46.

Schwab, J. J. (1962). The concept of the structure of a discipline. *Educational Record 40,* 197–205.

Sowell, E. J. (1996). *Curriculum: An integrative approach.* Upper Saddle River, NJ: Merrill / Prentice Hall.

Taba, H. (1962). *Curriculum development: Theory and practice.* New York: Harcourt, Brace, & World.

Tyler, R. W. (1949). *Basic principles of curriculum and instruction.* Chicago: University of Chicago Press.

Wilson, M. (Ed.). (2004). *Towards coherence between classroom assessment and accountability* (103rd Yearbook of the National Society for the Study of Education, Part II). Chicago: National Society for the Study of Education.

Winebrenner, S. (1992). *Teaching gifted kids in the regular classroom.* Minneapolis, MN: Free Spirit Press.

Zimmerman, J. (1999). Storms over the schoolhouse: Exploring popular influence upon American curriculum, 1890 1941. *Teachers College Record, 100*(3), 602–626.

Zucher, A., Kozma, R., Yarnell, L., & Morder, C. (2004). *The virtual high school: Teaching generation V.* New York: Teachers College Press.

Chapter 11

IMPLEMENTING AND MANAGING THE CURRICULUM

The 1983 publication of the National Commission on Educational Excellence, *A Nation at Risk,* began the series of school reform movements that continue to the present. If the purpose of these efforts can be captured in a word, it would be *accountability.* The problem is, accountable for what? Student learning? What is taught? A particular curriculum? On the surface, making schools accountable seems simple enough: It is agreeing on what schools are to do, specifying criteria or standards that represent what they are to do, and then linking expectations to outcomes. National polls, the annual Phi Delta Kappa educational poll, for example, sample public attitudes and expectations (see Rose & Gallop, 2003). Presidents and governors set goals for schools. There is no shortage of people with agendas about what schools should be doing. The problem is actually in two parts. First is agreeing on what ends are to be served and what curriculum will link expectations to outcomes. That thinking is fine as far it goes, but the historic record as noted in Chapter 7 demonstrates how difficult it is. The second part is setting up a process, a set of procedures, an ordered way of thinking and operating, that creates data to inform both the public and school professionals about the expectations-curriculum-outcomes relationship and dynamics. One word describes what is needed to pull all those elements together, *management.* The difficulty here, as you will come to understand, is the latent concern for and, until recently, the lack of sophisticated and comprehensive management that can serve accountability.

MANAGEMENT IN CURRICULUM WORK

Before exploring management as a form of curriculum work, it is important to make some clarifications about management. The term management is used so offhandedly that it carries different associations. Often it is nothing more that a casual expression such as, "I will manage my own affairs!" Or, "How did you manage that?" Occupations are often associated with management, the corporate manager, a general manager, or perhaps even a baseball manager. Then there is the corporate meaning of managing Ford Motor Company, IBM, or Enron. Management study courses and degrees in colleges and universities give a certain academic respectability to management as well. Given that sort of general sense of management, what, then, is management and what does it mean to manage something? Figure 11.1 presents five aspects of management, focusing on the mission, developing a profile, creating options, developing plans, and implementation; these are drawn freely from the management literature (e.g., Pearce & Robinson, 1997; Stolovitch & Keeps, 1996). Summarizing from those assigned characteristics, *management* can be described as activities organized to accomplish a specified mission (goals, ends) integrated into a process containing the necessary resources to accomplish that mission. In short, management embraces the set of organization and oversight activities, the *management process,* that provides a product or service.

Figure 11.1   Conceptualizing Management

- Identify the **mission** assigned or formulate one that includes the statements of purpose, goals and objectives, and the very important philosophical considerations that undergird the mission.
- Develop a **profile** of the service, activity, or product-creation process by cataloging existing intrinsic and contextual characteristics or conditions and capabilities as benchmarks of the starting point.
- Analyze the mission and profile to identify **options** toward achieving the mission commensurate with resources identified in the profile.
- Prioritize options into short-, intermediate-, and long-term **plans** that include allocation of resources, tasks, people, technology, facilities, and rewards.
- Prioritize the plans and **implement** the plan selected according to the analysis.

In the education field, references to educational management are discussed very broadly as part of leadership or supervision or more particularly as instructional or classroom management (Tucker & Codding, 2002). You encounter kinds of management actions for the classroom or school such as instructional management or classroom management, but rarely curriculum management. Thanks to the work of Margaret Preedy (1989, 1993, 2002) and others at the University of Leicester and the Open University, United Kingdom, there are some studies of management in education that focus specifically on school and curriculum management. Granted, the context is British national curriculum and school reform, but the ideas about curriculum management apply generally to any curriculum management work and are useful for several reasons. First, they are drawn from actual work with teachers and other practitioners in the field. Second, they stress the idea of the management process for each aspect of schooling, curriculum and instruction, for example, within a larger operational management framework of *strategic management,* an idea of management as a confluence of actions to form and implement plans to achieve specified objectives (Middlewood & Burton, 2001; Pearce & Robinson, 1997). Also, Preedy and others provide management with a structural-behavioral interpretation by focusing on management as what people do and what they apply in doing their work. The emphasis is on the management process, the collection of supervising activities, of oversight, that have a particular application, and the management tools, the ways of thinking and the objects for application that they use. Taken together, the thinking, the process, the tools, and how they are organized constitute a *management strategy.* Consider, for example, curriculum, instruction, and assessment, each a composite of activities and functions unto itself yet integrated and linked in a larger web of school management. In any management strategy, what you learn from managing one component can transfer across management of the whole and among various other management activities, as in managing instruction or the classroom. Considered in that way, different types of activities, documentation (discussed in Chapter 4) and research and evaluation (see Chapter 12), for example, can be viewed as special tools in curriculum management work. Strategic management conveys a sense of oversight, the overarching, seamless encompassing of both curriculum work and the management process itself. It acts to manage everything assigned to it and to alert management workers when some function is not performing or warn of a developing problem. This conceptualization of management as a dual process referred to earlier as strategic management can be found in such mundane activities in a school as encountering a mistake in a textbook, or discovering that test items, standards, and curriculum don't match up. Having a curriculum management strategy is vital in curriculum work to ensure that finding such problems is not serendipitous but results from preparation and having an actual operational management process in place. You have already been given one example of a management process in the preceding chapter, the example of a curriculum development process.

MANAGING THE CURRICULUM MISSION

Making schools accountable is contingent on effectively managing schooling, especially the curriculum. In this era of accountability, the schooling mission is to have learners learn and have a curriculum sufficient to that task. Getting there, linking curriculum and learning, requires some kind of relationship that is both curriculum specific and connected to the total strategy integrating all schooling functions (e.g., instruction, resource allocation, assessment, evaluation, and personnel), much like what has been mandated under the No Child Left Behind (NCLB) Act of 2001, the specifics of which are still being revealed. The ultimate aim of *curriculum management* is to establish a systematic approach that senses or detects how the curriculum is performing in order to make ongoing adjustments. That management framework entails identifying the mission, profiling the various curriculum-related resource components, identifying options, and developing a plan that will effectively monitor the curriculum both in its static, inert form as a set of documents or texts, and in the lived form as the curriculum-in-use. The features of management presented earlier in Figure 11.1 depict a general concept applicable in business or any other endeavor. Applied to curriculum work, the concept acquires particular meaning when reconceptualized as curriculum management. The management–curriculum management relationship and action examples presented in Figure 11.2 lead to several more observations about general curriculum management and managing changes as the curriculum mission proceeds. First is the relational nature of management in the strategic sense. Note in Figure 11.2 that curriculum management occurs in relation to other actions, such as instruction and assessment, that are part of a systematic approach to understanding how the curriculum is performing in order to make ongoing adjustments. In the case of the mathematics example, data collection could suggest that student learning discrepancies are not curriculum related but instructional, because the presentation across several teachers differs and the method of instruction could be the cause of discrepancies in learning. The critical point is not to assign responsibility or blame but to use management as an opportunity to remediate, change, or adjust the process and use the knowledge gained to ensure that other teachers will be aware of the pitfalls in teaching with a particular method, at least in this particular case. A second observation about management is that the activities covered can differ in operational complexity. Referring again to the action examples in Figure 11.2, there would probably be greater complexity in managing the total curriculum than in managing the two special projects. Because managing the curriculum is long term and continuous, you can expect that other special curriculum projects and programs will be added, deleted, retained, or incorporated from time to time, and the curriculum management process needs to be able to accommodate those changes as the curriculum management process is itself reviewed and reconstituted. For example, it is possible that the mathematics project, initially limited in scope, could prove out and become the new

Figure 11.2   Curriculum Management

Management	Curriculum Management	Action Examples
Establish the Mission	Identify and state schooling and curriculum outcomes.	Curriculum materials (state standards, courses of study, and district curriculum guides) detail the schooling mission.
Build Profiles	Create composite inventories of personnel (teachers, students, and support personnel), physical property (chairs, tables, etc.), consumables (pens, paper, etc.), nonconsumables (lab equipment, maps, software and hardware, etc.), curriculum resources (texts, etc.), for each school unit (classroom, etc.).	The physical classroom and its fixtures set a tone for learning that is suggested in a profile. This could suggest the need for renovations, reallocation of chairs and tables, or reconfiguring the room. Profiling teacher curriculum expertise can identify strengths and weaknesses and indicate future support needs. Curriculum resource profiles can identify material needs, such as text allocation problems.
Identify Options	Comparing profiles identifies curriculum options that can be prioritized for planning. This might reflect comparisons among personnel, specific curriculum content, and other profiles.	Profiles of the mathematics curriculum and teacher expertise suggest teachers need developmental activates for the new curriculum materials in sixth-grade mathematics prior to and at intervals during implementation.
Prepare a Plan	Prioritized options are the basis for a plan for managing curriculum activities. Plans include curriculum actions set to the rhythm of the school year and planning in timed intervals such as a 6-month or 2-year framework, depending on the priority level established in the plan and the implementation phases for various formative and summative assessments that provide data as implementation proceeds.	Curriculum management requires a reporting grid for gathering data about the curriculum generally and for each specific area (e.g., science, mathematics, or reading) and each grade level. The reporting process configures the plan for curriculum and is keyed to the prioritized options. All reporting about the reading curriculum is standardized and reviewed by the curriculum-reading specialist. For the mathematics curriculum, a special priority, the reporting process is more complex and the time line is different.
Detail the Implementation	The cycles and time lines for teaching curriculum, developing curriculum, assessment-evaluation, all the forms of curriculum work, are prepared and curriculum workers assigned for the level of implementation	The district curriculum specialist provides a software-reporting matrix for daily curriculum data gathering cued to aspects of the plan. Continuous data gathering is built into the plan through a daily teacher curriculum report. Special curriculum

(Continued)

Figure 11.2 (Continued)

	or action oversight. A data-gathering and reporting network connects all aspects of the plan through either a computer-assisted reporting process or planned, personnel-generated reports.	plans, such as implementing the new sixth-grade mathematics, are fitted with specific reporting and data-gathering requirements concentrating on the mathematics curriculum and how the new materials are working with the students. Weekly classroom paper assessments track progress and identify student learning problems. Quarterly formal assessments track weekly remediation or curriculum adjustments made as the curriculum progresses so it is consistent with daily implementation or similar actions.
Monitoring	Curriculum monitoring, the continuous and purposeful collection of data about how the curriculum is doing, provides insights into the curriculum-in-use.	Teachers and curriculum specialists can adjust the curriculum for the student as the data suggest in a timely manner that could include a curriculum-on-demand response from a curriculum specialist to differentiate curriculum on a very personal basis.

mathematics curriculum, falling within continuous oversight under curriculum management. Third is the interesting inclusiveness of curriculum management, the subsuming of forms of work that have to be managed within the curriculum. In the reading initiative example, there is the hint of curriculum development work in materials for the reading project. In both examples, assessment-evaluation activities will be included in the management effort. Thus, curriculum management forms an overlay of various forms of curriculum work linking workers in an operational network of different curriculum work activities. A final observation is that curriculum management should strive to be flexible by adjusting to the differences in scope, scale, and tempo inherent in oversight and special project aspects of curriculum work. The reading and mathematics examples are short term in comparison to the larger management process encompassing the total scope of the curriculum. The mix of scope and tempo is also reflected in the scale or comparative size of the management effort that is needed; small scale usually means a different scope of work and tempo in the work effort. Strategic management is intended to promote flexibility by accommodating differences in scope, scale, and tempo in the continuous management for the long term. The intent of any management is to promote work continuity, whether it is the large scale and tempo of managing the whole curriculum or the time-bound, small-scale tempo of the special project or priority curriculum undertaking (Hardie, 2001).

FORMING A CURRICULUM MANAGEMENT STRATEGY

Curriculum management work has several dimensions that suggest its complexity. One refers to the kind of management work, and the other to when that particular kind of work is most important, when it occurs. A standard characteristic of management is that it is constant and ongoing. In the classroom, management means the planning and preparation of lessons from the first to the last day of school. Everything in the management of learning and teaching is represented in that collection of lessons, whether formalized in some required format or informally recorded as notations or as prescribed entries in a software package on the computer. The rhythm of schooling, 180–200 days out of the year, gives a different meaning to management in curriculum work. With the exception of 12-month employees among whom might be some curriculum specialists, teachers and most other school personnel are only working for 9 or 10 months. During off times, activities such as ordering books and reviewing evaluations occur. These activities reflect a different perception of curriculum management continuity, one that includes a time of interim or preparatory activities when teachers, students, and others return and schools return to full operation. In a way, it is like the annual retooling or model change shutdown in the auto industry: management is still ongoing but the emphasis shifts. Unlike business or industrial management, curriculum management must adjust to the different rhythm of schooling.

There are special characteristics of curriculum and all aspects of curriculum work that bear consideration. These characteristics, what needs to be considered in a curriculum management strategy, are portrayed in Figure 11.3. They will be discussed at various points and in different contexts as the chapter continues. The curriculum mission and management as a process have been addressed earlier in this chapter. Useful tools in curriculum management, mapping and analysis, for example, will be discussed in the section that follows. Horizontal and vertical management characteristics refer to the layering of management activities (e.g., horizontally across all classrooms in a school or across all schools and vertically from classroom to school to district), the scope and sequence aspect of management. Environment encapsulates considerations about space use, furniture and other content artifacts in any classroom where curriculum engagement occurs, and connections to a book depository or a resource center for curriculum production, all special environments to be managed in support of the teacher-learner-curriculum mission.

Strategic management applied to curriculum requires thinking that emphasizes continuity, maintenance, and monitoring that is continuous, from policy making and

Figure 11.3   Characteristics to Consider in a Management Strategy

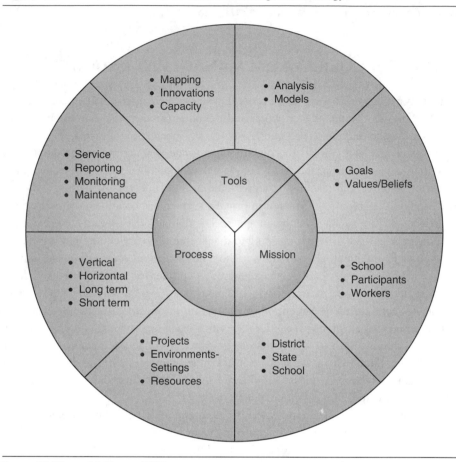

Source: Middlewood & Burton (2001).

planning to implementing and sustaining curriculum work. Obviously, an ideal curriculum management strategy would seek to resolve the discontinuities and other matters in curriculum management. The question would then be, what would comprehensive curriculum management look like and what would it entail? Viewed from another perspective, you might start by asking what knowledge exists about curriculum and practice that would be useful in creating a management strategy, and, concomitantly, what new knowledge needs to be created to continuously inform management and practice. That set of thoughts, thinking strategically, positions management as a critical function in all curriculum work, whether it is managing curriculum development, policy making and planning, assessment-evaluation, or management itself.

Figure 11.4 Examples of Curriculum Management Functions and Activities

Maintenance Activities	Monitoring Activities	Servicing Activities
• Specific worker assignments for system maintenance/oversight • Technical assistance to maintain data/reporting sites • Maintenance reporting system created and operational	• Reporting system/data collection process in place • Scheduled periodic analysis of the reporting/data process • Periodic external review of the monitoring process and activities	• Available material copying and production support • Curriculum/content and management specialists on call for assistance • Classroom and school district capacity available to support curriculum work

Development and Integration

All the various activities that constitute curriculum management can be placed in at least three functional categories. One involves actions to *maintain* the curriculum, another activities that *monitor* the curriculum, and a third those that *service* the curriculum. The kinds of activities that could be found under each category are suggested in Figure 11.4. Taken together, these sets of activities have the potential to provide two things, a systematic accounting of the curriculum process itself and a system for creating data about the curriculum-in-use and its effect with learners. The maintenance function keeps the curriculum operational. The curriculum management monitoring function focuses on performance, how both curriculum and the management of it are operating and doing what the mission intends them to do. Curriculum maintenance activities serve in a more immediate, formative way to inform workers as soon as possible about the curriculum and the management process. On the other hand, monitoring activities focus on management's summative use, the curriculum outcomes relationship, whether the curriculum is achieving assigned outcomes. All management activities, as you will note in the discussions that follow, including those that are summative and formative, are intended to create data about curriculum work in its various forms and about the impact of curriculum with those who use it.

Resource Allocation

Resource allocation, or resourcing, to use Middlewood and Burton's (2001) term, refers to the identification and effective use of a range of resources to support the overall curriculum and its operational contexts. Curriculum resourcing includes the environment, such as the classroom, the world of the child in that space and what he or she brings to it. That environment, as Briggs (2001) succinctly frames it, is not just the classroom but the world outside that "may be brought in to enhance the learning experience. Virtual worlds [that] may be set up within which learners can access knowledge and develop skills through the medium of information and learning technologies" (p. 175). That environment includes such other considerations as teacher collegiality, student behavior, other school human resources, and parents, all of which are visible, live signs of the school's social and cultural dimensions. Usually you think of resources as consumables, the pens and paper used, and nonconsumables, like a book, maps, or other curriculum expanders. Additionally, there are the taken-for-granted fixtures such as lights, trim, and window treatments, all of which taken together set a tone for curriculum and its engagement. Resources also include the psychological character and characteristics of place, location, and space, the constructed ways that the setting and everything included in it are culturally and socially created and understood. This is the holistic and symbiotic or confluent sense of looking at schooling and other processes that Bronfenbrenner (1976) called the ecological perspective, a way in which resources are more than the tangibles of pen and paper. Consider the ecological sense of resources in places as diverse as a Hopi school; a classroom of Hispanic children in Bisbee, Arizona; a school in affluent Webster Groves, Missouri; or a school in an economically distressed area of East St. Louis, Illinois, and you get a start in understanding the need to expand and explore the idea of resources and their allocation.

Maintenance and Monitoring

There is nothing sophisticated about curriculum maintenance activities; they are mostly mundane activities akin to maintaining a house, car, or your health. Activities are emphasized that support real-time curriculum work and curriculum-in-use. For the former, real-time curriculum work, this might mean managing a curriculum development project in a school district or the management scheme in place as a publisher brings a textbook to production. For curriculum-in-use, this might include keeping sufficient texts and other curriculum materials and supplies on hand (the textbook repository comes to mind), or maintaining a technology team to ensure student and teacher entrée to the Internet and access to online materials that support curriculum engagement. Keeping the library or media center up to date with newspapers and periodicals provides on-demand resources and makes available a quick-time curriculum response capability to serve teachers and others. You probably noticed that all those activities involve work that seems to supplement the actual curriculum. The tech support people perform other work besides curriculum; they may assist with computer-based administrative functions or assist with digital imaging and other instructional technology that assists curriculum engagement. The media center amplifies curriculum resources as well as providing instruction in how to use it or assisting students in actually using the facilities. Those are some examples of activities, curricular in nature, that assist engagement with the curriculum and keep curriculum operational.

Curriculum monitoring is also straightforward, managing the curriculum to determine the operational impact over time. Unlike the pulse-checking nature of maintenance work, monitoring has long-term longitudinal implications. It involves activities associated with education in general, terms like assessment, evaluation, research, and meta-analysis. In curriculum management, monitoring is used as an umbrella concept subsuming tools like research methods and evaluation used to study activities over the long term. Simply put, to monitor means to ride herd on the curriculum using those kinds of tools. Management activities to monitor the curriculum should focus on summative, longitudinal questions. Specifically, what you want to know is whether students are learning what is intended, particularly as that relates to standards and compliance with the NCLB Act of 2001. This suggests two concerns, the immediate and the long-term needs of monitoring. Either will require gathering information on or conducting studies about how the curriculum is structured so there is a baseline of data. In degree, and depending on the question asked or need expressed, it might also mean inquiring about other factors that interdict in curriculum work, things like instructional implementation, scheduling, teacher preparation in a given area of the curriculum, language, and cultural issues. The difficulty is that the past failure to understand the need for and to implement management strategies that link things together means that long-term monitoring and maintenance needs and work are still being charted and invented. In the immediate, present sense, curriculum management is also needed when updating curriculum that is already in use and needs to be monitored. Think of this as anticipating and having available the materials or actions for an onboard fix much like the technological repair of systems in space or corrective action in navigating a plane or ship. The monitoring systems alert and provide initial data, but the ultimate patch to be applied has its own developmental framework and management needs. In curriculum, developmental means to create, and that could be to make material to fill an informational void or, in a math book, for example, to provide supplemental or corrective materials where deficiencies are found or more examples are needed. These seem mundane examples to be sure, but many teachers find that they don't have the management system in place to support the vital center of learning, the interaction between teacher and students.

Formative and Summative Applications

You are probably most familiar with the use of the terms formative and summative in assessment and evaluation. They are also useful concepts in curriculum management. *Formative* management refers to activities at the front end in curriculum work. The front end is the closest place of immediate impact, the classroom, for example. The focus is on getting data and giving them to the teacher and students. Or, for example, if you were in a curriculum development project, the focus is on getting the pilot test data, discussed in Chapter 10, to the developers as soon as possible so the maintenance dimension of creating curriculum could impact curriculum decisions and changes in a timely manner. A publisher would benefit from field tests with materials in a similar fashion. Maintenance and monitoring management knowledge can apply in a formative sense. Monitoring activities are useful during formative aspects of curriculum work. For example, if a curriculum is going through a process of revision based on a preceding model, or a publisher's book is going through a second edition, the data secured from monitoring over a period of time can be useful in deciding what revisions are warranted or what content needs updating.

Summative applications might be thought of as a summing up, how something is actually working out over a period of time. This can be a short term of weeks or longer, or years, or a continuous longitudinal configuration with intervals to access the curriculum-in-use. Obviously, it is management to determine the end game, how a curriculum holds up and its effect. Summative considerations can take many forms. If, for example, you are using a 6-year-old textbook, there is going to be a large gap between the knowledge in the book and what is on a current standardized test. Management in the summative sense would mean building in monitoring alerts on a progressive basis as textbooks age and developing or securing materials to cover the gap until new texts are available. Summative applications in curriculum management can also include responses to public issues about curriculum. Claims about schools failing in particular curriculum areas, usually math and science, are perennial problems. Student performance data from local state or national tests are summative, and their use should be part of curriculum management. Year-to-year data offer a summative comparison and also can serve as an alert to curriculum problems. The caution about summative thinking is to keep in mind that what is summative in a concluding sense is a prelude to what follows. In curriculum management, the critical breakdown would be the failure to monitor changes in the knowledge base of what is in the curriculum or to ask particular questions and not follow up with some particular kind of action, a research study, assessment, evaluation, or some other form of inquiry.

CURRICULUM MANAGEMENT TOOLS

Performing maintenance on or monitoring the curriculum is in some ways like doing it on your vehicle. Your purpose is to keep the vehicle operating by attending to a set of basic operational features. You check the tires for air, the coolant and other fluids for appropriate levels, the battery for the charge, and the lights to make sure they're working. Simple. If any of those need attention (air for the tires, an oil change, etc.), you do it or take it in for servicing. The curriculum, like the car, needs occasional servicing, and you need to know what choices there are among available instruments. The idea of instrumentation is important because it refers to the tools that can be organized and used in various ways to manage curriculum. Tire gauges tell you about tire pressure, and the gauges on the dashboard about oil, water, and other fluid levels and whether the battery is charging. In addition, warning lights are ready to alert you to problems. In the same way, there are tools available for performing various kinds of management work. These tools range from using existing reporting systems in the school, the district, or commercial enterprises such as publishing, to various kinds of research strategies and curriculum-specific techniques like curriculum mapping. In discussing these tools and their possible applications, attention has been given to who the users might be and the complexity of use relative to type of work and where it is or would be useful.

Reporting Systems

Every school and school district has some formal reporting procedure. Today, it might be computerized, the classroom teacher having the capability to send specific information and requests to a central curriculum office. Often it is systemwide and sectored for gathering particular instructional, curriculum, or other information. It is the most obvious and taken-for-granted route for dealing with curriculum matters. Maintenance actions, such as requests for books or other curriculum materials and questions about specific curriculum matters, are routinely submitted through it. The reporting system is a communication process that takes many forms: e-mail, the traditional mailbag, phones, and couriers. It allows district curriculum supervisors and teachers to maintain contact. It is the process for information flow about ideas and problems.

Curriculum Analysis

Considered formally, analysis refers to the task of breaking something into its constituent parts. In a less formal sense, it means to unpack an idea, a process, a poem, a medical specimen, or perhaps evidence gathered during an investigation. William Pinar et al. (Pinar, Reynolds, Slattery, & Taubman, 2002, p. 584) seem to consider analysis to be similar to criticism in curriculum discourse, at least in the academic sense. As applied in other areas of scholarly inquiry, discourse analysis, sociology, linguistics, to cite a few, analysis seems less method than a particular perspective grounded in a particular knowledge and tradition of inquiry. This manner of proceeding is like choosing to think about something and needing to clarify the lens used and its color, such as looking through rose-colored glasses, what one chooses to think about and how one views it. Analysis used in curriculum work is about the fundamentals: scope, sequence, continuity, and balance. The inclusion of other thinking or focus elements would depend on whether what is being proposed for analysis is in the real curriculum-in-use, the world of practice, or part of the important but different philosophical-theoretical discussions of the academic curriculum community. By using the curriculum funda-mentals as the focal point, analysis lends itself as a practitioner tool for those who work with curriculum in the classroom and school, and up the ladder to include district and state workers. What are to be analyzed are the concerns of practice, the curriculum fundamentals and others such as curriculum integration and alignment. Curriculum analysis applied in such ways can provide practitioners with useful data about curriculum-in-use.

Curriculum Mapping

Teachers and curricularists, among others, want to understand the relationships among curriculum content and skills in classrooms and schools. That task calls for a method or technique connecting across the curriculum, one that ties things together and allows a survey of the landscape. The second use of such a method is to tie curriculum and teacher activity across classrooms and to connect various subjects where it is rele-vant to do so. A third need is to have a way of auditing what is happening across the curriculum compared to that which is planned or intended, the curriculum as actually taught or delivered or engaged and the curriculum as it is actually received and person-alized in learning. As a particular analytical procedure, curriculum mapping, according to Fenwick English, its author (1980), creates a curricular matrix set to the school year that gives a graphic representation of the curriculum as it unfolds. Tom DeClark (2002) provides a useful example of curriculum mapping applied in one school district. It is an auditing procedure for assessing the time, content, scope, and sequence of the curricu-lum based on teacher reports and back-up documentation. Curriculum mapping has become a useful method for auditing curriculum work at the practice level (Jacobs, 1997; Minkel, 2002).

Curriculum Workers

The instrumentations discussed to this point obviously reflect the mechanical or applied emphasis in doing management work. There is also the human side, which is to create a culture for management by supporting those roles that have a management function. Those might be the teacher in the classroom, the curriculum specialist at the district office, or perhaps the project director responsible for managing a federal or foundational grant to carry out some curriculum work.

The roles and work are many, and awareness of management tools and how to work with people could determine the success or failure. All this is familiar to people in schooling as the traditional array of activities variously called in-service, training, or staff development. Activities such as those are more generally thought of as human resource or professional development actions. The tendency, in the broader world of educational work and the particular one of curriculum, has been to understate the importance of a consistent, continuous effort to prepare people and provide for their long-term support as part of the management process. Jacky Lumby (2000) and others (see Middlewood & Burton, 2001; Preedy, 1989) have demonstrated this in practitioner research work in England. Because the United Kingdom's national school reform program is continuous, they are able to tap into the curriculum and management work in ways unavailable in America, where reform efforts are, by comparison, characterized by limited relationships across states, receive uneven funding and other resources, and are managed in a top-down manner. Results from the United Kingdom suggest the importance of the people factor in curriculum management. That is also consistent with Michael Fullan's (2001a, 2001b) observations on leadership in American school reform. Translating knowledge from those studies to the American experience will also require consideration of new ways of thinking about curriculum and management.

Innovation Studies

There is an important body of literature about implementing reforms and changes in schools and schooling. The general inquiry idea behind most of those studies was to find out what happens when expectations built into a reform or change meet reality when implemented in a school or inserted into the schooling process. These studies range across all aspects of schooling, from curriculum, instruction, assessment, and evaluation, to teacher performance and school and classroom climate. Innovation as used here means to introduce something that is new or different from what is already there. Gene Hall and Shirley Hord (2001) suggest three curriculum innovation characteristics:

1. The innovation is a new or revised *product,* a tangible innovation such as a textbook that treats some content in a new way.

2. The innovation is a new or revised *process,* the modification or radical reconstruction of a curriculum scope and sequence, or one that is totally new.

3. The innovation varies in *size and complexity,* from those individualized for the student or tailored for a special group or the classroom to large-scale ones for a school, a district, or a state.

As a rich body of information about curriculum change, innovation studies are a valuable tool for developing a curriculum management strategy. The knowledge about change that they contain can be used in developing a curriculum management strategy that avoids implementation pitfalls or builds on factors that enhance the potential for success. E. M. Rogers's *Diffusion of Innovations* (1995) and P. C. Schlechty's *Shaking up the School House* (2001) are useful resources and guides on how to support and sustain innovations.

MANAGING FOR QUALITY

In its fullest meaning, the mission of curriculum management is to achieve two goals—generate data about how the curriculum is operating in-use and determine whether the curriculum is doing what it was intended to do, in other words, answering the "how are we doing" and "are we getting there" kinds of questions. Whereas the importance of curriculum management is to achieve curricular ends, it also includes consideration of how they are achieved and the quality of the process in attaining them. Quality is about the value that something has attained. Quality refers to factors that attach to performance, a service, or a product. An ice skater in competition receives ratings that are the valuing of the performance by experts according to specific criteria about loops, spins, triple or quad jumps, and what the skater details in advance will be part of the performance. For a service, such as getting a tune-up on your vehicle, it could mean whether the garage did all the items on a service checklist. For a product, it might mean whether the toaster actually works and does all the individual operations the manufacturer claims it can do. And, for teachers, it could mean how well the students do on tests related to standards to which the curriculum speaks. In curriculum work, quality issues are about attention to the curriculum user, the acquisition process, its utility or usefulness, and the integrity of the curriculum itself.

Curriculum Consumer

Matters of quality are often ignored that affect the primary user, usually the teacher. Materials intended for the classroom that aren't subjected to pilot or field testing with real teachers, classrooms, and students might have integrity but never, in the curricular sense, fit the classroom and students for which they are intended. Students are first and foremost individuals who learn in idiosyncratic rather than prepackaged ways. The curriculum implementation discussed in Chapter 10 illustrates that designing materials from some one-text-fits-all approach doesn't always address the characteristics of the users, especially where cultural or special learner needs are evident. There is also the problem of the sophistication of a written text and its compatibility with users. Children from language-rich homes or environments have an advantage. The dilemma is that those with poor language backgrounds will be frustrated if materials are too sophisticated and those with a rich language base will be bored. Consider an elementary first-grade classroom of 20 students with varying language backgrounds and you get a sense of the problem. The matter of materials-to-audience fit is also a problem when instructions accompanying curriculum materials fail to address how teachers might use them.

Curriculum Integrity

One quality concern is how the curriculum holds together in use, its integrity. Whether it does or not is a reflection of wholeness in the curriculum process. A curriculum can be operational and need constant adjustment or refurbishing, as in finding that a text is inadequate and having to delay teaching to secure material that meets the need. A textbook publisher is concerned about the quality issue, not just that the text gets produced and sold but that it is accurate in its presentation of knowledge and composition. Integrity also means to have the best match of curriculum purposes and materials (books, etc.) and consistent availability of materials in the classroom for teacher and student use. The teacher should also have curriculum integrity, the appropriate subject expertise for what is being taught with regards to scope, sequence, continuity, balance, and other curriculum knowledge. It is also important to have integrity in curriculum assessment and evaluation. The process should be constructed with professional integrity so that outcomes and measures about curriculum are neutral and not skewed to accommodate partisan views or special interests.

Curriculum Acquisition

Another critical concern is acquisition, how curriculum is suited to a student's ways of learning. This is more than how curriculum and materials are organized and packaged for the teacher and student as users. It is about curriculum and learning idiosyncrasies ranging from personal learning styles to social, cultural, and language differences. Developers do address and try to account for such matters when curriculum and curriculum materials are developed. However, materials once delivered do not always deal with all the particular factors that make local schooling and particular classrooms so dynamically diverse. Converting embedded meaning from one language to another, from one cultural pattern to another, is place bound. For example, will there be an appropriate ESL program to support curriculum acquisition? Will the curriculum meanings be cross-culturally adaptable? Questions like these suggest that in the various kinds of curriculum work, from policy development to creating curriculum, attention to the nature and manner of acquisition is a quality concern. Elements that influence acquisition include learner and teacher sociocultural, cognitive, personal, and family backgrounds. A teacher of European ancestry from a language-rich home that emphasized learning must understand not only his or her background but also the range of differences in similar categories of the children in the classroom. It is not just the teacher's possessing an introspective sense, but having encountered knowledge appropriate to understanding those elements, the teacher in training should be able to adjust the curriculum for the learners. That will depend on having a curriculum management process in the classroom and across the school district.

Curriculum Effectiveness

A fourth quality concern is to establish an overall value scheme to interpret the curriculum. This is a quality issue beyond matters of process integrity, curriculum user, or acquisition; it is about how the curriculum is perceived and accepted. This quality of efficacy refers to curriculum usefulness, the degree to which the social, cultural, and possibly nationalistic purposes in the curriculum are met in the curriculum. A very simple national expectation is that schools will teach children to be competent readers. For example, that value is spelled out in the requirement that, consistent with developmental level, the child will be able to read at a particular proficiency level at the end of the third grade. Effectiveness is also partly a determination of the value a curriculum provides to a society and all its citizens. Is the curriculum seen as a valid representation of society? If that is so, is the curriculum doing what it is supposed to do? It is a utilitarian perception of how curriculum is serving society. Given the diversity of perceptions and their changing nature, concerns about efficacy are snapshots of how society views curriculum, the expectations, and if they are being met. Polls are associated with this, and the results taken over a period of time are useful tools for gauging public support. They are also effective in monitoring curriculum constants such as math and science as well as faddish, sporadic entrants that come and go.

PERSPECTIVE INTO PRACTICE: Quality Control in K–12 Curriculum Management		
Quality Concerns	*Elementary*	*Secondary*
Curriculum Consumer	The first-grade teacher is provided only with reading program A, which is at a reading readiness level above several of the students in the class. Requirements are that each student should be at the reading level in A. Should the teacher seek approval to use programs B and C, which would allow the students to move from where they are in readiness toward the standards required?	The new seventh-grade science class texts have been distributed. A student checks the index for the topic of evolution, finds it, and is concerned that there is nothing about creationism/intelligent design. State standards and assessments address only evolution as a theory in science. Should user/student interest be accommodated? To what extent?
Curriculum Integrity	In third-grade science, students are learning about weather patterns and types of storms. The teacher is focusing on	Student A submits a required report in the American Literature class on an assigned author and works. It is neatly

	pronouncing and spelling storm names like typhoon, monsoon, and hurricane. The teacher pronounces monsoon as "monson" and proceeds to spell it that way on the overhead transparency. A student speaks up about the discrepancy and the teacher corrects the spelling but continues to pronounce the word incorrectly. Curriculum integrity means that all aspects of what is being learned are accurate. Should the student again point out the pronunciation problem?	prepared on a word processing program, with appropriate citations and references, and it meets style requirements. The teacher checks each report with a commercial program that checks for plagiarism and other problems. The program identifies several plagiarisms in the report. Curriculum integrity applies to students as well as teachers. How should this integrity problem be handled to emphasize the need for accepting responsibility and marking personal honor as critical elements in curriculum integrity? Should curriculum integrity be defined in personal terms?
Curriculum Acquisition	Reading standards define skills and reading proficiency levels for students at given grade levels. Assessments check the proficiency. Disparities appear in levels of proficiency; learners from families with higher incomes do better than those from low-income families. What can a school provide to raise proficiency when it can't control for family income? Should acquisition be reconsidered as a quality factor?	A science course in physics developed for the college bound is required of all students and covered on the 12th-grade state assessment. Curriculum acquisition is thus dictated by special conditions that don't reflect individual differences in career choice. Should a college entrance requirement dictate curriculum for all?
Curriculum Effectiveness	Fifth graders are studying American history and settlement of the Western frontier. The social studies curriculum is keyed to both a specific standard and assessment questions about democratic ideals of fairness and the rule of law. Text examples and discussion focus on encounters among settlers,	The high school music appreciation course is designed to meet a state standard for students to have an understanding of various American music forms. One instructor provides a comprehensive list of examples (e.g., jazz, folk, country western, fusion) and uses a variety of compositions and

(Continued)

(Continued)

	the U.S. Army, and Native Americans by presenting facts about the battles of Little Bighorn and Wounded Knee but without commenting on the larger context of settler-U.S. Army policy and treaties with Native Americans. How should a teacher address this apparent discrepancy between text, standards, and assessments so the students will align their learning to respond appropriately? Should appropriateness, a correct response, be a value of effectiveness?	artists to illustrate the forms both in class and as homework. A second teacher with an interest in classical music (opera, symphonic music, etc.) uses the same list, provides examples for students to listen to as homework assignments, reviews those assignments each Friday, and spends the other four days exploring more classic forms of music. Both approaches square with the standard and would allow students to perform satisfactorily on the assessment. Should a teacher be allowed to stray in part from the course intent even though the students would be able to perform positively on the assessment? Does this compromise curriculum effectiveness?

KEY ISSUES IN MANAGEMENT: THE REALITY AND THE IDEAL

Considering the importance of schooling to any society, and particularly the emphasis placed on schooling in America, it would be reasonable to expect an extensive body of literature about various aspects of school management, particularly curriculum. The difficulty is the fragmented character of the literature into studies of broadly conceived "educational" management, or narrower concerns about classroom or school management. With the few exceptions noted earlier in this chapter, there is little that has been written or reported about management in curriculum work. Considering the importance of reforms involving curriculum, the standards-curriculum work that is ongoing, and the National Assessment of Educational Progress, that is an interesting paradox. Given the commitment in resources and work to creating standards and rubrics that can vary by state or as compiled by different curriculum interest groups, it is interesting that there is such weak coordination and no coherent strategy for thinking about curriculum or its management. If curriculum is at the center of schooling and learning, then curriculum management should be central to the function of schooling and learning.

Thinking Strategically

Curriculum management, as noted earlier in this chapter, involves oversight activities the purpose of which is to provide data for making decisions about curriculum as it is and in the longitudinal sense of how it performs with learners. In national approaches to schooling, those in the United Kingdom, Germany, and elsewhere, curriculum management is front and center. In the United States, the federal system and the American tradition of decentralized authority have tended to blunt consideration of comprehensive ways to manage curriculum. Maintaining and monitoring aspects of management have been parochial and disconnected. Even the textbook selection and approval processes, probably the most obvious example of state-local curriculum management activities, continue to be functional *intra*state anachronisms rather than sources of useful, shared *inter*state information. Even with organizations such as the Council of Chief State School Officers or the National Governors Association providing reports and information about standards, there is no useful central authority for managing the process. Despite admonitions that curriculum should serve "to provide information that agents, both teachers and students can use in making informed decisions about what to do in the multiple and varied contexts in which they work" (Olson, 2004, p. 25), the potential of curriculum management has not been realized. The primary reason, as Bush and Bell (2002) and Middlewood and Burton (2001) seem to suggest, is the lack of tactical or strategic thinking among school and academic practitioners about management as a critical element in schooling and curriculum work. The fix for all that has been referred to earlier: it is called strategic management (Middlewood & Burton, 2001; Pearce & Robinson, 1997), a confluence of decisions about capacity, personnel, continuity, policy making, and planning. If the record of its use in business and management science is any indication, using it to think through and conceptualize a curriculum management strategy could promote a capability for effective curriculum work of any kind by any agent or organization.

Continuity

One criticism of comprehensive school reform and accountability is the lack of any continuous and coherent management plan for studying and understanding it. This criticism applies as well to curriculum, instruction, learning, or assessment-evaluation as components in comprehensive school reform and accountability. Jacky Lumby (2001), who has extensive experience studying management in learning and schooling, notes two problems. One is that "the images, languages and concepts are retrospective and may be an inadequate basis for responding to the fast changing world" (p. 3). Second, since humans tend to think forward and backward from the moment, the images held about management tend to limit imagining other possibilities, much like "imagining a future high-tech virtual class room [when you] currently teach a class of 60 with no resources beyond a bare building, a blackboard and chalk" (p. 3). Continuity is difficult to achieve in large-scale ventures such as school reform when any strategic sense of how to manage it is missing. Take the National Assessment of Educational Progress, for example: not every state participates and among those that do, the degree of participation varies both in the numbers tested and the grades at which they are tested. The words *systematic* and *systemic* are important. A systematic example might be the linking of interstate and federal efforts in schooling. Systemic would refer to that systematic arrangement having defined and integrated curriculum management actions in a common framework that enhances monitoring and maintenance activities. National curriculum reform programs in England and other countries attempt to build continuity and defragment curriculum clutter. The key to those efforts is a management umbrella that is national in scale and scope, linking all levels and elements in curriculum work with instruction and assessment. The latest American reform effort, the NCLB Act, does not articulate any systematic or systemic management concept. The curriculum-instruction-assessment linkages go undefined when there is no management process common to all participants.

Curriculum work needs intrinsic as well as transcending management. Intrinsic as, for example, managing policy-planning work in itself, and transcending as in managing policy-making–planning across all work. Continuity and wholeness, as opposed to discontinuity and fragmentation, evolve from a coherent management that accepts differences in the scale, levels, and tempo of curriculum work like the differences in managing curriculum in a classroom, a school, a district, or a state. Current school reform studies suggest the importance of linkages among personnel, within and across schools and districts, and with various resource networks like the National Clearinghouse for Comprehensive School Reform at George Washington University (see the resources section at the end of this chapter). The linking of parts creates the network needed to share knowledge built from implementation. This emphasis on networking is an important new dimension of management thinking, as Douglas Schuler and Peter Day suggest in *Shaping the Network Society: The New Role of Civil Society in Cyberspace* (2004). Integrating capital resources (e.g., human, technical, material, and knowledge) is a key to building effective management and monitoring processes in curriculum work. Continuity in curriculum management is a function of both its technical capabilities, whether it can and does provide the data appropriate to understanding how the curriculum is operating, and building in self-monitoring characteristics that check the process itself. The vehicle you drive has gauges and sensors that are usually in a steady state but occasionally alert you to a problem. At the same time, there is built into your vehicle's management system other sensors that monitor the operation of the management system itself so it will warn you of problems. This layered cross monitoring increases the probability that the management process will function to get you where you want to go and warn you if there are problems as you travel toward your destination. Curriculum management is the same; it monitors the curriculum and itself to assure continuity.

Policy Planning

Reform movements seek change. Central to that effort is a need to create a climate for change, a reference to establishing public beliefs that accept proposals or specific reforms as reasonable and under which activities supporting change can occur. The creation of Head Start and special needs programs in the mid-1960s exemplify progressive policies under the ideals of the Great Society enunciated by the administration of President Lyndon Johnson. It meant extending curriculum into preschool years and creating curriculum for new special needs populations. There was, however, no comprehensive planning to outline how those initiatives would be extended into individual states and made truly national in scope. There was no systemic or systematic planning based on a common policy. Instead, there was federal policy planning and what each individual state chose to do. The problem was a failure to create management links and define the elements held in common that management would oversee. Management patterns differed because the missions were different and management processes were established differently.

Personnel

Managing curriculum or anything else requires knowledge. As the old adage goes, you have to know the territory, and that means grounding in both the cumulative formal knowledge base and the knowledge that comes from practice. Often, responsibility for managing curriculum is given to teachers who are unprepared because course work in preparing to teach is inadequate to the curriculum tasks of the classroom. School districts often make promotional assignments to curriculum specialist positions that are administrative rather than knowledge or work-needs based. A third problem is the lack of consistent, systematic, in-service or staff development to support practice, particularly the critical work of the classroom teacher. Often the in-service or staff development is ad hoc or faddish, appealing but functionally irrelevant.

Managing curriculum has two critical personnel aspects. One is to identify the personnel who are directly involved in managing curriculum and others directly affected by that management. The second aspect is to enable and support those who will manage curriculum. Enable means to be sure workers are qualified and receive preparatory instruction. Support means that after workers implement the management strategy, they have on-the-job support with the curriculum-in-use. In developing any management strategy, teachers, the critical, primary personnel involved, need to know what the management strategy is and how it is expected to work. Preparation should include knowledge about the management strategy and expectations for successful classroom implementation. For example, some teacher preparation programs offer a course in classroom management whereas others do not. Those with such a course may be better prepared to manage in a general sense; those without such knowledge are at a disadvantage. Teachers from any background are going to need differentiated preparation for understanding a specialized strategy in managing curriculum work. A management strategy should include staff development opportunities and continuing support during implementation. Workers will also need direct assistance by curriculum specialists with problems they encounter. Not everything can be anticipated for inclusion in preliminary staff development activities. Indeed, here is a good example of the dialectic between knowledge and practice; problems arising in practice and the knowledge added by their solution provide case examples of knowledge to be added to the curriculum knowledge base and as content in staff development. The reflexive relationship between knowledge creation and its use is important for implementing and sustaining a curriculum management strategy that might otherwise languish.

Capacity

In Chapter 4, you were introduced to the idea of capacity in schooling and curriculum work. This concept is about whether an organization, such as a school faculty or district administrative team, has the knowledge, materials, policy support, and other kinds of capital and resources to carry out their work. Put very simply, it is difficult to make a pie if you don't have the recipe and the ingredients. Curriculum management requires that a capacity should exist equal to the mission. While this may seem like nothing more than common sense, studies of school reform and change implementation document the failure to even consider capacity, or, if it is addressed, to accurately match what exists with what will be needed. The failure to consider capacity is cited as one of the common causes of failure in effecting school change (Elmore, 2002).

During the American Civil War, Confederate General Nathan Bedford Forrest was asked what was the success factor in winning battles. His reputed reply was that victory depends on whoever gets there first with the most. What he implied was that success depends on having the capacity at hand to accomplish the mission. Strategic management, as noted previously, is a perspective used in management science, a way of thinking that promotes development of a management plan. It can alert curriculum workers to the various aspects of curriculum roles, knowledge, and practice that must be considered in curriculum work and in the larger arena of schooling and educating. Equipping personnel to do the work expected of them is part of capacity building. Personnel who are ready to do any kind of curriculum work are just one part of the strategic management equation. Appropriate levels of funding, decision-making authority, on-call supporting agents, and services are essential components in capacity building.

Summary and Conclusions

Determining whether schooling is successful rests on creating and sustaining a reliable process of accountability for all aspects of schooling. In turn, that accountability depends on the curriculum students are to acquire and how their performance matches what is expected of the curriculum and what it delivers. Central to all that is the matter of managing the curriculum so it continuously delivers what is expected—high learner performance. What is reflected in that determination is how well learners acquired the curriculum compared with what was expected. Aside from excellent policy making and planning, or developing an exceptional curriculum, what holds curriculum practice together is the management web that in various ways maintains and monitors all curriculum work. The concept of strategic management is useful in curriculum work. Strategic management is a perspective, a framework, that envisions accomplishing a mission through effective development and integration of the curriculum process, the tools, and a management strategy. Through it, you can envision what important elements ought to be considered (e.g., resources and worker training) and the array of activities and tools that should be made available. Planning through strategic management thinking anticipates operational conditions, the character of the work, matching those features with descriptions of activities, and the qualities of methods and tools.

Critical Perspective

1. The text defines management in curriculum work in a particular way. When you think of managing and management, what definition or description comes to mind? If you were to use that to characterize management, how would it compare with the text definition? What would be the similarities and differences?

2. The classroom teacher has the important task of managing the curriculum. What other roles in the administrative organization of any school, or a larger public, private, or parochial unit such as a school district, are responsible for managing curriculum?

3. Using http://edstandards.org/standards.html or http://www.mcrel.org/standards or a site of your choice, compare several state standards for a particular curriculum area, reading, science, and so forth. Are they alike? Different? How would you describe the degree of congruence or fit across them?

4. If an innovation or new component is being considered for implementation in a curriculum and you were the curriculum specialist assigned, what quality considerations would you emphasize in developing a curriculum management strategy for your project?

5. Every application for a grant or any solicitation for funding from a foundation or government source requires a management plan. Usually, the sponsoring agent, school, or school district maintains a file of submitted proposals. If possible,

secure a copy of a proposal and study the management section. How are the mission, maintenance, monitoring, and implementation characteristics discussed in this chapter addressed in the proposal? Can the specifics of the management strategy be identified?

Resources for Curriculum Study

1. Literature in management science and about management models in business forms the largest body of work for studying management as a general concept. Any standard textbook such as Pearce and Robinson's *Strategic Management* (1997) will provide a useful introduction. Human resource management related to workplace performance presents another useful view of management that has implications for schools and schooling management. Stolovich and Keeps's *Handbook of Human Performance Technology* (1992) is useful in that regard. Gary Dessler's *A Framework for Management* (2002) offers a summary of management principles that may be more relevant in application than the detailed approach taken in the other textbooks.

2. Matthew Miles was a pioneer in studying the connections between school innovation and management. His early work *Innovations in Education* (1964) is still useful and is often considered the genesis for the study of management in American education.

3. An up-to-date resource on management is *The Principles and Practices of Educational Management* (2002), edited by Bush and Bell. In the same book, Margaret Preedy's chapter, "Managing the Curriculum for Student Learning," is a look at the practical side of curriculum management.

4. Discussions of strategic and operational management, roles and responsibilities, and resourcing in curriculum management are usefully presented in *Managing the Curriculum* (2001), edited by Middlewood and Burton. Curriculum management being a quite recent focus in schooling studies, this is one work that brings it all together. Another good resource is Briggs and Sommefeldt's *Managing Effective Learning and Teaching* (2002). Although the context is British, these initial conceptions by a variety of authors are applicable in America.

5. Phi Delta Kappa International has a Web site for its Curriculum Management Center at http://pdkintl.org. This is a fee-based service, but it is one of the few that addresses curriculum management. Another source of publications, reports, and references to other resources is the Clearinghouse on Educational Policy and Management at the University of Oregon, which can be accessed at

http://www.eric.uoregon.edu. The Directory of Organizations, an online list of organizations available at the same site, can be explored for a variety of public, nonprofit, and private institutes, associations, and so forth, with interests in educational management.

6. The North Central Regional Educational Laboratory (NCREL) has a Web site, http://www.ncrel.org, at which curriculum mapping and other tools and materials about management are available. NCREL is one of 10 regional members of the Regional Educational Laboratory (REL) Network supported by the U.S. Department of Education, Institute of Educational Sciences.

7. To access information about school reform, simply type in "school reform" on the Internet and go from there, or you can start with these two recommended sites, the Center for Comprehensive School Reform and Improvement at http://www.csrclearhinghouse.org and the American Association of School Administrators at http://www.aasa.org. In addition, state sites, the Colorado Department of Education, for example, are informative places for particulars about individual state reforms and management activities.

8. Innovation literature focuses on the role of change agents—the human and other factors, positive or negative—important in change. In addition to others cited in this chapter, Michael Fullan's *Leadership in a Culture of Change* (Jossey Bass, 2001a) and Hargreaves et al. *Learning to Change* (2001) are two good introductions to change and the change process.

9. INNODATA is a data bank of international innovations. You can access it at http://www.ibe.unesco.org. You will find it an excellent resource about practices, programs, and related activities throughout the world and an entrée to other useful sites.

References

Briggs, A. R. J. (2001). Managing the learning environment. In D. Middlewood & N. Burton (Eds.), *Managing the curriculum* (pp. 175–189). London: Paul Chapman/Sage.

Bronfenbrenner, U. (1976). The experimental ecology of education. *Educational Researcher, 5*(9), 5–15.

Bush, T., & Bell, L. A. (2002). *The principles and practice of educational management.* London: Paul Chapman/Sage.

DeClark, T. (2002). Curriculum mapping: A how to guide. *The Science Teacher, 69*(4), 29–31.

Elmore, R. F. (2002). Unwarranted intrusion. *Education Next, 2*(1), 30.

English, F. W. (1980). Curriculum mapping. *Educational Leadership, 37*(7), 558–559.

Fullan, M. (2001a). *Leadership in a culture of change.* San Francisco: Jossey-Bass.

Fullan, M. (2001b). *The new meaning of educational leadership* (3rd ed.). New York: Teachers College Press.

Hall, G. E., & Hord, S. M. (2001). *Implementing change: Patterns, principles, potholes.* New York: Allyn & Bacon.

Hardie, B. (2001). Managing monitoring of the curriculum. In D. Middlewood & N. Burton (Eds.), *Managing the curriculum* (pp. 70–88). London: Paul Chapman/Sage.

Jacobs, H. H. (1997). *Mapping the big picture: Integrating curriculum and assessment K-12.* Arlington, VA: Association for Supervision and Curriculum Development.

Lumby, J. (2000). Influencing the management of the curriculum. In D. Middlewood, M. Coleman, & J. Lumby (Eds.), *Practitioner research in education* (Vol. 4 in Educational Management Research and Practice Series). London: Paul Chapman/Sage.

Middlewood, D., & Burton, N. (2001). *Managing the curriculum.* London: Paul Chapman/Sage.

Minkel, W. (2002). Charting a clear course: Curriculum mapping takes the guesswork out of what students are learning—and what they're not. *School Library Journal, 48*(9), 60–61.

Olson, D. R. (2004). The triumph of hope over experience in the search for "what works": A response to Slavin. *Educational Researcher, 33*(1), 24–26.

Pearce, J. A., & Robinson, R. B. (1997). *Strategic management.* New York: Irwin McGraw-Hill.

Pinar, W. F., Reynolds, W. M., Slattery, P., & Taubman, P. M. (2002). *Understanding curriculum.* New York: Peter Lang.

Preedy, M. (Ed.). (1989). *Approaches to curriculum management.* London: Paul Chapman/Open University Press.

Preedy, M. (1993). *Managing the effective school.* London: Paul Chapman/Open University Press.

Preedy, M. (2002). Managing the curriculum for student learning. In T. Bush & L. A. Bell (Eds.), *The principles and practices of educational management.* London: Paul Chapman/Sage.

Rogers, E. M. (1995). *Diffusion of innovations* (4th ed.). New York: Free Press.

Rose, L. C., & Gallop, A. M. (2003). The 35th annual PDK/Gallop poll. *Phi Delta Kappan, 35*(1), 41–56.

Schlechty, P. (2000). *Shaking up the schoolhouse: How to support and sustain educational innovation.* San Francisco: Jossey-Bass/Wiley.

Schuler, D., & Day, P. (2004). *Shaping the network society: The new role of civil society in cyberspace.* Cambridge, MA: MIT Press.

Stolovitch, H. D., & Keeps, E. J. (1996). *Handbook of human performance technology.* San Francisco: Jossey-Bass.

Tucker, M. S., & Codding, J. B. (Eds.). (2002). *The principal challenge: Leading and managing schools in an era of accountability.* San Francisco: Jossey-Bass.

Chapter 12

EVALUATION IN CURRICULUM WORK

If you were to peruse the accumulated reports about American schooling over the last 50 or so years, certain persistent concerns emerge. One is the inconsistency of reporting itself, the failure to have a sustaining information-gathering approach and total participation, the National Assessment of Educational Progress (NAEP) being an example of effort but without full participation. Another is the tendency to sensationalize, as the *Nation at Risk* report did in the 1980s, without reliance on clearly agreed-on data devoid of political influences. A third is the inclination for a person or group to have an agenda, albeit for good social purposes, the good of society and the individual, as James Bryant Conant's *The Comprehensive High School* did in the 1950s. Finally, there is the basic problem of creating and fitting together information about 50 different state systems of schooling and a very dispersed unsystematic federal involvement. The No Child Left

Behind (NCLB) Act of 2001 proposes to solve that problem. In spite of NCLB, there is no discernable consensus on direction, and there are accompanying controversies over appropriateness of the methods employed in the studies to generate data and whether those procedures provide data that are useful in forming appraisals of schools and the conditions of schooling (Madaus, Stufflebeam, & Scriven, 1983).

The current and continuing reform proposals for schools and schooling and the host of new reports to come will, if the past record is any indicator, continue to reflect those discrepancies. There are several important observations to be drawn from the composite body of various commissioned and uncommissioned reports that are useful in considering how to implement effective procedures and generate useful data about schools, schooling, and curriculum work:

- First is the importance of creating data in whatever form: numbers, words, symbols, documents, anecdotes, or memories.
- Second is the need for a data collection process tied to a specified purpose.
- Third is the need to interpret the data, to give it some worth according to a set of values assembled in view of the purpose.
- Last and most important is the need to use the interpreted findings (the valued data) to inform work decisions and activities.

In summary, this means to have a purpose, gather data, determine a value for the data, and use the valued data in making decisions. In educational talk, this is usually referred to as assessment and evaluation. With the possible exception of disputes about curriculum content, no area of the educational enterprise is more fraught with difficulty and the subject of sharp exchanges than that of accountability and assembling an appropriate assessment and evaluation process.

CURRICULUM AND ACCOUNTABILITY

The public wants to know that school programs are effective; that the curriculum being learned achieves intended purposes; that if it isn't effective, it will be changed; and that part of curriculum work is to constantly monitor and improve the curriculum. Schooling is supposed to engage students with a curriculum they are to learn. As you recall from discussing policy making in Chapter 9, agreeing on which curriculum outcomes determine if schools are achieving those learning goals is often an interpretive venture. The work of school and curriculum professionals is directed toward maintaining and monitoring the curriculum. Given that what schools are doing for students is dependent on a lot of factors over which the school itself has little or no control, the public understands that what is assessable is the curriculum and the degree to which the learner has acquired it.

Figure 12.1 A Review of Critical Curriculum Concepts

Accountability	Responsibility for meeting the curriculum outcomes linked to standards, usually determined by data from standardized tests.
Standards	Statements that are clear, measurable descriptions of what students are to know or be able to do after engaging the curriculum. Usually stated as content-specific outcomes for specific areas of the curriculum such as mathematics, history, and so forth.
Learning	The school-based process of acquiring what skills and knowledge are in the curriculum and engaged through instruction.
Curriculum	The composite of content (e.g., science, literature) provided to learners as required by an authorized body responsible for schools and schooling, usually under state law.
Assessment	The process of creating data with tools such as tests, checklists, computers, and other instrumentation; the planned effort to collect data for evaluation.
Evaluation	Creating and applying indicators that provide a value interpretation of data from assessments for making judgments about various aspects of schooling, curriculum, learning, and other educational matters.

Purposes and Accountability

Curriculum accountability refers to the school and curriculum professionals' ability to accurately determine and report about the curriculum and student learning outcomes. Ideally, accountability efforts should include the expressed purposes schools serve, the representative standards and curriculum, instruction, assessment, and evaluation, all linked together. Those terms, discussed at various points in previous chapters, are part of the conversation about accountability and are recapped in Figure 12.1.

Those elements also apply to schooling in any context, whether it is public, parochial, or private. Of course, the particular religious or secular purpose in a parochial or private institution will be an additional purpose to be accounted for. Whatever the espoused purposes for schooling and therefore for what constitutes the curriculum, in the present, reform interests and accountability drive perceptions about schooling and curriculum and that takes form through what was referred to earlier as program evaluation.

Activities in Accountability

It is easy to talk about curriculum accountability; it is another matter to be specific about the kinds of activities it includes. Whatever the specific purpose or intent, all activities in curriculum geared toward accountability are usually included under the banner of *program evaluation,* which simply means finding out if and how something is working in the school and classroom. This meaning is distinct from *student evaluation,* which refers to the assessment of student performance and the giving of letter grades. The meaning here is that the totality of what a school does is its program, and the center of that program is curriculum. Decker Walker (1990, p. 384) identified six purposes (what he calls functions) that a program evaluation might serve. Those purposes, recast and rephrased with additional comments, suggest an interesting range of curriculum and program evaluation actions applicable to a district, school, or even a classroom:

1. *Curriculum review.* Studying curriculum scope and sequence documents and other curriculum materials to look for strengths and weaknesses is usually a school, district, or state undertaking rather than a classroom, although several teachers at a grade level might engage in a selective curriculum review.

2. *Considering a curriculum change.* Scale and location are important elements. Scale refers to the size of the contemplated changes and location to whether the change is limited to a classroom, school, or school district or encompasses a whole state. Changes might range from appraising an individual textbook to considering a classroom- and school-based curriculum change, or one for an entire district or state. Major changes might include engaging in a textbook review and adoption process for a school district or the entire state.

3. *Implementing a curriculum change.* Implementing or putting a curriculum change in place used to be a casual, personal matter, much like a teacher deciding to use a supplemental textbook. Fifty-plus years of reform have made that less likely and more probable that it will be a major project event with goals, deadlines, special meetings, added personnel assignments, a slew of approval requirements, and careful documentation of the project life.

4. *Evaluating curriculum change.* The proof of change, how it works out, will depend on gathering data about it and making a determination as to the change's effectiveness. This, as noted earlier, is program evaluation and requires some form of assessment-evaluation or another type of tool. The simpler the intended change, the less complex the program evaluation requirement. Of course, the reverse is true as the project becomes larger and entails more work.

5. *Long-range curriculum planning.* Curriculum accountability is not some ad hoc, occasional demand; it has a continuousness to it because constituencies demanding reform shift and the nature or kind of reforms changes. It is very fluid, and the most effective response to reform and demands on curriculum is to have a long-range planning process in place. This is a positive, transparent action that anticipates possible curriculum change scenarios. In addition to the rephrased purposes identified by Walker, there are at least two other important purposes for programmatic evaluation actions.

6. *Continuous monitoring of the curriculum.* The traditional idea of program evaluation was that it was a useful tool for looking at specific programs rather than in a more comprehensive way at the ongoing activities as well as new initiatives for change. That has shifted, and program evaluation has attained a more holistic and synergetic meaning. The word *programmatic* is suggestive of this change, implying all factors that attend to the main thing under consideration, the linkages among defined parts of the whole. What that means is that all those elements reviewed in Figure 12.1 interrelate but, at the same time, each can be viewed separately as a specific program aspect to be evaluated.

7. *Informed policy making and planning.* The importance of program evaluation or any effort to create knowledge is how the results are used. The critical need is to inform decision making, particularly about policy-making and planning actions in curriculum work. Informed curriculum work rests on continuous monitoring to produce data that can be interpreted and used by curriculum workers.

Keep in mind that these purposes have evolved and, as schooling and curriculum respond to change, others will probably emerge, especially as globalization and other leading-edge issues create new perspectives on schooling and curriculum.

Linkages in Accountability

Schooling is of a piece; it is made up of activities that can be placed in categories, with all the activities having links to each other. That connectedness means the parts and their relatedness can be understood. It also provides you with a structural sense of arrangements important to understanding the linkages between aspects of curriculum work and the complexity of curriculum-instruction-assessment reflected in the reality of the classroom. Those linkages, or their absence, are important. Consider, for example, the role instruction can play as it mediates among the curriculum, the student, and valuing his or her performance. It is common for elementary school students at some point to study their state and to learn about the state animal, bird, flower, rock, and so forth. Consider two teachers teaching the same list of state-designated items. Teacher A's instructional approach is to read about them in the textbook, write them on the board, and then have the children copy them from the board and memorize them. Teacher B has them read the same textbook, make up cards for each item with a picture and name and describe or explain them, then she has them periodically quiz each other and asks them to create a game using the cards. Both teachers give the same kind of paper-pencil fill-in-the-blank quiz. Here is the linking of the same curriculum, instruction in two different forms, and a common quiz as the assessment. Consider the importance of various critical factors, the linkages suggested in the example, and how they come together in accountability:

- *Curriculum and Standards.* The state standard is clear: students are to master designated specifics and are to be able to identify or describe them as appropriate. The knowledge is embedded in a state-approved textbook both teachers use.

- *Curriculum and Instruction.* The curriculum is contained in the same textbook the students read and discuss. Two different instructional approaches are used, and it might be inferred from the example that one teacher uses several techniques to ensure engagement takes place, whereas the other relies on memorization with little other apparent emphasis on the importance of the content.

- *Curriculum and Assessment.* Both teachers use the same quiz as their assessment instrument to gather data, which are the answers provided by the students. At this point, there is no value given to that data nor is there any proposed analysis to determine how different instructional approaches might have mediated the results.

- *Curriculum and Evaluation.* A common assessment tool, the quiz, is used to gather the data that has no intrinsic value or importance. What gives the data importance is the purpose for which it was gathered: to determine what learning has occurred in relation to a standard and the curriculum. That decision about creating and assigning a value is evaluation.

You could, of course, conjure up a scenario of results for the example, but, in reality, you can't know how it might end; that is a matter of establishing a value for accountability that factors in performance, curriculum, and the standard. First, there is the matter of the assessment-evaluation link being unclear. How will Teacher A or B use the data? How will it count in the overall scheme of giving a grade? Perhaps one teacher uses a cumulative total point system for each grading period, with an A equivalent to 90–100% of actual points. The other teacher might use a similar percentage system but based only on the correct number of points on the assessment. As the example tries to suggest, there are often inherent or built-in discrepancies (the lack of uniformity and consistency, for example) in connecting curriculum-instruction-assessment-evaluation.

Curriculum, Accountability, and Evaluation

As you can discern from the foregoing discussion, matters of accountability and creating a process for it that is uniform and consistent loom large in education. Parents hold the school responsible for teaching their children. Communities hold schools responsible for preparing functional, literate, civic-minded citizens; businessman and executives want competent employees; and politicians want accountability for political reasons. All those expectations have curriculum roots. Everybody holds the schools accountable but never in quite the same way, which makes it difficult to match the intent of programmatic evaluation as a process with the various interpretations of account-ability (Linn, 2003). Curriculum is at the heart of accountability because it is what is supposed to be learned, and the assessment-evaluation process should join what the curriculum is with what students reveal they have learned. Put another way, if there was no curriculum, what would be assessed and evaluated? Today's accountability has had previous manifestations and different policy connections. Whereas accountability and evaluation in the present occur on a large national scale, previous ventures differed in their purpose, scope, and effect. Present-day ideas about accountability depend on assessment and evaluation to determine school and curriculum effectiveness. The link-ing of accountability and assessment-evaluation evolved from two other important movements, one the emergence of evaluation, the other the objectification of schooling outcomes.

The Emergence of Evaluation

The original impetus for evaluation was arguably Ralph Tyler's proposal in 1949 (see Chapter 2) that specific learning objectives should be developed for individual courses in the curriculum and that tests be tied closely to those objectives. Tyler was proposing to link student performance and curriculum and to use tests, objective-based tests, to get a picture of the relationships. Creating objectives and matching them with tests was an early accounting exercise to look at expected outcomes, the learning that was assumed to occur and the actual outcomes revealed by the tests. Although there is no particular book or event that marks the convergence of concepts about testing, objec-tives, and evaluation, the 1967 monograph by Robert Stake and others for the American Educational Research Association, *Perspectives on Curriculum Evaluation* is a good benchmark. One chapter in particular, "The Methodology of Evaluation," by Michael Scriven, proposed that evaluation work should make distinctions between different kinds of evaluation, the *summative evaluation* that provided data and information at the end, and *formative evaluation* that provides ongoing results as the program or activity proceeds so that corrections or changes can be made in a timely manner. Scriven's artic-ulation of summative and formative evaluation helped clarify thinking by pointing out that evaluation comprised at least two things, types and processes. *Summative, forma-tive,* and *program* are names for types of evaluation. Processes are ways to do evalua-tion, the actions or activities, the methods that evaluators use. Further refinements were added as the matter of evaluation emerged in importance aside from the tests and mea-surements with which it was initially associated. Assessment, for example, began to refer to the actual tools, such as tests, that were used in evaluation. Further distinctions about assessment were made. *Formative assessment* referred to the daily, real-time, in-the-classroom use of tests or other data collection tools, whereas *summative assessment* referred to tests at the end of teaching and learning, the NAEP or other tests keyed to standards being examples. If the term evaluation became synonymous with objectives and testing, it was also being associated with accountability in school programs and curriculum. Add the issue of whether there could be other ways of looking at the curriculum-learning relationship, the impetus to broaden the idea of evaluation, the emergence of reforms, and growing programmatic rather than piecemeal approaches to improving curriculum and learning, and you have the forces in play for the coupling of assessment with evaluation as an important practice and as an emerging discipline of knowledge in the education field.

Objectives, Curriculum, and Evaluation

The starting point for evaluation is to identify what is to be evaluated. It sounds simple but it isn't. People in education, schooling, and curriculum try, in the spirit of Ralph Tyler, to objectify learning, to get things into measurable terms so they can be studied to find out what effect they have on learning and how they square with curriculum. The association of assessment-evaluation-curriculum begins with the idea of stating objectives about learning. The objectives movement had different lives under different names, such as performance objectives, behavioral objectives, instructional objectives, and learning objectives, down to its present incarnation. The core idea, whatever the term used, is that any plan about what the student is to learn, the learning a curriculum is to provide, should be specified clearly and concisely in the form of very precise objectives. This emphasis on objectives has had three episodes in its development. The earliest interest in objectivizing began with Franklin Bobbitt in the 1920s and the so-called scientific movement in education (refer to Chapter 7) that emphasized stating what students were to know in specific, defined terms. This *planning by objectives* was primarily to ensure that there was a clear curriculum-teacher-learner linkage through carefully crafted *teaching objectives*. The important thing about this idea of objectivity was that it was a microlinkage at the local level of the classroom-teacher-student rather than the macrolinkage of curriculum-teacher-learner across districts or as a policy leading to educational legislation enactments at state levels. This micro-macro distinction is important to keep in mind. Some 40 years later, Robert Mager published *Preparing Instructional Objectives* (1962), which, when used with the first volume of *Taxonomy of Educational Objectives* (Bloom et al., 1956), dealing with the cognitive domain as a taxonomic foundation, seemed to provide a convenient procedure for building more precise objectives. The taxonomy, arranged in six main levels, from simple-concrete at the knowledge level to complex-abstract at the evaluation level, is summarized in Figure 12.2.

Other taxonomies for the psychomotor (Harrow, 1970) and affective domains (Krathwohl, Bloom, Masia, & Masia, 1964) were also developed. Most recently, Marzano (2001) developed a taxonomy based on levels of thinking and kinds of knowledge, and Anderson and Krathwohl (2001) offered a revision of Bloom's original

Figure 12.2   A Summary of Bloom's Taxonomy

Level	Summary
Knowledge	Recalling specific elements of previously learned information
Comprehension	Recalling bits of information, organizing the information, transforming the form of information, and extrapolating from the information
Application	Using new information in different contexts from that in which it was initially learned
Analysis	Describing characteristics of something through identifying relationships between and among its parts
Synthesis	Putting together elements of something in a way that is new to the person engaged in the task
Evaluation	Making judgments about something in terms of specific and credible criteria

taxonomy. Bereiter and Scardamalia (1998) have also offered ideas that go beyond Bloom. Like its predecessor, planning by objectives, this educational objectives emphasis sought to create a more precise relationship between what is to be learned (curriculum), what a teacher should teach, and what a student could expect to learn at the microlevel of classroom application. Perhaps the greatest impact was in schools and colleges of teacher education, where writing behavioral objectives in lesson planning became an important function. The idea of writing objectives, whether in the form of Bobbitt's planning objectives, or using the Mager-*Taxonomy* approach, has an identifiable set of characteristics:

1. Objectives, whether labeled behavioral, instructional, or performance, are intended to describe observable student behavior or performance.

2. Objectives are about curriculum, not instruction, a key point. They are not about conduct or other classroom behavior; they are about what is to be learned.

3. Objectives have specifications for a demonstration or performance by the student so that a teacher can infer if learning in the classroom has taken place.

4. Objectives are composed of stated conditions, the context in which the behavior is to be performed, an action verb or word that connotes the behavior that should occur and be observable, and stated criteria or indicators for the acceptable range of behaviors.

Quite possibly you have encountered several of these taxonomies for creating *precision objectives* based on observable behaviors in lesson planning or in another course.

Figure 12.3   Analysis of a Behavioral Objective

A Behavioral Objective

After reading the poem "Katrina" by Chanteuse Clair, the students, working in their regular class cooperating teams, will collectively write an essay using the Loften Poem Analysis criteria and reporting format. Each team will have 45 minutes to deliberate and write the essay using their assigned computer and Microsoft Word software. In the next class period, the essays will be shared visually using a PowerPoint presentation and orally discussed and analyzed using the Loften scale.

Four-Point Analysis

- *Has a described set of behaviors:* work in teams, write, deliberate, discuss
- *Curriculum centered:* part of the high school curriculum in language arts and literature
- *Detailed performance:* read poem and write essay using specific criteria to critique the poem in a specific reporting format
- *Has specified conditions:* setting, subject, and instruction are specific and use action verbs (read, write, discuss); Loften Poem Analysis sets the criteria for critique and format for writing

---

An example of how the four characteristics might appear in a behavioral setting is provided in Figure 12.3.

Standards, Curriculum, and Evaluation

The third episode in the objectives movement is contemporary and subsumed in the standards movement and particularly with testing requirements under the 2001 NCLB Act. In 1989, President George H. W. Bush, with support from state governors, held a national education summit to identify academic achievement goals for American schools. Out of this came the National Educational Goals Panel and the National Council on Education Standards and Testing (NCEST), who were to determine the subject matter schools should teach (curriculum), the types of testing and tests that should occur (assessment), and the student performance standards (evaluation) that should be expected (Marzano & Kendall, 1996). This standards movement reflects the ideas and intent of the earlier episodes. The precision objectives emphasis in the development of test items and the linkage of tests to standards and curriculum have to be written in measurable terms: items on tests have to be clearly linked to what is to be learned (curriculum), taught (instruction), and engaged (learning) by the student. The data resulting have to be judged according to some value scheme supporting further judgments and decisions, in this instance, the NCEST preset student performance standards. All four characteristics of precision objectives discussed previously in this chapter are inherent in the new accountability expressed in standards and the NCLB Act of 2001. What is new and reflects the convergence of curriculum-assessment-evaluation in accountability is the articulation of performance standards, the values around which judgments of progress and identification of problems can be made. There are now standards about goals expressed through curriculum; there are now values for student performance as that allows a basis for possible judgments about schooling and curriculum and their worth in serving the nation. Several cautions about standards and accountability are needed. First, accountability through curriculum evaluation applies only to public schooling and those who participate in the assessment-evaluation. Second, there are at least 50 different state standards-curriculum-assessment-evaluation plans, and comparison across public schools regionally and nationally is suspect. Third, there is the matter of the private and parochial schools that have no assessment-evaluation processes linked to national assessment, so there is no way to know how *all* schools are doing. This state of affairs has possible implications for public policy making and allocation of resources to schools, public, private, or parochial. More will be said about that issue in Part IV, Trends and Issues. Finally, the only national test for assessment is the NAEP, and that test is not uniformly used across all states.

National Evaluation and the NAEP

The case in point, the NAEP, is the oldest formal assessment that is truly national in scope. Devised in the 1980s, it was originally intended to determine what students learn in specified areas of the curriculum, an early look at the connections between curriculum and learning. As experience with assessment-evaluation evolved, parallel reform movements came along as well. One was associated with the 1980s report *A Nation at Risk,* which selectively raised the specter of failing public schools but not those in the parochial or private sector. The defining and formalizing of accountability as a process of finding the problems and offering a fix followed, as did the gradual formulation of national policies about schooling and curriculum and how to determine accountability through assessment-evaluation. What starts out as various forms of aid to schools through the federal coffers turns into federal control through assessment-evaluation-based accountability. There is a discernable path of related developments, from policies aiding schools in the 1960s to the 2001 NCLB Act. The impression is that accountability has become assessment-evaluation driven and the knowledge, as well as the process developed in assessments like the NAEP, serves accountability however it is interpreted. The curriculum particulars, science and mathematics, continue to be used as the leading indicators of progress and accountability. The tendency to emphasize science and mathematics is also reinforced by the use of *high stakes tests,* those that are used for determining who graduates, who gets into college, and who receives merit scholarships. Reading and literacy are, of course, critical indicators of elementary school curriculum and performance quality. In addition to the national efforts, individual states have taken on extensive assessment-evaluation activities, devising their own standards and tests or hiring commercial firms to create a program. There are two ways to look at those developments. One is to see each state as an experiment and the total as a composite of efforts out of which the best or most useful can be selected, a best practices scenario. The other possibility is to view the process as uncontrolled and unconnected. The standards differ, the assessments also, the curriculum-instruction-assessment alignment is unclear, and the results are incomparable. Standards and evaluations follow no coherent policy. Take your pick; the discussion and arguments about those matters will continue for some time. Assessing for accountability is costly and time consuming, results are often open to interpretation, and, at times, the NAEP and national assessment are captured in politics outside of their intended use to guide decision making about schooling and curriculum.

THE PROCESSES OF ASSESSMENT AND EVALUATION

After following the evolution of accountability into standards and assessment-evaluation, questions about it still remain. Foremost is, what exactly are assessment and evaluation? Evaluation with an assessment component, or assessment *and* evaluation, or something else? Reading in the literature, you will often find the terms used interchangeably. W. James Popham (2004), Susan Brookhart (2004), and Black and William (1998) have all commented on the confusion and inconsistencies that occur. In order to understand assessment, evaluation, and their relationship, it is important to keep in mind two earlier observations. One is that evaluation activities (assessment implied) usually fall into two categories, those addressing students and learning and those about programs and learning. Second, those activities can occur at different levels, the classroom, state, and national, and have different implications. Classrooms involve activities, the working parts of the program like instruction-curriculum interactions, student and instructional variations that have to be valued, as in the giving of grades for reporting purposes and promotion. At the state level, the interest is in comparative performance by schools and districts. Nationally, it can be a comparative of state data usually set against standards or some other value of performance.

Conceptualizing Assessment-Evaluation

As a teacher or other practitioner, you want to know if the programs and activities are useful in promoting learning, which is the ultimate purpose of schooling. As you understand it, that means assessment, the use of instruments such as tests to produce data, and evaluation, the process of interpreting the data so they are useful in further deliberations and decisions about learning, what Lorrie Shepard (2000) refers to as the role of assessment in a learning culture. Expressed that way, assessment-evaluation applies to two different but complementary things often incorporated under the single word evaluation. The choices would seem to be either to use assessment-evaluation or evaluation separately or interchangeably. There is a third way of viewing assessment-evaluation and that is to think of them in tandem as a *curriculum appraisal* process, a way of including both while allowing each to retain its distinctive meaning. Consider, for example, how an antique dealer does appraisals. The dealer has to create data by taking into consideration a set of factors (e.g., age, condition, and provenance of the object), and has to develop a value commensurate with that data and current pricing and demand for the particular antique or family of antiques being appraised. Appraising educational and curriculum objects and programs through assessment and evaluation has similar requirements, a set of basic considerations or questions to bring into play, setting up criteria, collecting data, and interpreting and using the information. In application, that could range from something as simple as comparing two textbooks to determine how each fits the curriculum, or as complex as establishing the effects of a reading program using two different reading processes. As you will recall, the general use of assessment and evaluation to determine the effect of some innovation, technique, or new program on children in schools refers to program evaluation. In curriculum work, the focus of appraising is on questions about the curriculum fundamentals in a program, the scope, sequence, balance, and continuity matters referred to in Chapter 6 and elsewhere. Conceptualizing assessment and evaluation as curriculum appraisal also reflects the range of complexities regarding those factors. For example, comparing readability levels between textbooks in two third grades is far more specific than the more general interest in gathering information about a current elementary textbook series being used in science across Grades 1–6. Whether a curriculum program assessment-evaluation is broad or narrow in its focus does not, however, indicate the degree of complexity—the third-grade textbook appraisal process could be more multifaceted than that for the series in Grades 1–6. Also, each might differ in assessment and evaluation requirements. Awareness of that division and the differences that are possible is important because assessment and evaluation have become separate areas of knowledge and emerging disciplines in the education field. The quadrilateral implications of accountability, curriculum, assessment, and evaluation are just emerging as important issues in schooling and the appraisal of curriculum. The concept of curriculum appraisal offers a way to consider assessment and evaluation as essential parts of one process while also accepting that each can be considered separately without the other. It's hoped it will help you understand each separately and as applied together as a process whenever you think of assessment and evaluation as important curriculum work. Having suggested a reconceptualization of assessment and evaluation as appraisal solely for application in curriculum work, it will still be necessary to use the more familiar term evaluation in place of appraisal for discussion purposes in this text.

Tools for Curriculum Evaluation

As a classroom teacher, you want to know what students are learning about the curriculum you are teaching. The familiar pattern is to give a test or quiz, the scores being the results you need, and then interpret the results to provide a grade that places the results and individual performances in perspective. You have, in the simplest sense of it, appraised the student's performance with an assessment and evaluation of learning. At that point, there is no intended connection with curriculum; that would follow as a secondary concern. The crucial curriculum act that could follow would be to use the data about learning and performance to make judgments about the curriculum. The key is the intended purpose and the tools that then apply. Tools and purposes can be referred to by their direct or indirect application, the distance from the classroom, students, and teacher. Familiar classroom tools such as tests and quizzes are first about students and second about curriculum or other matters. Their use for curriculum would be secondary, or inferred and indirect, to develop some meanings or relationship about curriculum from the data on learning. Tools like curriculum analysis or a national test, on the other hand, may be intended and direct in their use; they are specifically in use for a curriculum purpose and not, as in the other example, by way of student learning. Given that distinction, a look at the various kinds of tools and categories is in order.

Classroom Teacher Tools

As a student, you are familiar with teacher-made tests and quizzes, the traditional assessment instruments. If you participated in art and used portfolios, you were also using another kind of assessment tool. Any method, procedure, or performance that is used to capture your work can be a form of assessment. The gathered data could also be used to identify problems with instruction or curriculum that perhaps contributed to discrepancies between expectations and results. The intent could also be to look specifically at just the curriculum outcomes of the learning relationship. Distinctions are also sometimes made between *traditional assessment* and *authentic assessment,* the former referring to pencil-paper teacher-made or commercially made tests typically used in the classroom and the latter to forms of assessments, such as performances or portfolios, that attempt to reflect real life and preferably real work situations. Whatever curriculum purpose they might serve will be as an indirect, inferred kind of appraisal because the intent is primarily to value the students' work and secondarily to make inferences about the curriculum.

Standardized Tests

According to Alfie Kohn (2000), standardized tests are used in the United States far more frequently than in the rest of the world. Those tests are obviously an important tool for gathering aggregate data and useful to state and national educational interests who want to make judgments about the relative excellence of schooling at various levels. The problem is that such data in the form of high or low scores tell nothing about the curriculum and particularly how standardized tests measure any curriculum-learning relationship. Data from standardized tests are also subject to political entanglements, which distract from their possible value in addressing problems or using results to improve teaching and curriculum. The main observation about standardized tests, however, is that they can't be clearly related to curriculum. This is a problem of coherence, that to link assessments from the classroom to national ones, they must share an underlying common model of learning and further, as Lorrie Shepard suggests, "coherence in assessment . . . cannot be achieved without agreed-upon curriculum . . . requiring much more substantive elaboration and congruence than is implied by the currently popular term *alignment*" (2004, p. 239). Reports such as *The Nation's Report Card: Mathematics 2000* (U.S. Department of Education, 2001) also suggest that other variables such as student poverty, parental education levels and expectations, and the school setting are strongly associated with results on standardized tests. Whether it is a lack of coherence, ties to curriculum, or other factors, standardized test results may have little relevance to teaching and learning at the classroom level. What the standardized test can tell about curriculum seems indirect and inferred at best.

Curriculum Analysis

Evaluation in curriculum usually infers concerns about scope, sequence, continuity, balance, and their relationship as the fundamental internal features of curriculum. Those aspects also apply to concerns about specific subjects or content in the curriculum, such as mathematics or art. *Curriculum analysis* is a collective term for different ways of probing curriculum. It can refer simply to a checklist or short guide for evaluating textbooks and curriculum guides (Zenger & Zenger, 1973, 1976) and other curriculum materials, or to more complex analysis of a total curriculum like the methods included in the volume *Guidebook to Examine School Curricula* (1997), published by the United States Department of Education. The use of curriculum analysis was also discussed in Chapter 6 as one set of important tools in curriculum work. Two newer approaches for analyzing are backward design and mapping, the aspects of which are summarized in Figure 12.4. *Backward design,* a concept introduced by Wiggins and McTighe (2001), could be considered to be both a model for developing curriculum and a means of analyzing curriculum, a template of factors for evaluating curriculum in terms of performance. A second analysis process is *curriculum mapping,* which began with the first formulation by Fenwick English (1980) and has since been popularized by Heidi H. Jacobs (1997) and the Association for Supervision and Curriculum Development. It is a way of moving horizontally and vertically in evaluating curriculum scope and sequence. The horizontal dimension refers, for example, to the curriculum across a grade, a school, and schools within a district, and the vertical refers to the curriculum as a whole or a particular part, such as science, and its K–12 grade progression. As a process, curriculum mapping reminds one of working with concept maps (Novak, 1993) and other kinds of graphic organizers but in a much more sophisticated and

Figure 12.4   Examples of Models for Curriculum Analysis

Backward Design	Curriculum Mapping
A series of steps defining a process for thinking through what the curriculum should be and then creating and implementing it with a mechanism for continuous refinement and revision: • Starts with identifying the desired results, as in stated goals/standards • Identifies the evidence of learning, the performance outcomes or indicators expressed in the standard • Performance expectations then define the curriculum to be constructed to meet the performance called for by the standard • Materials, technology, and all resources in whatever form are then identified for the teacher to prepare for and equip student performance capability	A technique for laying out the curriculum that connects all the elements and allows both vertical and horizontal relating of components (standards, performance, criteria, indicators, and resources)—the big picture with the small details: • Identify the objectives and assessment process, what is to be the enacted curriculum • Focus on what is taught, the content and skills of the taught curriculum • Determine what students get, the received curriculum • Mark and determine why certain performance results are achieved • Study relational factors among intentions expressed in objectives, performance as identified in assessment, student performance features, and resources provided to prepare for performance

extended way. Curriculum mapping has spawned a cottage industry of consultants and online resources that you can explore by going to the Resources for Curriculum Study section at the end of the chapter.

Evaluation Models

In the discipline of evaluation, the approach has been more toward development of particular models of how to execute an evaluation. These, as noted earlier, have been used particularly for educational program evaluation rather than specifics such as instruction or curriculum or others aspects of schooling and learning, except as those are part of some intended educational program. Although they could be used for appraising curriculum-specific programs or projects, the literature does not report such examples. Among the more widely known are Michael Scriven's Goal-Free Evaluation (1972), Malcolm Provus's Discrepancy Evaluation (1971), Robert Stake's (1975) Responsive Evaluation, Parlett & Dearden's Illuminative Evaluation (1977), and Daniel Stufflebeam's CIPP Evaluation Model (2000). These models are not necessarily appropriate for a solo evaluation of curriculum but are used when curriculum is part of the school program or activities being evaluated. Some models in curriculum have multiple uses. The often-referred-to Tyler-Taba model is useful in determining educational and curriculum objectives, devising lessons, organizing curriculum, and, interestingly, creating a simple evaluation process by looking through it at what it was used for in evaluating what was created. For example, to the question "was a needs assessment conducted?" a yes or no response is very simple; however, if, then, the needs assessment itself is studied to determine if it adequately assessed needs, you arrive at a deeper and more rigorous use of evaluation. Variations in purpose lead to using different models in curriculum evaluation work. Three are selected for discussion in Figure 12.5, the Tyler-Taba model (see Chapters 4 and 6); the Illuminative (Parlett & Dearden, 1977), which strives for description and interpretation; and the CIPP (Stufflebeam, 2000), which aims more for comprehensive measurement and prediction. Moving across the models, you can observe differences in depth of complexity and breadth of application. That should not be confused with simplicity but instead represent, as noted with Tyler-Taba, how the different characteristics of a model make it useful in different ways when there is a need for evaluation in curriculum work. A. V. Kelly (2004), in summarizing studies of the evaluation-curriculum relationship, suggests several up-front or threshold considerations in making decisions about curriculum evaluation and employing models:

1. *The purposes for devising an evaluation will vary.* There are multiple perceptions of purposes, those of the participants in or the operators of that which is to be evaluated and those of the evaluator or persons executing the evaluation. The size, scope, and level of the evaluating suggest matters of scale that might expand rather than narrow perceptions of the evaluation—the more the participants, the more the views of the evaluation.

2. *It is important to devise an evaluation or select a model that is as appropriate as possible.* The matter of fit is, of course, relative to the perceptions, but articulating the characteristics of the object of evaluation helps to establish criteria for creating an ad hoc evaluation process or selecting from among models. For example, if this is a developmental program, you might evaluate for its internal effectiveness (is it doing what it is supposed to do?) or you might evaluate for external effectiveness in terms of learning and outcomes; assessing and evaluating with high-stakes tests is an example. In addition to evaluating something in its development, there are evaluations that are formative and summative, which were discussed earlier in this chapter.

3. *Know what is being evaluated.* A process evaluation is different from a product evaluation. Put another way, evaluating a textbook production process is different from evaluating the textbook as a product. Field tests and piloting are useful forms of evaluation in product development, but they are probably not useful in determining if learning is occurring in the use of the textbook. Obviously, the questions to be asked should point to the differences in intent and form that a developmental, formative, summative, or other object of evaluation seeks to serve.

Figure 12.5   Selected Models in Curriculum Evaluation

Model	Characteristics	Curriculum Applications
CIPP Model		
Context Evaluation	• Consider what students do or do not know, their backgrounds • Identify institutional setting and service • Assess needs of target population • Do a comparative analysis of resources to opportunities, goals, and needs	Useful in constructing predevelopment profile and characteristics a curriculum or a textbook and other curriculum materials as products would need to address
Input Evaluation	• Provide information about planned or in-place procedures for meeting goals and objectives and whether they are appropriate • Consider alternative pedagogy	Important for curriculum scope and sequence development but not as critical for text or materials development unless they are a K–12 progression of content
Process Evaluation	• Useful for monitoring a new or revised program implementation • Useful for determining if the ongoing activities and actions need to be modified in-use or if correctives and enhancements are appropriate without critically altering what is intended	Similar to piloting and testing in developmental work and useful in curriculum adaptation when a more formal evaluation is envisioned
Product Evaluation	• The project or curriculum is at the end of its cycle of operation; it is now a product and can be viewed in a complete and detached way • A determination of its viability and decisions about continuation can be made before it is implemented again, as in thinking about the next school	Very important before putting a curriculum in place permanently and applies also to curriculum materials that are selected for use
Illuminative Model		
Observation	Observation to identify the factors and/or issues significant to the participants in a specified context	More restrictive and ad hoc use, for small-scale curriculum projects that pertain to the context of a classroom or classrooms in a school or small selection of classrooms for delineating context characteristics to guide development of a curriculum or materials in a classroom or school context

Description	Concerned with description and interpretation of the identified factors and elements, often relying on interviews and use of documents and other information about the context	In-depth, detailed characterizations of the context and factors observed for curriculum in specific places but perhaps not generalizable to other contexts; might be of use in developing differentiated textbook/materials that are the same in content but differentiated (e.g., for gifted or multilingual situations)
Exploratory	Useful when there are complex or hard-to-define goals, there is distortion because of the institutional setting, or there is uncertainty about the premise and nature of questions to be studied	Could be applied in unique contexts when experimenting with curriculum organization or ideas for content in curriculum materials and some preliminary evaluation is needed
Tyler-Taba Model		
Specific Sequence	• Diagnose needs (assessment) • State purposes—based on needs • Formulate objectives • Organize objectives • Identify experiences • Select experiences • Organize experiences	Proven sequence for thinking about curriculum, either as it is or to create new or alternative ones; a useful model, a tool that in addition to evaluation can be applied in many aspects of curriculum work and is flexible in application from the individual teacher's planning to district- and statewide curriculum development

Finally, it is important to differentiate between processes and methods. Evaluation is a process and is made up of techniques or methods. *Processes* are flows of actions, as in following a set of established instructions, or creating a sequence of actions to be followed. In the instance of the Tyler-Taba model, it is both a process and a method for evaluating; it is complete in itself. If you were to consider the Illuminative or CIPP approach, they can accommodate using various methods or techniques that might be available because they are open rather than closed evaluation processes that allow for inclusion in a particular phase or action.

Other Tools for Appraising Curriculum

The appraisal concept gives latitude in considering the selection and use of tools beyond the usual ones associated with assessment-evaluation. It also avoids entanglement with academic discussions about whether assessment and evaluation are separate disciplines or part of research. The tack taken here is that areas of work such as curriculum, instruction, and learning are areas for study unto themselves. Second, what matters are the purposes and contexts for appraisal, not the perceived academic legitimacy of some method, model, or tool. That seems consistent with L. R. Gay's observation that "educational research seeks control while evaluation assesses what is, and that the natural settings characteristics of evaluation essentially preclude that control" (1996, p. 10), although he comes down on the side of evaluation as a type of research used to inform decision making. Purpose, context, and expectations define discussions about perspective and choice of approach in the education field. Curriculum, being a defined discipline with particular work activities, has purposes, contexts, and expectations that may change the character of assessment-evaluation and selection of the tools to be used. That is also apparently the view as well in other fields and disciplines, such as human service technology (Stolovich & Keeps, 1996) and medicine (Barnes, Stein, & Rosenberg, 1999), among others (Yin, 2003).

Action Research

Even though purposes for appraising curriculum might seem to preclude selection of traditional educational qualitative or quantitative research methods, action research is another matter. Again, purpose, context, and use come into play. The purpose for *action research* is to solve practical problems, those that are matters of practice and work. The context is the local setting and its use is local. Being context specific, the findings are not intended to be generalizable to other settings. Action research is context and practitioner centered, be it the classroom and teacher or pilot testing and the curriculum developer. Because the activities are designed to inform decision making, some educational research authors, McMillan and Wergin (1998), for example, consider evaluation and practice-based research (teacher and classroom research) as variants of action research.

Other Research Methods

The idea of evaluating curriculum would not be complete without the mention of other inquiry traditions that are not usually applied in or associated with curriculum work. Although there are a number of inquiry traditions (see Chapter 5) and methods, the ones in the education field are usually classified into two families, the quantitative and qualitative. These families and some of the particular methods associated with each are sketched out in Figure 12.6.

The purpose here is to acknowledge that some of these methods, particularly those in the qualitative family like narratives and case studies, have been utilized modestly in studying curriculum questions and issues. The basic difference between quantitative

Figure 12.6   An Overview of Qualitative and Quantitative Inquiry

Quantitative Inquiry Method Examples	Qualitative Inquiry Method Examples
Experimental	Case Studies
Comparative	Narrative
Quasi-experimental	Grounded Theory
Quantitative Descriptive	Ethnographic
Features	*Features*
Uses numbers	Uses words
Seeks objectivity and methodological rigor	Interpretive
Positivistic-empirical	Recognizes subjectivity
Data externally derived	Data internally derived
Seeks to generalize findings to other areas	Findings are setting or context specific

and qualitative inquiry is that the data in quantitative inquiry appear in numerical form, whereas qualitative inquiry is descriptive and uses words. Although there is no specific scientific research method, the tendency is to associate quantitative inquiry with science. *Quantitative inquiry* methods attempt to draw conclusions, for example, gathering numerical data to determine correlations between pupil achievement and class size. The most common examples of *qualitative inquiry* methods are the case study methods and ethnography associated with research in anthropology (McMillan & Wergin, 1998; Patton, 2002). If you are interested in more in-depth treatment of these families and their particulars, several resources are suggested in the Resources for Curriculum Study at the end of the chapter.

Meta-Analysis

One of the most difficult problems in education is how to take a variety of studies done with different methods and make use of the findings collectively to inform education professionals about a problem, technique, or strategy of value in their work. Gene V. Glass and others (1981) conceived a process called meta-analysis, the analysis of analysis, to resolve that problem. Although his reference is for education generally, Robert Stake (2000) has used the term metaevaluation to describe its use in evaluation proper. The evaluation of evaluations is, of course, another tool for looking at grouped evaluation studies to inform decision makers and, it's hoped, improve the school curriculum. If there are a sufficient number of studies strictly about curriculum, then there could be a metaevaluation of curriculum evaluations. Recent calls for using scientific-based findings (Eisenhart & Towne, 2003; Mayer, 2000) in the education field would seem to suggest a very important future role for meta-analysis in evaluation studies both to identify those that are rigorous and increase the credibility of findings for practitioners.

DOING EVALUATION IN CURRICULUM WORK

Educational evaluation in general tends to be of two kinds, those of large scale, such as evaluating a districtwide program or a national evaluation like the NAEP or TIMSS (the international evaluation study in math and science), and small scale, such as a teacher's use of evaluation in the classroom. Evaluation work in curriculum has increasingly moved toward more systematic applications, especially in response to the standards movement in the various states. Interestingly, much of the latest literature about curriculum evaluation comes from the United Kingdom, Australia, and New Zealand. School reform actions in those countries have focused on curriculum as the critical change agent in reform (Gamoran, 1998; Kelly, 2004). A recurring theme in dealing with evaluation in curriculum work is the difficulty of identifying actual evaluation activities. Evaluation is most closely associated with curriculum development, less so with other areas of curriculum work. Additionally, the role of evaluation varies depending on the location or level of curriculum work. Obviously, national assessments come to mind but, as discussed earlier, the linkage to curriculum is problematic. Evaluation-curriculum linkages at local and state levels are more evident, but can vary according to state emphasis in pursuing standards and the testing carried out. These caveats aside, a discussion of the kinds of curriculum work and the levels of their occurrence can reveal the current and potential dynamics of the evaluation-curriculum relationship.

Curriculum Evaluation and Policy Work

Policy making refers to the laws, statutes, and other administrative warrants authorizing the planning activities leading to development of what the curriculum in schooling will look like and the kinds of knowledge it will represent for students to learn. Currently, there is no national or federally mandated policy about what the curriculum should contain. Under the current NCLB Act of 2001, there is an effort to influence the development of so-called standards that suggest indirectly what content students need to learn. This is a call for some national uniformity based on standards, not curriculum. The focus is on standards produced by individual states and a variety of organizations attempting to define what students should know as they pass through schooling, particularly public schooling. Among the groups weighing in about content and standards are the National Science Foundation, the National Council for Social Studies, the American Federation of Teachers, the National Education Association, and the Council of Chief State School Officers. As you might surmise from just this short list, the viewpoints and interests are multiple and varied. The continuing movement for a model national curriculum and agreement on what it will contain is both a trend and issue that will be developed in Part IV.

Evaluation and Curriculum Development

Curriculum development, as discussed in Chapter 10, is one of the most pervasive forms of curriculum work, occurring with a variety of different agents in places all across the United States. Curriculum development work done by teachers and other curriculum workers is a response both to locally perceived needs and the findings and viewpoints from state, regional, and nationally based organizations and other commercial and not-for-profit sources. There are three aspects of curriculum development that warrant discussion in relationship to evaluation. One is curriculum development as a generic process itself, a second has to do with evaluating curriculum materials for classroom use, and a third involves evaluation in commercially published curriculum materials. As you are aware, any curriculum development process includes pilot and field types of appraisal to make sure that both the process and the product are internally sound and that the latter works as intended with the specified audience of learners. That establishes accountability in the curriculum development process and for the product resulting from that process. Any materials developed by a schooling authority for classroom use should use such a curriculum development process. The next evaluative framework is the familiar curriculum materials or textbook review procedure that exists in states and usually in most school districts. That review should apply to materials developed by curriculum workers and by commercial and not-for-profit sources. Those two sets of actions, one during the curriculum development process by the developer, the second by the appropriate education authority, form an effective evaluation screen. Commercial publishers are also careful to evaluate materials during development. This is done in several ways. One is to use a panel of authorities on both the subject matter itself and curriculum development to guide development of textbooks and other materials. The materials as they are constructed are also subject to field and pilot testing. In addition, materials are subject to special reviews for a variety of other factors, such as readability for intended grade levels or audience and for balanced multicultural and gender presentation. During the development process and particularly its later phases, materials are scrutinized for accuracy by sending materials out to independent reviewers and real-life classroom teachers for comment. These examples of evaluation or appraisal activity in curriculum development work suggest the high degree of accountability that can be expected if those actions are taken.

Evaluation and Curriculum Management

Think of assessment-evaluation as a management tool. Again, the nature of the area of study and the particulars of working in that area, the need, for example, to consider curriculum commonplaces, condition the use of one tool or another. Evaluation as an informal and useful tool of first consideration in curriculum management work has certain advantages. First, simple and informally used tools such as tests and quizzes, portfolios, and performance settings are available for both traditional and authentic assessment. Those, if used casually in the classroom, can give a teacher informal snap-shots of the captured curriculum-student performance and provide insights about the possible need for curriculum changes or for instructional ones. The problem is that curriculum management has to occur both in and across classrooms, and the informal use by individual teachers does not lead to management in that larger standardized manner. One road to standardizing evaluation lies in the use of *rubrics,* a set of guides or guidelines that surrounds assessment data and provides the indicators for making judgments about the quality of student performance on a task or given set of tasks. The idea of rubrics emerged from the standardized testing movement. Rubrics in curriculum evaluation work help standardize interpretation so there is a possibility of like explanation by different persons from assessments directly linked to curriculum in and across a variety of classrooms. Because rubrics constrain judgment in useful ways, they lend certain respectability to whatever indicators of performance are used and to the information being used in managing curriculum. Student performance data from standardized tests can also be useful at the state and district levels. Schools performing below expected performance levels can be identified and resources shifted to assist classroom teachers with auxiliary support personnel and materials to enhance curriculum and to provide in-service and systematic staff development that focuses on specific identified problems from the assessment-evaluation. State departments of education can also use the data to identify particular districts having problems and, as in the case of a failing school, shift resources as required. Problems identified from standardized test assessments do not necessarily point to some curriculum problem. Often the analysis reveals other contributing factors, like levels of poverty, disintegrating human support such as a failing family, and inadequate public services such as police assistance in the communities served. Such factors outside the school conditions are not easily neutralized in the classroom. In schools with high numbers of migrant and immigrant students, language barriers often militate against students having the knowledge necessary to respond in class or perform successfully on tests. Those factors make it difficult not only to improve test scores but also to imply any connection directly to the curriculum or its management.

Informed management in curriculum work depends on the availability and quality of information derived from assessment-evaluation. Certainly one of the most promising is the use of the meta-analysis discussed earlier. Unfortunately, there are no applications to activities or studies that are strictly about curriculum, scope and sequence studies, for example. A few useful meta-analysis studies are appearing. One example is a study by Boorman, Hewes, Overman, and Brown (2003) that offers a timely meta-analysis of school reform studies. While not singularly curricular in focus, it exemplifies the procedure and suggests its effectiveness in gleaning findings that can be useful in practice, especially information to inform curriculum management.

PERSPECTIVE INTO PRACTICE: Examples of Curriculum Assessment-Evaluation Tasks at the Elementary and Secondary Level		
Assessment- *Evaluation Task*	*Elementary Level Application*	*Secondary Level Application*
Reviewing Textbooks	District specialist has sent three first- through sixth-grade social studies series for teachers to appraise for content and reading level appropriateness to the grade being taught. Using a state-approved checklist and readability scores for the texts, teachers must individually rate the text series for their level, then send the rating to the specialist for tallying before meeting to review and discuss the data and then make a recommendation.	Each biological science teacher has the same two books to evaluate for content and readability at the 10th-grade level consistent with state guidelines and standards. The assigned district curriculum specialist has prepared a checklist paralleling the state rubrics for evaluating textbooks in biology. Following the meeting, teachers individually evaluate the texts and return the completed form, and the specialist compiles the ratings. At a final meeting, ratings will be discussed and a textbook selected to complete the review.
Appraising Learning	Four third-grade elementary school teachers decide to use the same quiz about mathematics symbols (e.g., $<$, $>$, $=$) as a formative diagnostic tool prior to beginning work with equations. The quiz data reveal a wide range of student understandings, from those who know most or all of the symbols to those who know	David and Jesse are twins studying for tests in their high school American literature course. They have different teachers. David's teacher likes short essay-type tests; Jesse's teacher uses multiple-choice-type exams. After the tests, covering the same comparable content about late-20th-century American authors, David received a grade of B

(Continued)

(Continued)

	nothing or a little, depending on experiencing them (e.g., +, =) in nonmathematical contexts. The formative assessment allows teachers to choose alternative content materials about symbols to fit the various degrees of understanding. The data also suggest that a variety of instructional options, such as games and memory card exercises, would be useful.	on his short essay test and Jesse got 91 points out of a possible 100, for an A. Obviously, each teacher has a different view of the types of assessment that apply and the criteria for making judgments in assigning grades. As a department, the teachers decide to address how to standardize the assessment-evaluation process with rubrics that cocoon the test items for essays and objective tests so there is a uniformity of testing and criteria for judgments.
Creating Curriculum	Several students are in need of English-Spanish translation activities for words being used in language arts. No equivalent materials or assistance is available. Teachers develop examples of words arranged in two parallel lines, English above and Spanish below, and sample sentences. Teachers pilot the material with advanced Spanish-to-English-speaking students, make adjustments, and use the materials in a number of classrooms in that particular school for further development. The curriculum specialist then does field tests of the materials with all district elementary schools (as applicable). Following revisions, the materials are offered to teachers throughout the district.	In Zane Middle School, few parents come to teacher conferences to discuss their students' work. The PTA does a survey that indicates parental barriers include knowledge about key words like standards, curriculum, and alignment. District curriculum staff prepares a Talking With Teachers Guide for parents and a Talking to Parents Guide for teachers. The parent guide materials are piloted with parent volunteers, revised, and field-tested with parent sessions at all middle schools; the guide for teachers is piloted and field-tested similarly. In preparation for the next scheduled conferences, the staff develops an assessment checklist keyed to the materials for teachers and parents to use in evaluating the materials for further development.

Summary and Conclusions

Evaluation has emerged as an important concern in schooling and education. Ideas about accountability and the push for school reforms not only affect evaluation in general but also in thinking and working with the school curriculum. The use of the term evaluation is often confusing because it is applied at times as a collective term for both assessment and evaluation and the meaning intended is often unclear. The meaning of evaluation, compared to its earlier conception, has separated into two connected areas of work. Assessment, as part of the earlier meaning of evaluation, is concerned with tools of evaluation such as tests. Evaluation itself has come to mean the manner of judgment or placing of value on the data derived from assessment tools. To offset this potential for confusion, the idea of assessment-evaluation as appraisal is suggested for curriculum work. The conditions for appraisal in curriculum work are greatly hindered by the fragmentation of assessment and evaluation practices. For example, there is a national (NAEP) test and evaluation as well as 50 different state approaches to the same task. Such fragmentation in policy development, the lack of systematic and systemic management and curriculum development, suggests an incoherence that affects the attainment of real accountability in curriculum work and schooling.

Critical Perspectives

1. The importance of developing a systematic and comprehensive evaluation for any curriculum is now evident in many fields of knowledge. Access the Internet, type in "curriculum evaluation," select two or three sites, and compare the suggested approaches. What common elements can you find across the examples that might suggest a core of generic concepts in curriculum evaluation? How do those compare with the ideas in this chapter?

2. Assessment linked to purposes often means that the latter reflect some view of intelligence and learning, fixed, changeable, gender differentiated, and so forth. What view of intelligence do you have? If you are involved with a school community, what view prevails? Consider the kinds of assessments used in your experience or in the school community. What do they reflect about the view of intelligence and learning?

3. Confusion with using assessment and evaluation is often the case. Ask 10 people at random what the terms mean and how they are linked. How would you explain the terms to another person?

4. If a proposal were put forward to use student test scores from a state test to determine if the curriculum needs changing, would you consider this an acceptable way to evaluate the curriculum? Why or why not?

5. High-stakes tests, as they are called, are taken for college entrance and scholarships. Should they be used along with the NAEP as data for evaluating curriculum? Why or why not?

6. Various organizations and interest groups want to influence curriculum management and policy making through the sole use of tests. Do you think data from tests alone should be used to make judgments about the value or effectiveness of schooling? What arguments would you put forth one way or the other?

Resources for Curriculum Study

1. Resources are available online and from various organizations for assessments and standards (see also Chapter 8, resources section). Some places to start are the sites of the Council of Chief State School Officers (http://www.ccsso.org) and the Mid-continent Research of Education and Learning (http://www.mcrel.org). Other online resources can be found by simply typing in "standards" or "assessment-evaluation" on Google or other search engines.

2. There are many evaluation models. An older work but an excellent resource to earlier models is Sara M. Steele's *Contemporary Approaches to Program Evaluation* (1973). An excellent resource on current kinds of models and their use is http://www.otis.scotcit.ac.uk/onlinebook/. It is also a thorough discussion of evaluation with interesting online resources to explore.

3. Curriculum analysis can be a homegrown process by modifying and applying the curriculum mapping technique to fit local patterns. Just typing in "curriculum mapping" will provide you with a number of school district efforts. A particularly good site is http://www.glencoe.com/sec/teachingtoday/educationup close.phtml/35, which offers a succinct discussion with leads to school district examples. Greece Central School District in New York has used an integrated backward design and mapping approach and has detailed maps of their curriculum at www.greece.k12.ny.us/. The Appalachian Regional Educational Laboratory (AEL) has published a comprehensive book about mapping, R.C. Burns's (2001) *A Leader's Guide to Curriculum Mapping and Alignment* (Charleston, WV: Appalachian Education Laboratory).

4. Two good sources for further study of quantitative and qualitative inquiry are R. L. Gay's *Educational Research* (1996) and the third edition of M. Q. Patton's

Qualitative Research and Evaluation Methods (2002). A third form of educational inquiry, variously called mixed methods or mixed research, has been put forth as a way to bridge the quantitative-qualitative divide. A good introduction and discussion is the Johnson and Onwuegbuzie *Educational Researcher* article, "Mixed Methods Research: A Research Paradigm Whose Time Has Come" (2004).

5. The function of rubrics in evaluation is to guide judgment. As statements containing criteria on which judgment is based, rubrics attempt to constrain the possibility of other factors entering into the judgment-forming process. There are many online resources for exploring rubrics; the Association for Supervision and Curriculum Development's site at http://www.ascd.org/ is a good place to start. A good article with references to further reading is by Heidi Goodrich Andrade (2000), "Using Rubrics to Promote Thinking and Learning," in *Educational Leadership, 57*(5), 13–18.

6. Recent calls for scientifically based research standards seem to suggest that quantitative rather than qualitative educational research methods would be preferred. Much of the discussion has to do with the history of educational research and the kind of difficulties that arise in doing such research regardless of methods. An excellent introduction is E. C. Lagemann's (2000) *An Elusive Science: The Troubling History of Educational Research* (Chicago: University of Chicago Press).

References

Anderson, L. W., & Krathwohl, D. R. (2001). A taxonomy for learning, teaching, and assessing: A revision of Bloom's taxonomy of educational objectives. New York: Longman.

Barnes, J., Stein, A., & Rosenberg, W. (1999). Evidence based medicine and evaluation of mental health service: Methodological issues and future directions. *Archives of Diseases in Childhood, 80*(3), 280–285.

Bereiter, C., & Scardamalia, M. (1998). Beyond Bloom's Taxonomy: Rethinking knowledge for the knowledge age. In A. Hargreaves, A. Lieberman, M. Fullan, & D. Hopkins (Eds.), *International handbook of educational change* (pp. 675–692). Dorbrecht, Netherlands: Kluwer.

Black, P., & William, D. (1998). Assessment and classroom learning. *Assessment in Education, 5,* 7–74.

Bloom, B. J., & Krathwohl, D. (1956). *Taxonomy of educational objectives. Handbook I: Cognitive domain.* New York: Longman Green.

Boorman, G. D., Hewes, G. M., Overman, L. T., & Brown, S. (2003). Comprehensive school reform and achievement: A meta-analysis. *Review of Educational Research, 73*(2), 125–130.

Brookhart, S. M. (2004). Classroom assessment: Tensions and intersections in theory and practice. *Teachers College Record, 106*(3), 429–458.

Burns, R. C. (2001). *A leader's guide to curriculum mapping and alignment.* Charleston, WV: Appalachian Educational Laboratory.

Eisenhart, M., & Towne. L. (2003). Contestation and change in national policy on "scientifically based" education research. *Educational Researcher, 32*(7), 31–38.

English, F. W. (1980). Curriculum mapping. *Educational Leadership, 37*(7), 558–559.

Gamoran, A. (1998). Curriculum change as a reform strategy: Lessons from the United States and Scotland. *Teachers College Record, 98*(4), 608–628.

Gay, L. R. (1996). *Educational research.* Upper Saddle River, NJ: Merrill/Prentice Hall.

Glass, G. V., McCaw, B., & Smith, M. L. (1981). *Meta-analysis in social research.* Beverly Hills, CA: Sage.

Harrow, A. J. (1970). *Taxonomy of the psychomotor domain: A guide for the development of educational objectives.* New York: Macmillan.

Jacobs, H. H. (1997). *Mapping the big picture: Integrating curriculum and assessment K-12.* Arlington, VA: Association for Supervision and Curriculum Development.

Kelly, A.V. (2004). *The curriculum: Theory and practice* (5th ed.). London: Sage.

Kohn, A. (2000, September 27). Standardized testing and its victims. *Education Week, 20*(4), 46–60. Retrieved November 2004 from http://www.edweek.org/ew/articles/2000/09/27/04kohn.h20.html

Krathwohl, D. R., Bloom, B. S., & Masia, B. B. (1964). Taxonomy of educational objectives: The classification of educational goals (Handbook 2, Affective Domain). New York: McKay.

Linn, R. L. (2003). Accountability: Responsibility and reasonable expectations. *Educational Researcher, 32*(7), 3–13.

Madaus, G. F, Stufflebeam, D., & Scriven, M. S. (1983). Program evaluation: An historical overview. In G. F. Madaus, M. S. Scriven, & D. Stufflebeam (Eds.), *Evaluation models: Viewpoints on educational and human services evaluation* (pp. 3–22). Norwell, MA: Kluwer.

Mager, R. F. (1962). *Preparing instructional objectives.* Palo Alto, CA: Fearon.

Marzano, R. J. (2001). *Designing a new taxonomy of educational objectives.* Thousand Oaks, CA: Corwin.

Marzano, R. J., & Kendall, J. S. (1996). *A comprehensive guide to designing standards-based district, school and classroom.* Alexandria, VA: Association for Supervision and Curriculum Development.

Mayer, R. E. (2000). What is the place of science in educational research? *Educational Researcher, 29*(6), 38–39.

McMillan, H. J., & Wergin, J. F. (1998). *Understanding and evaluating educational research.* Upper Saddle River, NJ: Merrill/Prentice Hall.

Norris, N. (1998). Curriculum evaluation revisited. *Cambridge Journal of Education, 28*(2), 207–220.

Novack, J. D. (1993). Clarifying with concept maps: A tool for student and teacher. *The Science Teacher, 58*(7), 45–49.

Parlett, M. & Dearden, G. (Eds). (1977). *Introduction to illuminative evaluation: Studies in higher education.* Washington. DC: Council of Independent Colleges.

Patton, M. Q. (2002). *Qualitative research and evaluation vethods* (3rd ed.). Thousand Oaks, CA: Sage.

Popham, W. J. (2004). Curriculum, instruction, and assessment: Amiable allies or phony friends? *Teachers College Record, 106*(3), 417–428.

Provus, M. (1971). *Discrepancy evaluation for educational program improvement and assessment.* Berkeley, CA: McCutchan.

Scriven M. (1967). The methodology of evaluation. In R. W. Tyler, R. Gagne, & M. Scriven (Eds.), *Perspectives of curriculum evaluation* (American Educational Research Association Monograph Series on Curriculum Evaluation, No. 1, pp. 39–53). Chicago: Rand McNally.

Scriven, M. (1972). Pros and cons about goal-free evaluation. *Evaluation Comment, 3*(4), 1–7.

Shepard, L. A. (2000). The role of assessment in a learning culture. *Educational Researcher, 29*(7), 4–14.

Shepard, L. A. (2004). Curricular coherence in assessment design. In M. Wilson (Ed.), *Towards coherence between classroom assessment and accountability* (103rd Yearbook of the National Society for the Study of Education, Part II, pp. 239–249). Chicago: National Society for the Study of Education.

Stake, R. E. (1967). The countenance of educational evaluation. *Teachers College Record, 68*(7). Retrieved July 2004 from http://www.ed.uiuc.edu/circe/

Stake, R. E. (1975). *Program evaluation—Particularly responsive evaluation* (Paper No. 5, Occasional Paper Series). Urbana-Champaign: University of Illinois Center for Instructional Research and Curriculum Evaluation. Retrieved July 2004 from http://www.ed.uiuc.edu/circe/

Stake, R. E. (2000, January). *Evaluation and assessment: Discrimination against minorities?* Paper presented at the RACE 2000 Conference, Tempe, AZ. Retrieved July 2004 from http://www.ed.uiuc.edu/circe/

Steele, S. M. (1973). *Contemporary approaches to program evaluation.* Washington, DC: Education Resources Division Capitol Publications.

Stolovitch, H. D., & Keeps, E. J. (1996). *Handbook of human performance technology.* San Francisco, CA: Jossey-Bass.

Stufflebeam, D. L. (2000). The CIPP model for evaluation. In D. L. Stufflebeam, G. F. Madaus, & T. Kellaghan (Eds.), *Evaluation models* (2nd ed., pp. 279–317). Boston: Kluwer.

Tyler, R. W. (Ed.). (1976). *Prospects for research and development in education* (National Society for the Study of Education Series on Contemporary Educational Issues). Berkeley, CA: McCutchan.

United States Department of Education. (1997). *Guidebook to examine school criteria.* Washington, DC: Author.

United States Department of Education. (2001). *The nation's report card: Mathematics 2000.* Washington, DC: Author.

Walker, D. F. (1990). *Fundamentals of curriculum.* New York: Harcourt Brace Jovanovich.

Wiggins, G., & McTighe, J. (2001). *Understanding by design.* Upper Saddle River, NJ: Prentice Hall.

Yin, R. K. (2003). *Applications of case study research.* Thousand Oaks, CA: Sage.

Zenger, W. F., & Zenger, S. K. (1973). *Writing and evaluating curriculum guides.* Belmont, CA: Fearon.

Zenger, W. F., & Zenger, S. K. (1976). *Handbook for evaluating and selecting textbooks.* Belmont, CA: Fearon.

Part IV

CHALLENGES OF CURRICULUM CHANGE

In the time and place of your using this book, matters educational, in particular those about schooling and curriculum, will be changing, perhaps in degree, possibly dramatically. This Part IV, Challenges of Curriculum Change, is a speculative venture grounded in present-day ideas and studies. The discussions about curriculum, schooling, and society are suggestions, not predictions. Curriculum and the schooling process in which it is embedded will, like the American society it serves, continue to evolve.

Chapter 13

INTERPRETING CONTEMPORARY CURRICULUM ISSUES

The transition from the last years of the 19th century into the first of the 20th is marked by the challenge of the progressive movement to rethink the role of government and institutional needs for the public good. In the field of education, there was a general affirmation of the need for public schooling. Even with a consensus of the central role of schools as needed public institutions, there were still differing perspectives about what knowledge the curriculum should contain. Similarly, the years from 1983 through the first years of the 21st century are marked by another discussion about schools and curriculum. However, the contemporary dialogue is about issues that signal a deeper, more subtle consideration of the role of public institutions, particularly public schooling; American identity; the nature of civic culture; and the balance of power between private and individual and public and societal interests. In essence, it is a discussion as old as America, one about special interests, national identity, the degree of diversity that is acceptable, the role of schooling as an instrument of the people in a constitutional republic, and what kind of curriculum will serve those purposes.

Although often made up of diverse voices, contemporary discussions frame a host of issues too numerous to be addressed in a single chapter, so selectivity is a consideration. A second concern in framing a discussion of contemporary issues is the matter of interpreting the issue. Often there are multiple viewpoints, because the issue is still unfolding and the task of interpretation requires a synthesis of views. Synthesis, in turn, creates the risk of not remaining true to the issues or, at worst, seeming to slant what is written in accord with some ideology. Recognizing these inherent pitfalls, the approach in this chapter is thematic, clustering a set of issues around four themes: control, reform, accountability, and social change.

THEME: CONTROL OF SCHOOLING AND CURRICULUM

In 1983, the famous Bell Commission report *A Nation at Risk* presented an analysis of American public schooling suggesting that the schools were failing America and a drastic overhaul was needed. What followed was reminiscent of the shrill claims made after Sputnik 26 years earlier about the failure of schools and the need for reform. And, again, there was ample discussion from all quarters and a scramble among potential interests to become stakeholders in the movement. The question became one of who or what had the power to control and influence the direction the reform movement would take. Working through the power issue would determine who would control and set the agenda for school reform and which ideas would determine the policy from which actions would emerge. What has evolved to the present in this dialogue about school reform seems to reflect two policy thrusts: one concerning issues loosely associated with organizational structure for schools and schooling, and the other about setting a new direction in the control of schooling and curriculum.

Organization and Structural Issues

The organizational and structural issues are about location (where schooling takes place) and authority (under whose auspices schooling is carried out). Traditionally, schooling referred to institutional locations, teaching and learning in public, private, and parochial schools as matters of personal choice. Public funds provided for public schools, and secular public interests were separated from personal and religious ones. Individual states provided a constitutional framework respecting that structure while also allowing state or local variances or at least a paternalism for particular ethnic, language, cultural, and religion-based social and cultural traditions—such as education of blacks, new immigrant arrivals, Jews, Mormons, Mennonites, and Amish—in the way public schooling was supported and administered, particularly in local communities

(Boorstin, 1973; Degler, 1959; Spring, 1986). Such allowances constituted a benign looking-the-other-way that was publicly acceptable, recognizing the Judeo-Christian-based heritage of religious diversity and the exercise of school control in the best interests of the people at the local community level. Following World War II, local control very gradually ceded to state and federal governments as expectations about the organization of schooling and the curriculum changed. Since then, schooling organization has become in many ways a continuous yet de-centered process. Curriculum, initially adjusted to perceived local needs under an umbrella of very general state curriculum guides, has gradually assumed a more national character influenced by the National Assessment of Educational Progress (NAEP) and the movement for standards. The traditional K–12 structure has loosened from the triadic public, private, and parochial school organization to include other forms, such as home schooling, charter schools, and for-profit schools. Rather than beginning in kindergarten with graduation by Grade 12, schooling commences in various kinds of preschool and often extends past the 12th grade (the fifth-year senior phenomenon) and, despite compulsory schooling laws, can be exited in some states as early as 13 years of age. Magnet schools, schools-within-schools, open schools, gifted programs, and other organizational patterns represent a subtle effort, usually unspoken, to differentiate and track student ability while providing an appropriate curriculum. Along with these organizational and curriculum changes have come financial ones, with claims on public funds for extended educational services, such as those for students with exceptional needs, bus services, or participation in basic skills such as reading programs. Special services often mean busing children from nonpublic to public schools or assigning school district specialists, reading and special education teachers, for example, to the nonpublic school. Similar resources and service transfers also occur in middle and high school, particularly in hard-to-staff curriculum areas such as physics and chemistry.

The key point to keep in mind is that such accommodations ostensibly were for access to curriculum and not for other reasons such as supplanting staffing needs or offsetting other services that are costly to private, parochial, and other alternative schools. Two impressions can be drawn about schooling in the ongoing reform. First, authority over schools that used to reside in a diocese, district, or private board is now broader and more dispersed, inclusive of old and new school forms having different organizational and governance requirements; charter schools are a good example. Second, traditional images and ideas about schools—that they have particular shape, structure, location, and use—are questionable, perhaps even obsolete, especially in light of home schools, distance learning, and other nonprofit and for-profit options. Changes in perceptions mark shifts in thinking about schools as institutions and about schooling as a process (Apple, 1991). *The basis of these changes is a shift away from the traditional idea of the responsibility of government to provide basic public schooling with public funds to the idea that public funds for schooling students should follow the child as the parent wishes and should not be restricted specifically to public schooling.*

Control Issues

Control over schools and schooling is a political concern expressed through the process of allocating resources for different purposes. Those who decide the purposes determine the allocation of those resources. More subtly, those who control the purposes also control the curriculum. A reality of schooling is the allocation of public money for schools and programs. Political agendas reflect two main but contrasting sets of ideas. One holds that schooling is traditionally a public responsibility, with public monies for public schools. People have the choice of going to public or some other school. This idea is consistent with the idea of separation of religion and the state, the sacred and the secular, the public and the private. The other position is that public monies are collected for schooling that is a matter of personal choice. People use an allotted amount of money to educate their children where they please. There are, of course, variations on these two main ideas, but they summarize the politics involved.

The Curriculum Connection

The theme of control has been enlarged over the last 50 years through the consistent growth of federal government involvement in all aspects of civic life, including curriculum. That involvement has led to policies that use schools for social and cultural change in partnership with the states, which participate in federal programs to receive federal funds. Following the Bell Commission report of 1983, collaboration meant that states yielded control in the face of federal funding power for programs that had become entitlements, or at least popular expectations, as part of the daily school program. Some of those expectations were programs for the bright and gifted, school nutrition (breakfast and lunch), and special education. You can gain a sense of the imperatives or perhaps demands for reform that the commission recommended in the report from the excerpts in Figure 13.1.

The opposing idea—that services should follow the learner—promoted assistance to private and parochial schools, leading to extensive legal challenges concerning constitutionality in light of church, private, and state powers. Yet to emerge was a renewed concern about a common curriculum, regardless of the setting or the agent responsible for schooling. Historically, the tradition of public schooling and a common curriculum had served to unite citizens in, and assimilate others to, a common sense of nationhood. This rationale of inclusion and Americanization had been popularly accepted since the Declaration of Independence and became ingrained over time as a civic and patriotic duty. Since 1983, however, the nationhood thesis as a justification for public schools has been pushed to the background. What emerged refers to a "sectarian narcissism" (Lasch, 1979), promoting separateness over unity, the immediate over the long term, and dogmatic responses rather than reflection about alternatives.

Figure 13.1   Excerpts From the Bell Commission Report

1. Principals and superintendents must play a crucial leadership role in developing school and community support for the reforms we propose, and school boards must provide them with the professional development and other support required to carry out their leadership role effectively. The Commission stresses the distinction between leadership skills involving persuasion, setting goals and developing community consensus behind them, and managerial and supervisory skills. Although the latter are necessary, we believe that school boards must consciously develop leadership skills at the school and district levels if the reforms we propose are to be achieved.

2. State and local officials, including school board members, governors, and legislators, have *the primary responsibility* for financing and governing the schools, and should incorporate the reforms we propose in their educational policies and fiscal planning.

3. The Federal Government, in cooperation with States and localities, should help meet the needs of key groups of students such as the gifted and talented, the socioeconomically disadvantaged, minority and language minority students, and the handicapped. In combination these groups include both national resources and the Nation's youth who are most at risk.

4. In addition, we believe the Federal Government's role includes several functions of national consequence that States and localities alone are unlikely to be able to meet: protecting constitutional and civil rights for students and school personnel; collecting data, statistics, and information about education generally; supporting curriculum improvement and research on teaching, learning, and the management of schools; supporting teacher training in areas of critical shortage or key national needs; and providing student financial assistance and research and graduate training. We believe the assistance of the Federal Government should be provided with a minimum of administrative burden and intrusiveness.

5. The Federal Government has *the primary responsibility* to identify the national interest in education. It should also help fund and support efforts to protect and promote that interest. It must provide the national leadership to ensure that the Nation's public and private resources are marshaled to address the issues discussed in this report.

6. This Commission calls upon educators, parents, and public officials at all levels to assist in bringing about the educational reform proposed in this report. We also call upon citizens to provide the financial support necessary to accomplish these purposes. Excellence costs. But in the long run mediocrity costs far more.

In education, so-called sectarian narcissism led to political interest arguments known as the Culture Wars of the late 1980s and the 1990s (Gates, 1995; Hunter, 1991; Ravitch, 2000). These "wars" tended to avoid substantive issues about the curriculum, however. Instead, questions about cultural diversity, gender representation, and inclusion of minorities—the somewhat cosmetic matters involving curriculum—tended to be the issues discussed. For example, were minorities and cultural and gender variations proportionately represented in the pictures and examples used in curriculum materials? Although important, such questions did not touch deeper issues about curriculum content. As William Bennett (1993), E. D. Hirsch, Jr. (1996), and others have asserted, more significant questions had to do with what the content should be in the total mathematics or science curriculum, what should be taught as American history, and what should be the balance of mathematics, science, social studies, literature, and language arts for the school curriculum. What content should be included in the curriculum? And, most important, who decides? The people? Government? You personally? These are perennial issues, as old as the country, continually raised in different times and contexts.

THEME: SCHOOLING AND CURRICULUM REFORM

Pick up any newspaper and you will find some article dealing with schooling, whether it is an announcement about the rise or decline in school violence, student attitudes toward sex, or principal leadership; a complaint about school lunch menus; a report challenging another report about the effectiveness of a reading program; a discussion over the correct version of American history; or a new report that the content of textbooks in mathematics has no scientific basis. What do the matters of sex attitudes, leadership, lunch menus, or school violence have to do with curriculum reform? And, what do articles about interpretations of American history, reading program differences, or the scientific bases for mathematics content have to do with school reform?

Like control questions, reform questions are multifaceted and affect administrative processes of schooling as well as curriculum matters. Reform movements are never about just one issue; they birth a range of issues, some that disappear, others that survive and may become the focus of change later in the life of a movement. *Reform* means to take what exists—the curriculum, schools, and the kinds of work done—and re-form them, not do away with them. Discussing reforms is to engage in a debate about the merits, the pros and cons, of proposals for reform.

Patterns in Reform

Reform movements evolve as leadership, organizations, and people become party to the discussion. Earlier reform movements, like the one that grew out of the 1950s Sputnik challenge, centered in part on the hardening of the curriculum around science and discipline-based knowledge. Participants and leaders in the Sputnik era came from academic settings in colleges and universities and quasi-governmental agencies such as the National Science Foundation. Although the United States Congress provided important legislative and financial assistance, the essential leadership came from the public institutional centers outside of direct government control. The reform movement begun in 1983 is different. Between the Bell Commission report of 1983 and the enactment of the No Child Left Behind (NCLB) Act, signed into law in 2002, various waves of reform have been generated. As discussed in Chapter 7 and summarized in Figure 13.2, each wave had a particular emphasis that, in varying degrees, left some residual impact.

Figure 13.2   Waves in School Reform

Wave 1: Cosmetic changes

Wave 2: Organizational and structural changes

Wave 3: Emphasis on core changes in leadership, instruction, and curriculum

Wave 4: Changes in teacher preparation and professional development

Source: Based on Chapter 7, Figure 7.3.

Wave one, the cosmetics of reform, was simply a political reaction: do something, a quick and dirty response. Extend the day or the year so there is more contact time. Until a strategy and policy formation could be worked out, it was difficult to undertake the more in-depth, long-term work such as that in wave two. Wave one was obviously short lived, but waves two and three continue today, and the fourth, tinkering with teacher education and certification, is underway.

To date, contemporary reform activities that began nearly 20 years ago seem to reflect two themes. One theme is administrative in that it is about organizational and structural matters such as the arrangement between school units—the elementary or high school—and within those units, such as the creation of schools-within-schools. The second theme is about coherence, the consistencies or inconsistencies in schooling based on the linkages and relationships between school purposes and critical schooling processes: those involving learning, instruction, and curriculum (Shepard, 2004). Coherence is an emerging area of interest in reform. An interesting preliminary report of a study by Sandholtz, Ogawa, & Scribner (2004) suggests deeper problems of coherence possibly exist in the relationship of assessment to curriculum in reform efforts. Although one study alone does not make the case, an emerging issue is the matter of coherence, alignment, curriculum, and their interrelationships in reform.

Administrative Issues in Reform

Administrative reform centers on leadership and organization. Leadership studies (see Fullan, 2001a, 2001b) point to certain characteristics that a principal or other designated leader should emulate if he or she is to instill a reform spirit and reach set outcomes. There are perhaps two important perspectives. One position has it that the identified critical leadership elements, once implemented, will allow goal or outcome attainment and that the selection of a strong leader is important to success. Another perspective suggests that the implementation is more problematic, depending on the setting and context toward which the reforms are directed and that the honest—not contrived—involvement of the people who will become stakeholders in the reform efforts is important to success.

Figure 13.3   Comparative Leadership Qualities

Personal Qualities of Leadership	Positional Qualities of Leadership
Personal vision is important, having a scenario about what the ends are, what the start should be like, what might be expected between start and finish.	*Positional vision* refers to understanding the position role and responsibilities and seeing the assigned mission or tasks, such as reform requirements, in the context of responsibilities and authority of the position, such as a school principal.
Personal voice is presentation of self as leader, articulation and presentation of ideas, a sense of assuredness conveyed to others about filling a role, and fairness in dealings with them.	*Positional voice* is meshing self and expectations of the position, the traditions of behavior, the responsibilities, and the exercise of resident authority associated with roles, such as a school principal.
Personal knowledge is about your own held knowledge, what you have formally learned, what your degrees suggest, the quality and relevance of experience-gained knowledge that is yours to apply.	*Positional knowledge* includes the formal knowledge that degrees indicate you should have, the knowledge about a specific position, and other expectations, such as a principal being schooled in leadership and in curriculum and instruction knowledge.
Personal persona is the way you evidence humor, warmth, empathy, and character as a composite of values that surface in the manner of behavior.	*Positional persona* is actualized behavior of the person in the role and position, a congruence of role-position and self played out in perceptions by others of humor, fairness, empathy, and savvy.

Remember: reform means change, which can be a threatening experience, and handling change requires continuous conversation among the leader and change agents to establish a discourse community. Collaboration, openness, creating and reading from the same script is important in the leadership context. Reading widely in the literature, you will find most research-based findings summarized in either educational or business leadership models. There is a wide variety of business models in which leadership tends to emphasize the personal qualities of the individual leader (Covey, 2004) whereas those in education are more positional and applied. Educational models focus on explanations of leadership in reform (Fullan, 2001a) and administrative positions (Glanz, 2002) such as the principal and, more recently, the teacher (Lieberman & Miller, 2004).

Proposed qualities of personal and positional leadership are summarized in Figure 13.3. Of particular interest in the educational literature is the focus on what knowledge a leader should have (Stein & Nelson, 2003), which seems to separate into knowledge associated with the type of work or position—such as knowledge of the principalship—and formal or discipline knowledge—such as curriculum.

Fragmentation between personal and positional qualities raises the question of what is leadership? Is there a set of personal qualities common across all leadership? What is different about the personal qualities in a business leadership model and what a principalship requires? Are positional qualities the same for principals, say, in the different contexts of elementary, middle, or high school? And, applied to other administrative roles, does a curriculum specialist position have a particular set of attributes and, if so, are these attributes the same or different from those of other specialists? It is interesting in perusing the reform and accountability literature to find that the qualities of leadership for a principal include, among other things, knowledge about curriculum and instruction (Fullan, 2001b). The position is viewed as one of multiple areas of expertise in curriculum, instruction, assessment, and evaluation. What is required for curriculum aspects of leadership? Knowledge? A particular set of behaviors? It would seem worthwhile to explore such questions since leadership is deemed to be important to progress and fulfilling the assigned mission, whether in business or the education field.

Process Issues in Reform

Expectations in school reform extend beyond leadership. Ultimately, reformers look forward to implementing change in what is to be learned, or the curriculum; how it is to be learned, or instruction; and whether it has been acquired, or learning as indicated by some measure of student performance. In whatever guise they appear, reform proposals are about schooling as a process and its critical curricular, instructional, and learning functions. These are the gut issues of teaching and teacher performance. Articles about curriculum content in the subject areas and about the pros and cons of tests that drive curriculum in search of standards all relate to one issue: reforming the curriculum. However, as Lorrie Shepard (2004) and others point out, the tendency is to forget that most school reform proposals do not follow from decisions about what is to be taught and learned—the curriculum—but from institutional and political ones. Refer again to the excerpts from the 1983 *Nation at Risk* report recommendations in Figure 13.1 and note the few references to curriculum. Educational publications, such as the biweekly newspaper *Education Week* (www.edweek.org), present arrays of articles about pre-K and K–12 curriculum, instruction, assessment-evaluation, and federal and state policy initiatives, as well as opinion pieces on reform proposals or policy-based reforms in progress. Over time, these arrays suggest that tinkering with the schooling process has a long history. Periodically, for example, ideas surface, such as the open school, storefront school, and schools open for 24-hour instruction to accommodate different populations. These ideas have a period in the limelight and then fade, usually without any effort to establish a research agenda or to evaluate implementation. And, there are few discussions about curriculum and if or what kind of curriculum would be appropriate in those particular settings for the students that would attend them.

This "follow-the-fade" approach to understanding schooling yields little that can be called scientific-based results, a current aim of federal reform. The problem is the lack of an articulated and consistent long-term research agenda. Even if one were put in place, it would be years before that information could be put to use in response to issues needing immediate attention. There is, for example, some anecdotal evidence from school practice to suggest that boys and girls may learn better in certain curriculum subjects when placed in gender-segregated classes, particularly in mathematics and science (Parker, 1999; Sanders & Petersen, 1999). Little is known about any significant effect of such class configurations. For that matter, very little has been discussed about studies of gender-curriculum interactions at all. It may be fruitful to know more about gender-segregation classes and studies in literature, history, the arts, or other curriculum subjects. Should school schedules or any part of the schooling process be manipulated to accommodate a gender-based school reform proposal without a scientific research base? And, who—what body or agent—decides what is "scientific" in the entrepreneurial research marketplace? The present call for scientific-based research under the NCLB Act calls into question the scientific basis of educational research and whether the research community or the government in some capacity will make those determinations about what is or is not scientific. It has also led to a lively debate in the education field about the role of educational researchers and implications of second-class citizenship when contrasted with scientific work in other fields (Berliner, 2002; Eisenhart & Towne, 2003; Mayer, 2000, 2001; Olson, 2004). Advocacy for the scientific in educational research is not being dismissed; what is being challenged is whether the research that exists and the forms of research being proposed are "scientific." What is at issue is whether forms of research that are not quantitative are "good" science. You will recall from discussions in Chapters 5 and 12 that this question of what is scientific in research emerges periodically. The difference this time is that it is not a critique among scholars and researchers but a political one at the federal level that can affect the kinds of funding that will be allowed in the name of educational research, who will make those decisions, and who will get the funding support.

Organizational and Content Issues

Curriculum reform issues relate to the form or structuring of curriculum, what it should contain, and curriculum work. Structural issues reflect a desire by some interests to arrange curriculum in different ways. You may associate curriculum organization with the traditional divisions of the elementary, middle, and high school, the familiar K–12 scope and sequence. Other organizational suggestions would end schooling at the 10th grade and create a form of college that would encompass Grades 11 and 12 and the first two years of a regular college or community or junior college. Others, perhaps more radical, propose linking curriculum with testing to allow learners to proceed according to their levels of progress, a proposal that would provide a non-school-as-institution option for students. An example might be the school dropout who attends classes or prepares in other ways to take the GED (general educational development test) for a high school equivalency diploma. In view of existing honors courses, advance placement courses, early college entrance options, and the College Board's CLEP (college level examination program), such organizational reform proposals do not seem so far-fetched—at least for the college bound.

Organizational issues ultimately lead back to curriculum. If institutional schooling options were available for college, vocational, commercial, or other yet-to-be proposed kinds of careers, what curriculum core should be common to all? Or, should there be a common core? Here you address the critical issue of the content in the curriculum. Traditionally, schools and curriculum followed a standardized context in which to operate, manage, and use new standards and testing to set the scope of curriculum and particular core content. Quality assurance is delivered by regional accrediting agencies such as the Southern Association of Colleges and School, by state departments of education, and by testing programs. An issue that needs to be addressed is the relationship among standards, accreditation, and testing as factors in determining curriculum quality, which ensures that curriculum content provides what students need in becoming functional members of the society the curriculum serves. Assessment, for example, strives to establish some comparison of student knowledge, as determined by test results, with expectations of what they were supposed to master in school. Accreditation criteria seek to establish standards about such factors as class size, library-media facilities and holdings, staffing patterns, and support services. What relationships exist between the functions of assessment and accreditation? Experiencing an accreditation study makes you aware of the extensive preparation, money, and new resources necessary to bring things like library holdings up to standards, and the time that has to be dedicated to it by teachers, principals, and other district staff. What is not known, for example, is about accreditation-assessment relationships that might exist to suggest what effects on student learning or assessment might be associated with accreditation work. If, for example, it could be shown that accreditation enhances the organizational qualities of schooling, and how that supports curriculum, perhaps resulting in improvement of assessment scores, then there would be a defined set of factors to address in developing a continuous school and curriculum improvement process. You may wonder why little has been discussed about those relational issues. The answer in part is that the organizations associated with each particular endeavor have different memberships and purposes. There is also the possibility that particular research, accreditation, and governmental units have concerns about losing or sharing the role they perform in the schooling process. Curriculum work occurs at a variety of levels—local, state, and national—and sectors—such as private, business-commercial, and governmental. At the most fundamental level of schooling, the classroom, current reforms associated with the

NCLB Act of 2001 require teachers to have expertise in the subjects or areas in which they teach. Subject matter teaching is associated with teachers of history, mathematics, science, and so forth in middle and high school, those who teach knowledge in curriculum. Teachers in elementary schools teach in an area, a composite of knowledge including reading, language arts, arithmetic, social studies, and science. Depending on particular state requirements, elementary teachers may also be required to have a concentration or subject expertise that is part of the curriculum, in addition to elementary area requirements for teaching at that level. This would usually mean expertise in a knowledge area such as general science, social studies (history and social sciences), mathematics, or designated special skill areas such as reading or English as a second language (ESL). This is not to confuse content-skill teaching specifications and qualifications for regular curriculum assignments with those that may be required for special education teachers. Issues about curriculum expertise, teaching assignments, and the roles of other curriculum workers under laws like the NCLB will be contentious because they are entwined with the control issues discussed earlier. For example, is it the role of government or a professional organization to establish criteria for expertise and teaching competence? Currently, each state sets its own certification standards, and its programs are enhanced if accredited by the National Council on Accreditation in Teacher Education. To what degree should federal requirements trump the traditional authority and responsibilities of each state for certification in content areas of the curriculum? Whereas federal control might benefit standardizing certification and reciprocity, what are the trade-offs? And, if critics of NCLB are correct about unfounded mandates, what will states and local school districts do to comply with federal curriculum content requirements for teachers when the Congress in Washington fails to provide funds to bridge between a currently employed teacher's current expertise and what will need to be acquired in college courses or approved alternatives to meet the new requirements?

Debating School Reform

No reform movements are exactly the same; they vary in the reasons or events that compel them into being, the actions that constitute them, and their results. In their studies, such diverse chroniclers of public school reform as academic scholars and historians David Tyack (1995), Larry Cuban (1995, 1999), Diane Ravitch (1995), and M. R. Berube (1994) offer interesting perspectives on school reforms and what they did or did not achieve. What seems clear from their studies is that the various participants and observers in a reform movement have different views of it. There are the perspectives of parents and other citizens, professionals who work in the area of reform or are the subject of its focus, politicians, and academics who may be called on for their expertise and knowledge about something relevant to the reform. Within the various reform

Figure 13.4   Current Debates About Reform

The Pros	The Cons
Since the Revolution, renewal and consensus building through the political process have been a mark of American reform movements and are a sign of a vibrant democracy.	Reform movements are purely political and special interest driven. The discussions are rarely cool and detached or searches for best knowledge or practices based on evidence.
Public input for institutional change is usually participatory, sometimes coerced, rarely mandated, and seeks to create broad stakeholder equity in the reform process.	Reforms are agenda driven and often ideological. In either case, they can be coerced through slanted information, money or fund distribution, and influence peddling.
Reform fosters experimentation, innovation, and inclusion by encouraging citizen and group participation.	The envisioned reforms never are what results at the end; they are usually disjointed, complicated, and inefficient, often ending up as the dominion of special interests.

constituencies, there may be differing perspectives for and against some proposal, idea, action, or activity. Studies of reform movements suggest that those discussions share common patterns whatever the issues or whenever the movement occurred, and the pro- and antireform arguments summarized in Figure 13.4 are an interpretation based on the studies by the authors cited previously.

Remember that the commonalities are about the reform movements themselves, not the particular elements in a set of reform proposals. Reforms prior to the NCLB Act of 2001 were instigated by reports. *A Nation at Risk,* for example, influenced policy development rather than establishing it. Unlike previous reforms, the NCLB is both a law and a reform policy that seeds further policy development. In that sense, it represents a significant turn in the federal government's role in American schooling.

THEME: ACCOUNTABILITY IN SCHOOLING AND CURRICULUM

Today, discussions of school reform seem to center on ideas about accountability. Recall from earlier discussions in Chapters 7 and 12 that the calls for accountability that emerged in the contemporary reform movement were catalysts prompting the development of assessment-evaluation as a discipline and as a process critical to successful school reform. Accountability has taken on a life of its own apart from reform and may be the lasting feature when current reform work runs its course.

Curriculum Accountability

Accountability can be summed up in several ways. It is often depicted in a general sense as the linking of purposes to expectations through the evaluation of student performance as measured by tests. Accountability is also differentiated according to particular administrative, instructional, curricular, and professional functions in schooling. A principal is accountable for school performance and taking student achievement to the next level. The teacher is accountable for teaching a required curriculum. In those applications, accountability is a complex and multifaceted process that is continuous, repetitive, diagnostic, remedial, formative, summative, systemic, and systematic. These characteristics, as explained in Figure 13.5, are each issues in themselves and collectively suggest what curriculum accountability entails as an issue. Specifically applied to curriculum, those characteristics of accountability treat curriculum as a regenerative, self-correcting, systematic, and systemic process. As a consequence, accountability in any form (test scores, etc.) is ensured. That is, the issues are not limited to defining or determining accountability. Rather, they extend beyond into considering what a profile of curriculum accountability might be like—its shape, the elements that would constitute its structure, and the activities that would define accountability in curriculum work.

An Accountability Example

Curriculum accountability is not easily addressed because it is still unraveling conceptually as a bundle of issues. An example may be instructive. The profiled characteristics of continuity and repetition can be found in current curriculum assessment work. One example is the National Assessment of Educational Progress (NAEP), which has operated continuously for more than 30 years. Although not universally used in the United States as a source of accounting for curriculum, it is a model of *continuity* and *repetition* in that learning is tested in a scheduled way at designed intervals and at specific grades. The NAEP data can be used *diagnostically* to identify problems or successes that reflect on the curriculum indirectly through assessment of learning. Whether *remediation* occurs is another matter, because that is a function of the state or district or schooling unit to decide if they will use the data for curriculum analysis, to identify problems in the curriculum.

NAEP assessment results can suggest but cannot compel further curriculum analysis. The NAEP is not a required assessment, nor is it linked to the 50 different sets of state standards and curriculums. Also, the NAEP is not designed for daily or immediate feedback to the classroom, which would represent its *formative* use. It certainly can serve as a *summative* example in accountability, however. Whereas the NAEP is itself *systemic* and *systematic,* its deployment in curriculum accountability is not. Because the NAEP is not used for formative or remedial accountability, it is not systemic, even though the NAEP is administered systematically in continuous and repetitive

Figure 13.5   Profiling Accountability Functions in Curriculum

Continuous: Curriculum accountability means real-time, full-time operation of assessment in many forms with continuous data collection and entry. The operational ideal of curriculum-on-demand to the classroom is dependant on reporting, messaging, and delivering continuity. Curriculum work should not lie fallow during vacations or other down times; these are periods for analysis of data for real-time return to curriculum workers.	**Repetitive:** Key tasks in curriculum formulation and delivery, such as writing lesson plans and annotating the actual implementation of the lesson, mark a critical point in accountability between intent and reality. These are critical reporting points in a continuous process.
Diagnostic: To have accountability, actual performance of people in the process is important. Student performance assessment, such as tests, is one useful diagnostic tool. Others might include analysis of taught lesson documentation using particular rubrics allowing comparison with student performance data.	**Remedial:** A continuous, repetitive, diagnostic process provides accountability by identifying problems, anomalies in expectations-results, and possible fixes—for example, identifying student performance differences within one or across several classrooms in a single school and grade.
Formative: First-level accountability, the classroom or closest one-on-one curriculum-learning situation, is timely and important because in the flow of the accountability process, curriculum is most susceptible to correction or enhancement to influence final performance values.	**Summative:** Curriculum accountability is at present reflected in the end values attributed to student performance by using tests as the primary assessments. End results are a first step; the real need is for formative and intermediate assessments.
Systemic: This concept refers to the whole of a thing, the human body, for example. Systemic curriculum encompasses thinking about the whole of curriculum fundamentals, the scope, sequence, continuity, and balance. This may also be applied for a particular kind of curriculum, such as the science curriculum or the middle school curriculum. Curriculum accountability in the systemic sense is formative, summative, diagnostic, and all the other elements.	**Systematic:** Something that is systematic is characterized as being a series of regulated and orderly actions or activities. One example of curriculum accountability is to consider the degree of continuity in the curriculum scope and sequence. All the qualities of accountability, its diagnostic, continuous character, for example, give it a systematic quality.

assessment. As the NAEP example suggests, although curriculum accountability is an issue in itself, it is made so by the specific characteristics that shape it.

NCLB and Accountability

The latest chapter in accountability is the NCLB Act of 2001 and what it entails. This federal legislation is one of a series of acts since the landmark mid-60s Elementary and

Figure 13.6   A Summary of the NCLB Act of 2001

Standards and Assessments

- Establish reading standards
- Establish mathematics standards
- Implement annual assessment in reading and language arts
- Implement annual assessment in mathematics

Teaching and the Teacher

- Define a highly qualified teacher
- Establish indicators for subject-matter competence
- Develop tests for new elementary teachers
- Ensure highly qualified teachers are in every classroom
- Ensure high-quality professional development
- Use teaching tools based on scientific research

Secondary Assistance Act that has expanded federal involvement in American schooling. The effects of the NCLB are pervasive and, as noted earlier in this chapter and in various others, are entwined in most aspects of schooling, curriculum, and instruction. The many provisions of the act fall essentially into two main groups: those about creating standards and designing assessments, and those addressing teacher qualifications and teaching. These provisions are summarized in Figure 13.6.

The NCLB requirements are for the states and public schooling. Note the specific references to curriculum in mathematics, reading, and language arts. Along with science, those content areas of the curriculum have become the focus because the testing that is to be done emphasizes student performance in those areas. This raises potential curriculum issues about the purposes, scope, and balance in curriculum. As with any new law, implementation brings scrutiny, especially when the requirements "mandate" adherence to time lines into 2006 and beyond. Of course, as with any new law as significant as NCLB, controversies will arise as experiences with the law provide anecdotal evidence of its relevance in establishing accountability and renewal in public schooling. These controversies engage political partisans, academic and school experts, teachers, and assorted organizations and interest groups. Their opinions, however, are not based on any hard evidence external to the law or based on ongoing research under the law. The contentions are too numerous to mention and deserve your fresh exploration in emerging literature. What can be discerned seems to be a series of discussion points about the following:

1. The costs of implementation for the states, the adequacy of federal funding, and whether funds for testing are taking funds from other resources needed for schools.

2. Lack of accountability and standardization of standards across the states.

3. Balance in the curriculum for all students and subject areas, and the promotion of mathematics, science, reading, and language arts over other curriculum areas.

4. The meaning of scientific research and what exactly is educational practice guided by good, rigorous science.

5. Requirements for high-quality teachers and placement in subject-matter assignments—how and by whom requirements and placement are determined and how standardization in preparation across 50 different state requirements can be achieved.

6. The intent of the law and the appropriate federal role—that the law is too complex, and that the time lines for implementation and results are unreasonable.

The NCLB law is a lightning rod for conflicts about the federal and individual state roles in society. Present and future discussions about it raise very important questions about the American federal system, the separation and distribution of constitutional power and institutions, and the nature of civic culture in American society.

THEME: EFFECTS OF SOCIAL CHANGES ON SCHOOLING AND CURRICULUM

As a society changes, so do its institutional needs. America in the 20th century shifted from an agrarian society to an industrial one in urban settings connected by an extensive railroad network. Today, that centralizing of economic production and population has changed to decentralization in a continuous suburbia linked by highways, television, and the Internet. Older, traditional kinds of government units and governmental functions—the township, the village, the sheriff and constable—seem quaint and superfluous, bordering on the obsolete. The one-room rural school seems an agrarian myth, save for a school calendar dedicated to the Arcadian rhythms of the farm, which still hold sway over schooling. However, these general observations tend to obscure the complexity of changes that affect a society and its institutions at any given time. Of particular interest are those that affect schooling, as well as the teaching profession itself, such as technology in schooling and society, diversity in the population, and the implications of technology and diversity for schooling and curriculum.

Social and Cultural Diversity

Since the civil rights movement of the 1960s and 1970s, the struggle in the United States has been to balance understanding and appreciation of social and cultural diversity. The depiction of the partisan divide in the election of 2004—red Democratic states essentially covering the east and west coasts and blue Republican states covering the area between—is a simplistic but memorable portrait of national political divisions that does not reflect the reality of social, cultural, or economic demographics, which do not follow static state political boundaries. Migrations of American citizens from one place to another militate against generalizing about social and cultural change but do contain the seeds of future political actions. For example, the migration of non-English-speaking families to a new community can require a district or a single school to implement an English as a second language (ESL) program where none previously was needed. The presence of new minorities in local settings can trigger reactions much like the so-called white flight from city centers to the suburbs after desegregation. This is a common pattern that is very American and that followed the immigration of the Irish, Italians, and other Europeans into America's urban centers. Immigrants to the U.S. have encountered difficulties, especially non-European and nonwhite immigrants, particularly in the face of American nativism, which in any historical period tends to raise a specter of social contamination or the infiltration of dangerous foreign religious and political ideas (Higham, 1988).

Immigrants include children who have to be accommodated in schools. As noted earlier, there are usually language difficulties, and expectations that immigrant children can easily command English are usually false. In addition to language barriers, there are cultural customs that signal differences. For example, how a student addresses or approaches a teacher or another child, the matter of culturally cued use of personal space, and the wearing of different kinds of clothing often prompt prejudicial responses, either verbal or behavioral. It is important to remember that it is the public schools, not private, parochial, or other kinds of schools, that enroll approximately 90% of the eligible students in American schooling. Schools, particularly public schools, are the institutions that Americanize, and it is the curriculum that is the author of that process. At the same time, curriculum content has become more varied to reflect student diversity. Diversity is more often a subtle than overt influence, particularly when students make pizza, German cookies, or the like and then go to lunch in the cafeteria, which may be serving anything from southern fried chicken, hot dogs, chili, or tacos, to boc choi in the fresh salad. Also an influence is what a school does not acknowledge, such as a holiday or special event that is ethnically and culturally based. All those examples connect to curriculum and the social-cultural diversity of any school anywhere.

Technological Relevance

Technological change—computers, the Internet, cell phones, other forms of standardized Wi-Fi interconnect ability—contribute to social change and change in curriculum and schooling. These forms of technology create new ways of thinking about learning. Psychological space—that of the mind and thought—and the social and cultural dimensions of personal space are changed through technology challenging the traditional relevance of educational institutions. The observation is often made that schools and schooling follow a manufacturing and industrial model of work and learning that is obsolete (Illich, 1972; Kohn, 1999). Schools are thought of as buildings in which students learn in assembly-line fashion with the goal of attending college, regardless of student interests or needs relevant to working and living (Branson, 1988). However, technologies like the cell phone and the computer free up time, space, and personal resources because learning can be done on the fly and in multiple locations other than the traditional school. The success of distance learning, the increase in home schooling and other nontraditional settings that rely on the Internet, and access to commercial learning resources that are self-instructional—all these ways of repackaging schooling are available. The dilemma is techno-social, how to understand how the technology, the cell phone, for example, rearranges and constructs new social patterns among school-age children and adults (Jackson, Poole, & Kuhn, 2002). There are at least three considerations to the technology—student, curriculum, and school mix—and matters of relevance connect them all. School relevance is partly about how the school incorporates the external socializing and acculturating aspects of life as expressed in the mediated world in which students live. What is permissible about tattoos, other adornments, the use of cell phones, or the newest form of self-entertainment that can be hidden from the teacher in the classroom? To older people, especially those who dress in banker or lawyer blues and blacks, students may appear scruffy, whereas what they are reflecting is the dress and manners of their times created and interpreted through films, videos, TV, and the Internet. A second aspect of relevance is connecting students with curriculum, particularly the seemingly arcane subjects like literature when the words and tempos of rap and hip-hop are forms of prose and poetry themselves. Note that it is not a question of relevance as to the kind of form, as in reading a text, but as to the multilayered transmission that a technology makes instantaneous and simultaneous at the expense of other things and that most technology in schools can't come close to emulating. A third aspect of relevance has to do with the mobile nature of learning that personalized technology makes possible, the ability to get a lesson or assignments directly from the Internet site of a teacher, for example. That mobility brings into question the fixed nature of school-site learning and its relevance, at least for schooling of young adults. Is it really necessary for a high school class to meet for 60–90 minutes a day 5 days a week? Technological relevance is still an emerging issue, both as to the forms and how it is used to extend both the person and the capacity to learn. That latter aspect may be the most important one, how to effect learning and acquire ways to build the capacity for judgment that will allow students to control learning through technology rather than be controlled by it.

Social Institutions and Ideologies

Societies throughout the world birth a variety of ideologies and belief systems. Big ideas, like Hinduism, Christianity, Islam, democracy, and totalitarianism, have a broader, sustaining historical sweep and significance. During the 19th and 20th centuries, Marxism, communism, fascism, Nazism, and militarism were ideologies with far-reaching influences on national and international affairs. The Western-bred ideology of democracy has prevailed. Ideology, which includes, for example, conservative, progressive, and liberal, refers to any set of beliefs that characterizes the thinking of a group or nation (Ball & Dagger, 2004). Ideologies, as McClay (2000) suggests, are usually expressed in a series of statements or a creed about the way things should be and the social purposes that should be served.

Ideologies, whether viewed favorably or unfavorably, have had profound impacts on schooling and curriculum. Schools in any society exist to teach a curriculum to the young children and adults entering that society. That curriculum invariably represents an ideological agenda. In the United States, the American curriculum espouses democratic beliefs and values and strives to enact constitutional injunctions such as due process and the separation of church and state. At the same time, liberal or conservative ideological agendas modify schooling and the curriculum through educational policies (Apple, 1993). One of the concerns in democracy is the preservation of diversity in thinking. In curriculum work, discussion of competing ideologies, especially those that claim some religious purpose, are important to understand and monitor. Teachers and other curriculum workers need to be ideologically neutral in what they advocate but at the same time need to help learners think for themselves, to be solid inquirers. In America, the contemporary curriculum confrontation of Darwinian evolution and Christian creationism or intelligent design as theories in science courses is an issue that pits the secular and religious against one another. Compounding the issue is the interpretive problem of clearly stating what the Constitution's 1st Amendment in the Bill of Rights actually means by prohibiting the federal government and the states (through the 14th Amendment) from "establishing" a religion. These are ideological issues that can involve and trap teachers when the curriculum becomes the battleground.

Democracy accepts the rule of law—a constitution as established by the people, for example—as a basic tenet. It is this framework in which issues about evolution and intelligent design are hashed out. The discussions are about personal and public interests to serve society, which reflect choices about what knowledge is worthy of inclusion in the curriculum, what the sources of that knowledge are, and which knowledge is true. In any society, both religious and secular ideologies are used to support the dominant religion and culture, the government or elites in power, and prevalent social norms (the status quo). At the same time, ideologies underlie social change through calls for moral, social, or political reform. This historically complex interplay of ideology and society is reflected in the structure and content of schooling and curriculum and raises certain perennial questions. How should issues about ideologies be discussed in the school curriculum? How does the ongoing curriculum war over inclusion of theories about evolution and intelligent design reflect issues about truth, knowledge, and what knowledge is of most worth? Curriculum is always at the center of controversy, and how those kinds of curriculum questions are answered will dictate how the curriculum is configured and what learners will know. It is an awesome responsibility for teachers and curriculum workers, who turn on the beliefs, the ideologies, that define and justify society.

PERSPECTIVE INTO PRACTICE: **How Selected Issues Might Affect Elementary and Secondary Schooling**		
Themes and Examples	*Elementary Education*	*Secondary Education*
Control Issues: The extension of public services to nonpublic settings	Second-grade students in a private and a parochial school need specialized reading classes available only in public elementary schools. Two options are offered: (a) The public district will provide the class space and buses if the two schools will pay two thirds of the teacher salary or (b) the reading specialist will go to the two schools, which will provide space and materials, and the public school district will assume salary costs. Should services follow the child, and who should assume the costs?	Biology classes at Potts High can accept college prep students from Mission Christian High, which doesn't have a biology teacher. The Mission school offers to pay a fee to cover teacher time, materials, and busing, but wants intelligent design offered as a theory. Should discussion of the words *science, evolution,* or *intelligent design* and theory in the biology curriculum be avoided? What should the teacher who is trained in biological sciences decide?
Reform Issues: Teacher qualifications under the No Child Left Behind Act	Ms. Smith has an elementary school certification in reading and a regular elementary teaching assignment. Mrs. Johnson has elementary certification and is also assigned to an elementary classroom. The State Department of Education has interpreted expertise under the NCLB	Mr. Ellis has a secondary teaching certification in general science and can teach those courses at the middle school level. A vacancy has occurred in the high school's science department for a physics teacher. The district would like to move him to the high school vacancy, but the NCLB law stipulates

(Continued)

(Continued)

	law to be by certification. Is a reading certification an elementary certification? Consider the dilemma the school district has in figuring out what to do with Ms. Smith's assignment/certification.	expertise in the field of teaching. He has only two courses in physics on his transcript; the state requires a major (24 hours course work) in physics. Is this discriminatory? What flexibility should be allowed? What governmental unit should set criteria?
Accountability Issues: Tests as the measure in accountability	The state publishes all the state exam scores for the fourth grade for all five elementary schools in your city. The scores of two schools are below state mandates. Public concern is aroused, with extensive discussion at the school board meeting and in the newspapers. Some parents decide to move their children to local private and parochial schools. A newspaper article points out that those schools don't participate in any assessment programs, so there is no comparative data. Should all kinds of schools, whether public, private, parochial, or some other form, be required to participate in such testing? Should parents care?	Scores on state tests in 11th-grade mathematics for all five classes at Melvin High are very high. The class sections are taught by two separate teachers and are divided three sections to two. The students of the teacher with three sections all rank first through third, while the other teacher's sections rank fourth and fifth. The information appears in the local newspaper, and parents with students in the fourth- and fifth-ranked sections question the teacher's competence, even though all the scores are higher than most scores in the state. Mathematics is a diploma requirement and important for college entrance, so a number of factors are at play in the motives of concerned parents. Is a one-time test a fair indicator? Should the teacher of lower-ranking students be singled out? What does accountability mean in this context?
Social Change Issues: Immigration, local customs, history, and schooling	Twelve families from Indonesia have recently immigrated to your town, and the children are enrolled at the local neighborhood elementary school. The students are well behaved, learning English very rapidly, studious, and in general	The American history class is studying the Second World War and reading first-person accounts of people who fought in the Pacific theater. One account relates the horrors of enemy concentration camps for noncombatants and captured

	mixing well with the local children. The parents of the immigrant children object to the school dress code for religious reasons, especially the ban on headscarves for females and caps for the males, required dress for traditional Muslims. The study of peoples and cultures in the curriculum might educate the school and community to accept differences in custom and religion, which are democratic ideals. Should the dress code be set aside or modified for religious or other reasons of conscience or cultural identity? Or should the democratic ideals of consensus and compromise be enforced?	Allied fighters. One student raises the issue of forced internment camps for many Japanese Americans, and some German Americans and Italian Americans in the United States during wartime and the seeming contradiction those events raise in justifying the war as a fight to save democracy. This is an issue both about forthrightness in studying history, and about the way curriculum content is presented. The study of WW II usually is mandated. Should unpleasant events and episodes that contradict the assertions of American democratic ideology be emphasized or ignored? How should teachers treat events that appear to expose hypocrisies?

Summary and Conclusions

Issues affecting institutions in a society have important impacts that change as issues change. Interpreting those issues, culling among opinions and data cited as pertinent, is an important challenge. Issues generating public debate are often heated and polarized. Proposals for constitutional changes, for example, are often perceived as either political tinkering or solid fixing for the good of society—take your pick. Issues result in proposals for changes in school organization, the curriculum, or other aspects of schooling. Contemporary issues, such as charter and for-profit schools or curriculum accommodation for science and intelligent design theory, attest to strong differences. Polemical differences may arise over issues of control, reform, accountability, social and technological change, and ideological debates. Truth and evidence often seem the casualties in such discussions, but most issues are too complex and interlaced with others to resolve on that basis.

Critical Perspective

Theme: Control of Schooling and Curriculum

1. Suggested qualities of administrative leadership seem to imply that a principal can be a leader as an administrator, a curriculum expert, and an instructional expert. Do you think it is possible for a principal to be an expert in all three areas? Would it be equally or more possible at the elementary, middle, or high school level? What other contingencies might apply to leadership?

2. Administratively, as an elementary school principle, how would you address the task of implementing a comprehensive reading program reform? If you were a teacher, what questions would you have for your principal about such a proposed reform?

Theme: Schooling and Curriculum Reform

3. Administrative reform literature seems to suggest that the critical role in school reform is the school principal. Do you agree with that? What other roles might be critical to reform efforts? Why are those roles critical?

4. Select an issue of an educational periodical such as *Education Week*. On a piece of paper, make four columns, one each for administrative, curriculum, instructional, and other. Identify articles that seem to fit in each category. Indicate those that are specifically about reform, those that relate to reform, and opinion pieces about reform. What difficulties did you have in categorizing? What picture emerges from your efforts? What observations about reform efforts can you make?

Theme: Accountability in Schooling and Curriculum

5. Accountability as a general concept in education or schooling is still developing as a public idea. Based on an Internet search, identify and read resources about accountability in education. What types of accountability are discussed? Develop an annotated list of URLs to guide online study of this topic and share this resource with classmates or colleagues.

6. Review the eight functional characteristics of accountability presented in this chapter (continuous, repetitive, diagnostic, remedial, formative, summative, systemic, and systematic). Are there other characteristics that might be added?

Should any be deleted? What alternatives can you find for framing discussions of accountability, either generally or with particular application to schooling functions such as curriculum?

Theme: Effects of Social Changes on Schooling and Curriculum

7. In a democracy, should the curriculum be the same or common for all citizens regardless of location or differences? What are the arguments for or against a common curriculum? To what degree should cultural differences be reflected in the curriculum?

8. To what degree should curriculum accommodate the religious, social, or cultural beliefs of parents, guardians, organizations, or communities?

9. Define ideology and identify three ideologies by name that you think have had the most significant impact on curriculum and schooling issues during the past decade. What are some concrete examples of those impacts?

10. What ideological concepts do you think will have the greatest impacts on education in the 21st century, and why?

Resources for Curriculum Study

Education Week (http://www.edweek.org) is an excellent newspaper of record for issues related to schools, schooling, and curriculum. Local papers and education pages of national papers also will have relevant discussions. The American Educational Research Association, Phi Delta Kappa, International Reading Association, National Society for the Study of Education, and Association for Supervision and Curriculum Development are some organizations that provide resources on various schooling and curriculum issues and can be found online.

Theme: Control of Schooling and Curriculum

1. Understanding the political nature of control, the stakes, and the forces at play is important. As a professional, it is necessary to read across the literature and to understand partisan views and try to model appropriate habits of inquiry. Sources relevant to the politics and positions staked out are Joel Spring's *Conflict of Interest: The Politics of American Education* (4th ed., 2001) and Richard Elmore's *Redesigning Accountability Systems for Education* (2003).

Theme: Schooling and Curriculum Reform

2. Frederick M. Hess provides some interesting insights into school reform issues in *Commonsense School Reform* (2004). For insights into curriculum reform and other sources, S. T. Hopmann's article (2003) "On the Evaluation of Curriculum Reforms," *Journal of Curriculum Studies, 35*(4), 459–478, is useful.

3. A good resource for debates about reform is David Tyack and Larry Cuban's *Tinkering Toward Utopia* (1995). For curriculum reform in particular areas, mathematics and science, for example, try the Web sites of organizations such as the Association for Supervision and Curriculum Development (http://www .ascd.org) or the National Council of Teachers of Mathematics (http://www .nctm.org).

Theme: Accountability in Schooling and Curriculum

4. Accountability is a broad topic and includes school, teacher, and curriculum accountability. Education researcher E. R. Hanushek has written widely on economic aspects of accountability (see http://edpro.stanford.edu/hanushek/ content.asp?ContentId=61). Hanushek also edited a two-volume work, *The Economics of Schooling and School Quality* (2003).

5. The National Conference of State Legislatures' Web site (http://www.ncsl.org) can refer you to a trove of resources about various aspects of accountability. For a more academic treatment of accountability and the responsibilities and expectations it raises, see R. L. Linn's article (2003) "Accountability: Responsibility and Reasonable Expectations," in *Educational Researcher* [*32*(7), 3–13].

6. To find out about the No Child Left Behind (NCLB) Act, go to http://www .ed.gov/nclb at the U.S. Department of Education Web site. In addition, most state Web sites refer to their work and progress on the NCLB. Organizational sites such as those of the Council of Chief State School Officers (http://www .ccsso.org) and Mid-continent Research for Education and Learning (http://www .mcrel.org) are useful as well.

Theme: Effects of Social Change on Schooling and Curriculum

7. Appreciating wireless fidelity, or Wi-Fi, is important in light of the number of cell phones and computer interconnections that are being built into schools and classrooms. Technology frees up curriculum accessibility and options and allows students to function as self-instructional resources. For definitions and explanations of terms, see Webopedia at http://www.webopedia.com

8. Social change and shifting perspectives about schooling ultimately affect civic culture and the sense of America's national image. Among the many historical works available is Daniel Boorstin's *The Americans: The Democratic Experience* (Vintage, 1973) and Lawrence Cremin's *The Transformation of the School: Progressivism in American Education 1876–1976* (1961) and *Popular Education and Its Discontents* (1991). The American public has always accepted schooling and schools as the way to individual and national progress. The development and fusion of the idea of progress with society in America is chronicled in sociologist Robert Nisbet's *History of the Idea of Progress* (1980).

References

Apple, M. W. (1991). Conservative agendas and progressive possibilities: Understanding the wider politics of curriculum and teaching. *Education and Urban Society, 23*(3), 279–291.

Apple, M. W. (1993). *Official knowledge: Democratic education in a conservative age.* New York: Routledge.

Ball T., & Dagger, R. (2004). *Political ideologies and the democratic ideal.* New York: Longman.

Bennett, W. J. (1993). *The book of virtues.* New York: Simon & Schuster.

Berliner, D. C. (2002). Educational research: The hardest science of all. *Educational Researcher, 31*(8), 18–20.

Berube, M. R. (1994). *American school reform: Progressive, equity, and excellence movements, 1883–1983.* Westport, CT: Praeger.

Boorstin, D. (1973). *The Americans: The democratic experience.* New York: Random House.

Branson, R. K. (1988). Why the schools cannot improve: The upper limits hypothesis. *Journal of Instructional Development, 10*(4), 15–26.

Covey, S. R. (2004). *The eighth habit.* New York: Free Press.

Cuban, L. (1995). Forward. In D. Tanner & L. N. Tanner (Eds), *Curriculum development: Theory into practice* (3rd ed.). Upper Saddle River, NJ: Simon & Schuster.

Cuban, L. (1999). *How scholars trumped teachers.* New York: Teachers College Press.

Degler, C. N. (1959). *Out of our past.* New York: Harper & Row.

Eisenhart, M., & Towne, L. (2003). Contestation and change in national policy on "scientifically based" education research. *Educational Researcher, 32*(7), 31–38.

Fullan, M. (2001a). *Leadership in a culture of change.* San Francisco, CA: Jossey-Bass.

Fullan, M. (2001b). *The new meaning of educational leadership* (3rd ed.). New York: Teachers College Press.

Gates, H. L., Jr. (1995). *Loose cannon: Notes on the culture wars.* New York: Oxford University Press.

Glanz, J. (2002). *Finding your leadership style.* Arlington, VA: Association for Supervision and Curriculum Development.

Higham, J. (1988). *Strangers in the land* (2nd ed.). New Brunswick, NJ: Rutgers University Press.

Hirsch, E. D., Jr. (1996). *The schools we need.* New York: Anchor/Random House.

Hunter, J. D. (1991). *Culture wars.* New York: Basic Books.

Illich, I. (1972). *Deschooling society.* New York: Harper & Row, Harrow Books.

Jackson, M. H., Poole, M. S., & Kuhn, T. (2002). The social construction of technology in studies of the work place. In L. A. Lievrouw & S. Livingstone (Eds.), *The handbook of new media.* London: Sage.

Kohn, A. (1999). *The schools our children deserve.* New York: Houghton Mifflin.

Lasch, C. (1979). *The culture of narcissism.* New York: Norton.

Lieberman, A., & Miller, L. (2004). *Teacher leadership.* San Francisco, CA: Jossey-Bass / Wiley.

Mayer, R. E. (2000). What is the place of science in educational research? *Educational Researcher, 29*(6), 38–39.

Mayer, R. E. (2001). Resisting the assault on science: The case for evidence-based reasoning in educational research. *Educational Researcher, 30*(7), 29–30.

McClay, W. M. (2000). Two concepts of secularism. *Wilson Quarterly, 24*(3), 54–71.

Olson, D. R. (2004). The triumph of hope over experience in the search for "what works": A response to Slavin. *Educational Researcher, 33*(1), 24–26.

Parker, K. (1999). The impact of the textbook on girls' perception of mathematics. *Mathematics in School, 28*(4), 2–4.

Ravitch, D. (1995). *National standards in American education: A citizens guide.* Washington, DC: Brookings Institute.

Ravitch, D. (2000). *Left behind: A century of battles on school reform.* New York: Touchstone/ Simon & Schuster.

Sanders, J., & Petersen, K. (1999). Close the gap for girls in math related careers. *The Education Digest, 65*(4), 47–49.

Shepard, L. A. (2004). Curricular coherence in assessment design. In M. Wilson (Ed.), *Towards coherence between classroom assessment and accountability* (103rd Yearbook of the National Society for the Study of Education. Part II, pp. 239–249). Chicago: National Society for the Study of Education.

Spring, J. (1986). *The American school 1642–1985.* New York: McGraw-Hill.

Standholtz, J., Ogawa, R. T., & Scribner, S. P. (2004). Standards gaps: Unintended consequences of local standards-based reform. *Teachers College Record, 106*(6), 1177–1202.

Stein, M. K., & Nelson, B. S. (2003). Leadership content knowledge. *Educational Evaluation and Policy Analysis, 25*(4), 423–448.

Tyack, D. B., & Cuban L. (1995). *Tinkering toward Utopia.* Cambridge, MA: Harvard University Press.

Chapter 14

INTERPRETING TRENDS
IN CURRICULUM

It has been said that the more things change, the more they stay the same. That might be true as far as the living of a human life cycle is concerned, but the context and thinking during a life change. Ideas, inventions, technology, and new institutional forms alter the pace of life, how you live, and ultimately how you think as an individual and socially as collectively bound in the geopolitical sense of countries, states, and the world. You think about what will be or what is to come, projecting ideas and scenes that are futuristic. Jules Verne captured that tendency so well in his books about undersea adventures and going to the moon. Marshall McLuhan did it for technology and information; the Internet is doing it for everything else. Futurists, people who try to project what things will be like tomorrow, build future scenarios based on current trends and project their impact. In 1972, one futurist society, the Club of Rome, published *The Limits of Growth* (by Meadows, Meadows, Randers, & Behrens), a book that forecast the limitations of the earth's resources to support a rising population and made suggestions for resource consumption and other proposals to solve the problem. Similar books about the future, particularly those like *The Third Wave* by Alvin Toffler (1980), are widely read, quoted, and become part of public speculations about current trends and what they will lead to in the future.

WHAT IS A TREND?

Think of a *trend* as a prevailing inclination about some thing that persists in the long term. Demographers, for example, look for signals in population data. In the 1930s, they noted an out-migration of African Americans from the south to northern cities, where opportunities were greater. In the 1990s, demographers observed the start of a reverse in-migration back to southern roots. Trends are not fads. Current concerns about public obesity have led to a low-carbohydrate food emphasis. This phenomenon may prove to be nothing more than a passing social bubble, or it might be the first indicator of a major health style change affecting the American diet with untold implications for the American food industry. Such tendencies, migrations, dieting, and the like, will probably be affecting society for some time to come, and we can only glean some sense of what they will be like as they mature. Keep in mind in this discussion that the indicators, the conditions noted, facts cited, and ideas proposed, that suggest a trend may or may not prove out in the long term.

TREND: TECHNOLOGY AND RETICULATION

In 1829, the American James Bigelow, in his book *The Elements of Technology,* introduced the world to the concept of technology. Today that term is used universally without a need for explanation, implying everything from cell phones to the latest scientific frontiers of nanotechnology and synthetic materials for the skin of jet liners and the clothes you wear. It is the accrued meanings a word subsumes and the wealth of applications that give it importance. An old word but newer in use is *reticulation,* which means networking. When applied to such things as social patterns, economic distributions, government, schools and institutions, or linkages among those elements, it means the networking of networks. Why is reticulation an up-and-coming trend? Reticules (another word for networks) and reticulation, the process of networking networks, is the new perspective that provides a way for humans to conceptualize arrangements in a postmodernist rather than modernist way. C. A. Bayly (2004), in developing the historical importance of communication and complexity, suggests that a modernist perspective would have you think of nations and states, atoms, and culture, whereas the postmodernist perspective wants you to think of people and social groups in places, not nations and states, with global not national law, interconnected through information and communication technologies (Lievrouw & Livingstone, 2002); matter arranged through genomes (Margulis & Sagon, 2002); string theory (Greene, 1999); and culture by memetics (Gladwell, 2000). Wrapped together, you have the confluence of contemporary ideas that make up complexity at any historical time.

Techno-Social Impulses

Technological and social developments are connected through communication but not in the surface way of referring to communication as using a cell phone, viewing television, or other media as conduits or pathways. The deeper importance in the linkages is functional, the sharing and transfer of information, the capability and capacity to pass knowledge as information across distances to others with the possible consequence that it will contribute to their knowledge and social use in that place and time (Wellman, 1999). Cole (1999) describes this as "net-centric," or the centering of all devices around the social and learning needs of the person, group, and community, schooling without boundaries. This presents the possibility or at least the idea of global learning, which can be small, as in local and extending out in a region, or worldwide. Consider the possibility of a worldwide curriculum of global knowledge, one that can be translated simultaneously in your personal computer or by cell phone. Evolving clicker technology used at the university level now allows for instant and impersonal communication in the classroom between students using a computer and the instructor via a screen. This allows even the most reticent individual, perhaps one not wanting to raise a hand and risk a thought in class, to participate. The social and personal importance of this in a community of learners or in work settings could be profound (Danielson, 2004). Other techno-social impulses seem obvious as part of the contemporary culture. The social use of cell phones is not just for voice but for pictures and connectivity to computers—all those applications seem to expand our personal self into space from any location.

Space-Time-Learning

The techno-social impulse is also an extension of our senses and capabilities. During the early Apollo space program, astronauts took TV cameras into space and looked back at earth, the big blue marble in space. For the first time, humans stood outside and looked back at earth and themselves—a tranposition and extension of all our human senses and thought. The curriculum in the physical sciences was made real by pictures and computer-generated information. That early techno-social experience has now been transferred to you in the everyday everywhere use of your cell phone, the Internet, and other tools to advance human interconnectedness. Harnessed to schooling, technology has also provided greater access to knowledge and thus to the curriculum. School libraries and media centers can hook into the Internet to access classroom materials and presentations, CDs and videos now provide authentic lab experiments, and programs from PBS such as NOVA and other commercial sources expand access to knowledge. The more interesting possibilities, however, are in the uses outside the school, each student his or her own inquirer with Internet links to libraries in Australia or the United Kingdom, the resources of the world online, perusing e-journals and paper journal sites and newspapers—learning at the fingertips. The social link is maintained through blogs, chat rooms, direct e-mail, and other sites. The problem with all that is helping students attain and use standards of inquiry, not just knowing how to access but to make judgments about authenticity of knowledge and information, validity of sources, the what and why questions, the responsibilities and consequences in the disciplined sense of scholarly inquiry, not just for scholars but for everyone—learning how to learn in new dimensions. Blogs or personal Web journals allow for personal expression and immediate transmittal of ideas and experiences, written or with pictures or artifacts attached. How do you judge the validity of a blog message or the pictures or other artifacts? The composite of blogs is, in an interesting way, its own curriculum, an informal transmission of writings and experience in multiple media that has no specified center, organization, or authority that empowers it. It is not like going to a school or knowing that a TV network is located in New York. The Internet experience and blogs in particular can seem almost ethereal, otherworldly, detached, yet the medium and messages and what you understand about them are compelling because you can manipulate and personalize it all. The time-space-learning relationship suggests that one important trend will be the working out of the relationships between the place-bound school curriculum of the state, the personal curriculum of the learner through technology (Internet, etc.), and the shared curriculum of the global community.

Implications

Technological change is bringing interconnectivity to all aspects of work and life. It improves schooling by democratizing learning, making it available and accessible to more students, schools, and workers. It is also changing the way to think of knowledge and information, as unbounded rather than bounded by buildings and places, through reticulation, which is the new dimension of building social networks and, as some research suggests, is changing the form and dynamics of social relationships, personal empowerment, and how work is configured as a participatory involvement. Reticulation is also about knowledge networks, the networking of those knowledge networks and their relationships to and in curriculum.

TREND: SHIFTING IDEOLOGIES AND CHANGE

Historian David Tyack, in his classic study of American society and schooling institutions, *The One Best System* (1974), suggests that schools and schooling are central to the development of two important American traditions, the idea of the level playing field and the idea of local control. The first, the level playing field, refers to the establishment of opportunities to access the personal and social capital of a society through the use of universal schooling as a delivery system. The second, local control, is the matter of influencing how that delivery system operates, who controls it, and the messages that are carried by it; who controls determines the message and the messenger. Tyack's analysis is important. It is one of the first to emphasize both the pluralistic social character of America and the political nature of deciding schooling issues within such a society. What this means, quite simply, is that the curriculum is a political construction of compromises by interested parties with different perspectives, a floating plurality of ideas that may or may not coalesce but have a potential to do so depending on some catalyst.

Conflicting Ideologies

Some 80 years ago, several writers concerned about the corruption of America's traditions latched onto immigration as a threat to American nationalism. Such perceived or conjured threats to the self-identity of any majority are not unusual. Hitler used them in Germany, and there are numerous examples in American history that attest to this human penchant for appealing to nativistic purity (Handlin, 1990; Higham, 1988; Reimers, 2004). In the case of *nativism,* the social and political movement to establish policy favoring the interests of established inhabitants over those of immigrants, book titles tend to tell all that needs to be understood about the term. Several examples suffice. Madison Grant's *The Passing of the Great Race* published in 1916 and Lothrop Stoddard's *The Rising Tide of Color Against White World-Supremacy,* which appeared in 1924, eventually led to laws shutting off immigration. Except for selective countries and special laws for those seeking political asylum, it was not until the mid-1960s that new law would reopen and broaden the entry for immigrants.

Recently, distinguished scholar Samuel P. Huntington published *Who Are We? The Challenges to America's National Identity* (2004). Huntington's thesis is essentially this: The prevailing American culture, which is Eurocentric and Anglo-Protestant based, is under threat. Stated more starkly, the embracing of *pluralism,* meaning the acceptance of permanent cultural and social differences rather than assimilation of immigrants, undermines American society, which is based on a unique American culture that has evolved from Anglo-Protestantism and European traditions. That is what might be called "traditional" nativism; there is another nativistic perspective that goes farther. In another of his books, *The Clash of Civilizations and the Remaking of the World Order* (1998), Huntington suggests that what is unfolding is a clash between ethnic and religious forces. The "new" nativism sees the threat in terms of pluralism that is both cultural and religious, a Christian-Islamic encounter. What the new nativists see is the decline of the currently dominant Western Euro-Christian ethic. Is this a challenge to the prevailing pluralistic view of American society in which all ethnic and cultural groups are presented? Is it a metaphorical shift from the current pluralistic salad bowl conception of America to the early 20th-century assimilating melting-pot idea in response to the great immigrations of that time? Or, is this an evolving trend that, like a dialectic dialogue, is forming into a new thesis, a new trend?

How stories are told or not told influence what a society believes about itself. Even today, many Americans know little about the policy to essentially eliminate the Native American Indian populations in the 19th century before and after the Civil War or about the prison camps that were used to house American citizens of Japanese, German, and Italian ancestry during World War II. Until the civil rights movement of the 1960s, American history school texts either ignored such events or glossed over them. After all, it was only a few short years since the end of a war during which loyalty and patriotism were expected and necessary to the spirit of national unity. The contents of books and curriculum materials such as *My Weekly Reader* were selected to emphasize unity and support the war effort. The Pledge of Allegiance and singing of songs such as "My Country, 'Tis of Thee" among elementary school children exemplify the inculcation of such values. In plain and simple terms, the curriculum was used to indoctrinate, albeit in a benign and acceptable way. As scholars like Michael Doran (2004) point out, in the current context of the War on Terrorism, Saudi Arabian schools of the Wahhabi Islamic persuasion have been using a curriculum that paints a view of Western society and particularly the United States as corrupt and evil. At the same time, in the United States, there is no equivalent use of the curriculum or materials to convey an anti-Islamic view that counters that; indeed, some claim that there is a total lack of any understanding of the Middle East and Islamic civilization. What is implied in America is an emphasis on tolerance and understanding of social, cultural, and religious dissimilarities. What each example represents is a decision to use curriculum for reasons of the political state because it is the curriculum that can most effectively and continuously deliver a subtle message to large groups of citizens-to-be. In America, kindergarten to Grade 12 is a convenient, continuous, extended period of time in which to teach specified messages. As noted in Chapter 13, one important contemporary issue in curriculum thinking and work is the effort to have power over and control decisions concerning curriculum.

Currently, the pluralistic view holds sway in the curriculum consensus about America's social and cultural reflection. However, post-9/11 perceptions and a war outlook suggest a renewed struggle between pluralistic acceptance of difference, or unity through assimilation, and nativism.

Democratization

In a time of perceived cultural diversity, the momentum in politics is toward local community needs and what is called special interest and identity politics. In that context, schooling is best that serves and reflects local politics and ethnic-cultural identity. Indicators are the proliferation of special interest groups seeking to control schooling, efforts to change the scale of schooling by downsizing from large to small schools, and concerns over distances children have to travel to attend a school (which distances may be caused by some board action such as closing a local school as part of consolidation efforts or to economize when funding is perceived as inadequate and tax increases are unthinkable). In some states, there is also the shift of public funds from general schooling to charter schools, which often serve private, religious, and other special interests. Those kinds of actions, however justified, tend to lessen the use of schooling to unify or create a national sense of identity. The uncoupling de-centers the traditional approach, an informal, national consensus about common schooling that has been in place at least since the start of the 20th century. Does that mean the conception of democracy in the American image is changing and the place of schooling as the place for inculcating democratic ideology is diminishing? As suggested earlier in the discussion, the de-centering of the schools, the familiar bricks and mortar institution, is not an end to schooling as a process and curriculum as central to it. Institutional forms change, as do ideas of democracy. As noted in various chapters of this book, the idea of schooling in democracy has changed over the years, and that history suggests that, as an amoeba is still an amoeba even as it changes, so democracy is still democracy as it changes. Diamond and Molino (2004) have put forward an interesting thesis about democracy and change. They suggest that a series of eight elements (see Figure 14.1) are common to all democracies, and the relationships among them provide two important insights about democratization as a process. First, there is a range of possible democracies depending on how many of the dimensions a particular democracy claims or exhibits. Second, of the dimensions or factors identified or claimed, assessments have to be made about the degree of their robustness: Are they new, mature, somewhere in between, static, or accommodating to change? As John Higham (1988) and Oscar Handlin (1990) have chronicled, the response American society made to the great immigration from Europe at the beginning of the 20th century compared to that of today offers some instructive examples of democratic accommodation and institutional change. One of the critical responses early-20th-century progressives made to the immigration crisis at that time was to use schools and schooling as a tool for assimilation. Nearly 100 years later at the

Figure 14.1   Dimensions of Democracy

- **Participation:** Who participates as indicated by the percentage of voters who vote among those who are eligible
- **Competition:** Rules and practices encourage competition and create a level playing field
- **Rule of Law:** Fundamental use of laws as the boundaries of life and engagement
- **Freedom:** Citizenry has mobility and can move unfettered among political units, such as within or between states
- **Equality:** Citizenship and civic life based on social and legal principles of ethics and fairness with equal treatment of all citizens under law and toleration of differences
- **Responsiveness:** Government and other institutions serve citizens and respond to requests
- **Vertical Accountability:** The top-to-bottom and bottom-to-top relationship of citizen-elected servants and their sense of obligation to serve the public good
- **Horizontal Accountability:** Same as vertical accountability but across units such as towns, cities, and counties or parishes, and from state to state, or in regional compacts

start of the 21st century, immigration once again symbolizes a crisis. What is the discernable response? Bruce Fuller (2003), a long-time student of policy trends in schooling, argues that the matter is a cultural de-centering. The word *cultural* in this sense refers to the diversity of ethnic communities that have been created and empowered since the civil rights movement of the 1960s, particularly community-based organizations. Accepting or rejecting pluralism is a personal decision that enters the public sphere when the individual person becomes involved politically by voting for a particular candidate or seeks out and supports some local party or group with similar interests. The traditional pathway for groups and minorities to influence schooling has been through advocacy, putting forth an agenda of ideas and then convincing a majority to act on them. Since the 1960s, public protest and political action to influence or to control decision making, electing people of like interests to the school board, for example, has tended toward a confrontational process in contrast to the old tradition of persuasion, debate, and consensus. The essential institutional roles schools played to stabilize society and include newcomers attest to their important role as both transmitters of democracy as a concept and democratization as a social process of inclusion.

Curriculum-as-Message

A recurring theme about curriculum is that it is a mirror of the larger society. This idea refers to what the people and institutions of the society consider important to the perpetuation of that society. Schooling, as noted in the preceding discussion of democracy, serves as a messenger, with the curriculum as the message, about the society. *Curriculum-as-message* is about what is important to know and to be able to do, the beliefs that center on a sense of nationhood and how to participate effectively in society.

If assimilation of human cultural differences in a new social whole is the purpose, then the emphasis is on confluence, creating a national culture. If the purpose is to accept and perpetuate a sense of nationhood based on diverse social and cultural forms, ethnic affiliations, and lifestyles, then for those who acquire the curriculum, the purpose is diversity. Schooling and schools through the curriculum-as-message help a society negotiate change for both the immigrant and the citizen. The message must also be periodically reconstituted to reflect the social, political, economic, and ideological movements that change the dynamics of democracy. The perceived relevance or nonrelevance of schooling, its social worth, lies in the message the curriculum conveys.

Implications

Societies are always changing, and studying their institutions helps to reveal possible trends. Schools as institutions at the center of a society reflect the changing social patterns that indicate trends. The curriculum-as-message both records transitions in the society and conveys what is evolving, the synthesis of old to new; changes in a society, any society, are reflected in the curriculum-as-message the school provides. If there is a perceived discrepancy between the message received in the school and the life experienced outside it, the social fabric in a democracy will be stressed. Ideologies often affect individual and group interpretations of democracy, and the role of schooling is to bridge those differences through the curriculum. The currents of social change, the trends of tomorrow, are reflected in themes of clashing civilizations, cultural pluralism versus assimilation and group-individual identity versus nationalism. How they play out will be what is both recorded in and conveyed through the school curriculum.

TREND: THE IMPULSE OF GLOBALIZATION

Someplace in your high school or undergraduate years, you encountered the study of nations, nationalism, and international relations. Those concepts evolved from viewing the world as made up of nation *states,* and as social and monocultural units. That perspective is like studying government as a static structure, the president, the congress, and the judiciary, for example. An important trend that developed after World War II was to study institutions like governments or nations as living entities. For example, the Presidency of the United States is an office with powers and so forth, but more important, it is what it is by the president's behavior, what the person in the office of president does—that is a shift from the structural study to the behavioral study of things. That's the importance of the trend called *globalization;* it is a shift away from looking at the world as a study of nations and international relations as structural arrangements to looking at the world holistically as a global interface of human actors, actions, and interactions. Globalization also implies an economic dimension, referring to the increasing integration of business activities across borders and continents, sped and spread by the Internet.

Globalism and the Global Village

A trend discussed earlier is the interconnectedness through technology that has made humans more separate yet closer together. And that is essentially the meaning of the *global village*, an idea hatched some time ago by Marshall McLuhan (1967/2005). Think of a village and you probably imagine a grid of a few streets with homes and a town center, everything easily accessible, everyone a neighbor, and casual frequent conversation; all this evokes closeness and simplicity of life, a near bucolic existence. Think of a city and you conjure up images of continuous residential and commercial strips extending for miles, crowded roads, endless commutes, limited human interaction, a hectic flow of life. *Globalism* asks you to forget those images and assume a different perspective, one about separated connectedness that links place, institutions, time, and people through technology and economic and social interactions.

Recentering Economic and Political Power

At the mid-20th century, the cold war represented a contesting between imperial conglomerates the Soviet Union, China, the United States, and their allies. Ideologically, it was a showdown between communism with its planned economies and democracy with its entrepreneurial capitalism. That description evokes memories of iron curtain boundaries like the Berlin Wall, concertina wire, guard towers, and spies, the clash of nations and ideologies. Globalization is different because it invokes a seamless, boundaryless way of thinking about the world. Consider, for example, the economics of global corporations that have no boundaries, that possess diverse patterns of economic distribution, that form regional economic cooperatives like the North American Free Trade Agreement (NAFTA), and that are operated by a global social collective of chief executive officers and shared corporate board memberships relatively unconstrained by any individual nation's laws or any enforced international agreements; goods, services, and money pass more freely between nations and continents than people do.

Curriculum and Globalism

Pick up a school history, civics, or geography textbook and you will notice that regions, countries, and continents that portray the world are identified by whatever political boundaries are current. Think of what you know about the Middle East. You can identify countries (Iran, Iraq, Jordan, Syria, etc.), but consider ethnic and cultural sharing groups located in those areas, and boundaries go out the window. That is the way you were taught to think of the world internationally, as a set of permanent facts. Globalism asks you to view that world as made up of people in groups that identify themselves in various ways, operate as a society according to a specific set of rules, and are not slotted into already-created categories as states or nations that array from first to third world status. Think of the nice configured facts students learn: this country is here, that one is there, the capitals are these, and the products produced and the economies are thus and so. That is often referred to as the old modernist European empires approach, or Eurocentric perspective, which glossed over the reality of ethnic and cultural place. Globalism, the emphasis on presenting the world as a holistic entity, might be called the sociocultural turn in globalization, as it asks you to think in a boundaryless way by accepting the necessity of political boundaries, but only as temporary configurations for purposes of locating and identifying people, a social GPS or a global geo-positioning system. The world is accessible to anyone via the Internet, television, and air travel. In seconds, you can be in London or Tokyo on the Internet, and in 28 hours or less, you can travel by scheduled commercial jet service from the United States to China. The messages, pictures, and so forth carried over a wireless world in a few seconds create the possibilities for real-time curriculum-on-demand from any place in the world to any other place. The moral and ethical dimensions of this new curriculum-on-demand are just being glimpsed. Who or what will control it and what guidelines and policies will need to be in place? In a time of a War on Terror, what subtle uses are there for training terrorists or encoding messages? As the Nazis used propaganda as a crowd technique to configure thinking, so the Internet, as the potential global curriculum, can be a force for good or evil, depending on purpose and perspective.

Implications

Often dismissed by critics, Marshall McLuhan's idea of the global village has new life and reality in the idea of globalization. Globalism, the social and cultural dimensions of globalization; the boundaryless world of trade and commerce; and the technology-connected world of people, events, and things in places flesh out the emerging idea of globalization. The static ideas of internationalism represented by state and nation currently dominate in curriculum. The irony of globalization as a boundary-free perspective is that it will require states and nations to redefine both the control of and content for curriculum; currently, any learner can go beyond the school and the presented curriculum of the text, video, and classroom using the Internet from home, the library, or any other location. Globalization could be a techno-social revolution.

TREND: RETHINKING SCHOOLS AND SCHOOLING

Institutions and systems in any society take many forms. Some acquire a concrete expression, as in a building or facility. Hospitals, for example, are institutions for the care of the sick and applied medical practice that evolved from the much simpler ideas about care that began with the Hospitaler movement during medieval times and the religious crusades. Today, the movement in health care has been away from single hospitals and doctor-based private sector service into units of health care systems, managed health care, that are a mix of nonprofit, for-profit, public, private, and university-based hospitals and medical centers. Reflect now on schooling, a collection of systems, predominately public, with varying degrees of local private and parochial school options. Unlike hospitals and health care that is paid for by you directly or by participating in a health insurance plan, most schooling services are public and funded through taxes. If you want to choose a different schooling option, that is your choice, and you pay for it. When schools and hospitals are thought of, most think of the brick-and-mortar buildings, the buildings' footprints, and the grounds around them that would be familiar to anyone. The structural image of a school is one of little change; new buildings are transitions from old ones—nothing radical, just separated boxes of classrooms, perhaps wider hallways and better lighting and colors and a new cafeteria or gymnasium or all-events room—the patterns are the same. However, change is in the offing and a trend is discernable. What are the forces shaping this trend and giving it direction? They lie in changing social and service patterns, technology, work, and career patterns; schools as presently constituted evolved to serve a society of time, mind, and scale that no longer exists.

The Institution of Schooling

Schools as institutions are socially important because they provide a significant service. Both abstract and concrete representations, a diploma and the building, symbolize schooling and the school. Consider other symbolizing objects, such as phone booths, newspaper stands, television studios, and satellite dishes, that collectively convey a loose, yet representative meaning about communication as a socially useful and important institution and service. Now there are cell phones, the Internet, Wi-Fi, and other interoperative technologies Jules Verne never thought of. Communication as a social system has changed in terms of the forms that symbolize it, and some would say it has increased in its social importance as it becomes more pervasive. Schools also have a communication function; they are a collection point for communicating curriculum and, most important, the curriculum-as-message mentioned in the earlier discussion of democracy. This has been the reason for the bricks and mortar, fixed or static sites and hierarchical organizations from kindergarten to Grade 12. This has been the prevailing schooling model since the 1900s. It has been a useful, serviceable, functional arrangement consistent with the pattern, pace, and structure of society in another time. Expanded communications, increased personal mobility, accessible transportation, the option to live where you please, and changes in personal lifestyles have created a different society, one in which institutions are no longer fixed but movable, their services or functions not something you go to but that come to you. Traditionally, children and other learners "went" to school; now, you can still go to school but, increasingly, schooling can come to you. Family used to mean kin, brothers, sisters, parents, grandparents, aunts, uncles, cousins, and so forth; it may still mean that, but it often also means a collective of people who come together to support one another, much like the posse in the old movie Westerns, a collection of good guys who came to the rescue, mutual support in a common cause. Traditional institutional schooling is synonymous with family; the new schooling will be synonymous with the individual person. Schooling will become less institutionally fixed and more a diversity of services provided on demand and delivered to a variety of locations. This is the sort of civic and social scenario suggested by several scholars in the future network or cyber society (Meyrowitz, 1996; Schuler & Day, 2004; Wellman, 1999); perhaps the space cities of Star Wars are not just imaginary.

Chasing Obsolescence

In any American community, a school building is easily recognized. Schools symbolize schooling as an important sanctioned activity. Over time, change has come to the image of schools and the functions of schooling in society. Like its institutional counterpart, communications, which evolved from rudimentary forms of signaling over distance to the use of telephones and stand-alone, portable cell phones, schooling as an institution has changed. The one-room school has given way to the consolidated school and multiple rooms. The curriculum has been transformed from simple primers and a few subjects to multimedia materials and multiple subjects. New technology—online learning—offers the possibility to rethink the need for expensive school facilities and consider ways to streamline the learning process that is schooling—but at what loss or gain? A third critical aspect is what Norman Denzin (1973) described as the caretaking function that schooling acquired. Students generally are, by law, in school for about 8 clock hours between 180–200 days a year. That is an expected, taken-for-granted pattern. What do you do with students if you modify that pattern and schooling at specific sites? The fixed day for students—usually from 8 to 3 o'clock with possible on-site after-school options—supports the needs of parents or other responsible adults in their work patterns, especially where the parents need two incomes to maintain a middle-class standard of living. How, for example, would you vote if there were a referendum to change the school year to a year-round model? What are the ramifications for a family? How would changes alter the commercial, civic, and work rhythms in a community? Those are important questions that have social, economic, and political ramifications for the society and the social conception of nationhood. Where is the knowledge, where are the studies that can inform judgments about obsolescence and the need for change?

Power and Control

Institutional changes often bring seismic political and economic consequences of scale to societies. The disintegration of the Soviet Union in 1990 to 1991 and the subsequent political, social, and economic changes exemplify large-scale disruption and change. A small-scale change, the introduction of instructional videos and other software packs on school bus routes, particularly in rural areas, allowed for more efficient time use, improved instructional options, and enhanced curriculum engagement. Other small changes have enhanced curriculum delivery—videos can be played during lunch hours, and taped teacher discussion of classes can be given to students who missed school or be used by the homebound. These and a variety of other ways to package the curriculum are available and location independent. Schools in the existing facilities may become obsolete because new technology allows for learning-on-demand in diverse places. This suggests a need to rethink buildings, the need for them and their physical layout. If traditional school buildings are not needed, what will take their place? Storefront schools and other structural alternatives have been around for years. Can public monies collected for schools be more efficiently applied if the emphasis is not on buildings but on schooling as a process and service? Such a question possesses the possibility to both rethink the physical side of schooling, the building itself, and schooling as a process, so the flexible delivery of required curriculum can be interactive and done in any location.

Rethinking is not just about curriculum flexibility in the form the message-embedded materials take and the means of delivery, it is also about control of these processes. Moving from traditional site-based to multiple nontraditional sites will require a shift in control from the traditional megalithic school board and bureaucratic control at the local level. Recently, governors and legislatures in states such as Michigan and New York have taken control of school districts, reconstituted authority, and vested it in new boards, superintendents, and even mayors. Whether such actions can make existing schools work has yet to be shown. What is worth noting is that efforts to implement reforms or experiment with alternate forms, such as the charter school, require new power and control arrangements. If there is any relevant knowledge from reform or school-change studies, it is that there has to be some accommodation to top-down and bottom-up control and decision making in schooling, both institutionally and as a process (Coffield, 1998; Glennen, Bodily, Galegher, & Kerr, 2004). Ignoring those considerations will gloss over the real power and control issues and ignore the need to rethink schools and schooling.

Entrepreneurship

Your school textbooks were commercially published materials that had to conform to whatever state standards about text selection prevail. High-volume sales states such as New York, Texas, California, and Illinois tend to set the standards other states watch. What is required in California night be modified for a different market and set of standards, but the likelihood is that it will reflect which standards are more stringent. The on-and-off curriculum wars (referred to in several previous chapters) and who wins them influence how text and, therefore, curriculum content are managed (Dimick & Apple, 2005). A war won in Texas over the content of American history will still be reflected in the text adopted in another state; whether it is a commanding and contentious issue there depends on the politics in that other state. There are also specialized publishing houses representing diverse interests that cater to the private and parochial school market. In the growing alternative school market, home schooling offers a new and interesting venture because publishers are usually unconstrained by the adoption requirements for the public schools. The more there is alternativization and privatization, the more likely this market segment will grow. As noted in Chapter 10, special interest publishing houses, political action groups, and not-for-profit and other organizations prepare materials for school use. Subject to state adoption standards, those other materials may or may not be adoptable for public schools. In the private, parochial, and alternative school markets, the adoption requirements for the particular state usually don't apply, so there is no mechanism to ensure a standard curriculum across all learners in a state. What has tended to ensure some degree of desirable consistency in school curriculum are the college admissions policies of state colleges and universities: those of prestigious private universities such as Chicago, Princeton, and Stanford; and the degree requirements for professional study, the medical field, for example, that require the teaching of specialized curriculum in sciences and math as early as elementary school. Schools, as central places for communicating curriculum, are still the dominant market for texts and other curriculum materials. However, as schools become more diverse, and the private, parochial, and alternative school sector grows, new markets and specialization will emerge.

Textbooks publishers have relied on academic and professional specialists for writing and reviewing materials as well as for giving an air of legitimacy by institutional affiliation and expertise in a particular field or discipline of knowledge. That entrepreneurial professionalism rested on the credentialing and standing of the writer, reviewer, or consultant (Brint, 1994). The entrepreneurial expert has come under fire in the curriculum wars and in the ideological debates over curriculum matters. The literature on school reform is replete with controversies over differing expert testimony; often that expertise appears as advocacy for one approach over another. The unfortunate result seems to be a devaluing of the expert and the professional's role as one who can provide an informed, balanced view about a matter at hand. The increasingly polarized and entrepreneurial role of experts and professionals has been at a cost of social trust in society. What has been lost is a sense of propriety and reserve in presentation, the key elements you might have learned in forensics and debate courses were they still part of the high school curriculum.

Implications

The prevailing model of schooling in the United States evolved at the beginning of the 20th century and has changed little in form and function. Often referred to as the factory and assembly line model, a series of reform efforts since the mid-1950s seem to have had limited impact in correcting perceived shortcomings or changing opinions about its relevance. Calls for charter schools and other alternatives still mirror the belief in fixed sites and traditional hours and months of schooling. The alternative is to rethink schooling: Acknowledge that obsolescence is still being pursued, reconstitute ideas of power and control, and examine the influence of social, economic, business, and personal entrepreneurship in a democracy.

TREND: THE RISING IMPORTANCE OF CURRICULUM

Central to any society and culture is the transfer of the group's wisdom to the new members. This refers to its body of accepted knowledge (what it knows), rules and procedures governing social arrangements, and the ways to interact with the world. These take various forms from simple to complex reifications as spoken truth, rituals, and some iconic representations like hieroglyphs to more sophisticated mediums such as books, CDs, or videos. It is the curriculum, what is to be learned. In this text, you have explored curriculum and schooling. Regardless of whether discussions were about academies, common schools, funding, and other issues captured in particular eras of reform, the resilient feature of schooling has always been the curriculum. The interesting aspect of all the years of discussion about schooling and the tinkering with kinds of schools and their organization is that the curriculum has been the one factor in schooling generally ignored, at least until the latest round of reforms.

Curriculum as Social Glue

Any society wants the word to get out about the importance of conducting one's behavior in an acceptable, preferably civil, manner. The social rules of the road tend to constrain bizarre and threatening kinds of behaviors. As learners move across settings, from family to neighborhood to school and outward into the larger community, each learns how to behave in those settings and which rules transfer across and which ones are unique to a setting; you take your shoes off at the door when in Nancy's house, at Tadjeka's, the food is always spicy. Beginning in elementary school from the first time you line up to go to lunch, visit the media center, or wash your hands, you learn the hidden but expected curriculum of manners and behavior that are part of the school experience. This is the social glue aspect of curriculum, the passing of the curriculum as social message, formalized sometimes in studies of other cultures, historical episodes about the Native American cultures, for example, and less formal in the lunchroom, hall, and classroom.

Nationalization

An earlier historian of sorts, one Parson Weems, gave us the mythic tales about George Washington chopping down the cherry tree and throwing the dollar across the Potomac. His attempt to glorify Washington was all a piece of building images of American nationhood and defining the American character and the qualities of the good citizen. Periodically, politicians and eager citizens raise up new images of character and a sense of national commitment by the individual. Franklin Roosevelt appealed to that when he said, deep in the Great Depression, that Americans had nothing to fear but fear itself. John F. Kennedy made a similar appeal to patriotic and national image when, during his first inaugural address, he asked Americans to ask not what the country could do for themselves, but what they could do for their country. President Bush has called for unity, dedication, and perseverance in the post-9/11 War on Terror. What is currently missing is any discussion about patriotic renewal in the curriculum, which is usually a characteristic of wartime efforts to create a nationalistic sense of purpose and resolve. This theme of building nationhood has subtly defined and glorified particular traits of the American character: generosity, civility, loyalty, individuality, and general friendliness toward others. Schools have been centralizing places for students to learn and practice these messages. As the society and its institutions changes, it is the curriculum to which society will turn to carry the message.

Changing Knowledge and Work

One perennial discussion is about general education for all and what should be included in that curriculum. Grounding in science, mathematics, history, and the social studies in the form of studies in geography, civics, and government has been the standard. The question has always been how much of each to include and, as you are probably aware, the determining measure has been the idea of using Carnegie units of time and designating so much study time for this or that area of the curriculum. That was sufficient for the old, centralized learning concept of schooling, when there was little that could be done outside of school time. Technology and access to knowledge have changed all that. It is questionable if the Carnegie unit is still useful. However, there is currently no replacement, and using time-based units doesn't ensure learning anyway. It is the quality of the knowledge form, the curriculum, fitted to the characteristics of the learner and what assessments indicate has been learned, that is important. Knowledge held is the new currency of exchange and the arbiter of control and power in a society. And, the acceleration in new knowledge and its development as a product for distribution in society can occur outside traditional school patterns. Not only is the knowledge creation process more democratic and outside the traditional work of the scholar and the university, it is entrepreneurial and interconnected. What is found about schooling, knowledge, or curriculum in the United Kingdom, New Zealand, Scandinavia, or Japan has important and possibly immediate applications elsewhere. The particular British experience in creating a national curriculum has important knowledge that might be useful in the United States as it grapples with whether and how to create a national American curriculum. There is also the changing pattern of curriculum specialization. Although there are projections for a continuing need for teachers, especially in mathematics and science, and the NCLB requires that content teachers meet mastery criteria, increasing the need for specialization, the increasing number of nonpublic, commercial, and private curriculum producers will also need persons with curriculum expertise that university faculty and staff can't fill. This suggests an expanding need for curriculum and content-specific knowledge experts, and, if school districts really begin to take curriculum and curriculum work seriously, an expanding role and importance for the school district specialists.

Implications

Curriculum is the social glue that potentially provides a common knowledge for all segments of a society. It is limited only by the failure to recognize the central importance of curriculum to schooling and to refocus on reforms envisioned to date as architectural rather than structural and in support of curriculum. It is the potential engine for inculcating nationalistic values such as patriotism and loyalty, and carrying the message of democracy, freedom, and unfettered inquiry. The rising importance of curriculum signals changes in the nature and types of curriculum work needs, from the teacher to the curriculum specialist. As technology and reticulation forces make curriculum pervasive and readily accessible, they raise its importance and elevate the specter of who or what will control it and constitute it for the future.

	PERSPECTIVE INTO PRACTICE: Selected Trends and Their Possible Impact at the Elementary and Secondary Level	
Trend	*A Possible Scenario for the Elementary Level*	*A Possible Scenario for the Secondary Level*
Technology and Reticulation	The elementary teacher in a district does not impart knowledge and skills in the traditional sense but is a coach and manager of student inquiry into acquiring knowledge and skills. Some students interact from home and other sites, whereas others, who may have limited access to the necessary smart technology, attend at the school site.	The secondary teacher coordinates the curriculum, differentiating it to specific student needs, facilitates curriculum-on-demand applications, and schedules students' contacts, all based in a centralized location. Assessment tracks student knowledge performance and calibrates lesson-student interface.
Globalization and Shifting Ideologies	Reading and language learning requirements for all students mean basic reading begins in a bilingual common language and second selection. Simultaneous translation software facilitates immediate assessment. The teacher acts as the coach, facilitator, and technical coordinator.	Wi-Fi pathways facilitate communication that links the study of biology with resource centers throughout the world. Translation software permits immediate contact and response at any validated site for students who can work in a flexible but coordinated time frame.
Curriculum and Schooling	Expanded curriculum and staffing make the elementary school a center for learning and meeting total needs of all students. Children are not learning by age cohort but individualized and rotated for play and other learning activities.	Individualized ID tags contain student schedules, information, assignments, and interactive student-teacher contact during the designated school time frame. Curriculum exists in multiple media formats that can be integrated or renewed by the teacher, whose role is coordination and acting as a knowledge and resource expert.

Summary and Conclusions

Trends develop from a confluence of forces, take on a life of their own, have a reasonably long existence, and achieve some impact across numerous institutions and other aspects of a society. Five trends, technology and reticulation, ideological shifts, globalization, school obsolescence, and the rising importance of curriculum, were identified and discussed. These are, of course, one person's prognostications about where schooling and curriculum are headed. The old model of schooling is dead and a new one will emerge. The critical need will be to find a way to deconstruct elementary school in the public mind and recast it in some preschool configuration that allows parents to have multiple site choices with guaranteed quality assurance and credentialed caregivers/teachers. The perceived baby-sitting function schools have acquired will be a difficult obstacle to overcome. The old assumption that a fixed site for schooling is important as a collection point for efficient teaching and learning no longer holds currency if the diversity of location and choice options for preschool is considered. Adult responsibilities for schooling children in their care are more easily addressed when multiple sites or centers for schooling are presented and parents have choices. The thread that links, the crucial reticule, is the curriculum. It can be the standard, the social glue that links people in anyplace anywhere in the world, exclusive of boundaries, real, political, or imagined. What message the curriculum will carry as defined by the actions of power elites is yet to be determined. That will be a first-order political act of immense potential and importance.

Critical Perspective

Critical perspectives are about selected key questions and things to think about pertinent to a particular topic. In this chapter, the perspectives are keyed to the particular trend or a particular aspect of it that may have more relevance to curriculum. The selections are, of course, arbitrary as befits speculating about trends.

Trend: Technology and Reticulation

1. What do you know about nanotechnology and memetics? Are they separate concepts or are they connected?

2. Networking and reticulation are important words in describing interconnectivity. The former implies linear connections and vertical or horizontal thinking, and the latter implies multidimensional interconnectivity and pliable thinking. The key difference is that the place of humans and their capabilities is central to one but not the other. Of the two approaches to interconnectivity, networking and reticulation, which is predicated on the role of humans?

Trend: Shifting Ideologies and Change

3. The text takes the position that ideologies are neither good nor bad, they are what the actors make of them. Do you agree with that assertion? What evidence would you offer one way or the other?

4. Democracy is portrayed as an ideology much like the totalitarian ones of fascism or communism. Do you agree or disagree with that assertion? Why?

5. The set of characteristics for democracy suggests that democracies can be sorted according to the number of those characteristics they have. If schools are expected to mirror democracy, which of the criteria relate to schooling and what implications are there for the development of curriculum content?

Trend: The Impulse of Globalization

6. Globalism and internationalism are two perspectives for viewing and thinking about the world. How does each view the world and how are they alike or different?

7. The predominant power in the world today is the United States. One trend is the shifting power relationships and the economic and political rise of the European Union, India, and China. This group can pressure other countries to usually act in ways parallel to their individual interests. Given that scenario, how should globalization be addressed in the curriculum?

Trend: Rethinking Schools and Schooling

8. The claim is made that schooling as it exists, whether it is public, parochial, private, or alternative, is failing; reforms to date have not worked; and it is essentially a problem of an obsolete early-20th-century industrial factory assembly line process. Do you agree that it is obsolete? Why or why not?

9. Critics such as Ivan Illich suggest we should begin de-schooling society. What does that mean to you? What are the implications for schooling and curriculum as they exist today and what should take their place?

Trend: The Rising Importance of Curriculum

10. Consideration of the other trends suggests that the key to human interconnectivity is the creation of a world form of schooling and curriculum. This would

involve globalization, technological extension of human capabilities, and the new knowledge disciplines of networking and information. What other ideas and new knowledge areas should be included?

11. It is suggested that curriculum work will diversify, require more expertise, and become more entrepreneurial. So far, in your studies and experiences as you prepare to teach, do you have any evidence to suggest if and how those claims are realistic or unrealistic?

12. The rise of curriculum importance is perhaps best seen in the national curriculum movements in the United Kingdom and elsewhere. Why do you think a similar movement has not begun in the United States?

Resources for Curriculum Study

As previously noted, *Education Week* is an excellent newspaper of record for any and all issues related to schools, schooling, and curriculum. Trends and prognostication are, of course, the meat of journalists in December and January of any year. Most major national newspapers and, often, local ones that take stories from Reuters and AP wires, get into the end-of-year recap. Major publications, *Newsweek, Time, U.S. News and World Report,* and *The Week,* recap the year's main events and offer opinion pieces about which stories or events will be critical in the coming year; of course, no one foresaw 9/11. Efficient inquiry suggests you keep in mind that it is important to sample across various publications and perhaps compile lists for comparison when studying about or looking for trends.

General Ways to Search Out Trends

Most schooling and curriculum-oriented journals will have dedicated theme issues or a theme-oriented section. Sampling across the table of contents for several months of these, preferably a year's worth, will give you a sense of what topics sustain or fade away from year to year. A good start is the Internet; just try Google or other search engine of choice to surface a variety of journals and articles. For a quick start in the education field or in topics specific to schooling and curriculum, *Phi Delta Kappan* and *Educational Leadership* are useful. Be sure to check the reference section in any article of interest for additional resources. Whereas references to particular sources in the text bibliography have been identified at relevant points in each chapter, additional resources are provided in the following discussion of each trend.

Trend: Technology and Reticulation

1. There are many books and online resources as well about technology and education, schooling, and curriculum; most are practical and utilitarian. Technology connects and extends and bypasses boundaries and awakens discontinuities in the perceived order of things. Two insightful works are Neil Postman's *Technopoly: The Surrender of Culture to Technology* (1993) and Arnold Pacey's *The Culture of Technology* (1985). Both authors offer a prescient discussion of the technology-culture collide that anticipated most of the views expressed over the past 20 years.

2. Reticulation is a newer conception as befits an emerging trend, but it links with technology through the study of interconnectedness of reticules (parts or elements) in a network. Find and look at a woman's string purse and note how all the strands interconnect and you get the idea in its simplest form. Reticulation has a wider use in sciences and engineering, and the few applications of it have been by historian Althea Hayter, particularly in *The Wreck of the "Abergavenny"* (2002), in which she develops a social dimension of reticulation, the reticule of social relationships.

Trends: Shifting Ideologies and Change

3. The 20th century saw a clash between totalitarian and democratic ideologies. Framing it in a more inclusive perspective, Bruce Mazlish, in *The Fourth Discontinuity* (1993), discusses what can be described as four discontinuities, the Copernican, Darwinian, psychoanalytical, and now the technological, that frame human development. Each is a super idea in the way Thomas Kuhn, in *The Structure of Scientific Revolutions* (1970), fashioned paradigms as overarching conceptions of how scientists think about and relate to their world and work. Ideologies tend to be the focus of philosophy and political science rather than of scholars in education or curriculum, although an argument could be made that the postmodernist turn in curriculum thinking is ideological.

4. An excellent introductory source to ideologies is Macridis and Hulliung's *Contemporary Political Ideologies* (1996). More in depth and challenging work is Michael Freeden's *Ideologies and Political Theory* (1998). Michael Apple's *Ideology and Curriculum* (1979) is an older but still useful discussion about American ideologies.

Trend: The Impulse of Globalization

5. Globalization and the idea of globalism is the subject of a growing body of literature in a variety of fields, from discussion about its history to its ecological

and geological dimensions. Most of the discussions are explorations of what it means or the various meanings ascribed to it. John Keane's *Global Civil Society* (2003) and Tony Shirato and Jen Webb's *Understanding Globalization* (2003) are useful starting points.

6. The relationship of globalism, the idea, and globalization, the process, to education in general and to schooling and curriculum is at the cutting edge. An interesting report about curriculum, schooling, and the implications of globalization by the Association of International Educators (2003) is available on their Web site at http://www.nafsa.org/public_policy.sec/public_policy_document/study_abroad_ 1/securing_america_s_future. See also David Selby's work cited in the next section on schooling.

Trend: Rethinking Schools and Schooling

7. Wayne Gersen, in his *Education Week* commentary article "The Networked School" (2003), offers a thoughtful critique of school change and offers some examples of how school districts are responding to obsolescence and alternate school forms.

8. David Selby, of the Ontario Institute for Studies in Education and Director of the University of Toronto International Institute for Global Education, in his article "Global Education as Transformative Education" (online at http://www.citi- zens4change .org/global/intro/intro2.htm), offers a useful model for thinking about the future of schooling.

Trend: The Rising Importance of Curriculum

9. Discussions of reform all seem to address everything else about schools and school- ing but curriculum. Lois Weiner (2000) points out in a discussion of trends in teacher education research in the 1990s that there is a contradiction among what researchers and scholars see as important, the various contexts of schooling, the drive for curriculum standardization that is motivated by political agendas, and globalism. Andy Hargreaves, in *Teaching in the Knowledge Society* (2003), explores the new knowledge society and possible future implications for curriculum.

10. The rising interest in the importance of curriculum is just beginning. References to the centrality of curriculum in schooling and reform are usually secondary or incidental comments in assessment and evaluation discussions. Lorie A. Shepard's suggestion, in her article "Curricular Coherence in Assessment Design" (2004), that assessments must be founded on an "agreed-upon curricu- lum" (p. 239) is an important acknowledgement. That particular volume, *Towards Coherence Between Classroom Assessment and Accountability,* a yearbook of the

National Society for the Study of Education (Wilson, 2004), along with Pelligrino, Chudowsky, and Glaser's *Knowing What Students Know* (2001), are two books that hint at the growing recognition of curriculum's importance in schooling and beyond. Some interesting implications of globalism for curriculum development are discussed by Cross and Molnar in their article "Global Issues in Curriculum Development" (1994).

References

Apple, M. W. (1979). *Ideology and curriculum.* London: Routledge.

Association of International Educators. (2003, November 18). *Securing America's future: Global education for a global age.* Retrieved August 2005 from http://www.nafsa.org/public_policy.sec/ public_policy_document/study_abroad_1/securing_america_s_future

Bayly, C. A. (2004). *The birth of the modern world, 1780–1914.* Oxford, UK: Blackwell.

Brint, S. (1994). *In an age of experts: The changing role of professionals in politics and public life.* Princeton, NJ: Princeton University Press.

Coffield, F. (1998). A tale of three little pigs: Building the learning society with straw. *Evaluation and Research in Policy Analysis, 12*(1), 44–58.

Cole, B. C. (1999). *The emergence of net-centric computing.* Upper Saddle River, NJ: Prentice Hall.

Cross, B. E., & Molnar, A. (1994). Global issues in curriculum development. *Peabody Journal of Education, 69*(4), 131–140.

Danielson, M. M. (2004). Theory of continuous socialization for organizational renewal. *Human Resource Development Review, 3*(4), 354–384.

Denzin, N. K. (1973). *Children and their caretakers.* New Brunswick, NJ: Transaction Books.

Diamond, L., & Molino, L. (2004). The quality of democracy. *Journal of Democracy, 15*(4), 20–31.

Dimick, A. S., & Apple, M. W. (2005, May 2). *Texas and the politics of abstinence-only textbooks.* Retrieved June 30, 2005, from www.tcrecord.org [ID Number 11855].

Doran, M. S. (2004). The Saudi paradox. *Foreign Affairs, 83*(1), 35 51.

Freeden, M. (1998). *Ideologies and political theory.* London: Oxford University Press.

Fuller, B. (2003). Education policy under cultural pluralism. *Educational Researcher, 32*(9), 15–24.

Gersen, W. (2003, December 3). The networked school [Electronic version]. *Education Week, 23*(14), 30–31.

Gladwell, M. (2000). *The tipping point.* Boston: Little, Brown.

Glennen, T. K., Bodily, S. J., Galegher, J. R., & Kerr, K. A. (Eds.). (2004). *Expanding the reach of educational reforms.* Santa Monica, CA: Rand Corporation.

Greene, B. R. (1999). *The elegant universe.* New York: Vintage.

Handlin, O. (1990). *The uprooted.* New York: Little, Brown/Rei.

Hargreaves, A. (2003). *Teaching in the knowledge society.* New York: Teachers College Press.

Hayter, A. (2002). *The wreck of the "Abergavenny."* New York: Macmillan.

Higham, J. (1988). *Strangers in the land* (2nd ed.). New Brunswick, NJ: Rutgers University Press.

Huntington, S. P. (1998). *The clash of civilizations and the remaking of the world order.* New York: Simon & Schuster.

Huntington, S. P. (2004). *Who are we? The challenges to American national identity.* New York: Simon & Schuster.

Keane, J. (2003). *Global civil society.* Cambridge, UK: Cambridge University Press.

Kuhn, T. (1970). *The structure of scientific revolutions.* Chicago: University of Chicago Press.

Lievrouw, L. A., & Livingstone, S. (2002). *The handbook of new media: Social change and consequences of ICTs.* London: Sage.

Macridis, R. C., & Hulliung, M. (1996). *Contemporary political ideologies: Movements and regimes* (6th ed.). New York: Prentice Hall.

Mazlish, B. (1993). *The fourth discontinuity: The co-evolution of humans and machines.* New Haven, CT: Yale University Press.

McLuhan, M., & Fiore, Q. (2005). *The medium is the message.* New York: Bantam Books. Corte Madera, CA: Gingko Press. (Original work published 1967)

Meadows, D. H., Meadows, D. L., Randers, J., & Behrens, W. W. (1972). *The limits to growth.* London: Earth Island.

Meyrowitz, J. (1996). Taking McLuhan and "medium theory" seriously: Technological change and the evolution of education. In Stephen T. Kerr (Ed.), *Technology and the future of schooling* (95th Yearbook of the National Society for the Study of Education, Part II, pp. 73–110). Chicago: National Society for the Study of Education.

Pacey, A. (1985). *The culture of technology.* Boston: MIT Press.

Pelligrino, J., Chudowsky, N, & Glaser, R. (Eds). (2001). *Knowing what students know: The science and design of educational assessment* (National Research Council Committee on the Foundations of Assessment). Washington, DC: National Academy Press.

Postman, N. (1993). *Technopoly: The surrender of culture to technology.* New York: Vintage.

Reimers, D. H. (2004). *Other immigrants: The global origins of the American people.* New York: New York University Press.

Schuler, D., & Day, P. (2004). *Shaping the network society: The new role of civil society in cyberspace.* Cambridge, MA: MIT Press.

Selby, D. (n.d.). Global education as transformative education. Retrieved August 2005 from http://www.citizens4change.org/global/intro/intro2.htm

Shepard, L. A. (2004). Curricular coherence in assessment design. In M. Wilson (Ed.), *Towards coherence between classroom assessment and accountability* (103rd Yearbook of the National Society for the Study of Education, Part II, pp. 239–249). Chicago: National Society for the Study of Education.

Shirato, T., & Webb, J. (2003). *Understanding globalization.* Thousand Oaks, CA: Sage.

Toffler, A. (1980). *The third wave.* New York: Bantam Books.

Tyack, D. B. (1974). *The one best system: A history of American urban education.* Cambridge, MA: Harvard University Press.

Weiner, L. (2000). Research in the 90s: Implications for urban teacher preparation. *Review of Educational Research, 70*(3), 369–406.

Wellman, B. (1999). *Networks in the global village: Life in contemporary communities.* Boulder, CO: Westview Press.

Wilson, M. (Ed.). (2004). *Towards coherence between classroom assessment and accountability* (103rd Yearbook of the National Society for the Study of Education, Part II). Chicago: National Society for the Study of Education.

A Glossary of Curriculum Terms

The terms with their definitions or descriptions set forth in this glossary are based primarily on their use in this text. Some terms are included because they are part of a family of terms or a different way of expressing a term found in curriculum. For example, academic-subject curriculum is sometimes referred to as subject-matter curriculum. To assist the reader, the italicized words in a particular definition or description cross-reference those relationships and meanings.

A

Academic-subject curriculum is a curriculum organized around traditional academic subjects such as mathematics and history. Often referred to as *subject-matter curriculum* and organized in different ways, such as *broad-fields, fusion, structure-of-the discipline,* and *correlation.*

Academy is a 19th-century kind of secondary school, usually private, often considered the precursor of the contemporary high school. It eventually declined in importance when legal precedents established public funding for secondary schooling.

Accountability in schooling and education means establishing data to determine whether results meet expectations. It is envisioned as a complex and multifaceted process that is continuous, repetitive, diagnostic, remedial, formative, summative, systemic, and systematic. It includes curriculum-instruction-assessment-evaluation accountability and agent or agency responsibility.

Action research is an applied form of research in the interpretivist-qualitative tradition. Action research seeks to understand the setting or environment and improve practice. Both practitioners and researchers, often in concert, employ it.

Affective domain refers to one domain of an approach to organizing educational objectives. The affective focuses on attitudes and values. The other domains are *cognitive* and *psychomotor.*

Alignment in curriculum usually refers to the relationship of scope, sequence, continuity, and balance. The expression "curriculum fit" implies a satisfactory relationship among the elements. Also see *coherence,* which is similar in meaning but not in application.

Appraisal process is a conception in curriculum that views assessment-evaluation as a single process for making judgments as to the worth or value of some action or product.

Articulation in curriculum development work is the focus on relationships across and among curriculum content, particularly the *curriculum fundamentals* of *scope, sequence, continuity,* and *balance.*

Assessment is the gathering of data in some form for *evaluation* purposes. Traditional forms are tests, particularly classroom and *high-stakes tests.* Authentic assessment refers to a performance, a demonstration, or some other tool that is keyed to demonstrating something in a specified live context. Curriculum can be assessed using either traditional or authentic modes. See also *traditional assessment* and *authentic assessment.*

Authentic assessment is a particular form of assessment, such as performances or portfolios, that attempts to reflect real life and preferably real work situations. See also *assessment* and *traditional assessment.*

B

Backward design is a series of steps defining a process for thinking through what the curriculum should be and then creating and implementing it with a mechanism for continuous refinement and revision. It can also be a tool for *curriculum analysis.*

Balance is a concept used in developing and managing curriculum. It refers to both the curriculum-learner relationship and, along with *scope, sequence* and *continuity,* it forms the *curriculum fundamentals.*

Behavioral psychology or **behaviorism,** as it is sometimes referred to, is a perspective or school of psychology that explores animal and human behavior in terms of observable and measurable responses to environmental stimuli and excludes subjective phenomena such as emotions and motives.

Benchmarks are used in *standards-based education* and in *school reform* discussions. They refer to what students are to know and be able to do in consideration of such variables as the student's age, developmental characteristics, and grade level.

Broad-fields curriculum refers to creating a new curriculum patterned from a wide range of sources from all branches of knowledge. See *academic-subject curriculum.*

C

Capacity refers to being able to accomplish what has been assigned in curriculum work by having the necessary human, technical, and other kinds of resources necessary.

Cardinal principles refers to seven principles that should guide curriculum and instruction in schools. These principles, health, command of fundamental processes, worthy home membership, vocational preparation, citizenship, ethical character, and worthy use of leisure time, came from the 1918 report of the National Education Association's Commission on the Reorganization of Secondary Education.

Cognitive domain is one of three classifications for educational goals and objectives, the others being the *affective* and *psychomotor domains*. The idea was to use these domains to standardize the focus on what should be taught in schools. Collectively, the three are usually referred to as Bloom's Taxonomy of Educational Objectives.

Cognitive psychology is another school of thought or perspective in psychology that seeks to understand the mental processes that occur between stimulation and response. These might include problem solving, memory, information processing, and how humans receive, process, store, and retrieve and use information.

Coherence refers to the totality of schooling as a process of curriculum-instruction-learning-assessment-evaluation-context linkages and relationships. The idea of coherence is to all those elements in schooling as articulation is to scope-sequence-continuity-balance in curriculum.

Common places refer to a set of considerations that is assumed or inferred in thinking about education and curriculum. These were first set out as educational commonplaces by Joseph Schwab and, as used in this text, are reframed as educational, teaching, and curriculum commonplaces.

Common school was a publicly supported type of school dedicated to the schooling of all members in a society. It is usually associated with the work of Horace Mann.

Content standards are specific statements that identify what students are to do or should know resulting from instruction. The actual curriculum devised to address the standard is what is to be taught. It is a term often found in discussions about *standards-based education* and *reform*. Standards are usually compiled in official documents to guide workers in their use.

Context analysis refers to the need to identify as many variables as possible in the setting so those factors are taken into account when creating new curriculum or adopting or adapting curriculum, because, in curriculum work, the use of curriculum in classroom and other live settings occurs in a very fluid manner with many variables.

Contextual knowledge refers to what can be known in the possible, immediate, social, artificial, and natural setting or environment: place, person(s), and their attributes considered together as a unit that is timebound in the ecological framing of the relationship between an organism and its environment.

Continuity is a concept in curriculum study and work referring to the completeness of the curriculum so there are no gaps and there is a sustaining flow without interruption in the content of the curriculum; the curriculum is itself complete and not missing elements that will affect its being learned. One of the *curriculum fundamentals*.

Core curriculum is a form of curriculum that is deemed central and mandatory for all students to learn. There can be a core within a curriculum or the total curriculum can be the core. What the core contains is not prescribed and can vary.

Correlation is a curriculum idea referring to the simultaneous relationship of content elements in a curriculum. The content may seem radically different, as in the correlation of selected mathematics and literature elements. See *academic-subject curriculum.*

Critical perspective is a distinct formulated manner of thinking about things that is grounded in knowledge and has a mechanism for reflection and self-correction. It is an element in developing a professional perspective in curriculum work.

Critical theory is an academic perspective that studies relationships about power, the interests that use power, elites of control, and social justice. The connection with curriculum work is to influence curriculum thinking and development that frees and empowers rather than subjugates people, particularly through schooling.

Curricularist is a general term for workers in curriculum that includes roles such as the teacher and the curriculum supervisor. The qualifier is the degree to which their work assignment involves curriculum.

Curriculum is a term used to represent the central purpose of schooling, the presentation of specified content for learning. Curriculum means the content, what is taught in schools, in a general, collective sense. It is also used to signify curriculum as a discipline, a specific area of knowledge and academic study.

Curriculum accountability refers to the school and curriculum professional's ability to accurately determine and report about the curriculum and student learning outcomes. Ideally, accountability efforts should include the expressed purposes schools serve, the representative standards and curriculum, instruction, assessment, and evaluation, all linked together.

Curriculum adaptation means to take a curriculum as it exists and change it either before, during, or after implementation to adjust or adapt it to fit the circumstances.

Curriculum adoption is to take a curriculum as it has been produced and implement it without change.

Curriculum alignment. See *alignment.*

Curriculum analysis is a collective term for different ways of probing curriculum. It can refer simply to a checklist or short guide for evaluating textbooks and curriculum guides as well as to specific techniques like *curriculum mapping* and *backward design.*

Curriculum appraisal is the application of assessment-evaluation specifically to curriculum and curriculum work needs. The idea is to remove it from the other contexts of assessment-evaluation, for example, program assessment-evaluation. See also *appraisal process.*

Curriculum-as-message is about what is important to know, to be able to do, for example, the beliefs that center a sense of nationhood and how to participate effectively in society that are conveyed through the curriculum.

Curriculum critique is a form of presentation, a written, scholarly perspective on some curriculum matter stating the perspective being used or presented, identifying particulars, conditions, and criteria or qualities about the topic, problem, or issue, or presenting the pluses and minuses about it. The critique is often a comparative analysis in the style of a written, reasoned appraisal of some aspect of the state of the discipline, a proposal, trend, tradition, and a theory or model, for example.

Curriculum design usually refers to patterns for developing curriculum, such as *broad-fields, fusion,* and *academic-subject curriculum.* In curriculum work, usually development, a design is a creative process of representing something before it is articulated in its details, as in a house design before it is drawn architecturally in its details. Designs occur after a *plan* has been formulated and are based on the particulars set forth in a plan.

Curriculum development is one kind of curriculum work that refers to the creating of curriculum and can also refer to the adoption and adaptive activities when implementing curriculum. It can range from the informality of a classroom teacher's handwritten paragraph for learners to the formal commercial venture creating a set of curriculum materials. See also *curriculum adaptation* and *curriculum adoption.*

Curriculum differentiation occurs when trying to match student characteristics, and curriculum requires breaking up or arranging curriculum in different ways to match or fit such things as learning styles or ways of learning like multiple intelligences.

Curriculum evaluation. See *evaluation, summative, formative.*

Curriculum fundamentals, *scope, sequence, continuity,* and *balance,* considered collectively, form a set of interrelated concepts basic to curriculum work.

Curriculum guide is an official document usually published by some sanctioned agent such as a state department of education or a recognized authority like the National Science Foundation that contains the scope and sequence for a curriculum. It may also contain *curriculum standards, rubrics,* or other protocols to guide curriculum work.

Curriculum-in-use, sometimes referred to as the *enacted curriculum,* means the actual ongoing engagement of curriculum by the teacher and students.

Curriculum maintenance is about those activities that support the *curriculum-in-use;* it is in tandem with *curriculum management.*

Curriculum management is to establish a systematic approach that senses or detects how the curriculum is performing in order to make ongoing adjustments.

Curriculum mapping is a tool for monitoring and evaluation work in curriculum, a way of moving horizontally and vertically in evaluating curriculum scope and sequence. The horizontal dimension refers, for example, to the curriculum across a grade, a school, and schools within a district, and the vertical refers to the curriculum as a whole or a particular part, such as science and its K–12 grade progression. See also *curriculum analysis.*

Curriculum monitoring refers to continuously watching over the curriculum with different tools, such as assessment data or management and maintenance operations.

Curriculum orientations refer to sets of flexible, malleable ideas in curriculum thinking that may or may not have a philosophical basis or be fixed, as in adherence to a specific philosophy such as *humanism, technological, postmodernism, cognitive,* or *developmental.*

Curriculum plan refers to the actual document or documents that represent how going from a policy to implementation in curriculum work is to occur. It usually flows from curriculum *policy making* and *planning.*

Curriculum planning is the set of activities in curriculum work that results in a *curriculum plan.*

Curriculum process refers to a flow of activities inclusive of decisions, tools, or any created series of actions particular to some kind of curriculum, most often in curriculum development.

Curriculum product refers to what results from some type of curriculum work. A product can range from a textbook that results from curriculum development to a K–12 mathematics curriculum that results from policy making and planning work and exists as a curriculum document.

Curriculum reform. See *reform.*

Curriculum standards are stated, written specifications of content that form the curriculum. These curriculum standards are usually found in *curriculum guides* and other important curriculum documents.

Curriculum theory is a form of theory particular to curriculum with certain features that separate it from other meanings of theory in academic work. It is a set of propositions, observations, facts, beliefs, policies, or procedures proposed or followed as a basis for curriculum action.

Curriculum tools refer to the *curriculum theory, models,* and *critique,* as key techniques or methods used in curriculum work.

Curriculum units refer to how a curriculum is broken out into workable sections or chunks, usually comprising a time line of lessons with some thematic or other organizing feature.

Critique is a type of tool in curriculum work usually engaged in by curriculum scholars. It is not a criticism from a particular perspective or philosophical position but a carefully drawn formal discussion based on a set of announced criteria related to curriculum knowledge and practice. See *curriculum critique.*

D

Declarative knowledge, also known as information, is a kind of content knowledge in curriculum that students are expected to learn. It is one of several delineations in different ways to categorize and organize knowledge for efficient learning. See also *modes of knowing.*

Design. See *curriculum design.*

Discipline refers to the designation of a special collection of knowledge, such as mathematics or history, that has a definable *discipline structure* of logics (ways of thinking) and a distinct literature, inquiry tradition, tools, and perspective(s) that govern work in the discipline.

Discipline structure. See *discipline.*

Documentation system in curriculum work refers to developing and implementing any notational process that establishes a systematic way of recording the work process to including actions taken, accessing and correlating curriculum documents, and work activities particular to a kind of work, as in piloting and field-testing in curriculum development, adaptation, and adoption.

E

Educational philosophy refers to the application of ideas from established schools of philosophy (e.g., humanism, existentialism, etc.) to education in general or with particular application to curriculum. For examples, see *essentialism, pragmatism,* or *progressivism.*

Eight-Year Study is the famous study done by the Progressive Education Association in the 1930s. It is important as the first longitudinal, comprehensive attempt to study curriculum and schooling effects.

Enacted curriculum means the same thing as the *curriculum-in-use,* referring to the teacher and students' real-time engagement of the curriculum.

Epistemology is an area of Western philosophy concerned with the nature of knowledge. Its particular importance in curriculum is the emphasis on the creation and organization of knowledge that would then be the basis for the curriculum.

Essentialism is an applied philosophy associated with late-19th- and early-20th-century educational progressivism in the United States that values the teaching of basic or "essential" information for effective citizenship, work, and life pursuits.

Evaluation is the process of determining a value for something based on specified criteria. In its broadest meaning, it refers to evaluating programs. In its narrower meaning, it refers to specific aspects of schooling such as student achievement, instruction, curriculum, contextual factors, or some combination of those aspects of schooling.

Existentialism is the philosophical position that posits reality as personal and subjective. The implication is that the curriculum and the school should avoid imposing other perspectives on learners.

F

Faculty psychology. See *mental discipline.*

Field test is a phase of curriculum development that may occur in a new development, adoption, or adaptation. The purpose is to try out the curriculum or a specific element of it on a large scale during development with the intended users to determine if it is doing what it was intended to do. See also *piloting.*

Focus or explicit knowledge refers to what you know about something that is in focus from its characteristics, as you perceive and think about it. This explicit kind of knowledge and *tacit knowledge* are ways of knowing from a personal perspective.

Formal knowledge is a term referring to any body of knowledge accepted as proven and that forms the basis of disciplines and is what schools in a modified version are expected to teach to the students. See also *informal knowledge.*

Formative in various kinds of curriculum work refers to what occurs in the early phases of development activity. It is most closely associated with evaluation and assessment activities in themselves and as activities within policy making, management, and curriculum development work.

Formative assessment. See *assessment.*

Formative evaluation. See *evaluation.*

Functionalism is a psychological school that holds that the school and curriculum should represent the contemporary social, economic, and political arrangements as real and appropriate, and should prepare students with the experiences to maintain the present patterns.

Fusion curriculum refers to a curriculum pattern in which elements of two or more disciplines of knowledge are formed into a new entity. The new curriculum achieves its own identity and defining characteristics over time. See *academic-subject curriculum.*

G

Generalization is a statement using the best available knowledge about a topic or issue that summarizes the relationship between two or more ideas in that knowledge. Generalization concept development activities were central to the *inquiry-based curriculum* movement in the 1960s reform era.

Globalism refers to the school of thought that holds that *globalization* is the active process for change in the world.

Globalization is the process of interconnectivity that brings into contact all parts of the world, particularly those supported by computer and other electronic communications. It also includes economic, social, and political interactions without regard to states or boundaries, as in a *global village.*

Global village is the image of a world wired together or interconnected by electronic communication. It was first put forward by Marshall McLuhan and has since come to metaphorically represent the process of *globalization* in *globalism.*

Grounded knowledge refers to that which is real and essential as in, for example, the basic formal knowledge to be learned in becoming a teacher. Applied to a single body of knowledge, curriculum, for example, it is the foundational or first level of knowledge, the *grounding,* upon and from which other levels of knowledge building occur up to that level where the newest knowledge is being produced.

Grounding refers to obtaining or being introduced to a general level of knowledge, as in being grounded in physics, acquiring an essential and verifiable rather than contrived or speculative knowledge.

H

High-stakes test refers to a particular test and a particular score on that test being used to make decisions about student retention and advancement. If the test is used to decide such questions as whether a diploma will be granted or what kind, then that is a high-stakes test because the results are of extreme importance to the individual who takes the test and the decision based on the test has significant social, academic, and economic impact both immediate and long term.

Humanistic psychology is a school of psychology concerned with the subjective nature of experience, knowing, and other aspects of being human. It eschews quantitative methods of research for those that are qualitative because what is real consists of that which is perceived and understood through human consciousness and not by other means.

I

Idealism is a school of philosophy tracing back to Plato. The central idea in idealism is that reality, what can be known, exists in the mental world of ideas, not in the senses.

Informal knowledge is knowledge that is personal and usually idiosyncratic meaning derived form everyday experience and often mixed with popular knowledge, as in being "streetwise." See also *formal knowledge.*

Inquiry-based curriculum encompasses the view that curriculum should be based on investigative or inquiry activities about topics and issues to develop critical concepts and generalizations from the disciplines of knowledge. Characteristics in this approach include active student learning, *spiraling,* knowledge based on the *structure-of-the-discipline,* and modeling the activity of scholars in the disciplines. See also *academic-subject curriculum.*

Instruction in schooling is the process of activating the curriculum. It is the engagement of the curriculum by the student as directed by the teacher or other assigned person. Instruction and curriculum are two different but confluent aspects of schooling.

Interstate Education Agent is a neutral term used to refer to other organizations outside of specific government or quasi-governmental standing that can be either regional or national in their scope of activity and their memberships.

K

Knowledge cycle refers to a series of actions by which knowledge is created and validated in the work of disciplines, as in *knowledge production and use.*

Knowledge production and use refers to one of the tasks of scholars in a discipline, to produce and use knowledge. The process is usually depicted as a cyclical form often referred to simply as the *knowledge cycle.*

Knowledge tools are the theories, methods, and models to be learned in the formal knowledge of disciplines like curriculum where work is creating and validating useful knowledge through scholarly and practice activities.

L

Learner-centered curriculum refers to a curriculum orientation in which the emphasis is on the human being as central to all curriculum considerations. This approach in curriculum essentially grew out of the early-20th-century child study movement and emphasis on curriculum arising from the needs of the child, a child-centered curriculum. It is sometimes referred to as *student-centered.* See also *knowledge-centered curriculum* and *social-centered curriculum*

Legitimacy is a criterion in curriculum that refers to the authority and legal standing behind policy making and practice in curriculum work.

Lesson plan is one of the most important documents in curriculum work because the teacher's lesson plan details the curriculum that is to be taught. As it is implemented, it becomes the *curriculum-in-use.* See also *curriculum units.*

Logics in philosophy refer to what can be known as functions of the mind. Thinking, as the work of the mind, operates in a logical manner either inductively or deductively according to their formulations in philosophy. In curriculum, it refers to the way of thinking in the discipline, the learned forms of thinking practitioners use in doing curriculum work. See *structure-of-the-discipline.*

M

Management can be described as activities organized to accomplish a specified mission (goals, ends) integrated into a process containing the necessary resources to accomplish that mission. In short, management is the organization and oversight activities of the process that provides a product or service.

Management process consists of that set of organization and oversight activities that ensures a coherent and consistent procedure from which a product or service will result. It is important curriculum work like policy making, planning, and curriculum development.

Management strategy is the *management process,* the collection of supervising activities, of oversight, that have a particular application, and the *management tools,* the ways of thinking and the objects for application that they use, that are organized to constitute a strategic plan of management.

Management tools are the specific tools, curriculum mapping or assessment-evaluation techniques, for example, in the management process.

Mental discipline was a dominant learning theory of the 19th and early 20th centuries in which the mind was viewed as composed of discrete faculties or areas connected to kinds of knowledge. Students could acquire the designated knowledge through specific learning experiences that "exercised" the particular faculty being addressed.

Metaphysics refers to an area in philosophy focusing on the nature of reality; it is also referred to as *ontology.*

Modernism is associated with a scientific, logical, positivist discourse with its emphasis on quantitative methods of inquiry.

Modes of knowing are ways of thinking that produce knowledge for the individual. To understand thinking as a process of creating knowledge, behavior can be studied and kinds of knowledge (e.g., tacit, experience, procedural) can be inferred and classified in various ways, modes or intelligence, for example.

N

Nativism is any social and political movement to establish policy favoring the interests of the established inhabitants over those of immigrants.

Needs assessment is most often associated with the curriculum work of Hilda Taba. The idea is to build curriculum based on the needs of community, students, or some other social unit by systematically gathering information about what students ought to know or schools ought to teach so that can be the basis for curriculum in schooling.

NGOs, or non-governmental organizations, are noneducational and humanitarian agencies, such as the Red Cross, in the larger national and international scene, and educational organizations like UNESCO, the United Nations Educational, Scientific, and Cultural Organization, which also operates at that level.

Niche curriculum is a curriculum developed for a special purpose or requirement. A drug education or character education curriculum is an example. These can vary in their use across states, within districts, or within schools, based on the authority requesting the curriculum.

Normal school refers to a kind of institution created in the 19th century to train teachers for schools. They varied in the length of time required for study, what was studied, and the kind of certificate given and enrolled mostly women. State governments created many, whereas others were private. They were not always equivalent to other institutions of higher education such as colleges and the later universities.

Norms are established scores resulting from examination of many scores from students in similar groups or having a similar set of characteristics. See *standardized tests.*

O

Objectives-based testing refers to the formulation of tests based on curriculum objectives that guide curriculum work, as in development or policy making, and are intended to assess the level at which the curriculum objective has been attained.

Ontology is an area in philosophy that deals with questions about the nature of reality. *Metaphysics* has the same meaning.

P

Paradigm refers to the set of assumptions, concepts, values, and practices that constitutes a way of looking at things, usually shared in common by a community of scholars. The concept of a paradigm is most closely associated with the work of Thomas Kuhn.

Perennialism is a school of philosophy that views certain kinds of knowledge as having been validated historically, a kind of eternal wisdom that should make up the curriculum.

Performance indicators are markers, or pieces of evidence, that mean something has been attained. Applied to performance, the appearance of a designated indicator or cluster of indicators is the measure of attainment.

Philosophy refers to an ancient discipline in the humanities field that relies on logic to understand knowledge, ethics, values, and other eternal, basic questions of being and existence. Those are fundamental questions in any area of knowledge, and there are philosophies such as *essentialism, existentialism, idealism, realism, perennialism,* and *pragmatism* that have application in education and curriculum, usually as *philosophical statements* incorporated in a curriculum theory or perspective. See also *epistemology, metaphysics (ontology),* and *logic.*

Philosophy or philosophical statements in curriculum work, particularly in policy making and development, refer to some statement or statements about values and vision that reflect the purposes and worldviews of the person, people, or community involved.

Philosophy of science is the systematic study of its (science's) structure and components (data, theories, and guiding principles), techniques, assumptions, and limitations. The scientific method, the way of doing science, has been at various times associated with fashionable thinkers such as Francis Bacon (inductive) and Isaac Newton (deductive) and their particular systems of reasoning, both of which espoused an empiricism or verification by observation and experiment.

Piloting in curriculum development projects is a phase to assess and evaluate with a target population that will use the curriculum. A pilot phase is small scale as contrasted with *field-testing,* which is large scale. Both are scaled to the intent and size of the development and the population that would use the curriculum.

Plan segues from policy to implementation and is usually in some written form in curriculum work, with statements about goals or objectives, a series of steps to implement them, identification of curriculum to be taught, instructional tools to use, and some immediate feedback loop for evaluation of the experience. See *lesson plan.*

Planning can be thought of as the process of creating an image, graphic, or textual representation of how the intent of the policy will be carried out and how the tools will be used.

Planning by objectives refers to developing a curriculum plan based on the stated objectives to be achieved. See also *teaching objectives.*

Pluralism is a concept meaning the acceptance of permanent cultural and social differences rather than assimilation into one cultural or social entity.

Policy enactment refers to that part of *policy making* where the policy sets up the actions and identifies the agent that will implement what is intended in the statement.

Policy making is the process of taking an idea into action by interpreting what institutions and the people in them should do and then stating what it is they will do while giving them the tools to do it. It includes both a *policy statement* and *policy enactment.*

Policy statement is the expression of intent in *policy making* by some agent or agency and precedes *policy enactment.*

Postmodernism is a representation of ideas and events as beyond modernism. It is a post–World War II school of philosophy that values and promotes human uniqueness while criticizing technology and power as injurious to human progress. Postmodernism is suspicious of positivistic science traditions and the search for objective truth in view of the subjective nature of human existence.

Practice knowledge is knowledge created from the actual actions taken, as in becoming a good golfer through repetitive play, and learning from that experience. In curriculum, it is the knowledge that informs the discipline from the practice, or applied, side of curriculum work.

Pragmatism is a school of philosophy based on realities such as the changing nature of the universe, knowledge itself, and the human condition. It rejects the idea that there is one body of unchanging knowledge that guides existence and should be learned by all.

Procedural knowledge is knowledge about how to do something. It is often cited as one of the *modes of knowing.*

Process refers to a flow of actions, as in following a set of established instructions, or it could refer to creating a sequence of actions to be followed. See *curriculum process.*

Program evaluation simply means finding out if and how something is working in the school and classroom by using assessment tools and creating a value for the results.

Progressive Education Association existed during the early-20th-century progressive movement as an arm of that movement concerned with schools and schooling.

Progressivism is a mainly American multifaceted political, social, economic, and educational movement of the late 19th and early 20th centuries that accepted change as the main constant in life. A progressive curriculum would emphasize the student as an active learner and use the most current scholarly and scientific knowledge. Of critical importance was the readiness of the learner and a supportive family context. Educational progressivism sought to shift curriculum away from *mental discipline* and traditional knowledge by emphasizing newer physical, biological, and social science knowledge.

Psychomotor domain refers to creating educational objectives around skills broadly conceived as in the development of the body's small and large muscle systems. The curriculum should reflect psychomotor development through physical and performance activities. See also the *cognitive* and *affective* domains.

Q

Qualitative is a term used to represent a set of research methods in the interpretivist inquiry tradition that seek to reveal meaning in a situation, context, or setting, and includes case studies, narratives, grounded theory, and the ethnographic.

Quantitative is a term referring to a set of methods associated with scientific or positivistic inquiry that includes experimental, quasi-experimental, comparative, and qualitative descriptive forms of research.

R

Realism is a Western philosophy associated with Aristotle that knowledge consists of unchanging truths that can be verified and learned through powers of rational thought. A curriculum based on Realism would consist of the truths and the process of verification.

Reconstructionism is a particular philosophical view holding that the current political, economic, and social arrangements need to be changed to promote progress and a just society. The school and curriculum should be shaped to promote that reconstruction of society.

Reform means to take what exists and change it. The change might be modest or extensive. Applied to the contemporary reform movement, it refers to changing schools, the schooling process, curriculum, and any other aspect that will bring accountability.

Rubrics are guidelines or sets of guidelines that frame how something is to be done. In education, these are usually associated with assessments and developing curriculum based on standards. Rubrics are also used in making qualitative judgments about performances.

S

Schema refers to an interpretation of cognitive processes as the internal thought structures used in processing new information. Inferring schemas that would be required in learning something would assist a worker in developing or planning a curriculum.

School is a word referring to an institution or system of institutions established under the authority of a society, usually through the political unit of the state, for the education of the young in that society.

Schooling refers to the formal process of learning a specified curriculum that usually occurs in schools but can also be found in other settings, such as the home. Schooling derives from learning in schools, an implied sanctioning of that process in settings authorized under the auspices of the state.

Scope refers to the breadth and depth of what the curriculum contains. It is one of the *curriculum fundamentals.*

Sequence is another *curriculum fundamental,* referring to the ordering of curriculum content.

Skills in curriculum refer to procedural and psychomotor learning that would be prefaced in the curriculum content. It also can mean the motor aspects of thinking and the *psychomotor domain.*

Social-centered curriculum is one of three overarching perspectives that emphasize the society, learner, and subject matter as central to any curriculum organization. The social-centered curriculum refers to those proposals that see the need to prepare the young for the continuation and betterment of society. See also *student-centered* and *academic-subject curriculum.*

Social efficiency movement refers to an emphasis on schooling and learning for economic benefits to the individual and society through specialization and building expertise. At the core is a reliance on technology in the mechanical form, a typewriter, for example, that later included other developments such as computers. It is a blend or confluence of the social and student-centered curriculum orientations advocated by Franklin Bobbitt.

Spiral curriculum is a conceptualization that curriculum should be organized from simple to complex and concrete to abstract in how content is ordered at each level and in moving through the K–12 grades. This creates a spiraling effect of knowledge development and sophistication in the curriculum. This is associated with *inquiry-based curriculum, structure-of-the-discipline* and *structure-of-the intellect* ideas.

Standardized tests are tests constructed from other test scores to create *norms* or expected scores. These are constructed from scientifically selected samples of students as a group.

Standards-based education is the development of educational practices based on (a) clearly stated and measurable descriptions of what students are to know and do as a result of schooling, (b) a curriculum allowing students to meet those descriptions, and (c) assessments developed to evaluate student achievement or attainment levels.

Strategic management is an idea of management as a confluence of actions to form and implement plans to achieve specified objectives. See also *curriculum management* and *management strategy.*

Structure refers to the framework or skeletal arrangements of something. In curriculum, it refers to the logics, literature, perspectives, and so forth embedded in the knowledge base and serving as tools in curriculum practice.

Structure-of-the-discipline is a way to organize the curriculum based on disciplines of knowledge and how they are structured. The emphasis is on the *processes* or ways that discipline workers (scholars and practitioners) organize their work, how they think, and what knowledge they use in doing their work in creating new knowledge. It is associated with *spiraling inquiry-based curriculum,* and *structure-of- the- intellect* ideas for organizing curriculum.

Structure-of-the-intellect is a multidimensional model of human intellect developed by J. P. Guilford to identify the elements in intellectual thought that could be a basis for considering how to plan and develop curriculum. It is one of the approaches to organizing curriculum based on interpretations and models of intellect like *spiraling,* or the *spiral curriculum,* and *inquiry-based curriculum.*

Student-centered curriculum is an orientation that wants curriculum focused on all aspects of student needs for their development. The term *learner-centered* is often used to mean the same thing. See also *social-centered* and *academic-subject curriculum.*

Subject-centered or **subject-matter curriculum.** See *academic subject curriculum.*

Summative refers to a determination about something made at the end. Although most often used with *assessment* or *evaluation* to mean a look at the results at the end, it can also be associated with new curriculum development or adaptation work. See *formative.*

T

Tacit knowledge is personally held knowledge about how to do something that doesn't require explanation or other outward elaboration. It is also knowledge embedded in organizational and group relationships that is personally held and shared but unspoken. It is hard to identify, map, or signify in other ways, much in the way that attaining élan or esprit de corps marks the military person and unit by its unconscious exhibition.

Taxonomy is a type of classification system that indicates the order of relationships among elements. In education, taxonomies have been constructed for three domains, *cognitive, affective, and psychomotor,* particularly for developing objectives for instruction and curriculum.

Teaching refers to the learned process and practice of making and implementing decisions about curriculum, instruction, learning, assessment, and evaluation for learners.

Teaching objectives are the ends to be achieved when the teaching is complete. They should guide the development of the *lesson plan, unit,* and curriculum choices in planning. Planning in this way is sometimes referred to as teaching-by-objectives.

Technological refers to a type of orientation about curriculum based on the use of *technology.*

Technology is a term referring to constructing tools to make and use tools, as in moving from hand creation, or manufacturing, to industrialization, or tools used to create tools. In the 19th century, scientific applications gave technology its contemporary meaning as scientific tool making. The term has become widely used and has acquired different social, cultural, and commercial meanings.

Theory in curriculum work refers to *curriculum theory.*

Trend is a prevailing inclination about some thing that persists in the long term.

Traditional assessment is a term referring to particular and well-known tools used in assessment such as teacher-created paper-pencil, commercially produced, and standardized tests.

V

Validation in curriculum work means to determine the degree to which expectations in the form of outcomes and the curriculum or curriculum materials that manifest those outcomes match performance represented in some form of data.

Recommended Readings

Adams, J. E., Jr. (2000). *Taking charge of curriculum.* New York: Teachers College Press.

Aldridge, J., & Goldman, R. (2002). *Current issues and trends in education.* New York: Allyn & Bacon/Longman.

Alexander, P. A. (2003). Can we get there from here? *Educational Researcher, 32*(8), 3–4.

Bagley, W. C. (1910). *Educational values.* New York: Macmillan.

Bagley, W. C. (1941). The case for essentialism in education. *National Education Association Journal, 30*(7), 202–220.

Bailyn, B. (1960). *Education in the forming of the American society.* New York: Vintage Books.

Baker, B. D., & Friedman-Nimz, R. (2004). State policies and equal opportunity: The example of gifted education. *Educational Evaluation and Policy Analysis, 26*(1), 39–64.

Ball, D. L., & Cohen, D. K. (1996). Reform by the book: What is—or might be—the role of curriculum materials in teacher learning and instructional reform? *Educational Researcher, 25*(9), 6–8.

Bauer, H. H. (1995). *Scientific literacy and the myth of the scientific method.* Urbana: University of Illinois Press.

Behar, L. S. (1994). *The knowledge base of curriculum: An empirical analysis.* Lanham, MD: University Press of America.

Bereiter, C., & Scardamalia, M. (1992). Cognition and curriculum. In P. W. Jackson (Ed.), *Handbook of research on curriculum.* New York: American Educational Research Association/Macmillan.

Bereiter, C., Scardamalia, M., Cassell, C., & Hewitt, J. (1997). Postmodernism, knowledge building, and elementary science. *Elementary School Journal, 97*(4), 329–340.

Berliner, D. C. (1994). The wonder of exemplary performance. In J. N. Mangieri & C. C. Block (Eds.), *Creating powerful thinking in teachers and students* (Chap. 7). Fort Worth, TX: Harcourt Brace College.

Berliner, D. C. (2003, April 15). Educational psychology as a policy science: Thoughts on the distinction between a discipline and a profession. *Canadian Journal of Educational Administration and Policy.* Retrieved February 2004 from www.umanitoba.ca/publications/cjeap/

Bestor, A. (1953). *Wastelands: The retreat from learning in our public schools.* Urbana: University of Illinois Press.

Bohm, D., & Peat, F. D. (2000). *Science, order, and creativity.* New York: Routledge.

Boostrom, R. E. (2005). *Thinking: The foundation of critical and creative learning in the classroom.* New York: Teachers College Press.

Bronfenbrenner, U. (1979). *The ecology of human development: Experiments by nature and design.* Cambridge, MA: Harvard University Press.

Bronowski, J., & Mazlish, B. (1960). *Western intellectual thought from Leonardo to Hegel.* New York: Harper & Row.

Broudy, H. S. (1988). *The uses of schooling.* New York: Routledge.

Broudy, H. S., Smith, B. O., & Burnett, J. R. (1963). *Democracy and excellence in American secondary education.* Chicago: Rand McNally.

Bruner, J. (1971, September). The process of education revisited. *Phi Delta Kappan, 53,* 18–21.

Bruner, J. (1993). *The culture of education.* Cambridge, MA: Harvard University Press.

Burbes, N. C. (1993). *Dialogue in teaching: Theory and practice.* New York: Teachers College Press.

Burtless, G. (Ed.). (1996). *Does money matter: The effect of school resources on student achievement and adult success.* Washington, DC: Brookings Institution Press.

Carlsen, A., Klev, R., & Von Krogh, G. (Eds.). (2004). *Living knowledge: The dynamics of professional service work.* London: Palgrave Macmillan.

Chi, M. T. H., Glower, R., & Farr, M. J. (Eds.). (1988). *The nature of expertise.* Hillside, NJ: Lawrence Erlbaum.

Chua, A. (2002). The suicide of free-market democracy? *Wilson Quarterly, 29*(4), 62–77.

Cobb, P., McLain, K., de Dilva Lamberg, T., & Dean, C. (2003). Situating teacher's instructional practices in the institutional setting of the school. *Educational Researcher, 32*(6), 13–24.

Coburn, C. E. (2005). The role of nonsystem actors in the relationship between policy and practice: The case of reading instruction in California. *Educational Evaluation and Policy Analysis, 27*(1), 23–52.

Cole, M. (1995). The supra-individual envelope of development: Activity and practice, situation and context. In J. J. Goodnow, P. J. Miller, & F. Kessel (Eds.), *Cultural practices and contexts for development* (pp. 105–118). San Francisco: Jossey-Bass.

Combs, A. W. (1979). *Myths in education.* Boston: Allyn & Bacon.

Costa, A. L., & Loveall, R. A. (2002). The legacy of Hilda Taba. *Journal of Curriculum and Supervision, 18*(1), 56–62.

Cross, C. T. (2004). *Political education.* New York: Teachers College Press.

Cross, R., & Parker, A. (2004a). Staying close to the teacher. *Teachers College Record, 105*(8), 1586–1605.

Cross, R., & Parker, A. (2004b). *The hidden power of social networks: Understanding how work really gets done in organizations.* Boston: Harvard Business School Press.

Cuban, L. (2004). Assessing the 20-year impact of Multiple Intelligences on schooling. *Teachers College Record, 106*(1), 140–146.

Curriculum Development Associates. (1970). *Man: A course of study.* New York: Author.

De Alba, A., Gonzalez-Gaudiano, E., Lankshear, C., & Peters, M. (1999). *Curriculum in the post modern condition.* New York: Peter Lang.

Deets, J. (2000). Maps and curriculum decision-making. *Journal of Curriculum and Supervision, 15*(4), 359–371.

Denzin, N. K., & Lincoln, Y. S. (1994). Introduction: Entering the field of qualitative research. In N. K. Denzin & Y. S. Lincoln (Eds.), *Handbook of qualitative research* (pp. 1–17). London: Sage.

Donaldson, L. (2001). *The contingency theory of organizations.* Thousand Oaks, CA: Sage.

Downing, D. B. (2005). *The knowledge contract: Politics and paradigms in the academic work place.* Lincoln: University of Nebraska Press.

Drucker, P. F. (1999, October). Beyond the information revolution. *Atlantic, 284*(4), 47–57.

Drucker, P. F. (2001, November 3). The next society. *The Economist,* 13–20.

Early, M. J., & Rehage, K. J. (Eds.). (1999). *Issues in curriculum: A selection of chapters from past NSSE yearbooks* (Ninety-Eighth Yearbook of the National Society for the Study of Education, Part II). Chicago: National Society for the Study of Education.

Educational Policy Commission. (1947, March). The imperative needs of youth of secondary school age. *Bulletin of the National Association of Secondary School Principals, 31,* 145.

Educational Research Service. (2003). *Handbook of research on improving student achievement* (3rd ed.). Arlington, VA: Educational Research Service.

Eisner, E. (1991). *The enlightened eye: Qualitative inquiry and the enhancement of educational practice.* New York: Macmillan.

Eisner, E. (1992). Curriculum ideologies. In P. W. Jackson (Ed.), *Handbook of research on curriculum* (pp. 302–326). New York: Macmillan.

Evans, R. W. (2004). *The social studies wars.* New York: Teachers College Press.

Ewert, G. D. (1991) Habermas and education: A comprehensive overview of the influence of Habermas in educational literature. *Review of Educational Research, 61*(3), 345–378.

Fein, L. J. (1971). *The ecology of the public schools: An inquiry into community control.* New York: Pegasus.

Feltovich, P., Ford, K. M., & Hoffman, R. R. (Eds.). (1997). *Expertise in context: Man and machine.* Cambridge, MA: AAAI/MIT Press.

Fennema, E., & Leder, R. (1998). *Mathematics and gender: Influences on teachers and students.* New York: Teachers College Press.

Fisher, M. (1967). *Workshops in the wilderness.* New York: Oxford University Press.

Foray, D. (2004). *The economics of knowledge.* Cambridge, MA: MIT Press.

Fusarelli, L. D. (2003). *The political dynamics of school choice.* New York: Palgrave Macmillan.

Garibaldi, W. (2000). *Negotiating postmodernism.* Minneapolis: University of Minnesota Press.

Gee, J. P. (1999a). *An introduction to discourse analysis: Theory and method.* London: Routledge.

Gee, J. P. (1999b). The future of the social turn. *Research in Language and Social Interaction, 32*(1 & 2), 61–68.

Gee, J. P. (2000). Communities of practice in the new capitalism. *Journal of Learning Sciences, 9*(4), 515–523.

Gee, J. P., Hull, G., & Lankshear, C. (2003). *The new work order.* Boulder, CO: Westview Press.

Geis, G. L., & Smith, M. E. (1992). The function of evaluation. In H. D. Stolovitch & E. J. Keep (Eds.), *Handbook of human performance technology* (pp.130–150). San Francisco: Jossey-Bass.

Gill, B. P., Timpane, M., Ross, K. E., & Brewer, D. J. (2001). *Rhetoric versus reality*. Santa Monica, CA: Rand.

Glanz, J. (2002). *Finding your leadership style*. Arlington, VA: Association for Supervision and Curriculum Development.

Glass, R. D. (2001). On Paulo Freire's philosophy of praxis and the foundations of liberation education. *Educational Researcher, 30*(2), 15–25.

Glesne, C. (1999). *Becoming qualitative researchers* (2nd ed.). New York: Longman.

Glossop, R. G. (1988). Bronfenbrenner's ecology of human development: A reappreciation. In A. R. Spence (Ed.), *Ecological research with children and families* (pp. 1–15). New York: Teachers College Press.

Goddard, R. G. (2003). Relational networks, social trust, and norms: A social capital perspective on students' chances of academic success. *Educational Evaluation and Policy Analysis, 25*(1), 59–74.

Gonzalez, N. (2004). Disciplining the discipline: Anthropology and the pursuit of quality education. *Educational Researcher, 33*(5), 17–25.

Goodson, I. F. (1997). *The changing curriculum*. New York: Peter Lang.

Graham, P. A. (2005). *Schooling America: How the public schools meet the nations's changing needs*. New York: Oxford University Press.

Grant, M. (1916). *The passing of the great race: Or, the racial basis of European history*. New York: C. Scribner.

Griffin, E. M. (1997). *A first look at communication theory*. New York: McGraw-Hill.

Halpern, D. P. (2003). *Thought and knowledge: An introduction to critical thinking* (4th ed.). New York: Lawrence Erlbaum.

Hart, B., & Risley, T. R. (1995). *Meaningful differences in the everyday experience of young American children*. Baltimore: Paul H. Brookes.

Hart, B., & Risley, T. R. (1999). *The social world of children learning to talk*. Baltimore: Paul H. Brookes.

Hatano, G., & Oura, Y. (2003). Commentary: Reconceptualizing school learning using insights from expertise research. *Educational Researcher, 32*(8), 26–29.

Hatch, T., White, M. E., & Faigenbaum, D. (2005). Expertise, credibility, and influence: How teachers can influence policy, advance research, and improve performance. *Teachers College Record, 107*(5), 1004–1035.

Hawthorne, R. K. (1992). *Curriculum in the making: Teacher choice and the classroom experience*. New York: Teachers College Press.

Henderson, J. G. (2001). Deepening democratic curriculum work. *Educational Researcher, 30*(9), 18–21.

Hess, F. M. (1998). *Spinning wheels: The politics of urban school reform*. Washington, DC: Brookings Institute.

Hillocks, G. (2002). *The testing trap: How state writing assessments control learning*. New York: Teachers College Press.

Hittleman, D. R., & Simon, A. J. (1997). *Interpreting educational research*. Columbus, OH: Merrill/Prentice Hall.

Hlebowitsh, P. S. (1997). The search for the curriculum field. *Journal of Curriculum Studies, 29*(5), 507–511.

Honig, M. L., & Hatch T. C. (2004). Crafting coherence: How schools strategically manage multiple, external demands. *Educational Researcher, 33*(8), 3–15.

Huebner, D. (1966). Curricular language and classroom meaning. In J. B. Macdonald & R. S. Leeper (Eds.), *Language and meaning* (pp. 8–26). Washington, DC: Association for Supervision and Curriculum Development.

Hull, G., & Schultz, K. (2001). Literacy and learning out of school: A review of theory and research. *Review of Educational Research, 71*(4), 575–611.

Jackson, P. W. (1980). Curriculum and its discontents. *Curriculum Inquiry, 1,* 28–43.

Jackson, P. W. (1990). The functions of educational research. *Educational Researcher, 19*(7), 3–9.

Jacobs, H. H. (2003). Connecting curriculum mapping and technology. *Curriculum Technology Quarterly, 12*(3), 1–4.

Jacobs, H. H. (2004). *Getting results with curriculum mapping.* Alexandria, VA: Association for Supervision and Curriculum Development.

Johnson, R. B., & Christensen, L. (2004). *Educational research: Quantitative and qualitative approaches* (2nd ed.). New York: Allyn & Bacon.

Jones, L.V., & Olkin, I. (Eds.). (2004). *The nation's report card: Evolution and perspectives.* Bloomington, IN: Phi Delta Kappa Educational Foundation.

Kanpol, B. (1999). *Critical pedagogy.* Westport, CT: Bergin & Harvey.

Kaplan, A. (1964). *The conduct of inquiry.* San Francisco: Chandler.

Kendall, J. S., & Marzano, R. J. (1996). *Content knowledge: A compendium of standards and benchmarks for K–12 education.* Alexandria, VA: Association for Supervision and Curriculum Development.

Kennan, G. F. (1950). *American diplomacy, 1900–1950.* Chicago: University of Chicago Press.

Kincheloe, J. L. (1997). Introduction. In I. Goodson (Ed.), *The changing curriculum: Studies in social construction* (pp. ix-xl). New York: Peter Lang.

Kincheloe, J. L., Steinberg, S., & Villaverde, L. (1999). *Rethinking intelligence: Confronting psychological assumptions about teaching and learning.* New York: Routledge.

Kirk, D. (1990). School knowledge and the curriculum package-as-text. *Journal of Curriculum Studies, 22*(5), 409–425.

Kirst, M. W. (2000). Bridging educational research and educational policymaking. *Oxford Review of Education, 26*(3/4), 379–391.

Kliebard, H. M. (1999). The liberal arts curriculum and its enemies: The effort to redefine general education. In M. J. Early & K. J. Rehage (Eds.), *Issues in curriculum: A selection of chapters from past NSSE yearbooks* (Ninety-Eighth Yearbook of the National Society for the Study of Education, pp. 1–26). Chicago: National Society for the Study of Education.

Kornbalm, M. L. (2004). Appropriate and inappropriate forms of testing, assessment, accountability. *Educational Policy, 18*(1), 45–70.

Kuhn, T. S. (1977). *The essential tension: Selected studies in scientific traditions and change.* Chicago: University of Chicago Press.

Lankshear, C. (1997). Language and the new capitalism. *International Journal of Inclusive Education, 1*(4), 309–321.

Lasch, C. (1965). *The new radicalism in America: 1889–1963.* New York: Alfred A. Knopf.

Lasch, C. (1995). *Revolt of the elites.* New York: Norton.

Lines, P. M. (2003). *Support for home-based education: Promising partnerships between public schools and families who instruct their children at home.* Eugene: Clearinghouse for Educational Management, College of Education, University of Oregon.

Linn, R. L., & Haug, C. (2002). Stability of school-building accountability scores and gains. *Educational Evaluation and Policy Analysis, 24*(1), 29–36.

Logan, K. M. (1997). *Getting the school you want.* Thousand Oaks, CA: Corwin.

Luke, A. (1995). Text and discourse in education: An introduction to critical discourse analysis. In M. W. Apple (Ed.), *Review of research in education* (pp. 3–48). Washington, DC: American Educational Research Association.

Marshall, C., Mitchell, D., & Wirt, F. (1989). *Culture and educational policy in the American states.* New York: Falmer.

Marx, L. (1997). The emergence of hazardous concept. *Social Research, 64*(5), 965–988.

Mazlish, B. (2005). *Civilization and its contents.* Palo Alto, CA: Stanford University Press.

McDonnell, L. M. (2005). Assessment and accountability from the policymaker's perspective. In J. L. Herman & E. H. Haertel (Eds.), *Uses and misuses of data for educational accountability and improvement* (104th Yearbook of the National Society for the Study of Education, Part II, pp. 35–54). Malden, MA: National Society for the Study of Education/Blackwell.

McEwan, E. K., & McEwan, P. J. (2003). *Making sense of research: What's good, what's not, and how to tell the difference.* Thousand Oaks, CA: Corwin.

McLaren, P. (1999). A pedagogy of possibility: Reflecting upon Paulo Freire's politics of education. *Educational Researcher, 28*(2), 49–54.

Merriam-Webster. (1988). *Webster's ninth new collegiate dictionary.* Springfield, MA: Merriam-Webster.

Morrison, K. R. B. (2004). The poverty of curriculum theory: A critique of Wraga and Hlebowitsh. *Journal of Curriculum Studies, 36*(4), 487–494.

Moss, P. A. (2004). Curricular coherence in assessment design. In M. Wilson (Ed.), *Toward coherence between classroom assessment and accountability* (103rd Yearbook of the National Society for the Study of Education, pp. 217–238). Chicago: National Society for the Study of Education.

Murphy, J. (2000). Governing American schools: The shifting playing field. *Teachers College Record, 102*(1), 576–584.

National Research Council. (2002). *Scientific research in education.* Washington, DC: National Academy Press.

Nelson, M. R. (1978). Rugg on Rugg: His theories and his curriculum. *Curriculum Inquiry, 8*(2), 119–153.

Newman, J. W. (2002). *American teacher: An introduction* (4th ed.). New York: Allyn & Bacon.

No Child Left Behind Act of 2001. (2002). Pub L. No. 107–110.

Nobel, T. (2004). Integrating the revised Bloom's Taxonomy with Multiple Intelligences: A planning tool for curriculum differentiation. *Teachers College Record, 106*(1), 193–211.

Oliva, P. F. (2004). *Developing the curriculum* (6th ed.). New York: Pearson Allyn & Bacon.

Orlofsky, D. D. (2002). *Redefining teacher education: The theories of Jerome Bruner and the training of teachers.* New York: Peter Lang.

Ornstein, A. C., & Hunkins, F. P. (2004). *Curriculum: Foundations, principles, and issues* (4th ed.). New York: Pearson Allyn & Bacon.

Ozman, H. D., & Craver, S. M. (2002). *Philosophical foundations of education* (7th ed.). Upper Saddle River, NJ: Prentice Hall / Wiley.

Paavola, S., Lipponen, L., & Hakkarainen, K. (2004). Models of innovative knowledge communities and three metaphors of learning. *Review of Educational Research, 74*(4), 557–576.

Paul, J. L., & Kofi, M. (2001). Preparation of educational researchers in philosophical foundations of inquiry. *Review of Educational Research, 71*(4), 525–547.

Pillow, W. S. (2000). Deciphering attempts to decipher postmodern educational research. *Educational Researcher, 29*(5), 21–24.

Placier, M. L. (1993). The semantics of state policy making: The case of "at risk." *Educational Evaluation and Policy Analysis, 15*(4), 380–395.

Popkewitz, T. S. (1987). The formation of school subjects and the political context of schooling. In T. S. Popkewitz (Ed.), *The formation of the school subjects* (pp. 1–24). New York: Falmer Press.

Popkewitz, T. S. (1997). A changing terrain of knowledge and power: A social epistemology of educational research. *Educational Researcher, 26*(9), 18–29.

Portelli, J. P. (1987). On defining curriculum. *Journal of Supervision and Curriculum Development, 2*(4), 354–367.

Posner, G. F. (1998). Models of curriculum planning. In L. E. Byers & M. W. Apple (Eds.), *The curriculum* (2nd ed., pp. 79–100). Albany: State University of New York Press.

Postman, N (1995). *The end of education: Redefining the value of school.* New York: A. A. Knopf.

Pratt, D. O. (2004). *Shipshewana: An Indiana Amish community.* Indianapolis: Quarry Books/ University of Indiana Press.

Preedy, M. (2001). Curriculum evaluation: Measuring what we value. In D. Middlewood & N. Burton (Eds.), *Managing the curriculum* (pp. 89–103). London: Paul Chapman/Sage.

Puryear, J. M. (2005). Building education research capacity in developing countries: Some fundamental issues. *Peabody Journal of Education, 80*(1), 93–99.

Reid, W. A. (1998). "Reconceptualist" and "dominant" perspectives in curriculum theory: What do they have to say to each other? *Journal of Supervision and Curriculum, 13*(3), 287–296.

Reid, W. A. (2000). Curriculum as an expression of national identity. *Journal of Curriculum and Supervision, 15*(20), 113–122.

Reid, W. A. (2001). Rethinking Schwab: Curriculum theorizing as a visionary activity. *Journal of Curriculum and Supervision, 17*(1), 35–44.

Reil, M. (1993). Global education through learning circles. In L. M. Harasin (Ed.), *Global networks* (pp. 221–236). Cambridge, MA: MIT Press.

Reimers, D. H. (2004). *Other immigrants: The global origins of the American people.* New York: New York University Press.

Rickover, H. (1959). *Education and freedom.* New York: E. P. Dutton.

Riley-Taylor, E. (2003). Relational knowing: An ecological perspective on curriculum. *Journal of Curriculum Theory, 19*(3), 39–50.

Robertson, J. (1980). *American myth, American reality.* New York: Hill & Wang.

Robinson, F. G., White, F., & Ross, J. (1983). *Curriculum analysis for effective instruction.* Toronto: Ontario Institute for Studies in Education.

Ross, D., Skinner, Q., Tulley, J., & Daston, L. (Eds.). (1991). *The origins of American social science.* London: Cambridge University Press.

Rothman, R. (1995). *Measuring up: Standards, assessment, and school reform.* San Francisco: Jossey-Bass.

Rotman, B. (2005, January 17). Monobeing. *London Review of Books, 27*(4), 29–30.

Rudolph, J. (2002). From world war to Woods Hole: The impact of wartime research models on curriculum reform. *Teachers College Record, 104*(2), 212–241.

Ruff, W. G., Hansen, C. C., & Gable, K. (2004). Beyond research: Improving how we improve reading. *Academic Exchange Quarterly, 8*(2), 40–44.

Sabatier, P. A. (1988). An advocacy coalition framework of policy change and the role of policy-oriented learning therein. *Policy Sciences, 21*(2–3), 129–168.

Sandholtz, J. H., Ogawa, R. T., & Scribner, S. P. (2004). Standards gaps: Unintentional coverage of local school-based reform. *Teachers College Record, 106*(6), 1177–1202.

Sassover, R. (1995). *Cultural collisions: Postmodern technoscience.* New York: Routledge.

Scardamalia, M., & Bereiter, C. (1989). Conceptions of teaching and approaches to core problems. In M. C. Reynolds (Ed.), *Knowledge base for beginning teachers* (pp. 37–46). New York: Pergamon.

Scardamalia, M., & Bereiter, C. (1994). Computer support for knowledge-building communities. *Journal of the Learning Sciences, 3*(3), 265–283.

Schatzki, T. R., Cetina, K. K., & von Savigny, E. (Eds.). (2001). *The practice turn in contemporary theory.* New York: Routledge.

Schlecty, P. (2000). *Shaking up the schoolhouse: How to support and sustain educational innovation.* San Francisco: Jossey-Bass / Wiley.

Schwab, J. J. (1964). Problems, topics, and issues. In Stanley Elam (Ed.), *Education and the structure of knowledge: Fifth annual Phi Delta Kappa Symposium on Educational Research* (pp. 4–42). Chicago: Rand McNally.

Schwab, J. J. (1969). The practical: A language for curriculum. *School Review, 78*(5), 1–23.

Scribner, S., & Cole, M. (1981). *The psychology of literacy.* Cambridge, MA: Harvard University Press.

Scriven, M. (1972). Pros and cons about goal-free evaluation. *Evaluation Comment, 3*(4), 1–7.

Searle, J. (1995). *The construction of social reality.* New York: Free Press.

Senge, P. (2000). *Schools that learn.* New York: Currency-Doubleday.

Sennett, R. (2000). *The erosion of chara*cter. New York: W. W. Norton.

Short, E. C. (1993). Three levels of questions addressed in the field of curriculum research and practice. *Journal of Curriculum and Supervision, 9*(1), 77–86.

Silin, J., & Schwartz, F. (2003). *The hidden power of social networks: Understanding how work really gets done in organizations.* Boston: Harvard Business School Press.

Sleeter, C. E. (1999). Curriculum controversies in multicultural education. In M. J. Early & K. J. Rehage (Eds.), *Issues in curriculum: A selection of chapters from past yearbooks of the National Society for the Study of Education* (pp. 255–280). Chicago: National Society for the Study of Education.

Smagorinsky, P. (2001). If meaning is constructed, what is it made from? Toward a cultural theory of reading. *Review of Educational Research, 71*(1), 133–169.

Smith, P. J. (2003). Workplace learning and flexible delivery. *Review of Educational Research, 73*(1), 53–88.

Smithson, J. L., & Porter, A. C. (2004). From policy to practice: The evolution of one approach to describing and using curriculum data. In Mark Wilson (Ed.), *Toward coherence between classroom assessment and accountability* (103rd Yearbook of the National Society for the Study of Education, Part II, pp. 105–131). Chicago: National Society for the Study of Education.

Soltis, J. F. (1981). Introduction. In J. F. Soltis (Ed.), *Philosophy and education* (Eightieth Yearbook of the National Society for the Study of Education, Part I, pp. 1–12). Chicago: National Society for the Study of Education.

Spence, A. R. (Ed.). (1988). *Ecological research with children and families.* New York: Teachers College Press.

Spencer, D. A. (2000). Teachers' work: Yesterday, today, and tomorrow. In T. L. Good (Ed.), *American education: Yesterday, today, and tomorrow* (Ninety-Ninth Yearbook of the National Society for the Study of Education, Part II, pp. 53–83). Chicago: National Society for the Study of Education.

Spillane, J. P., Reiser, B. J., & Reimer, T. (2002). Policy implementation and cognition: Reframing and refocusing implementation research. *Review of Educational Research, 72*(3), 387–431.

Spring, J. (2004). *American education* (11th ed.). New York: McGraw-Hill.

Sproull, L., & Kiesler, S. (1991). *Connections: New ways of working in the networked organization.* Cambridge, MA: MIT Press.

Stake, R. E. (1999, April). *The representation of quality in evaluation.* Paper presented at the Annual Meeting of the American Educational Research Association, Montreal, Canada. Retrieved June 2004 from www.ed.uiuc.edu/circe/

Sternberg, R. J. (2003). *Wisdom intelligence creativity synthesized.* New York: Cambridge University Press.

Sternberg, R. J., & Horvath, J. A. (Eds.). (1999). *Tacit knowledge in professional practice: Researcher and practitioner perspectives.* Mahwah, NJ: Lawrence Erlbaum.

Stevens, R., Wineburg, S., Herrenkohl, L. R., & Bell, P. (2005). Comparative understanding of school subjects: Past, present, and future. *Review of Educational Research, 75*(2), 125–157.

Stoddard, L. (1920). *The rising tide of color against white world-supremacy.* London: Chapman & Hall.

Stoodley, B. H. (1959). *The concepts of Sigmund Freud.* Glencoe, IL: Free Press.

Tanner, D. (1999). The textbook controversies. In M. J. Early & K. J. Rehage (Eds.), *Issues in curriculum: A selection of chapters from past NSSE yearbooks* (Ninety-Eighth Yearbook of the National Society for the Study of Education, pp. 113–140). Chicago: National Society for the Study of Education.

Tanner, D., & Tanner, L. (1995). *Curriculum development: Theory into practice* (3rd ed.). New York: Macmillan.

Taylor, L., Nelson, P., & Adelman, H. S. (1999). Scaling-up reform across a school district. *Reading & Writing Quarterly, 15*(4), 303–325.

Tesch, R. (1990). *Qualitative research: Analysis types and software tools.* New York: Falmer Press.

Tombs, W. E., & Tierney, W. G. (1997). Curriculum definitions and reference points. *Journal of Curriculum and Supervision, 8*(3), 175–195.

Turner, S. (1994). *The social theory of practices: Tradition, tacit knowledge, and presuppositions.* Chicago: University of Chicago Press.

Turvey, M. (1992). Foundations of cognition: Invariant of perception and actions. In H. L. Pick, Jr., P. van den Broek, & D. C. Knell (Eds.), *Cognition* (pp. 85–117). Washington, DC: American Psychological Association.

Tyack, D. B. (2003). *Seeking common ground.* Cambridge, MA: Harvard University Press.

Tye, B. B. (2000). *Hard truths: Discovering the deep structure of schooling.* New York: Teachers College Press.

Tyler, R. W. (Ed.). (1976). *Prospects for research and development in education* (National Society for the Study of Education Series on Contemporary Educational Issues). Berkeley, CA: McCutchan.

Tyler, R. W., Gagne, R., & Scriven, M. (Eds.). (1967). *Perspectives of curriculum evaluation* (American Educational Research Association Monograph Series on Curriculum Evaluation, No 1). Chicago: Rand McNally.

Udelhofen, S. (2004). *Keys to curriculum mapping.* Thousand Oaks, CA: Corwin.

United States Code, Title 28 (2003). Testimony by Experts. Sec. 702, 426–430. United States Department of Education. (1987). *James Madison High School.* Washington, DC: Author.

United States Department of Education. (1988). *James Madison Elementary School.* Washington, DC: Author.

United States Office of Education, Department of Health, Education, and Welfare. (1960). *Final report: The development of designs for curriculum research.* Implication of the Conference on Fundamental Processes in Education, sponsored by the National Academy Of Sciences, Woods Hole, Massachusetts, September 9–18, 1959. Jerome S. Bruner, Principal Investigator. Cambridge, MA: Laboratory of Social Relations, Harvard University.

Usdan, M., & Cuban, L. (2002). *Powerful reforms with shallow roots.* New York: Teachers College Press.

Wegner, G. (2002). *Anti-Semitism and schooling under the Third Reich.* New York: Routledge Falmer.

Wells, A. S. (1993). The sociology of school choice: Why some win and others lose in the educational marketplace. In E. Rasell & R. Rothstein (Eds.), *School choice: Examining the evidence* (pp. 47–48). Washington, DC: Economic Policy Institute.

Whipple, G. (Ed.). (1926). *The foundations and techniques of curriculum-construction, the foundations of curriculum-making* (Twenty-Sixth Yearbook of the National Society for the Study of Education, Part II). Bloomington, IL: Public School Publishing.

Wideen, M., Mayer-Smith, J., & Moon, B. (1998). A critical analysis of the research on learning to teach: Making the case for an ecological perspective on inquiry. *Review of Educational Research, 68*(2), 130–178.

Wilson, J. Q. (2002). *American government* (6th ed.). New York: DC Heath / Houghton Mifflin.

Wirth, A. G. (1994). An emerging perspective on policies for American work and education for the year 2000: Choices we face. *Journal of Industrial Teacher Education, 31*(4), 9–21.

Wodak, R., & Meyers, M. (Eds). (2001). *Methods of critical discourse analysis.* London: Sage.

Wolcott, H. (1992). Posturing in qualitative research. In M. LeCompte, W. Millroy, & J. Preissle (Eds.), *The handbook of qualitative research in education* (pp. 3–52). San Diego, CA: Academic Press.

Wolfe, M. P., & Pryor, C. R. (2002). *The mission of the scholar.* New York: Peter Lang.

Wong, K. (1991). The politics of education as a field of study: An interpretive analysis. In J. G. Cibulka, R. J. Reed, & K. K. Wong (Eds.), *The politics of education in the United States.* Washington, DC: Falmer Press.

Worthen, B. R. (1999). Critical challenges confronting certification of evaluators. *American Journal of Evaluation, 20*(3), 533–555.

Zeichner, K. M. (1981–1982). Reflective teaching and field-based experience in teacher education. *Interchange, 12*(4), 1–22.

Index

About the Author

Thomas Hewitt was born and raised in Michigan. He received his Bachelor of Arts degree in Political Science and History from Western Michigan University in 1960. Following a tour of duty as a Lieutenant in the US Army he completed his Masters in History at WMU, taught in middle school and then at Oakland Community College in Detroit. In 1968, he married Sheri and moved to Texas where he earned his EdD in Curriculum and Instruction at the University of Houston. He worked for a foundation in San Antonio, Texas, for three years and then took a faculty position at Kansas State University. In 1979, he accepted a position at the University of South Alabama in Mobile, where he served a term as chairperson of the University Faculty Senate and chaired the Department of Elementary and Early Childhood Education. At KSU and USA he was a successful grant writer, taught courses in elementary and secondary social studies and curriculum for the undergraduate, masters, and doctoral programs. Opting for an offer of early retirement in 1999, he segued into a new career of consulting, writing, traveling, reading, surfing the Internet, bird watching, and tending his flower garden. He also enjoys cooking, dinner parties with friends, Mardi Gras, singing tenor with his wife in the church choir, sharing life with their married children, and contemplating future ventures.